In Defense of Monopoly

In Defense of Monopoly

HOW MARKET POWER FOSTERS
CREATIVE PRODUCTION

Richard B. McKenzie
and Dwight R. Lee

The University of Michigan Press
Ann Arbor

Copyright © by the University of Michigan 2008
All rights reserved
Published in the United States of America by
The University of Michigan Press
Manufactured in the United States of America
⊗ Printed on acid-free paper

2011   2010   2009   2008   4   3   2   1

A CIP catalog record for this book is available from the British Library.

Library of Congress Cataloging-in-Publication Data

McKenzie, Richard B.
    In defense of monopoly : how market power fosters creative
production / Richard B. McKenzie and Dwight R. Lee.
        p.   cm.
    Includes bibliographical references and index.
    ISBN-13: 978-0-472-11615-7 (cloth : alk. paper)
    ISBN-10: 0-472-11615-0 (cloth : alk. paper)
    1. Monopolies.   2. Production (Economic theory) I. Lee, Dwight R.
II. Title.

HD2757.2.M34   2007
338.8'2—dc22   2007035404

FOR
CHARLIE

A system—any system, economic or other—that at *every* given point of time fully utilizes its possibilities to the best advantage may yet in the long run be inferior to a system that does so at *no* given point of time, because the latter's failure to do so may be a condition for the level or speed of long-run performance.

JOSEPH A. SCHUMPETER
Capitalism, Socialism, and Democracy
(1942, 83; emphasis in the original)

Contents

Preface

Most adults in the United States and much of the industrialized world today can vividly remember as children playing their way through marathon Monopoly games. Few have come close, however, to challenging the length of the longest Monopoly game in history (which dragged on for 1,680 hours, or seventy straight days).[1]

Although the board game involves key market institutions—money, a bank and banker, deeds, trades, and wealth accumulation—only a modicum of business savvy is required to win. Accordingly, ten-year-old kids can beat their parents, who may be astute, seasoned business people, mainly because the competition among the players is highly constrained by detailed rules, the layout of the board, and elements of luck that are introduced through required tosses of the dice and draws of the "cards of chance." The game's popularity is probably attributable in no small way to the fact that it taps into twin passions: to win and to acquire wealth (even play wealth).

Each player's best strategy for winning is often to buy up all properties of given colors—for example, all the green properties of Pennsylvania, North Carolina, and Pacific Avenues—and then add (plastic) houses or hotels to them. We can only surmise that the game is called Monopoly because the rent that property owners can charge when another player lands on any particular property escalates both with the number of properties of a given color owned and with the number of houses and hotels that owners buy for each property. Market dominance translates into a form of "monopoly rents," loosely defined.

The player who is able to buy both Boardwalk and Park Place (the only two blue properties) and put the maximum of four hotels on each has a good chance of winning, given that the rents on those properties are then the highest on the board. Of course, the owner of those two properties can be assured of their monopoly in the game because the players are trapped: They each in turn must throw the die and must follow in lockstep the route, square by square, around the board, which means that players must run the risk of landing on the monopolized properties. However, winning by developing monopolies on properties of given colors is never assured, mainly because of the properties' costs and the several elements of chance.

Economists play another monopoly "game" in their textbooks (and classroom lectures) that is not totally unlike the board game. Like the board game, the economists' textbook monopoly game is also highly constrained—not, of course, by the printed surface of a piece of cardboard, but by an underlying, explicitly stated set of assumptions. Economists start by loosely attributing the status of monopoly to any firm that has "market power," that is, the firm is sufficiently dominant in its market and sufficiently protected by barriers to the entry of potential rivals that the monopoly can raise its prices and capture "economic rents" or "monopoly profits" by restricting output below the ideal-ized competitive output level.[2] The assumption underlying the economists' monopoly game that lines up best with the Monopoly board game is that the more control a firm has over a carefully defined, given market (or the greater the firm's "market dominance," often defined as percentage of all market sales) and the more the firm is protected from market entry of rivals, the more eco-nomic rents the monopolist can earn.

But there is another way the two games align: The prospects for creativity and improvement in both games are nil. In the case of the board game, the board and the properties on the board are given. That is to say, they are not created by the players in the course of the play. Their market values are also predetermined and fixed. The rent to be made on each property is also given and fixed, which is to say that the rent is merely *extracted* by the property own-ers, as opposed to being created by them. No new properties can be added, and neither can the existing properties be subdivided and reconfigured to enhance the value of all properties. It follows that a player's rent from becoming a "monopolist" over Boardwalk and Park Place will never affect the creation of new properties by others, which, of course, means that players have every rea-son to charge what the game (and market) will bear at the time of play. Because nothing is created or destroyed by the play of the Monopoly, the game can always be used again, with everything (rules, property values, and rents) remaining exactly the same.

In the case of the economists' monopoly game, the monopolized good is also *given* to the textbook (and blackboard) analytics. That is, by assumption, the monopolist has nothing to do with its own emergence as a monopoly or the creation of its good and its market. The monopoly and its good and market are simply assumed into existence. With the shapes and locations of the monopo-list's demand and cost functions also given, again by assumption, there is not much more for economists to do in playing their model-building games other than move around their "boards" and deduce the monopoly's output and price levels that maximize economic profits (or rents).

In the narrow context of the model, because the monopolist necessarily restricts output below the (idealized) competitive level, a self-evident inefficiency exists in the allocation of resources mandated by the underlying assumptions and the rules of the monopoly model. The monopoly rent is merely *extracted* from the consumer surplus that is presumed to exist independent of whatever the monopolist may have done in the past or proposes to do in the future. Under such conditions, the fairness of the rent extraction is, at best, suspect. Again, this is because the monopolist, by assumption, had absolutely nothing to do with the creation of the monopolized good, the good's market, the protective entry barriers (which, under the model, serve only a negative economic function, that of permitting a curb in output), and the resulting consumer surplus and (hence) the monopoly rent that is extracted. Prices above marginal cost of production, of course, serve no value-creating function.

The welfare consequences of the play of Monopoly are harmless. Everything about the game (all the properties, money, and pieces) remains fixed, no matter how many monopolies the players are able to create. If anything, the development of monopolies adds to the players' received value from play. Obviously, public policies are not subject to change because of the Monopoly game's rules or the manner in which the game is played. Monopoly is a game that simply would not sell if consumer gains from play (and the development of monopolies among the various properties) were absent.

That is hardly the case with the monopoly game economists play out in their models. This is because the economists' monopoly game carries a direct and powerful lesson: Monopolies everywhere are "bad." They are bad in terms of what they *fail* to do in the production of goods and, consequently, in terms of what they do to the allocation of countries' scarce and therefore valuable resources. They are also bad because of what they do to countries' income distributions. Monopoly rents can only be construed as an unnecessary grab on *consumers'* (not the *monopolist's*) surplus by firms that have absolutely no prior or justifiable claim on the surplus value. Monopolies everywhere, in other words, have no redeeming virtue (a central lesson all too frequently exposited with only minor and easily dismissed qualifications).

Because judges, journalists, politicians, policymakers, bureaucrats, and researchers (and economists) thoroughly absorbed the monopoly model in their college classes, it should surprise no one that welfare-destroying monopolies are seen everywhere.

- Microsoft is a monopolist because its Windows operating system and Office suite of productivity applications for personal computers are used on nearly all of the world's personal computers (i.e., those that use Intel-compatible microprocessors).[3]

- Clear Channel has monopoly power because it has more than 1,200 radio stations (of the 10,000-plus stations in the country) in its network.
- Intel has market power because its Pentium chips dominate the microprocessor market.
- The Irvine Company, a major property owner in Southern California, has monopoly power simply because of its large size and the strategic locations of its properties in a high-growth area of the country.
- Even J. K. Rowling, author of the Harry Potter series, has been accused of having a monopoly presence in the book market because she has sold so many books (hundreds of millions), which obviously gives her publisher the option of selling fewer than could have been sold to charge higher than competitive prices (Blais 2005).

Indeed, the economists' model has been learned so well by many commentators that they are able to nimbly reverse the model's logic: Any firm that makes a lot of money—or more than is required to keep the firm doing what it is doing—must have monopoly market power. Otherwise, the excess earnings would have been eroded by competition. Hence, people's riches (Bill Gates's billions) are prima facie evidence of an unseen inefficiency in the allocation of resources—a welfare loss that need not have been. Never mind that Gates's fortune may amount to a small fraction of the societal welfare gains that have been, and will continue to be, realized because of key decisions he made with regard to the development of Microsoft years ago.

The public policy implication from the "play" of the economists' monopoly game is equally clear: When the cost of antitrust action is lower than the monopoly's deadweight loss imposed on its market, monopolies should be abolished wherever and whenever sighted. When the cost of such antitrust action is higher than the expected efficiency improvement, monopolies must be endured, but only as a "necessary evil." Monopolies should never be welcomed for what they contribute to the development of human welfare. This is because, to restate our point, monopolies cannot be seen as beneficial, on balance, to human welfare—at least not from the perspective of the standard static monopoly model.

As economists over the past two hundred years have lamented the almost complete absence of any real-world market matching their competitive ideal market structure, "perfect competition," and as economists have bemoaned the prevalence of monopolies, oligopolies, monopolistic competitors, and monopsonies in the economy, something very curious has occurred: The American economy has prospered as no other economy has prospered before in human history. This is because the past two hundred years have stood witness to a record of discovery, invention, and innovativeness not matched in earlier epochs. Moreover, three-quarters or more of the welfare gains from all the innovativeness have been garnered not by the innovators (and all the firms built around the innovations) but by the consuming public.[4] It is no exaggeration to suggest that economists' myopic focus on monopolies' wrongs is comparable to observers of the play of the Monopoly board game stressing how unreasonable the rent on Boardwalk is without ever recognizing that the players are having a lot of fun and that the prospects of each player acquiring the rights to the rent on Boardwalk is very likely one of the forces that inspires their continued play.

In this book, we develop at length two arguments that represent a frontal assault on conventional economic wisdom as related to monopolies: First, economists' conventional, widely accepted, and parroted static model of monopoly greatly exaggerates the economic harm done by real-world monopolies in real-world markets, which are necessarily evolutionary, dynamic, creative processes that do not square well with the static, noncreative nature of economists' monopoly model.

Second, contrary to conventional wisdom among economists (for reasons that are explored at length in this book), some degree of monopoly presence in an economy is "good" because without some monopoly presence no economy can ever hope to maximize human welfare improvement over time. In this regard, we argue that a perfectly fluid, perfectly competitive economy, idealized and idolized by economists, must be decidedly inferior to an economy that is beset with some degree of market entry and exit restrictions (or costs). In making these points, we repeatedly defer to the wisdom of the late Harvard economist Joseph Schumpeter, who observed succinctly and prophetically in his classic work *Capitalism, Socialism, and Democracy* more than six decades ago that market imperfections can be a source of an economy's long-term progress (see the epigraph to this volume). Readers who appreciate the wisdom in that passage need not read on. However, we have written this book on the presumption that many economists and professionals in related fields (e.g., law and public policy) will view the passage with some skepticism. As documented throughout this book, much conventional criticism directed at monopoly ignores this Schumpeterian insight.

Our purpose in this book is to expound and then to extend Schumpeter's key insight in ways that he failed to develop as fully as he could have. We seek to explain why we believe Schumpeter was actually too timid in making his point. Our essential position is stronger: An economic system's failure to efficiently allocate its resources at all points in time *is* a necessary precondition for the maximization of the system's long-term performance.

Our reasoning is at times complex, but more often it is elementary. In the main, much of what we write in this book reduces to the proposition that an economy is unlike a board game in which players compete for a limited number of given properties. It is unlike the blackboard games in which economists develop their monopoly models. In real-world economies, goods and services are not given, as is the case in both the board game Monopoly and in economists' treatment of monopoly in their blackboard games. Goods and services are created, and the process by which goods and services are created and enhanced requires competition, but any process involving truly creative production also requires the prospects of gains beyond a "normal competitive rate of return." In no small way creative production drives, in unheralded forms and to an unheralded extent, Schumpeter's much-heralded "creative destruction."

Monopolies (and their built-in monopoly rents, as well as their entry and exit barriers that inspire the rents) are an underappreciated inspiration for the development of new goods and services that enhance human value and, at the same time, undermine their (the monopolies') own existence. This is to say that, unlike the board game Monopoly, monopolies in real-world economies can inspire new and more valuable properties and can give rise to players moving off the beaten path around the board and into uncharted territories. Even when given monopolies are said to be bad in their markets (as Standard Oil and Microsoft have been found to be by antitrust authorities and the courts),[5] they can contribute much to the advancement of human welfare, primarily because they inspire others in close-by and far-removed markets to try to become like them, monopolies with above-competitive returns. The long-run improvements in human welfare from a greater variety of and higher quality products, inspired by the "bad" monopolies' profits, can easily exceed any short-term loss in welfare due to "bad" monopolies' restrictions on output.

Moreover, monopolies and their profits are absolutely essential and expected in real-world markets beset with risk and uncertainty, which make business failures not only a possibility but also a persistent fact of market life. In order for individuals and firms to venture forth in such real-world markets, they must have a realistic prospect of temporary monopoly profits just so that in an array—or a portfolio—of ventures, at least a competitive rate of return can, on balance, be expected.

Besides, in a world beset with risk and uncertainty, good luck is bound to happen, with the luck revealing itself in monopoly profits, enabled by natural and unexpected barriers to entry that emerge with the development of products. No doubt, J. K. Rowling never expected to sell hundreds of millions of books, and to have the degree of reader royalty that her Harry Potter series inspired among young and adult readers. Similarly, Apple could not have known that its iPod would become the standard for digital music players and would, for so long, dominate its market segment. In an imperfect world, the prospects of monopoly profits, from anticipated or unanticipated sources, surely inspires more risk taking than would otherwise occur, which should be expected to pay off in an economy that, over the long run, is more innovative than it could otherwise be.

So what if firms' allocative efficiency in every product line is not achieved with perfection, when the resource base is expanded at the same time that consumer value is enhanced *because* of the incentive effects built into the prospects of monopolized markets? Clearly, as we shall argue repeatedly in this book, if antitrust enforcement were "perfect" in all regards, wiping out all monopolies and returning all markets to perfectly competitive market conditions, innovation and long-term prosperity would surely be undermined since we would replace an economy that is more productive over time with one that is as productive as possible at every point in time.

Before they take up monopoly in their classes, economists often review with their students Adam Smith's clever metaphor, the "invisible hand," which he used to explain how people's drive to serve their own private ends results in the advancement of society's ends. Our arguments represent an extension of Smith's profound point, for we see monopoly as a crucial activating force behind the invisible hand. Take out the prospect of monopoly (and the attendant monopoly profits) from a market economy, and the invisible hand will likely go limp, a position that appears to be ironic only because of how monopoly has been caricatured for so long in economic models.

Our analysis leads to another transparent conclusion: The world of perfectly fluid, perfectly competitive markets (or any close approximation) is first of all *unachievable* (because of the unattainability of perfection) and furthermore *undesirable* even if it were achievable. The kind of competition in real-world markets is far superior to the competition in perfectly competitive markets precisely *because* the competition is not restricted solely to price competition. Rather, competition in real-world markets is multidimensional, with the avenues of competition constantly being created and redefined with the advent of new products and production processes, a point fully appreciated by Schumpeter, who asserted the far greater importance of nonprice competition over price competition in determining the allocative efficiency of resources over time.[6]

Clearly, if the good that is subject to monopolization is *given*—that is, not actually created by the monopoly—nothing much can be said about the morality of any distribution of the surplus value from the good's production and sale. This is true even when, assuming constant cost of production, the surplus value would go entirely to consumers, under conditions of perfect competition. So what if consumers get all of the gains from trade? There is no necessary justification for the monopoly getting any of the net gains, because the monopoly had no role in creating the good and bringing the net value into existence.

However, if the good is actually created by the monopoly, then surely the monopoly's claim, on fairness or justice grounds, for a portion of the net gains is strengthened, while the consumers' claim to all of the gains is undermined. Because successful real-world economies are advancing evolutionary processes marked by innovations developed by individuals and firms, we argue in the following pages that monopoly profits have far more moral merit than they are commonly accorded when viewed from the perspective of static models. And, we should never forget, above-competitive profits are the incentive that innovators need to innovate, and they are the cause of far more intense and meaningful forms of competition than price competition isolated from all other forms of competition.

Economists make much to-do about how competitive market prices are important signals to firms as they try to decide what to produce and what resources to employ (and pull away from other uses). Prices supposedly lead entrepreneurs as if by Adam Smith's invisible hand into an efficient allocation of resources and maximization of human well-being. We ask in this book, following the lead of Paul Romer (1994), how can that be, given that, as economists themselves stress, the prices set in perfectly competitive markets only reflect goods' marginal values, which means that prices in such markets do not and cannot reflect the full consumer value of the goods that are produced?

That question is irrelevant when the goods are *given*, that is, do not need to be created. However, if the goods need to be created and produced, perfectly competitive prices can lead to impaired incentives to create new and superior goods and improve old products and, hence, to an underallocation of resources toward economic progress that benefits us all. The failure to develop new and improved products that cost less than they are worth is a market inefficiency that easily goes unrecognized (it is difficult to recognize the lack of something that has never been available) and surely one that is as important as the short-run deadweight loss economists focus on in their static models of markets. To paraphrase Romer, a new good not produced is as easy (perhaps easier) to overlook as the dog that did not bark—and apparently for economists, far more difficult to conceptualize than the units of *given* goods that are not produced in monopolized markets.[7] True competitive prices are particularly problematic when the marginal cost of production is close to zero, if not zero, as is the case for the burgeoning array of digital (or electronic) goods and services today.

Our arguments, in other words, lead to the observation that monopolies might create one form of short-run inefficiency, deadweight loss, but they also lead to a more-than-offsetting improvement in the efficiency with which goods are created and improved over time. Again, this is the point Schumpeter had in mind when he suggested that short-run inefficiencies could establish the conditions for improving "the level and speed of [an economy's] long-run performance."

From our reexamination of monopoly theory, we can only deduce that human welfare is today superior to what it would have been had policymakers followed, over the past couple hundred years, more assiduously the monopoly teachings of economists. At the same time, the world today would likely have been superior to what we see around us had more policymakers over the past six decades read carefully Professor Schumpeter's seminal tract on the required market foundation for progress in free-market economies.

To avoid any misunderstanding and to be clear, we hasten to add that our arguments do not lead recklessly to the conclusion that all monopolies are good or that the more monopolies an economy encourages, the better. We can easily imagine that some level of monopolization of markets can be, on balance, welfare destroying. Our point is that not all monopolies and not all levels of monopolization are welfare destroying, a perspective that suggests economists should pay more attention to the institutional conditions for what might be called *optimum monopoly*. We acknowledge that optimum monopoly (discussed later) lacks the level of analytical precision that economists' market models have. Nevertheless, we are proposing that the issue of monopolies of all kinds in a market economy should be addressed analytically, in the way that the terms for copyrights and patents have historically been addressed: Those forms of market protection are needed to inspire greater creativity than would otherwise exist, but the extent and term of the protection need not be unlimited. We suggest that optimum monopoly is no less relevant to public policy than optimum pollution or optimum crime rate.

In completing this book, we are deeply indebted to Tyler Cowen, Kenneth Elzinga, and Thomas Sullivan for their incisive and very helpful reviews of early drafts of the book.

Chapter 1

"The Wretched Spirit of Monopoly"

Historically, monopoly has, with limited exceptions, been seen by economists as a bane of markets, one of the more prominent forms of so-called market failure. Across time, economists have equated the "evils" of monopoly with theft and taxation, given that monopoly can impair an economy's vigor just as theft and taxation can. Unfortunately, countries have, either all too willingly, with malice or political intention, created and nurtured monopolies, or else inadvertently, from ignorance of monopolies' economic consequences, allowed them to arise and persist.[1]

In contemporary economics, monopoly is treated as a source of "inefficiency," or "deadweight loss." That is, monopoly forces a misallocation of resources, with too few resources being used in the monopolized industries and too many resources used to lesser advantage in other competitive markets.[2] The chief modern standard of comparison for assessing the welfare loss of monopoly is "perfect competition," a hypothetical market structure, developed mainly for analytical purposes, in which all potential gains from trade are realized—all resources are allocated among alternative uses with "perfection" (by assumptions of the model).

At the same time, many economists as far back as Adam Smith have doubted that the economic damage done by monopolies could long endure without the protective arm of government heeding the monopolies' political demands for market protections. The main change in economists' overall appraisal of monopoly through history has been the growing formalization of the monopoly model that shows ever more clearly the economic harm monopolies cause, a point that can be seen with a review of the treatment of monopoly by classical economists (covered in this chapter) and their more contemporary neoclassical counterparts (covered in the following chapters).

In this book, our central goal is to undertake a critical and extensive (but not exhaustive) reexamination of contemporary monopoly theory, though not with an eye toward dispensing with the theory altogether. We would be the first to argue that the monopoly model that economists widely employ has many good uses. However, we suggest that the model has been overused and abused, given that it has almost everywhere been employed to show that monopoly power— or the capacity of firms to affect market price and firm profits (or "monopoly rents")—is prima facie evidence of a "market failure," or a sign of "inefficiency" and consumer "welfare loss," which amounts to the same thing. On the contrary, we suggest that there is much wisdom in a widely unappreci-ated position taken by Joseph Schumpeter (1883–1950) in his classic 1942 work *Capitalism, Socialism, and Democracy*, in which he observed, partly in an effort to explain why capitalism would not survive, that an economic system is necessarily an imperfect evolutionary process of "creative destruction," which makes it ill-suited for ultimate appraisal by the static analysis of conventional economic theory.

> Since we are dealing with a process whose every element takes considerable time in revealing its true features and ultimate effects, there is no point in appraising its performance of that process *ex visu* of a given point of time; we must judge its performance over time, as it unfolds through decades or centuries. A system—any system, economic or other—that at *every* point of time fully utilizes its possibilities to the best advantage may yet in the long run be inferior to a system that does so at *no* given point in time, because the latter's failure to do so may be a condition for the level or speed of long-run performance. (1942, 83; emphasis in the original)

In taking a page from Schumpeter, we suggest that monopoly, or the prospect of monopoly, is an engine of creative production, which necessarily undergirds economic progress, in contrast to much ingrained wisdom that sug-gests that monopoly is a drag on economic progress. Take monopoly, and con-comitant monopoly rents, out of a market economy—that is, convert all mar-kets to ones of perfectly fluid (and perfectly efficient) competition, or some close approximation, eliminating all prospect of economically significant monopoly rents in the process—and the system will likely stagnate. Any short-run efficiency gains achieved by such a conversion, even if such were possible without massive disruption in economic relationships, would likely be swamped by the long-term losses from the absence of what Schumpeter con-sidered the far more potent force of "creative destruction."

In short, we suggest that market economies need some optimum level of monopoly presence to achieve maximum growth in consumer welfare over time. The concept of optimum monopoly, albeit ill-defined, could better direct policy-level discussions on copyrights, patents, and antitrust than the current view that elevates "perfect competition" (or, again, some close approximation) and the intentional destruction of all monopoly vestiges as a societal goal of the highest order. "The only good monopoly is a dead one" is a quip, in other words, that contains a mountain of fallacies.

As will be seen, we extend our criticisms of current monopoly theory by showing that monopoly pricing can increase consumer surplus under specified market conditions (e.g., network effects) at the same time that it spawns the so-called deadweight loss (a concept that needs to be discarded in much economic analysis as irrelevant). Of course, our analysis leads inexorably to the conclusion that market entry barriers can be welfare enhancing, in spite of their giving rise to a deadweight loss, as described in conventional analysis.

We show that even when the conventional monopoly model is taken as the basis for analysis, the monopoly profits and deadweight loss of monopoly are not nearly so large as economists' blackboard models indicate, simply because conventional analysis does not recognize that achievement of the monopoly objective of restricting sales to raise price and profits is a managerial problem of major proportions. It is a coordination problem, differing from the coordination problems faced by cartels of independent producers only in degree.

Moreover, conventional analysis in which a fully competitive market is somehow magically cartelized does not consider an obvious problem, that the individual producers who are brought under a cartel's umbrella of market control can switch roles, from being independent entrepreneurs, or principals, to being employees (or bureaucrats), or rather agents, the net effect of which is to change dramatically their incentives to produce efficiently. This means that much monopoly "rent seeking" (or the pursuit of monopoly profits through government-backed restrictions) must be revised. If monopoly rents are reduced by so-called principal-agent problems in managing monopolies, then less rent seeking must be the consequence, which implies less inefficiency than conventional monopoly rent-seeking theory suggests.

In the conventional analysis of monopoly, consumers would never want to be subjected to monopoly pricing. They would pay higher prices as well as transfer a portion of their consumer surplus to the monopoly owners. We suggest this is only the case in static analysis, when the product is a given and when there is no interplay between the actual, or anticipated, consumption of the good and future consumer demand for the product over time. Indeed, we suggest that under some realistic market conditions, consumers would actually want to face the prospects of monopoly pricing at some future point in time, as such prospects can affect the monopolist's pricing decisions between now and when the monopoly rents are actually extracted. This isn't to say that consumers aren't worse off from monopoly pricing. On the contrary, they are *when it occurs,* but a producer's initial pricing policies that lead to the monopoly prices can more than compensate consumers for the costs they incur from the so-called future monopoly prices.

All of these points, understandably, lead to a need for a revamping of modern antitrust thinking that is heavily guided (and misguided) by the conventional microeconomic theory of monopoly under which so many legal scholars and judges have mistakenly equated market dominance with monopoly—monopoly as a problem that requires a government-imposed solution.[3]

Finally, we point out that the theory of monopoly on the buyer's side of the market—monopsony—is as defective as monopoly on the seller's side. For reasons we will explain, it is hard for us to imagine how a monopsony would ever be able to emerge in labor (or other input) markets without paying above what were, before the monopsony emerged, competitive wage rates. Hence, from the perspective of arguments marshaled in chapter 7 of this book, monopsony should more correctly be viewed as expanding labor's employment and income opportunities, not contracting them. In chapter 8, we expand on our discussion of problems with monopsony theory with a discussion of how the NCAA, an acclaimed monopsony of collegiate athletic (mainly football and basketball) talent, could be actually improving the welfare of those athletes whom other economic and legal scholars presume are being exploited. If this view is correct (or to the extent it is), any proposal that would force the NCAA to pay market wages for college and university athletes would have the exact opposite impact of the one intended.

To put these points in historical context, we begin in this chapter an examination of the monopoly views of key economists in history, starting with Adam Smith and going through Schumpeter. This review of monopoly thinking is intended to be indicative only of how economists' thinking on monopoly has evolved over time. It is not intended to be exhaustive of all positions taken by economists on monopoly. In the following chapter, we will present the contemporary monopoly model in some graphical detail with the purpose of laying the foundation for critiques of monopoly theory developed by Donald Dewey (1959) and John McGee (1971) on which we expand in a variety of ways in following chapters. In the main, however, our critique follows in the Schumpeterian tradition (Schumpeter 1942).

SMITH, BENTHAM, AND RICARDO ON THE "EVILS" OF MONOPOLY

The venerable Adam Smith (1723–90), the recognized founder of economics as a discipline, viewed monopoly not much differently than contemporary economists now do, although, as might be expected, Smith was less exact in the way he chose to discuss the economic harm done by a monopoly. In his *Wealth of Nations*, he used the term *monopoly* to describe a range of market structures, with the critical feature being the capacity of a firm or firms within a protected industry to raise the selling price above the competitive—or "natural"—price. More specifically, he equated the grant of a monopoly with a trade secret that allowed the producer to control supply and, hence, price (Smith 1776, bk. 1, chap. 7).

By controlling supply—or "keeping the market under-stocked, by never fully supplying the effectual demand"—Smith reasoned that monopolists can "sell their commodities much above the natural price, and raise their emoluments, whether they consist in wages or profit, greatly above their natural rate" (1776; bk. 1, chap. 7, ¶ 26). On the one hand, the monopolist's price "is upon every occasion the highest which can be squeezed out of buyers, or which, it is supposed, they will consent to give." On the other, the "natural" or competitive price "is the lowest which the sellers can commonly afford to take, and at the same time continue in business" (bk. 1, chap. 7, ¶ 27).

To Smith, as well as to other early economists, the word *monopoly* was not exclusively used to characterize a single seller of a good or service protected by barriers to entry, as is often the case in modern discussions of monopoly. Rather, monopoly applied more loosely to any firm that was capable of elevating its price above cost and that could generate monopoly rent, or an income over and above what was required to keep the resources in their current employment. This meant that Smith used monopoly to describe any firm capable of restricting sales with the intent of raising its price, but it also applied to firms that were protected by, say, import restrictions and that, as a consequence, were able to elevate their prices above competitive levels, as well as expand their sales. (Our discussion of monopoly will follow Smith in this regard. We will talk about monopolies as being firms that have some control over price through control over market supply, even though they may not be the only seller in their market.)

Accordingly, Smith was concerned with the monopoly consequences of mercantilism, which gave rise to a host of trade restrictions designed (mistakenly) to build the nation's economic well-being. The British Navigation Act of 1660 specified that "no merchandise shall be imported into the plantation but in English vessels, navigated by Englishmen, under the penalty of forfeiture" (Little 1886, ¶ 3693). Another law prohibited the importation of all European commodities into the colonies except in British ships manned by Englishmen. There were other times in which kings used patents and exclusive franchises as revenue sources. For example, Charles I, circa 1630, issued a patent on soap to a "company of soap-makers" on the condition that the soap-makers pay him £10,000 and £8 per ton of soap they sold (¶ 3689). In the Act of 1672, New England producers were forbidden to compete with the English on the produce from Southern plantations. Moreover, American firms were forbidden to manufacture goods that would compete with English goods in foreign markets (¶ 3699).

Among monopoly's many vagaries—which caused Smith to summarize them as the "wretched spirit of monopoly"—Smith cited how the creation of monopoly by, say, import restrictions oppresses the poor, and, at the same time, the oppression of the poor invariably gives rise to "the monopoly of the rich, who, by engrossing the whole trade to themselves, will be able to make very large profits" (1776, bk. 1, chap. 9, ¶ 15). He also noted how monopolies are "a great enemy to good management" because, protected as they are, monopolists don't have to work as hard at improving, as a matter of market self-defense, their management ways in response to "free and universal competition" (1776, bk. 1, chap. 11, ¶ 14).

Moreover, whereas monopolies might well improve the profits of the protected industry, they necessarily undercut state tax revenue precisely because aggregate national income is diminished (1776, bk. 4, chap. 7, ¶ 143).[4] And then there is the one flaw of every monopoly that Smith characterized as "fatal": "The high rate of profit seems every where to destroy that parsimony which in other circumstances is natural to the character of the merchant. When profits are high that sober virtue seems to be superfluous and expensive luxury to suit better the affluence of his situation" (1776, bk. 4, chap. 7, ¶ 147). Because the protected "owners of great mercantile capitals" are often political and commercial leaders of communities and, hence, set examples for others by how they act, a monopoly can also cause the masses of workers to be less parsimonious than they would be otherwise.

> Accumulation is thus prevented in the hands of all those who are naturally the most disposed to accumulate, and the funds destined for the maintenance of productive labour receive no augmentation from the revenue of those who ought naturally to augment them the most. The capital of the country, instead of increasing, gradually dwindles away, and the quantity of productive labour maintained in it grows every day less and less. (1776, bk. 4, chap. 7, ¶ 147)

Finally, Smith is well known for having written,

> People of the same trade seldom meet together, even for merriment and diversion, but the conversation ends in a conspiracy against the public, or

in some contrivance to raise prices. It is impossible indeed to prevent such meetings, by any law which either could be executed, or would be consistent with liberty and justice. But though the law cannot hinder people of the same trade from sometimes assembling together, it ought to do nothing to facilitate such assemblies; much less to render them necessary. (1776, bk. 1, chap. 10, ¶ 82)

Smith is also well known (and revered) for his emphasizing the value of markets freed of government interferences—aside for a short list of potential interferences, including certain goods, like roads, characterized as "public goods" in modern literature. What is not so widely appreciated is that Smith argued for public provision of cross-country roads in part because they would ease the flow of trade across local markets and thereby would make cartels more difficult to maintain.[5]

Because Smith presumed that privately organized cartels would be short lived, due to the forces of competition that would arise, his major concern in the *Wealth of Nations* was with monopolies that were either directly approved by the state or those that arose in the domestic economy because of government-imposed restrictions on international trade that gave the protected domestic firms a degree of monopoly pricing power (a concern we share in spite of our defense of monopolies that arise from unfettered market forces). Smith recognized that "country gentlemen and farmers" have a more difficult time than merchants and manufacturers in colluding against the general public. As a consequence, "they accordingly seem to have been the original inventors of those restraints upon the importation of foreign goods which secure to them the monopoly of the home-market" (1976, bk. 4, chap. 2, ¶ 21). The monopoly profits to be garnered with the trade restrictions are all the "encouragement" domestic firms need to press for the protection, which, in the process, distorts the allocation of resources, especially the employment of labor.[6]

In this regard, Smith seemed to understand economic tenets that, in modern times, form the basis of public choice economics, which uses economic theory—including monopoly theory—to understand governmental policy processes. Monopoly, in other words, was an important engine of interest group politics, or what has come to be called, following the work of twentieth-century economists Gordon Tullock (1967) and Anne Krueger (1974), rent seeking, the political search for monopoly profits from government-imposed market restrictions or other forms of government-provided largess with the added profits being the motivation, or what Smith called "encouragement."

Ultimately, the problems of monopoly, according to Smith, are compounded by government being made "subservient to the interest of monopoly" (1776, bk. 4, chap. 7, ¶ 190), and the restrictive laws, passed at the urging of monopoly-seeking interest groups, are "written in blood."[7] So what if the import taxes encouraged smuggling that, in turn, reduced government revenues from what they would have been had a lower import tax been imposed? Smith understood that tax revenues were not the point of the import restrictions; monopoly privileges were.[8]

Of course, protected industries would like nothing better than to have their domestic monopoly extended to markets in foreign countries, Smith mused. However, any government's jurisdictional boundaries necessarily limit the geographical reach of any monopoly protection, which is why the protected industries have pressed for export subsidies that can be expected to have the same production and profit effects for the favored domestic firm or industry as the import restrictions. In Smith's view, firms that benefited from export subsidies were no less monopolies than the firms that were favored with import restrictions. Both sets of favored firms received monopoly rents that were, in some sense, unearned and that gave rise to the misallocation of resources, as well as to all the other harms Smith noted that flowed from the presence of monopoly.[9]

Contrary to what might be deduced from reading about Smith's hostility to market protections in general, he was not totally opposed to all monopolies under all circumstances. According to Jeremy Bentham (1748–1832), Smith once wrote (in a publication Bentham did not identify),

> When a company of merchants undertake at their own risk and expence to establish a new trade, with some remote and barbarous nation, it may not be unreasonable to incorporate them into a joint-stock company, and to grant them, in case of their success, a monopoly of the trade for a certain number of years. It is the easiest and most natural way, in which the state can recompense them, for hazarding a dangerous and expensive experiment, of which the public is afterwards to reap the benefit. A temporary monopoly of this kind may be vindicated, upon the same principles, upon which a like monopoly of a new machine is granted to its inventor, and that of a new book to its author. (Bentham 1787, Letter 13, ¶ 38)

Bentham scolded Smith for being inconsistent, given that Smith had in other forums denounced all other monopolies. Bentham added, "Private respect must not stop me from embracing this occasion of giving a warning, which is so much needed by mankind. If so original and independent a spirit [as Adam Smith] has not been always able to save itself from being drawn aside by the fascination of sounds, into the paths of vulgar prejudice, how strict a watch ought not men of common mould to set over their judgments, to save themselves from being led astray by similar delusions?" (¶ 39). Bentham suggested that Smith could use his logic for his monopoly exception to support usury laws, which Smith, Bentham noted, had opposed (¶ 44).

David Ricardo (1772–1823) added to Smith's view of monopoly in only marginal ways. In his *Principles of Political Economy*, Ricardo noted, like Smith, that the monopoly price "is at the very highest price at which the consumers are willing to purchase it," but this monopoly price could change from time period to time period and product to product. However, that price, according to Ricardo, "is nowhere regulated by the cost of production" (1817, chap. 17, ¶ 8). Ricardo's main concern was elaborating on an argument pushed by Smith, Thomas Robert Malthus (1776–1834),[10] and others, that private property in land was a source of monopoly, that the price of land is necessarily a monopoly price, and that the prices of crops—barley or wheat, for example— produced on the land contain monopoly rent that, if taxed away, would fall totally on the landlord, or so argued Ricardo: "If all rent were relinquished by landlords, I am of opinion, that the commodities produced on the land would be no cheaper, because there is always a portion of the same commodities produced on land, for which no rent is or can be paid, as the surplus produce is only sufficient to pay the profits of stock" (1817, chap. 20, ¶ 12).

Ricardo corrected Smith, and others who adopted Smith's position on trade restrictions as a source of monopoly rents, in one substantial way. He stressed that trade restrictions do not afford domestic producers the power to charge monopoly prices and to garner monopoly rents as Smith had maintained. This is because such restrictions do not cut out domestic competition, which could be intense. The "real evil" from such restrictions, Ricardo argued incisively, is not that the restrictions enable the supposed "monopolies" to charge more than the competitive price, but that the restrictions actually raise the "natural price" (meaning competitive, cost-based price) because they increase market inefficiency: "By increasing the cost of production, a portion of the labour of the country is less productively employed" (1817, n. 54).[11] Ricardo seemed to understand a point often overlooked in even modern treatments of monopoly, namely, that monopoly rents can be capitalized in the market value of tradable monopoly, rent-producing assets (e.g., land or franchise), the effect of which can be to hike implicit opportunity costs and to drop profits net of the value of tradable asset prices, returning rates of return on investments to competitive levels.

BASTIAT AND MARX ON MONOPOLY AS "PLUNDER"

French economist Frédéric Bastiat (1801–50) is renowned for his incisive satirical opposition to import restrictions, as in his "petition" to the French Chamber of Deputies on behalf of his country's "Manufacturers of Candles, Tapers, Lanterns, Candlesticks, Street Lamps, Snuffers, and Extinguishers, and from the Producers of Tallow, Oil, Resin, Alcohol, and Generally of Everything Connected with Lighting." In his petition, he urged his fellow deputies to pass laws that would require people to block out the sun during the entire day for no higher purpose than to increase the demand for candles and everything else his supposed clients produced. Such laws would have essentially the same effects as all other laws designed to thwart the free flow of trade founded on cost advantages.[12]

Obviously, Bastiat had no more respect for monopolies, especially government-created ones, than did Smith and Ricardo. We will consider in some detail Bastiat's views on monopoly in chapter 10 (when we consider how writers have equated, wrongly, property rights with monopoly privileges). Here we can note that in various publications, Bastiat placed monopoly among a changing list of "evils of society," along with war, slavery, unethical practices, theocracy, colonialism, impostures, inequitable taxation and excesses of government, frauds of every kind, and privilege (1850, chap. 1, ¶ 32; chap. 8, ¶ 9; 1845, ser. 2, chap. 2, ¶ 12). Bastiat saw government-sanctioned "plunder" as a common denominator of his "evils": "Plunder not only *redistributes* wealth; it always, at the same time, *destroys* a part of it. War annihilates many values. Slavery paralyzes many capabilities. Theocracy diverts many energies toward childish or injurious ends. Monopoly too transfers wealth from one pocket to another, but much of it is lost in the process" (1845, ser. 2, chap. 1, ¶ 21).

When Bastiat wrote about monopoly, he was most concerned about the then widely expressed contentions that (1) private property gave the owners monopoly power and (2) "Liberty begets monopoly," along with "Oppression is born of freedom" (1850, chap. 1, ¶ 87). With regard to the latter, what he called a "socialistic pretext," Bastiat scoffed that the argument is "fatal" for human history because the claim implied that for people "to learn to choose is to learn to commit suicide" and then there would be no satisfactory governmental means of correction, given that government would have to call upon human beings who are, by the nature of the claims, fatally flawed.[13] Bastiat maintained that the "laws of competition" would see to it that there is no "permanent monopoly," "since the product of their labor, by an inevitable dispensation of Providence, tends to become the common, gratuitous, and consequently equal heritage of all mankind" with the result "in mankind a basic tendency toward *equality*" (1850, chap. 16, ¶ 110). By this he seemed to mean that any temporary market advantage, owing to some unique ability, would dissolve with the emergence of competition from the spread of the advantage with duplication.[14]

With regard to the claim that private property affords owners monopoly privileges, Bastiat first quoted a number of prominent writers of his time, including Smith, Ricardo, Considerant, and Jean-Baptiste Say (1767–1832), as well as lesser known individuals, all of whom maintained that land is productive in and of itself, independent of what owners do to it, and hence gives rise to unearned returns, treated synonymously with monopoly profits and monopoly rents. According to pre-Bastiat scholars, when crops are sold, the workers get paid for the value they add to what is produced, but landowners are paid for what is rightly the contribution of the land, not the owner.[15] No economic purpose was seen to be served by the payment to property, just as there is no positive societal economic purpose served by the rent of monopolists who are able to control market supply. Bastiat points out that any value contributed by the land, which is truly "gratuitous" (an adjective that seems to be synonymous with "unearned") will be competed away: "Land as a means of production, in so far as it is the work of God, produces *utility*, and this utility is gratuitous; it is not within the owner's power to charge for it. The land, as a means of production, in so far as the landowner has prepared it, worked on it, enclosed it, drained it, improved it, added other necessary implements to it, produces *value*, which represents human *services* made available, and this is the only thing he charges for. Either you must recognize the justice of this demand, or you must reject your own principle of *reciprocal services*" (1850, chap. 9, ¶ 111; emphasis in the original). Bastiat continues by arguing that the landowner receives a return only for the improvements he has made.[16]

With regard to the claim that scarcity of resources or goods affords their owners monopoly power, which is destructive of social welfare, Bastiat acknowledges that nature's scarcity enables the resource and good owners to extract higher prices than otherwise. However, he dispenses with the argument by drawing a distinction between "natural monopoly" (that which emanates from nature) and "artificial monopoly" (that which is contrived by firms or government). Bastiat notes that "the favors bestowed by Nature do no harm to society. At the very most we could say that they bring to light an evil that already existed and can in no way be imputed to them. It is too bad, perhaps, that tokay wine is not as plentiful, and therefore not as cheap, as ordinary red wine. But this is not a social evil; it was imposed on us by Nature," to which he adds, "Mankind would be childish indeed if it became upset, or if it rebelled, because there is only one Jenny Lind, one Clos-Vougeot, or one Regent [talented people of Bastiat's era]" (1850, fn. 13).

For Bastiat, what should be of major concern is when people impose an artificial scarcity on themselves through governmental grants of monopoly privileges, which can only add to social and economic impoverishment, especially as monopoly privileges are widely extended to industry groups.[17] When monopoly privileges become widespread, Bastiat saw a form of creeping socialism with ever more monopoly privileges, as well as other forms of government largesse—"education, employment, credit, assistance, at the people's expense"—provided to the "masses." The "masses" understandably justified their political press for government benefits by all the other extant government-based privileges and largesse. Although Bastiat never used the expression Prisoner's Dilemma,[18] he certainly saw that dilemma at work as the political process helped one group after another, with the end result being a loss for (practically) everyone: "But how the people, once they have won their battle, can imagine that they too can enter as a body into the ranks of the privileged, create monopolies for themselves and over themselves, extend abuses widely enough to provide for their livelihood; how they can fail to see that there is nobody below them to support these injustices, is one of the most amazing phenomena of this or any age" (1850, chap. 12, ¶ 28).

Karl Marx (1818–83) had much to say, of course, about how capitalism favored the capitalists over the workers, given that the capitalists got rich by extracting a "surplus value" from the productive contributions of labor. However, according to Marx, Malthus's dreadful population theory was much to blame. People's sexual proclivities would ensure a supply of labor that would press worker wages toward, if not exactly to, subsistence levels, except for short periods of time. Capitalists could take the differential between the market value of what the workers produced and what they were paid. Marx had little to say about monopoly per se.[19] However, he shared Smith's and Ricardo's complaint that many firms were able to extract more than a competitive surplus value because they were often protected from competition.

> Manufacturing was constantly protected in the domestic market by protective tariffs, in colonial markets by monopolies, and in foreign markets, to the maximum extent possible, by differential tariffs. The processing of domestically produced materials (wool and linen in England, silk in France) was favoured, the export of raw materials generated at home was prohibited (wool in England) and the [processing] of imported materials was either neglected or suppressed (cotton in England) . . . In general, manufacturing could not dispense with protection, because the slightest change occurring in other countries can cause it to lose markets and be ruined. (1845, 162–63)

Elsewhere, Marx chided the political parties in England for not having an adequate explanation for the "pauperism" of the masses. Each of the two dominant parties, Whigs and Tories, considered the other party the cause, with the

Whig Party pointing to the "large-scale ownership and the prohibitive legislation against the import of corn," and the Tory Party claiming that the "entire evil lies in liberalism, in competition, in a factory system that has been carried too far," points that allowed Marx to note that neither party understood that the source of poverty lies in politics in general and that the solution lies in "the reform of society" (1844, 100). In this regard, Marx shared with Bastiat a healthy disrespect for the conduct of politics.

MARSHALL ON THE "NET REVENUES" OF MONOPOLY

Alfred Marshall (1842–1924) is widely recognized for having formalized much of the economic theory of his time in his textbook, *Principles of Economics*, first published in 1890. In that work, he introduced the concepts of supply and demand curves, equilibrium, price-elasticity of demand, consumer surplus, and producer surplus. Moreover, he made full use of marginal analysis (which dates to the work of Stanley Jevons [1835–82], Leon Walras [1834–1910], and Carl Menger [1840–1921], the three economists generally credited with explaining prices with reference to *marginal* utility and, thus, founding the "marginal revolution"). Marshall explored market adjustments under three periods: the "market period," the amount of time in which the amount of a good cannot be varied; the "short period," or the amount of time in which labor and other inputs can be changed but capital cannot; and the "long period," or the amount of time in which all resources, capital included, can be varied.[20]

With respect to monopoly, Marshall accepted the general view that a monopoly was any firm able to "fix an artificial monopoly price; that is, a price determined with little direct reference to cost of production, but chiefly by a consideration of what the market will bear" (1890, bk. 5, chap. 1, ¶ 17). He then set about describing in some detail, with the aid of graphs (relegated to footnotes), how a monopolist, which disregards the interests of society, including consumers, would choose its price-output combination in order to maximize "net revenues," or monopoly profits, which he defined to be revenues minus all explicit and implicit costs, including risk cost, and "normal profits." This means that he defined monopoly profit in much the same way it is defined in contemporary economics.

Marshall also pointed out that the monopolist's profit-maximizing price would be left unaffected by a change in the firm's fixed costs or by a tax applied solely to "net revenues."[21] Of course, a change in variable costs or a tax applied to total revenue (or the "amount produced") or to book profit (not "net revenue") would cause the monopolist to reduce its output and raise its price.[22]

Marshall recognized that the monopolist's pricing could be tempered by a number of factors, not the least of which is that the monopolist might be duty-bound to be concerned about the welfare of consumers.[23] However, it might also be concerned with how its pricing decision could affect the entry of competitors, which led him to suggest an early, albeit brief, form of the more contemporary theory of "limit pricing," that is, "of a monopoly limited by the consideration that a very high price would bring rival producers into the field" (1890, bk. 4, chap. 11, ¶ 16)—a theory of monopoly pricing brought back into vogue among economists in the 1940s and 1950s by Joe Bain (1949, 1956) and Franco Modigliani (1958) in the form of "entry forestalling prices."[24] However, Marshall also suggested that the monopolist might temper its *current* price demands in order to develop its market and the *future* demand for its product that would, at that time, allow the monopolist to charge a higher price.

> But, in fact, even if he [the monopolist] does not concern himself with the interests of the consumers, he is likely to reflect that the demand for a thing depends in a great measure on people's familiarity with it; and that if he can increase his sales by taking a price a little below that which would afford him the maximum net revenue, the increased use of his commodity will before long recoup him for his present loss. The lower the price of gas, the more likely people are to have it laid on to their houses; and when once it is there, they are likely to go on making some use of it, even though a rival, such as electricity or mineral oil, may be competing closely with it. The case is stronger when a railway company has a practical monopoly of the transport of persons and goods to a sea-port, or to a suburban district which is as yet but partly built over; the railway company may then find it worth while, as a matter of business, to levy charges much below those which would afford the maximum net revenue, in order to get merchants into the habit of using the port, to encourage the inhabitants of the port to develop their docks and warehouses; or to assist speculative builders in the new suburb to build houses cheaply and to fill them quickly with tenants, thus giving to the suburb an air of early prosperity which goes far towards insuring its permanent success. This sacrifice by a monopolist of part of his present gains in order to develop future business differs in extent rather than kind from the sacrifices which a young firm commonly makes in order to establish a connection. (1890, bk. 5, chap. 14, ¶ 20)

In making these observations about the interconnectedness of demand over time, Marshall was anticipating more involved theories that came nearly a century later and will be considered in following chapters in this volume: the theories of experience goods (Nelson 1970), rational addition (Becker and Murphy 1988), lagged demand (Lee and Kreutzer 1982), and network effects (Arthur 1996). However, Marshall obviously failed to consider in his textbook that consumers might anticipate how current pricing could affect the future monopoly power of the firm achieved from lowering its current prices and, therefore, how consumers' current purchases might be tempered without some assurance by the firm that it would not act like a monopolist in the future.

Modern refinements on monopoly theory in the form of imperfectly competitive or monopolistically competitive market structures developed by Edward Chamberlin (1933) and Joan Robinson (1933) have not given rise to a fundamentally different treatment of the way firms facing a downward sloping demand can curb production and give rise to a misallocation of resources. The difference in the distortion is a matter of degree, not of kind. The principal difference is that imperfect monopolies cannot count on earning monopoly rents in the long run. Still, such firms have excess capacities. The issue of whether the product variations spawned under imperfect monopoly market structures compensate, or more than compensate, for the supposed resource misallocation is left as a question that economists cannot answer, and should not pretend that they can (or so conventional, contemporary economic thinking holds).

SCHUMPETER ON THE VITAL ROLE OF
THE "MONOPOLOID SPECIE"

When Joseph Schumpeter said that any economic system that is fully efficient at every point in time will likely be inferior to a system that is efficient at no point in time, he was dramatically parting ways with what had, through time, developed into the conventional view of monopoly, or what he tagged as the "monopoloid species"[25] (1942, 106): Any level of monopoly (or any market structure "less perfect" than perfect competition) should be the object of economists' scorn (with the degree of scorn related to a firm's "monopoly power," or ability to hike prices above marginal cost). In Schumpeter's view, "monopoly had become the father of almost all [market and societal] abuses—in fact it became his [the economist's] pet bogey" and had become "almost synonymous with any large-scale business" (1942, 100). He noted that Adam Smith had "frowned" on monopolies with "awful dignity" (1942, 100). By using perfect competition as the standard of market efficiency, or cost-based competitive pricing, Schumpeter argued that "literally anyone is a monopolist that sells anything not in every respect, and wrapping and location and service included, exactly like what other people sell; every grocer, or every haberdasher, or every seller of 'Good Humor' on a road that is not simply lined with sellers of the same brand of ice cream" (1942, 99). To him, "pure competition" was no less than a "hallowed ideal," and its use by economists to divine policy positions (especially relating to antitrust policy) was "futile" (1949, 358). Because of virtually all economists' myopic focus on perfect competition, Schumpeter concluded that an economist could be "a very good theorist and yet talk absolute nonsense whenever confronted with the task of diagnosing a concrete histori- cal pattern as a whole" (1942, 83, fn. 3). Edward Mason reports that Schum- peter once confided that "he [Schumpeter] was anxious to clear existing work out of the way in order to undertake a study of the question whether anything could be said about the 'monopoly problem' that was anything other than 'sheer ideology'" (Mason 1951, 141), a study on which, by the time of Schum- peter's death, he had already drawn strong conclusions.[26]

Schumpeter reasoned that economists' static models of markets—whether competitive or monopoly—were directed narrowly toward explaining how firms in markets "administer" existing known and available resources, "whereas the relevant problem is how it [capitalism] creates and destroys them" (1942, 84). In his "creative destruction" process of long-term economic improvement, price competition or its absence, the focus of standard compet- itive and monopoly models, is not inconsequential, but price competition obvi- ously pales in comparison with the importance of actual competition, or the threat of competition, from innovations, which can cover new products, new technologies, and new types of organizational structures. Competition from these sources strikes "not at the margins of the profits and the output of the existing firms but at their [the firms'] foundations and their very lives" (1942, 84).[27] According to Schumpeter, without including an analysis of this type of nonprice competition, any discussion of markets, even though technically cor- rect, is as empty as a performance of "Hamlet without the Danish prince" (1942, 86).

Schumpeter's "perennial gale of creative destruction" can easily, although mistakenly, be viewed solely as a positive commentary on the role of firms in highly competitive market environments, not monopoly, under capitalism. Schumpeter, however, saw the market process in more complex and complete terms, which ultimately made monopoly a strategically important force for social good in any dynamic, or would-be dynamic, economy. Firms that are able to charge above-competitive prices might indeed earn, for a time, monop- oly profits.[28] However, if firms could not hope to earn more than "normal profits" (or the minimal return capital must have to stay in place), they might not emerge with the same frequency that they do, because they would have drastically impaired incentives to innovate (1942, 102).[29] Besides, monopolies "largely create what they exploit. Hence, the usual conclusion about their influence on long-run output [that overall economic growth should be choked] would be invalid even if they were genuine monopolies in the technical sense of the term" (1942, 101).[30]

Moreover, the monopoly profits "might still prove to be the easiest and most effective way of collecting the means by which to finance additional investment [i.e., expansion]" (1942, 87), a line of argument that underlies the granting of monopoly privileges through copyrights and patents.[31] Surely, Schumpeter also understood (as did Smith) that the prospects of monopoly profits would make the financing of initial forays into markets all the easier and cheaper. Just as surely, he understood that the probability of monopoly profits over a range of entrepreneurial ventures—whether taken up in a single firm or across an array of entrepreneurial investments—could encourage the development of investment portfolios, which can reduce investment risks and, thereby, encourage investments and innovations.

In an important way, Schumpeter appears to be arguing that the instances of monopoly, or market power, in a broader economy are an unheralded force behind Adam Smith's "invisible hand." Monopolies actually energize "creative destruction." In seeking to create monopolies and earn above-competitive profits, new firms are forever destroying existing monopolies. In the process, these new entrants may, by accident or direct intention, be giving rise to new and improved products, technologies, and organizational forms, or over time the economy is able to grow faster because at each point in time, monopolies are holding it back. Put another way, monopolies are a "necessary evil" (1942, 106).[32] In drawing what many might see as a paradoxical conclusion, Schumpeter suggests, "There is no more paradox in this [case for monopolies] than there is in saying that motorcars are traveling faster than they otherwise would *because* they are provided with brakes" (88; emphasis in the original).

But then, Schumpeter could rest comfortably in what he believed to be the reality of market life: Monopolies were short-lived practically everywhere—at least when unprotected by governments, precisely because of the "gale of creative destruction": "The power to exploit at pleasure a given pattern of demand . . . can under the condition of intact capitalism hardly persist for a period long enough to matter for the analysis of total output, unless buttressed by public authority" (1942, 99). In contrast to Smith and others, Schumpeter doubts that even firms protected by significant entry restrictions can long endure if they do what monopolies are supposed to do, restrict their outputs to raise their prices (99).[33]

Schumpeter concludes, "Perfectly free entry into a *new* field may make it impossible to enter it at all. The introduction of new methods of production and new commodities is hardly conceivable with perfect—and perfectly prompt—competition from the start. And this means that the bulk of what we call economic progress is incompatible with it" (1942, 104–5; emphasis in the original). That is to say, economic progress is compatible only with the existence of monopoly profits of some (unstated) degree. It follows that entry barriers have social value, at least up to a point.

Why, then, is there so much talk about the "evils" of monopoly? Schumpeter suggested that it is largely unrecognized demagoguery at work: "Economists, government agents, journalists, and politicians in this country obviously love the word because it has come to be a term of opprobrium which is sure to rouse the public hostility against any interest so labeled" (1942, 100). At the same time, he clearly believed that monopolies' ease of movement among markets and of arising in new markets, and thereby destroying others, would inevitably cause large firms with market power to be frequently subjected to "vindictive harassment" by antitrust authorities (Mason 1951, 144).[34]

But then, Schumpeter was not the first to focus on the destructive side of markets or the integral role monopolies play in that process, a point most recently stressed by Michael Perelman (1995). David Wells (1828–89)—a chemist by training but acclaimed as one of the more important economists of the last quarter of the nineteenth century (Ferleger 1977), in spite of working for the federal government as Special Commissioner of Revenue—saw competition pushing capitalism to the brink of self-destruction. The source of the self-destructive competition was rapid technological advances, spawned principally by "great industrial enterprises," pushing the economy relentlessly toward excess capacity, overproduction, and deflation (and the country's price index did fall by nearly half during the last third of the century). Wells saw an integral connection between progress and the destruction of wealth, which he characterized as an "economic law," which has all the markings of Schumpeter's "perennial gale": "All material progress is affected through the destruction of capital by invention and discovery, and the rapidity of such destruction is the best indicator of the rapidity of progress" (1889, 146).[35]

For Schumpeter, monopolies were collectors of investment funds, which made them a wellspring of new innovations that ultimately fuel the creative destruction process, a part of which was the dethroning of existing monopolies by new ones. Wells also saw monopolies as a wellspring of inventions and discoveries. However, he also saw in them another source of social value, the only potential check on overproduction: "There appears to be no other means of avoiding such results than that the great producers come to an understanding as to the prices they will ask; which, in turn naturally implies agreements to the extent to which they will produce" (Wells 1889, 74), an advantage of monopoly that Schumpeter specifically rejected (1942, 106). Like Schumpeter, Wells worried that antitrust laws would have the opposite effect of the one intended. In Wells's case, he feared that antitrust enforcement would ensure the continuation of self-destructiveness (through overproduction) of supracompetitive markets (unless they were used to thwart trusts, such as Standard Oil, that have used their ability to raise capital to drive up output and drive down prices).[36] Schumpeter, on the other hand, emphasized how the indiscriminate pursuit of trust busting would undermine the innovative vitality of the economy (1942, 91).

THE SCHUMPETER HYPOTHESIS

If Schumpeter had left his assessment of the relative merits of competitive and monopoly markets totally conceptual, without concrete direction on the nature of the testable facts, he would have certainly retained his honored status within the annals of economic thought. However, just as surely, the generations of economists and policymakers who followed him would not have seen Schumpeter's thinking subjected to as much following econometric work, nor cited as frequently. Over the past sixty-some years, econometricians have created a nonconsequential competitive industry of their own as they have sought to test the so-called Schumpeter hypothesis, which was best stated by Schumpeter in this way: "As soon as we go into the details and inquire into the individual items in which progress has been most conspicuous, the trail leads not to the doors of those firms that work under conditions of comparatively free competition but precisely to the doors of the large concerns" (1942, 82).

The Schumpeter hypothesis has, of course, been reformulated by a series of economists for their own research needs.[37] Econometricians have also produced a sizable number of studies that have attempted to draw statistically validated connections between various measures of, on the one hand, firm size, industry concentration, market power, or retained business earnings and, on the other hand, various input measures of innovativeness of firms (e.g., their R&D expenditures) and output measures of their inventiveness (e.g., patents awarded firms). The statistical deductions drawn have been, unfortunately, all over the econometric map, with some studies showing a growth in R&D expenditures or patents awarded with growth in firm size, and other studies showing the opposite (Baumol 1990; Scherer 1965; Hamberg 1964; Horriwitz 1962; Jennings 1989; Jennings and Lumpkin 1995).[38] Then, more studies have shown an initial increase in input and output measures of the innovativeness and inventiveness of firms with growth in size, only to be followed by a decline.[39]

Of course, the researchers have also found that the relationship between firm size and measures of innovativeness and inventiveness differs by industry (Worley 1961; Schmookler 1959; Mansfield 1963, 1964).[40] However, economists who have reviewed this literature have found the Schumpeter hypothesis wanting at best. Moreover, Scherer (1970, 377) deduced from all the work done through the late 1960s that "new entrants contribute a disproportionately high share of all really revolutionary new industrial products and processes," although he had earlier cautioned that "perhaps a bevy of fact-mechanics can still rescue the Schumpeterian engine from disgrace" (1965, 1122). In their extensive review of the studies on the Schumpeter hypothesis through the early 1970s, Kamien and Schwartz concluded that "the evidence indicates that research output intensity does tend to increase and then decrease with increasing firm size" (1975, 3).[41]

Link (1980) could have been one such "fact-mechanic," given that he has argued that the rate of return on firms' R&D expenditures is a far better test of the Schumpeter hypothesis than, say, R&D expenditures and patents awarded. After all, the payoff from innovative activity is of greater interest to owners than the absolute real level of their expenditures or the count of patents (whose worth can vary greatly). In his study of firms in the chemical and allied products industry using 1975 data, Link found substantial economies of scale on R&D expenditures, as measured by their rate of returns. Small firms (those with less than $300 million in sales) had a rate of return on their collective R&D expenditures of 30 percent. Large firms had a rate of return of 78 percent, which should imply greater innovative activity among larger firms—at least in the chemical industry (and Link chose the chemical industry to study because the industry's R&D expenditures were affected only to a limited extent by government funding).[42]

A number of empirical problems arise in testing the Schumpeter hypothesis. For example, we can't be confident that measured variables—for example, firm size measured by sales or industry concentration ratios—are reasonable surrogates for the kind of market power Schumpeter had in mind. Moreover, R&D expenditures are hardly the only use to which large firms can put their (monopoly) profits (Markham 1965; Fisher and Temin 1965; Cohen and Levin 1989). After all, Schumpeter stressed that innovation could come in the form of changes in firm organization or, for that matter, advertising campaigns. In addition, it is not altogether clear whether the R&D expenditures were the result or cause of firm size and market dominance. Indeed, as Nelson and Winter (1982) have argued, the market structure is endogenous to Schumpeterian competition, suggesting that R&D expenditures and firm size emerge together.

Finally, the full impact of large firms, or firms with measures of monopoly power, may be more indirect than researchers have imagined. With technology in product and process development progressing along so many avenues, the top 100 or 500 largest firms in an industry, or even the entire economy, which are the focus of a number of econometric studies, can hardly be expected to investigate all avenues of innovation. They must pick and choose their innovation avenues (and their risks), often with an eye to how their R&D work will complement their existing product line, leaving much for outsiders to do that breaks with existing product lines.[43] Top firms' own bureaucracies can hold them back on the range and depth of their entrepreneurial activities. They can, however, set themselves up as cherry pickers, that is, they can wait and see what products emerge from much smaller and newer firms and show signs of becoming successful. They can then step in and buy up the successful smaller firms, with the larger firms using their well-established distribution systems to make the newly developed products and processes more successful than they otherwise would be. The existence of the large firms, along with their willingness and ability to pay supracompetitive prices (because of their market power) for demonstrated successful innovations, can inspire much entrepreneurial activity among smaller firms—and, hence, can be viewed as an important force for innovation among small firms and new entrants.

Having said all of this, it is important to note that Schumpeter was careful to stress that any assessments of the impact of the monopoly power of large firms could be properly made only over a long stretch of time, covering decades, at the very least, and perhaps a century or more. Even then, he was careful to add addenda to his so-called hypothesis: (1) that "mere size is neither necessary nor sufficient for the superiority of the monopoly firm" (1942, 101) and (2) that the critical dependent variable would be some variant of the overall "standard of living," not some narrowly conceived measure of firm size or industry concentration.[44]

Researchers have done their studies, apparently assuming that Schumpeter was fixated exclusively on firm size. Although he often wrote about large firms in *Capitalism, Socialism, and Democracy*, his principal concern throughout his major book-length works was really the "character and quality" of entrepreneurship and leadership within firms, large or small, as McNulty (1974) has argued in some detail.[45] Indeed, as Chamberlin (1951) argued early in the debate, Schumpeter practically dismissed altogether economies of scale per se as a source of firm size (and therefore didn't give much credence to the theory of monopolistic competition). If there was any initial fall in long-run average cost, the source was the lumpiness of plant and equipment, not any technical advantage that firms achieve from expanding all factors of production. In Schumpeter's world, firms might appear to face decreasing long-run cost functions, which might appear to be the source of their size, but appearances can be deceiving. The ongoing pace of innovation in production processes, which lower firms' cost curves, is a key cause of lower costs with expanded size.[46]

CONCLUDING COMMENTS

Obviously, the word *monopoly* has been used in a variety of contexts throughout the history of economic thought. The term has been used to describe (if not denigrate) the inherent privileges of property owners, given that no one else has access to the owners' rights without dealing with the owner. *Monopoly* has been used to characterize large business firms (without regard to their market shares), as well as firms that are the dominant, if not the only, producers in their markets. A key unifying feature of firms tagged as monopolies has been the firms' ability to significantly affect total market supply of their products, enough at least for them to have some choice over their selling prices. This choice gives them the capacity to seek maximum profits, within the constraints of their cost and demand schedules. Of course, *monopoly* and *cartel* have been used synonymously, because a cartel can supposedly do, once it has been organized, what a single (or dominant) producer can do with almost the same facility (which, as we will argue later, is not likely to be the case).

However, *monopoly* has also been used to describe firms that have been able to raise their prices, as well as production levels, because of imposed governmental restrictions on competition, for example, through copyrights, patents, tariffs, and quotas, or, for that matter, trade secrets, trademarks, and brands. Such firms are said to be monopolies because with the market protections, they all can sell their goods above cost.

In the views of the economic masters covered in this chapter, except for Schumpeter (and, to a lesser extent, Wells), one feature stands out: No matter how the term has been used, monopoly has been viewed at best as a "necessary evil," as in the cases of land property rights, and at worst in other cases (with few exceptions, such as in Smith's argument that monopoly might be a useful device for encouraging especially hazardous market ventures) as a drag on consumer welfare, disposable income, and economic progress. At the same time, all writers covered appear to be unified on an important point: Absent government support, monopolies that endure for long are likely to be rare, which implies that any damage done is not likely to persist, mainly because in raising their prices above costs, monopolists inspire competitors to enter their markets.

Schumpeter clearly agrees that monopolies that spring solely from market strategies, unsupported by government protection, are likely to be relatively short-lived. Indeed, he suggests that the only market structure likely to be rarer than perfect competition in the world outside economists' classrooms is a firm that persistently behaves like a monopoly, that is, restricts its sales to push up its prices, and then survives.[47] That claim allows Schumpeter to stress the largely unheralded role of monopolies in fueling the "capitalist achievement," not so much price competition, in which consumer values remain constant, but rather in promoting nonprice competition, in which the value of available goods is constantly being upgraded, but with price competition ever-present, albeit derivative factors that make innovations accessible to the masses.[48] So what if the monopolist doesn't produce with the efficiency of a perfectly competitive market? That idealized standard is unachievable. Moreover, even if it were achievable, any harm done by any monopoly's restriction on output must be juxtaposed with the gains from product and production process improvements. Otherwise, reconciling the growth in human welfare in the latter part of the nineteenth century and early part of the twentieth century (if not beyond), a time when many companies were expanding rapidly and gaining control over price, is difficult, as Schumpeter stressed.[49]

Although much is to be gained from using perfect competition for evaluating price competition and from standard monopoly models, which help illustrate the standard negative assessment of monopoly that extends back to Smith and forward to the prevailing sentiment among modern textbook writers, it is the Schumpeterian view of monopoly that drives the development of this book and, to the extent adopted, forces a change in the perception of policies related to monopoly.[50] Under the Smithian view of monopoly, all trade restrictions, regulations, and private efforts to monopolize markets have a single policy solution: Get rid of them.[51]

From the Schumpeterian perspective, however, the solution is not so easy. Hidden in Schumpeter's analysis is a theory of *optimum monopoly* required for maximum economic growth.[52] Such a theory necessarily implies that a "delicate" (Schumpeter's word) balance be struck not only in matters of antitrust enforcement but also in all other government policies relating to market restrictions and regulation, whether they spring from private or public sources.[53]

We take up in this book a largely Schumpeterian view of monopoly—perhaps more accurately dubbed and widely known as Schumpeterian competition—in part because his view has been lost on many economists and policymakers, especially in the antitrust area, as seen in monopoly presentations in modern textbooks that we lay out in the following chapter. We also take up the Schumpeterian perspective because Schumpeter was, in our view, actually overly conservative in his criticisms of monopoly theory as it existed in his day, and as that theory has been brought forward with updates and extensions. A critique of modern monopoly theory should include a reexamination of the impact of the emergence of monopoly on the net inefficiency—and extent of failure—in markets. This reexamination acknowledges that price changes, up or down, affect the marginal value of the last unit buyers consume, but reexamination directly challenges the conventional microeconomic claim that price changes have no effect on the *schedule* of consumers' marginal values of various units, a claim that necessarily implies that price changes do not affect market demand.[54] The adjustments we propose in basic monopoly theory have been all the more relevant because of the emergence of many modern goods, the value of which is founded on such considerations as networks, experience, and trust.

Moreover, there has been a long-term decline in the marginal cost of production in many industries relative to total cost. Today, a growing number of goods can be reproduced at zero or close to zero marginal cost (as in the case of electronic goods: e-books, e-music, e-movies, and so on). These cost factors force a reconsideration of the social value of monopolies and their protective entry barriers, as we will argue at practically every step in this book. This means that our critique of monopoly theory stands on, but then moves beyond, Schumpeter's key insights.

Chapter 2

Deadweight-Loss Monopoly

Contemporary economists' classroom and textbook considerations of monopoly are formal and precise, subject to exacting mathematical specifications. However, informal and legal discussions of monopoly among economists and those who use monopoly theory (e.g., antitrust lawyers) are typically no more precise than Adam Smith's and David Ricardo's views.

The word *monopoly* is used in various venues to refer to a single seller of a product; a producer that has an overwhelming market share; a firm that is just large (perhaps with substantially less than half of market sales); or any firm with "market power" (meaning any firm other than a "price taker"). All these treatments of monopoly have one unifying feature, however: The monopolist is capable of influencing market price by substantially affecting market supply via its own production decisions.

The monopolist is seen to impose harm in two ways: It gives rise to a form of market inadequacy or failure, and the monopolist extracts consumer surplus for the benefit of its owners.

The widely touted inefficiency of monopoly is necessarily judged in almost all settings, to one extent or another, explicitly or implicitly, by an independent theoretical standard, perfect competition. Hence, we must start our critique of monopoly theory by laying out this market standard by which monopoly is evaluated and, often, condemned, with an eye toward theoretical corrections and market insights. We will see that it is not at all difficult to condemn any real-world market, monopoly or otherwise, that necessarily emerges in an imperfect world to solve pressing real-world problems, if the criterion is perfection. However, we will also press the case for a renewed appreciation for the net gains to be had from the emergence and persistence of monopoly under some real-world market conditions, in spite of any imagined inefficiency that might remain, given the extreme standard for judgment.

We fully understand that both perfect competition and monopoly are theoretical constructs, which are not intended to mirror real-world market conditions. As economist Milton Friedman pointed out decades ago, the test of an economist's model is, or should be, the validity of the predictions, not the correspondence of the model's assumptions with real-world market conditions (1953, 3–43). That said, the problem with the perfect competition/monopoly dichotomy is the common assumption that any monopoly that exists is necessarily a net drag on the economy. Thus, an improvement would necessarily be forthcoming were an identified monopoly subjected to competition, or more accurately more competition. Also, from the perspective of conventional treatments of monopoly, no amount of collusion could conceivably result in a market improvement. Likewise, all market entry and exit barriers give rise to a form of market loss.

Our reassessment of monopoly goes to the heart of monopoly theory because our central conclusion is that these tenets are all wrong, at least to one degree or another. To see these points, we need to lay out how economists see perfect competition and, therefore, assess monopoly. (Those readers steeped in standard microeconomic theory can skip or quickly skim the following two sections.)

THE EFFICIENCY OF PERFECT COMPETITION

The perfection of perfect competition is created through five notable market characteristics: (1) numerous producers are in the market; (2) all producers produce the same product, meaning all producers' products are identical in all regards; (3) the cost of entry into and exit from the market is zero; (4) the cost of information about the prices and products, both current and future, is also zero to both producers and consumers, which implies that everyone in the market is perfectly informed; and (5) no costs and benefits can be externalized to parties not involved in the market transactions.[1] The effect of these market features is, not surprisingly, a market that operates with unblemished perfection—by definition. Although we question the perfectly competitive model later, all trades that are mutually beneficial to consumers and producers are exploited. Producers are necessarily price takers. This means that the producers have no ability to charge more than the going market price and have no reason to charge less, since they can sell all they can justify producing at the going market price.[2]

All these results mean that the marginal value of the last unit sold to consumers just equals the marginal cost of its production to producers, which also just equals the market price. Hence, net welfare gains are maximized, meaning that the consumer and producer surplus combined cannot be exceeded by any conceivable market restructuring or resource reallocation. The complicated details of the efficiency of perfect competition can be left to textbooks (e.g., Pindyck and Rubinfeld 2005, chap. 8).

For our purposes, we can hold the discussion to the basic supply and demand model (which is built on an assumption of an underlying perfectly competitive market) as captured in figure 2.1. The downward sloping curve, the demand, captures how much all consumers are willing to buy from all producers at all prices indicated on the vertical axis. The curve that is upward sloping to the right, the supply, reflects the horizontal summation of all firms' marginal cost curves, or how much the producers are willing to provide in the aggregate at all prices indicated, again on the vertical axis. Because of the extreme degree of competition, the price necessarily gravitates toward the intersection of the two curves, or equilibrium.[3]

The producers are not able to hold the price above the intersection, given all the other forms of perfection embedded in the perfectly competitive model (that is, zero cost of movement in and out of the market and zero cost of information). At the same time, producers would face prohibitively high transaction costs in forming and maintaining a producer cartel intent on operating like a unified monopoly, which is one way of restricting the aggregate market supply for the purpose of raising their market price and the firms' individual and collective profits.

Moreover, if by some odd chance a cartel were ever formed, it would immediately dissolve as the producers cheated at zero cost on the cartel's restrictive production rules. In addition, zero cost of entry would ensure that firms outside the market would enter to take unexploited profitable production opportunities, which would leave the quantity of the good on the market at the intersection (equilibrium) level, leaving the price at the intersection level. The problems of making a cartel work are so overwhelming under perfect competition that no firm would even contemplate forming one, which means the perfection of perfect competition would not be sullied by cartel costs.

If the price ever happened to be below the intersection, a market shortage would emerge, resulting in competition among buyers, which would drive the price up to, not just toward, the intersection price. If the price were not quite up to the intersection level, some of the throngs of consumers, who would then value additional units of the good more than the price charged, would demand more and would, through competition, press the price to the intersection price.

As was true of the producers, consumers would not be able to form a buyer cartel, which in the consumers' case would be intent on suppressing their collective demand, holding the price below the intersection level. As

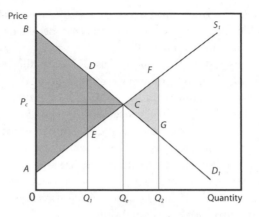

Figure 2.1. Market efficiency

true of producers, consumers would face prohibitive transaction costs in organizing and maintaining the buyer cartel; the prospects of cartel cheating would be rampant.

Interestingly, if transaction costs for forming supplier or buyer cartels were zero, perfect competition would not necessarily be so perfect, in the terms that economists hold dear. This is because collusion would be rampant on both sides of the market, and the market outcome would be indeterminate. The market outcome would then be a consequence of the bargaining skills of the two cartelized sides of the market. In short, if bargaining costs are zero, "perfect competition," to have this type of settled and determinate outcome, requires this one consequential imperfection, nonzero transaction costs in the formation of collusive efforts on either side of the market.[4]

Nonetheless, this extreme competitive process can be shown to maximize market outcomes, following Gary Becker's elegantly simple classroom pedagogy (1971, lecture 19). He starts by noting that all price-quantity combinations on the demand curve in figure 2.1 are acceptable to consumers, by definition. It follows that all price-quantity combinations below the demand curve are acceptable to consumers. After all, consumers should be willing to pay lower prices for any given quantity that is indicated by the price on their demand curve.

Similarly, all price-quantity combinations on the supply curve are acceptable to producers, by definition. Hence, all price-quantity combinations above the supply curve are acceptable to the producers. After all, if producers were willing to accept a price for a given quantity that is on the supply curve, then surely they would be willing to accept higher prices for the same quantity.

Notice that the price-quantity combinations within the triangular area *ABC* are acceptable to *both* producers and consumers. Of all those combinations, the one selected by the intense competition of perfect competition is the one furthest right, Q_e. This means that perfect competition maximizes output, given the consumer value and producer cost constraints underlying the supply and demand curves.

Moreover, notice that for every unit produced and sold up to Q_e, the point on the demand curve for that quantity, which indicates the unit's marginal value, is above the point for the same quantity on the supply curve, which indicates that unit's marginal cost. Put another way, for each unit of the good up to the intersection quantity Q_e, the marginal value of the unit exceeds its marginal cost, with the difference being the gain to be had from trade, that is, from producing and selling that unit.

Since the marginal *cost* of each unit indicates the value of what could have been done with the resources used to produce the unit, this gap between points on the supply and demand curves indicates the added value from using the resources in the production of this good over the value that could have been realized from using the resources in the production of some other good (the next best alternative). The triangular area *ABC* is the maximum aggregate gain to be obtained from production and trade of this good. That triangular area is the net welfare gain—surplus value—from having an unobstructed, perfectly competitive market.[5]

If production were (for purposes of argument) to fall below the intersection level, then mutually beneficial trades would be left unexploited. A part of the triangular area *ABC* would be lost. More precisely, *ABC* would not be fully realized. For example, if output was restricted to Q_1, the welfare gain from trades would be limited to the trapezoid *ABDE*, meaning that the triangular area *EDC* would be unrealized. This smaller triangular area *EDC* is the inefficiency or the deadweight loss of producing at Q_1.[6]

In a similar manner, if the production were above the intersection/equilibrium quantity, say Q_n, the *net* welfare gain from *all* trades would be undercut. The *ABC* triangular area would be realized, but this gain would be offset by another triangular area on the other side of the intersection output level, *CFG*, which would capture the extent to which the marginal cost of producing the units beyond Q_e exceeded the consumers' assessed value of the goods. This means that something more valuable could have been produced by the resources used to produce any units beyond the intersection level.

All in all, perfect competition leads to the market price being as low as it can be (given the constraint of marginal cost), resources being perfectly allocated (given what consumers value), and firms' realizing zero *economic profits* (as distinct from *normal profits*, or the minimum return on capital for the owners) at all times. If economic profits were positive, then firms outside the market would move in the market at, of course, zero entry costs. Outside firms would have no justification to stay out of the market. Accordingly, the market supply would expand as firms moved in, the market price would fall, and the economic profits would evaporate. Maximum efficiency would once again be the outcome.

THE INEFFICIENCY OF MONOPOLY

Microeconomic textbook authors always follow their presentations of perfect competition with discussions of the polar opposite market structure: pure monopoly. The pedagogical purpose of using *pure* is to simplify the analysis, sharpen the contrast, and crystallize the meaning of a key attribute of a profit-maximizing monopoly, the market structure's inefficiency.[7]

A pure monopoly is a market that is served exclusively by a single producer whose market position is protected by barriers to entry that are prohibitively costly to surmount for would-be competitors. The pure monopolist, unlike the perfect competitor, faces the downward-sloping market demand curve for its product, meaning it can choose any price combination along the demand curve. If its intent is to maximize profits, it will necessarily weigh off the marginal (or additional) revenue of each unit with the marginal (or additional) cost of producing each unit to determine its output level. After all, if the marginal revenue of any unit is greater than its marginal cost, firm profits can be raised by producing the unit. Production should expand as long as that is the case, or up until the marginal revenue of the last unit equals the marginal cost of the last unit. Production beyond equality of marginal cost and revenue will mean that profits decline, since marginal revenue on all additional units will then be below the units' marginal cost of production.[8]

If the pure monopoly is able to make a profit (by which we mean, strictly speaking, economic profit, or that part of book profit above normal profit),[9] it does not have to worry about its market ever being eroded by the entry of competitors. Other producers can't get in the pure monopolist's market, which is to say that the entry costs are prohibitive. Technically, this means only that the costs of entry exceed the present discounted value of the future stream of monopoly profits that entering firms could possibly garner.

To see all these points and others, let's simplify the monopoly model as much as possible. First, we consider only the monopolist's position in the long run (meaning it has worked its way through the nontrivial problem of optimizing its scale and scope of production), an assumption that allows us to count all costs as variable. Second, we assume for simplicity's sake that the marginal cost of producing each unit is positive and constant (the same for every unit). This means that average cost equals marginal cost at all output levels. We can make these simplifying assumptions because they do not disturb the central points we wish to make, and which are often made in conventional textbook discussions of monopoly.

These assumptions are embedded in the curves in figure 2.2. The monopolist's demand curve takes on its normal downward slope in figure 2.2. The monopolist's marginal revenue curve is, thus, downward sloping and inside the demand curve. That is to say that marginal revenue is below the price at every output level.[10] The assumption of constant cost is reflected in the horizontal curve, tagged as $MC = AC$, to signal the equality between marginal and average cost.

The central question the monopolist faces is, what price-quantity combination on its demand curve will maximize profits? It can answer the question by weighing off the marginal cost of production against its marginal revenue, or by comparing points on the MC and MR curves in figure 2.2. As long as the points on the MR curve are above the points on the MC curve, the monopolist's profits rise by extending production. That is, the monopolist should extend production up to Q_m for maximum profits. Beyond Q_m, profits fall, because MC is then above MR.

The monopolist's economic profits are equal to the area bounded by $P_c P_m XZ$. Its total revenue is $P_m \times Q_m$, or rectangular area $0 P_m X Q_m$. Its total cost is $AC \times Q_m$, or the area bounded by $0 P_c Z Q_m$. The economic profit is, of course, total revenue minus total cost, or the difference between those two identified areas.

The inefficiency of the monopolist's restricted output level can be represented by the shaded triangular area XYZ. This inefficiency occurs because perfect competition would lead (according to conventional treatment of perfect competition) to a production level of Q_c at a price of P_c. As we saw earlier, a perfectly competitive market would yield a production level at the intersection of supply and demand, or the industry's marginal cost curve and the demand. This area of inefficiency attributable to production at Q_m is the difference between the total additional value and total additional cost of the units produced under perfect competition and not produced by the monopolist, or $Q_c - Q_m$. The area of total value of these $(Q_c - Q_m)$ units is bounded by $Q_m X Y Q_c$. The area of total cost of these units is bounded by $Q_m Z Y Q_c$. The difference between those two areas is the inefficiency XYZ.

Consumers lose consumer surplus equal to the area bounded by $P_c P_m XY$, of which $P_c P_m XZ$ is shifted to the monopolist in the form of profits. The difference between those two areas is, again, the inefficiency, also dubbed dead-

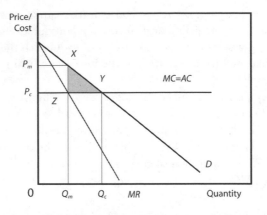

Figure 2.2. Monopoly model basics

weight loss of monopoly. This deadweight loss is the *net* amount of value lost because of a monopoly-induced underproduction of the good—and, hence, a misallocation of resources.

When the monopolist doesn't produce $Q_c - Q_m$ units, resources are released to be employed elsewhere. The problem of resource *misallocation*—sometimes characterized as the market failure of monopoly—occurs because the value of the resources released to their next best line of production is less than their value in the production of the monopolist's good. In short, the monopoly problem has universally been characterized as one of too little of the monopolized good. It could just as easily be characterized as one of too much of goods produced elsewhere in other competitive markets.

This basic monopoly model is extended with a number of refinements for real-world, less than fully competitive markets in a number of ways. Firms can have more or less monopoly power. It all depends on the count of competitors, the extent to which goods in a market are substitutes, and the cost of entry. The greater the count of competitors and the closer the substitutes, the greater the elasticity of demand (beyond some point) of any monopolist (or any firm with market power), the lower the profitability of the monopolist, and the lower the inefficiency caused by the monopolist.[11] The lower the entry costs, the lower the so-called limit prices (or market-forestalling prices) the monopolist can charge without attracting competitors (Bain 1956). Such adjustments in theory, however, only affect the extent of the damage done by monopoly; they do not, in any way, suggest that monopoly could conceivably be a positive (or neutral) force for growth in human welfare.

Under *monopolistic competition* (a market structure in which there may be a number, but not numerous, other firms in the market, which can be selling an identical or differentiated product), each firm with monopoly power can still charge a monopoly price, but only in the sense of the price being above marginal cost, by restricting sales. However, the firm may not be able to make an economic profit or produce at its long-term minimum average cost.[12] Under *oligopoly* (a market structure that may contain only a handful of competitors, so few in fact that competitors' pricing and output decisions are said to be interdependent), outcomes are necessarily somewhat indeterminate, mainly because the oligopolists must react sequentially to each other's unspecified but evolving strategies.[13]

Of course, monopoly theory lends itself to an analysis of cartels, or collusive efforts of would-be competitors to act *as if* they were a monopoly. Indeed, the basic cartel theory holds that competitors, as long as they are few in number, can act exactly like monopolists with no change in the cost curve. That is to say, competitors who collectively have cost curves equal to the $MC = AC$ curve in figure 2.2 can cartelize their market to reduce market output from Q_c to Q_m. With the cost curves held in place with cartelization, the underlying presumption is that the restricted output can be achieved without any shift in incentives within the industry to conserve and efficiently allocate firm resources, a theoretical treatment that is surely subject to challenge (and we undertake such a challenge in the next chapter) because of the problems cartels have in controlling cheating among cartel members on cartel production and sales quotas. The conventional presumption is that the greater the number of colluders and the lower the entry barriers, the more difficulty cartels have in hanging together and achieving monopoly market outcomes.

Still, under all less-than-pure-monopoly markets, the key attribute of the pure monopolist model—that the firm (or firms) with monopoly or market power kills off some consumer surplus at the same time that it transfers consumer surplus to itself—almost always is said to hold. Only the extent of damage done varies across less-than-pure market models. By the construction of the model, consumers do not attribute any additional value whatsoever from price increases, which means that market entry barriers that can inspire higher prices can mean only two things, some market inefficiency and loss by consumers of their surplus value. If for some reason, a monopoly firm decides not to maximize profits, the market price of a firm's stock will be suppressed below what it could be, meaning the monopoly firm is subject to takeover by investors willing to do what is necessary to maximize monopoly price and the firm's stock price.

Understandably, people who use the monopoly models see the potential for monopoly-induced market inefficiency whenever self-evident barriers to entry exist. These might come in the form of government regulations, but they can also come in the form of privately developed entry barriers such as may (or may not) be the case with scale economies, or just market dominances, first-mover advantages, frequent buyer (or flyer) programs, branding, and long-term contracts—because all such devices increase the entry costs for would-be competitors and reduce the elasticity of demand by increasing the switching costs of consumers. Needless to say, building on Schumpeter (1942) and McGee (1971) at various points in this book, we intend to challenge the validity of the underlying arguments, stressing again and again that such privately erected entry barriers could be a boon to the development of markets—and long-term growth in human welfare.

Of course, economists have introduced a couple of caveats that under some market circumstances, monopoly has the potential for being welfare enhancing. If an industry is beset with external costs (pollution, for example), the restricted output of monopoly can be welfare enhancing, on balance. The monopoly restriction on output can curb the overproduction that results from negative externalities. More generally, while a monopoly in the production of a "good" can be construed as "bad" (welfare destroying), a monopoly in the production of a "bad" (e.g., a criminal good, such as heroin), can be viewed as good. As Buchanan has argued (1973), there is a defense of the Mafia to be made from monopoly theory, since the monopoly can restrict production of criminalized goods (thus aiding and abetting the work of the police).[14]

THE LOCUS OF MARKET FAILURE: FIRMS?

If all (or virtually all) markets in an economy suffer from various degrees of competitive imperfections, realized in all firms facing downward sloping demand curves, we must wonder, from the perspective of economists' treatment of monopoly in their models, how it is that an economy can progress over time. The simple point is that, given the limitations of the monopoly model, an economy can't advance because of any mechanism for the creation of new and improved goods and services. The goods and services are, again, given.

The so-called monopoly problem, captured by the deadweight-loss or Harberger triangle (named after economist Arnold Harberger), is almost everywhere considered to be a serious, consequential *problem*—elevated to a market failure—caused solely by the monopoly (Harberger 1954). This is the case because there is no chance for the market inefficiency to be juxtaposed against any other social good (e.g., goods creation and enhancement) that the monopoly might provide apart from the pricing decision it makes in economists' monopoly model.

Perhaps this view is justified when the monopolist, as an unmitigated source of economic harm that is assumed into existence, has actually erected and maintained the barriers to entry, whatever those barriers might be.[15] Indeed, if monopoly is founded on the entry barriers, and the entry barriers are costly to erect (and have no value to consumers, an assumption to be critically evaluated later in the book), the triangular area *XYZ* in figure 2.2 clearly understates the inefficiency of monopoly, because it doesn't account for the cost of constructing entry barriers. That is, *XYZ* doesn't include the value of resources diverted from producing valued goods to erecting and maintaining entry barriers.

However, if the entry barriers are just there, or have their source in nature and are not the product of the monopolist's efforts, then it might be said that no inefficiency exists (as Bastiat recognized more than a century ago). This is because entry barriers invariably translate into costs. Seen from this perspective, the problem is not a consequence of what the monopolist does—that is, restrict sales—but rather is a consequence of nature. By this we mean simply that entry costs for outside firms are higher than the expected gains from market entry.

When deals between buyers and sellers are not made because the sellers' resource costs are higher than what the buyers are willing to pay, economists never suggest that the absence of the trades is a mark of the inefficiency, or failure, of the market. Indeed, the conclusion generally drawn is that inefficiency would result if the trades were ever actually consummated. This inefficiency occurs because the goods that would then be traded would be worth less than the goods that could have been produced with the resources devoted to surmounting entry barriers.

Such a monopoly problem has no conceivable solution, short of having government insist that firms in such market settings not profit-maximize or that the firms' prices and/or output levels be regulated, which can be no solution at all. As economists have long argued, the imposed regulations have their own costs both in terms of government's monitoring the regulated firm and in terms of abating entrepreneurial incentives to find and create such profitable opportunities (Stigler 1975).

So, we have here our first problem with conventional monopoly theory: In the case of natural (as distinct from created) barriers to entry, the theory leads inextricably to a form of "inefficiency" that is inappropriately labeled as such. It would be inefficient if outsiders incurred the costs of entry, expanded market supply, and pushed the price down to the (imagined) competitive level that cannot and should not exist (if the ultimate goal of the economy is that which is at the foundation of monopoly theory, to rationally allocate resources only to the point where the gains from the allocation are greater than the costs, with both gains and costs all-inclusive). In a sense, monopoly theory can be said to be founded on wishful thinking, or a pretense that entry costs either are not real or are irrelevant.

Some products spring into existence with fully formed entry barriers that are in the minds of many (if not all) consumers who associate the product with its creator. Picasso paintings are valued for their intrinsic worth as art, but they carry at least some value in the minds of consumers because they were done by Picasso, who had exclusive control of how many paintings were available. The treatment of monopoly in economic literature is tantamount to condemning Picasso for not supplying more paintings even though he had a long and prolific career. Why? No one other than Picasso could satisfy consumer demand for Picasso paintings. It is hard for us to imagine even economists drawing such a deduction, that Picasso was a negative force in the art world, on balance, because he refused to work as long and hard as the competitive equilibrium would dictate he should to maximize his buyers' welfare. Nevertheless, branding is seen as a source of monopoly inefficiency. Apple's iPod can be thought of as a source of inefficiency because a sizable majority (over 75 percent at this writing) of consumers *want* iPods and do not view alternative MP3 and MP4 players as a perfect substitute, a truly strange deduction for any theory founded on the value assessments of individual consumers for model building. In this regard, the inefficiency of at least some monopolies amounts to a contention that consumer values are not what they should be, a truly remarkable position for economists who insist that their analysis is positive and who object to theorists imposing their own evaluations on their model building.

THE LOCUS OF MARKET FAILURE: CONSUMERS?

The source of the monopoly problem could also be laid on consumers. They could, in a manner of speaking, collectively bribe the monopolist to extend its production beyond Q_m, say, all the way to Q_c in figure 2.2. Consumers would merely have to pay the monopolist more than the monopolist incurs in cost for the additional units (which for $Q_c - Q_m$ units equals, as noted before, Q_mZYQ_c). Consumers certainly value additional units more than those units cost the monopolist (or else there would be no deadweight loss). Conceptually speaking, consumers should be willing to pay for $Q_c - Q_m$ units as much as the area under the demand curve, or the area Q_mXYQ_c. The reason they don't buy off the monopolist is the presumed transaction cost of their getting together to strike a deal and to collect apportioned payments from all consumers. The likely free riding among consumers on such a deal would make such a cartel-like consumer buyoff prohibitively expensive on many goods. By *prohibitively expensive* we mean only that the transaction costs would exceed the triangular area *XYZ*, which makes such a deal a nonstarter.[16]

Seen from this perspective, the monopolist's curb in production results in what we see as nothing more than an *imagined* inefficiency, which is imaginary because the triangular area does not account for the full costs of consumers moving the monopoly from Q_m to Q_c. Granted, *if* consumers could get together to buy off the monopolist, and have more produced, all without cost, or very little cost, then the world would be a better place. However, such a claim is no less flawed than a claim that the world would be better fed if bakers didn't have to incur the cost of their flour. Transaction costs are no less real, or no less a market constraint, than the costs captured in the *MC* cost curves of either figure 2.1 or 2.2. Transaction costs must be accommodated in any *complete* assessment of market efficiency or lack thereof. In short, economists can claim that monopolies are everywhere inefficient only because key costs are ignored.

Of course, if we assume away transaction costs to enable consumers to buy off the monopolist, then consumers have no reason to stop with bargaining for the $Q_c - Q_m$ on some mutually beneficial terms. They should be expected to bargain for the lower, competitive price on all Q_c units, which means the monopolist would lose its pricing power. In such a world, monopoly would cease to be a problem.

If we assume zero transaction costs for consumers, then we would have to assume, for consistency's sake, that the monopolist had no transaction costs (or encountered far fewer such costs than it does). However, that would surely mean that figure 2.2 grossly overstates the monopolist's production costs, since so much of production is caught up in dealing with and minimizing transaction costs. The outcome that must then be imagined could easily be better than perfect competition, as captured in figure 2.2. By such a comparative standard, perfect competition, as normally constructed on the assumption of positive transaction costs, could easily be seen as inferior (implying a deadweight loss) when compared to a monopolized market with transaction costs assumed away.

THE ADDED WASTE OF RENT SEEKING

Granted, monopolies can be created by governments through the erection of artificial entry barriers at the behest of the would-be monopolies, in which case the inefficiency of the created monopolies can have real meaning. The government would then be preventing mutually beneficial trades, those for which the all-inclusive costs (as assessed by would-be producers of the additional units) would be less than the all-inclusive benefits (as assessed by would-be consumers).

But such market restrictions are not what is at stake when monopoly theory is developed in textbooks and on blackboards and when that theory is developed for policy purposes, such as antitrust policy and enforcement (Sullivan and Harrison 1988; Hovenkamp 1985). In those textbooks and blackboard venues, the monopoly is typically discussed as already existing, protected by barriers to entry that often have unspecified sources. The monopoly exists as if by magic. Granted, sometimes textbook treatments note that the monopoly may have been created by the establishment of entry barriers, for example, by government through an exclusive franchise, patent, or copyright. Another acknowledged possibility is a firm's growth, through mergers, to market domination or monopoly because of economies of scale and scope or by the firm's cornering of some critical resource that it doesn't make available to other firms. Clearly, such entry barriers can exist and give a firm monopoly power, or the ability to price above marginal cost.

The problem with such lines of argument is twofold.

- First, the presumption is that the firm that acquires the monopoly powers does so at no cost. That is to say, the cost curves and demand curve in figure 2.2 do not shift as a consequence of a movement from a competitive to a monopoly market structure. Hence, the monopoly profits remain equal to $P_c P_m XZ$. That cannot be the case, as we stress in this chapter and in the following chapter.
- Second, the presumption is that any firm that acquires its monopoly power always imposes a net loss on the world equal to the deadweight-loss triangle. The point made toward the end of the last section is that private monopolies—for example, those that emerge because some new product is developed—give rise to the deadweight loss because they are protected by barriers to entry that can be nothing more than a superior product that no one has yet been able to duplicate. In such cases, the supposed inefficiency of monopoly is blown all out of proportion. Indeed, without more attention to the supposed barriers (and we give entry barriers more attention in a later chapter), we have good reason to believe that the "natural" emergence of some monopolies under some conditions gives rise to welfare gains, in spite of any deadweight loss that might be identified on a graph that doesn't properly and fully account for all costs and benefits.

Now, when monopolies are the product or consequence of rent seeking, what amounts to competitive efforts of firms to acquire monopoly privileges through government, the actual inefficiency of monopoly, typically identified as triangle XYZ in figure 2.2, is understated. This is because the rent seekers will employ real resources in political lobbying, and in other ways, to acquire the monopoly privileges, as Tullock (1967), Krueger (1974), and others (Buchanan, Tollison, and Tullock 1980) have made clear. Indeed, if the monopoly profits of a government-created monopoly are equal to the area P_cP_mXZ in figure 2.2, rent seekers should be expected to expend in their competitive rent-seeking efforts that amount discounted for the time lag and by the probability that the monopoly rents will actually be realized. The competitive rent-seeking process can result in competitors for the monopoly privileges escalating their bids for the monopoly privileges, the net result of which is that the resources expended can equal (if not exceed) the actual monopoly profits.[17]

Of course, this means that the total drag of monopolies on the economy is a function of just how open government is to conferring monopoly privileges. The more open government is to extending monopoly privileges, the greater the deadweight loss from restricted production and from rent seeking. The welfare loss, it needs to be stressed, is then a product of government failure, not market failure.

This could also mean that the total drag of monopoly on the economy is a function of how effective the government is in responding to any and all interest groups; by way of devising policies to redistribute income to, say, poor people, it can open itself to exploitation to monopoly interest groups that can shroud their claims for monopoly privileges in the pursuit of some greater public good. From this perspective, the drag of monopoly on the economy from contrived government entry barriers can be viewed as an unavoidable cost of government pursuing the broader good under imperfect democratic institutions, a line of argument we have explored in an earlier work (Lee and McKenzie 1987).

THE IMPERFECTION OF PERFECTION

In his presidential talk to the Southern Economics Association, James Buchanan began by quoting a passing comment that Lord Acton made in one of his many letters to Mary Gladstone, daughter of the famous British prime minister: "It is not the popular movement, but the traveling of the minds of men who sit in the seat of Adam Smith that is really serious and worthy of all attention" (1964, 213). Buchanan's intention was to use the Acton comment to launch a critique of economic thinking that has relevance to our reassessment of monopoly theory. Buchanan noted how Lionel Robbins, through his highly successful 1930s book *An Essay on the Nature and Significance of Economic Science* (1946), converted economists to think of their discipline as a *science* that deals with the problem of the allocation of scarce resources that have competing uses. Thus, the discipline deals with the "science of choice," according to Robbins.[18]

Buchanan has several problems with characterizing economics the way Robbins's followers (not so much Robbins himself) have, not the least of which is that the person or entity doing the allocating is often not made clear. Moreover, the criteria for assessing any given allocation are uncertain. If the criterion is society's wants, then we run headlong into an old conundrum of economists, that of defining and computing a social welfare function. If we use individuals' valuations of goods, then the problem of assessing any allocation of resources doesn't go away because individuals' wants are not given to anyone. Moreover, people's wants often emerge in the process of their determining what resources are available, how the available resources can be used, and what (eventually) will be produced. Adam Smith's key insight is especially important at this juncture because, as Buchanan noted, Smith suggested that what an economy accomplishes "is not originally the effect of any human wisdom, which foresees and intends that general opulence to which it gives occasion" (1776, bk. 1, chap. 2, ¶ 1), a point familiar to students of Frederick Hayek's work (1945). Do we judge the allocation of resources by the standards of what people can't originally imagine? By the standards of that which emerges? Compared to what?

Economists—"men who sit in the seat of Adam Smith"—have developed *efficiency* as the standard for assessing market systems. However, the standard set forth is not just any kind or level of efficiency. It is that level of efficiency that emerges from the allocation of resources when it is assumed that people *know* from the start what they want, what resources are available, and how to use the resources in the best possible ways. *All* they have to do, within the Robbins construction of the discipline, is choose how to move the available known resources to the production of goods and services that satisfy extant wants. But this construction of the discipline is contradictory, as Buchanan has insisted. No real *choice* is involved in such an allocative scheme. Everything is already determined going into the so-called choices, which means the end allocation is predetermined by the conditions set beforehand for the allocation.[19] In fact, everything is settled instantaneously, as if by mathematical computation, or by the static nature of the analysis. But meaningful real-world choices are carried out in real time, and require time.

No possibility exists that the outcome of the allocative system could ever be "not originally the effects of any human wisdom," that is, could be better (or more efficient) than what people could imagine before the allocative process commences. There certainly is no "free lunch," as virtually all economists always insist is the case in real life. However, when economists repeat that familiar refrain, they are hardly doing so from the vantage point of the chair that Smith used, for his whole book was about the "free lunch" of markets, or, rather, the "general opulence" that no one can foresee from the way markets actually do operate, as distinct from the way economists have come to describe them. The free lunch is in the palm of Smith's "invisible hand," but that lunch is no less invisible, beforehand, than the palm of the hand itself.

Buchanan suggests that economists should discard Robbins's characterization of the discipline as hopelessly flawed. He makes a case for those who sit in Smith's chair to take up the more interesting problem of catallactics, or the process by which people try to solve their mutual problems through economic and political systems of exchanges.[20]

We don't wish to sidetrack our discussion by becoming embroiled in a debate over what economists should do. We simply note that it is certainly venturesome of economists to judge the efficiency, or lack thereof, of monopoly by the standard of perfect competition. Certainly, perfect competition is efficient, perfectly so—or so economists like to think. The model is not intended to describe the real world. Indeed, it is intended to describe a world that cannot exist, because it is founded on a degree of perfection—totally unblemished, even by one missed trade—that can exist only in the minds of economists or their mathematical models. Why? Very simply because the model itself grew out of a system of thought that starts with all-pervasive scarcity. In such a world, no one would want any market to be perfect any more than they would want any product to be perfect in all evaluative dimensions. Such a perfect product would cost too much, meaning other, more valuable things could be done with the resources devoted to achieving perfection in any given market, if perfection were not assumed.

Then again, economists who tout the importance of cost in restricting behavior on every dimension have no problem assuming away entry and exit costs or costs of information for purposes of setting up a standard by which real-world monopolies would be judged. If any costs were involved in moving the real-world markets to match the dictates of perfect competition, they no doubt would stop short of going that far (and incurring as many costs as would be required) to achieve *perfect competition*. That is to say, they would at some point have to agree that some degree of imperfection—some degree of monopoly—in markets is to be preferred to perfect competition. In those terms, perfection can't spring from scarcity. This necessarily implies that perfect competition is not perfect, meaning it must be suboptimal to most real-world markets.

Put differently, perfect competition as a market structure would, if ever realized, be defective, assuming any rising costs at all to the achievement of a perfect state of a market. Perfect competition is very likely more defective than a state of real-world markets in which price is above marginal cost and in which deadweight-loss triangles arise, as conceived by economists in their textbooks and on their blackboards. The achievement of perfect fluidity in any given market would very likely restrict the array of markets in any given economy.[21]

It is all too easy to deduce that we are proposing the trashing of supply-and-demand-curve analysis, because the analysis is based on an underlying assumption of perfect competition. That is not the case. We readily admit the usefulness of such curves to illustrate central price and output tendencies of many real-world markets. We also agree that they can be used to discuss directional changes in market price and quantity, given exogenous changes in market conditions (e.g., a change in production costs or the imposition of an excise tax). We are, however, highlighting the difficulties encountered when economists begin to use the underlying perfectly competitive model to evaluate less than perfect markets in terms of perfect efficiency, when that construct has no real-world counterpart. The damage done is doubled when economists propose corrective actions, such as making markets more competitive, when in fact the competitiveness of the imperfect real-world markets may be, as the saying goes, "as good as it gets."

ZERO ECONOMIC PROFITS

A presumption of perfect competition is that a market state in which firms everywhere and at all times earn zero economic profits is the best of all possible worlds. Why? Because if efficiency is maximized, then surely that means that the limited available resources are used to the greatest possible extent. Hence, monopoly can be condemned because of inefficiency and because of the presumably unnecessary transfer of consumer surplus from where it belongs—with the consumers—to the monopolist. At the very least, the consumer surplus transfer has no consequence other than, perhaps, its harboring the potential for another market negative, the waste of resources in counterproductive rent seeking by political competitors.

In standard blackboard and textbook static analysis, the implied presumption that *economic profits* (as distinct from normal or book profits) are simply a sign of inefficiency suggests that they cannot possibly serve a productive purpose. After all, the goods in economic models that are the subject of analysis are *given.* That is, they do not have to be created, and no one needs an incentive to create them. They exist, and the entire purview of the analysis is limited to exactly what the equilibrium conditions will be in that narrow, static framework. Such a framework allows for no risks, no uncertainty, and no array of entrepreneurial opportunities that must be appraised and pursued by would-be entrepreneurs who are constrained by the most pressing of all constraints outside the static models and inside the real world of markets: imperfect information.

If the world were completely covered with perfectly competitive markets—with all the attendant efficiency attributes contained by completely costless mobility of resources that resulted in instantaneous adjustments with no hope of earning supranormal profits—entrepreneurs would have absolutely no incentive to move off their proverbial dimes. Economic profits would emerge only in an infinitely small flash in time because market supplies would *instantaneously* adjust with costless resource movements, which brings us to an internal contradiction embedded in the perfectly competitive model, an assumption of resource movements when little (actually, absolutely no) incentive exists for anyone to move resources.[22] For the sake of argument, we might imagine that economic profits would emerge, but if they did, they would be wiped out so quickly that people might as well stay where they are. That means no economic development would occur at all. The world would remain as it is, a point central to Schumpeter's critique of perfect competition (1942, 104–5).

This matter of lack of incentives is particularly pressing when we consider the predicament of the entrepreneur who is contemplating the creation of one or more new products. A new product can't come into existence under perfect competition because individual competitors could reason, given the perfect fluidity of resource movement implied in zero entry and exit costs, that the creation of the new product would lead only to more of the same—with instantaneous adjustment to zero economic profits. Why bother?

One might think that a perfect competitor could reason that if he or she does not create new products (or new, less costly ways of doing things), then someone else might do just that and run competitors who don't engage in such product development out of business. Granted, if a new, improved, and cheaper product were to spring into existence as if by magic (or in the same way any product in a perfect competitive market is assumed to come into existence), without any *development* on the part of anyone being incurred, and there were no costs associated with developing the market for the product, then competitors would have to adopt the new and improved product. The reason is that under the two conditions just specified, there would be no costs of developing the product, and its product and market development costs would not need to be recovered. This would suggest that absolutely no reason would exist for anyone to hesitate developing the product and its market. And there would be one very good reason for developing the product and its market: Each competitor could reason that if he or she didn't adopt it, someone else would, and the competitors who failed to follow suit would be run out of business. Note, however, that everything is critically dependent on the magical appearance of the product along with its well-developed market (which is so well developed that information costs about the product are *zero*).

On the other hand, if the availability of the product required that some firm develop the product, incur costs of adopting the product, and incur additional costs to develop the market for the product, then the new, improved, and cheaper product would never emerge in a world of perfect competition that is characterized by zero entry costs. The firm developing the product and making a market for it would not be able to recover its up-front or sunk development costs.

Hence, as recognized by John McGee (1971), absent the prospects of economic profits (that which is over and above what is necessary to keep a firm in the market *after* the product and its market are well developed and exploitable by all competitors), each individual competitor has zero incentive to develop the product and its market. Each competitor can rest comfortably in the (perfect) knowledge (obtained at zero cost) that a perfectly fluid state of market affairs means that no one inside or outside the market has any more incentive than anyone else has to innovate. As a consequence, each individual competitor can rest assured that there will be no innovation—no new products coming onto the market and no new and less costly production processes (other than those products that descend as if from heaven, that is, without the energizing force of economic incentives).[23]

Even if readers don't completely buy our vision of perfect competitive markets as a stagnant state of affairs, surely we are right to conclude that perfect competition would lead to less innovation than would be the case if *durable* economic profits were a reality or a real prospect. The economic profits would energize entrepreneurs to create added consumer value as well as added inefficiency (as represented by the hypothetical Harberger, deadweight-loss triangle), with the latter form of lost value being potentially (and probably more than) offset by the former form of added value.

To see this point (and others), consider figure 2.3, which duplicates the demand and cost curves of figure 2.2, but adds a higher demand, the curve labeled D_2. This higher demand results from the monopolist being inspired by the potential of added economic profits to improve in some way the quality of its product, as far as consumers evaluate the product. Hence, the demand rises from D_1 to D_2. Cost also rises, but only from MC_1 to MC_2, or by less than the

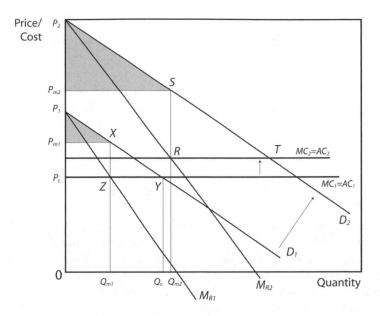

Figure 2.3. Monopoly model basics—extended

vertical shift in the demand curve.[24] To make the further development of the product profitable, the increase in the price consumers would be willing to pay must exceed the monopolist's added cost.

Discussions of monopoly are almost everywhere narrowly focused on the inefficiency or Harberger triangle XYZ when demand is D_1. What is too often missed is the net welfare gain that consumers receive from actually having the product in the first place, which is that area above the monopolist's economic profits rectangle and below the demand curve D_1, or area P_1XP_{m1}—an area dubbed the Dupuit triangle (for Jules Dupuit who in an 1844 article first recognized its importance). We point out that net consumer surplus area because it must exactly equal the deadweight-loss triangle (assuming straight lines for the cost curves, or a constant marginal cost, an assumption we make for simplicity). This means that consumers are not worse off by having the monopolized product. Indeed, they are better off to the extent of the Dupuit triangular area P_1XP_{m1}. They just aren't as well off as they *could* be, hypothetically speaking—*if* the monopolist were not out to maximize its economic profit.

Is there a defect in the system? It all depends on perspective. If we could assume that the product in question could come into being independently of the economic profit motive, the answer is yes. But we are hardly persuaded that such products could magically appear (in great numbers) under alternative real-world systems that rely on nonprofit motives. Consider the development of the Soviet Union, and its ultimate collapse under the weight of monumental economic stagnation inspired largely by the absence of private entrepreneurial leeway and profit, economic or otherwise. If the volume and value of created goods and services are unrelated to economic profit, then innovation is the only market outcome to which economists do not apply their upward sloping supply curve.

Similarly, as posited for figure 2.3, the profit motive leads to the increase in the cost and demand curves, the net effect of which is that the monopoly price rises from P_{m1} to P_{m2} as the quantity of the product produced rises from Q_{m1} to Q_{m2}. The deadweight loss rises from XYZ to RST. However, the consumers' aggregate leftover surplus (the Dupuit triangle) rises from P_1XP_{m1} to P_2SP_{m2}. This means that the world is a better place *because* of the profit motive, *because of the actual economic profits that are extracted*, and, therefore, *because* of the inefficiency.

Here, we interject that much is made in textbook discussions of how economic profits induce would-be competitors to surmount the walls of the entry barriers to get at the economic profits. We don't wish to detract from such a line of analysis. Rather, we wish to stress that monopoly profits can have motivational content even if the walls of the entry-barrier protection of a particular monopoly cannot be surmounted. This is because the existence and persistence of economic profits in any identified monopolized industry can encourage entrepreneurs to search out other, similar monopoly opportunities in *other product lines* (not just the product line that is the subject of the monopoly model), which implies that an inefficiency in one monopolized product line can give rise to added consumer value in other product lines, with the added value in these product lines potentially (and, we suspect, very likely) far exceeding the inefficiency of the monopolized line.

Schumpeter and many other economists who have followed in his footsteps have argued that monopoly unsupported by government market protections would not long endure. This is because by restricting sales to raise prices and profits, a monopoly created by private devices alone sows the seeds of its own destruction, given the incentive of the economic profits for other firms to enter the market. Schumpeter sees the "creative destruction" of monopolies, or their nondurability, as something of a market blessing. Private entrepreneurs would diligently find ways to surmount or circumvent any existing monopoly. But he also acknowledged and held dear the creative force of economic profits, however long they might endure.

We recognize that we tend to agree with Schumpeter at every step, but with a caveat. Having a privately created monopoly that endures, if it ever happens, cannot be summarily dismissed as necessarily a net loss for the economy. This is because the permanent monopoly, with its long-standing economic profits, can inspire greater creative production—more product creation and development—by other entrepreneurs who would like nothing better than to duplicate the market position of the permanent monopoly in another product line.[25] If a permanent monopoly were never realized, it is not at all clear that economic development—and growth in human welfare—would be higher. It could be. The imagined *prospect*, as opposed to the *reality*, of a permanent monopoly could have motivational content. But certainly the *reality* of a permanent monopoly would have more motivational content. Without the actuality of monopoly, it is doubtful that the *prospect* of monopoly would be a meaningful concept, or a motivation to do anything. Obviously, the matter of the *net damage* or *net gain* from the presence of monopoly in an economy is something economists have shied away from considering, given their narrow focus on the damage done by monopoly when compared with a nonachievable market outcome. We insist that economists have been dead wrong to argue without qualification that monopolies, durable or not, can only be welfare destroying.

TRANSITIONARY ECONOMIC PROFITS

Granted, many economists raise in their lectures (as Schumpeter did in his writings) the prospects of transitionary economic profits, resulting from, say, a shift in consumer preferences. However, in making that admission, they are necessarily stepping outside the strict confines of their perfect competition model. That model allows no prospects of such profits even in transition, because no time is allowed for transitions of any sort. The perfectly competitive model has no time dimension. It is *static* by design. In addition, such an admission of transitionary economic profits plays to the point that we seek to make here, which is that some level of economic profits is *good* for the economy. This means that some level of inefficiency is, on balance, *good* for the economy—and this, it must be stressed, means that some prevalence and degree of monopolized markets, with their required entry barriers, is on balance good for the economy.

The admission also plays to Schumpeter's key and unheralded insight noted in the epigraph, an insight that summarizes our point better than we could: "A system—any system, economic or other—that at *every* given point of time fully utilizes its possibilities to the best advantage may yet in the long run be inferior to a system that does so at *no* given point in time, because the latter's failure to do so may be a condition for the level or speed of long-run performance" (1942, 83).

In our way of thinking, Schumpeter's use of *may be* is overly guarded. We are arguing here that some inefficiency is a *necessary* condition for the "level and speed of long-run performance." From our perspective, the only relevant and contestable issue is how much monopoly presence in an economy is a good thing, or how much is too little and too much. That is to say, for the people who sit in Smith's seat, the relevant question is, or should be, what is the *optimum presence of monopoly* (in terms of prevalence and durability) for maximum long-run performance of an economy? That question is as relevant as the scope and length of copyright terms for artistic works and patent terms for inventors. Indeed, such debates presume that maximum human welfare growth requires some optimum prevalence of monopoly.

And we insist that monopolies must actually exist, and must actually impose inefficiencies on their market, for monopoly to have its desired incentive effect. This means that monopoly profits cannot simply be an illusion. Otherwise, the notion of economic profits cannot have any motivational content. Illusory profits would understandably and necessarily be discounted by a 100 percent probability of never being realized, which means their expected discounted value would be zero.

ECONOMIC PROFIT AS A SOURCE OF CAPITAL

Under conventional models of perfect competition, the product already exists. The market for the product also exists. This means that the required capital has already been raised in some unstated way. Any monopoly profits in any product line can do only two things: give rise to an inefficiency and extract consumer surplus. However, consider the real-world predicament of investors. They often have grossly imperfect knowledge of their markets. They are never sure what it is that consumers really want before they go to market with their product or products. They can develop educated assessments, but such assessments will often be no more than informed hunches, which means that the probability of product failure looms large for any firm. One way that firms solve their risk and uncertainty problems is to go to market with an array of products, knowing full well that most (if not almost all) of the products they put on the market will fail to cover the firm's costs for those products.

To remain in business, the firm must cover its economic losses on most products with economic profits on one or more products. It must anticipate achieving a monopoly position—with all the attendant attributes of higher-than-competitive prices, market entry barriers, and deadweight loss—in something, just to go into the market with its range of products. The prospect of a true monopoly position in the market at a later time is what the firm counts on to raise its required up-front capital as well as the capital it needs to expand its array of product offerings.

We understand that many economists—especially those who specialize in portfolio analysis—would concede that such realized monopoly results can be efficiency enhancing for the firm. Besides, the firm might not make more than a competitive rate of return across all product lines. However, that is the point we seek to push for the economy as a whole: To have an array of firms to develop a far greater array of products, monopoly positions are absolutely essential in a world beset with risk and uncertainty. This is because such a world is bound to have product (and firm) failures. Such a world *must also have* monopolies just to ensure that across all markets, entrepreneurs can *expect* to earn, at the very least, *normal profits.*

Besides, monopolies are absolutely unavoidable in a world in which a multitude of people are doing an even greater multitude of things, all with an eye toward making a profit or just pursuing the betterment of humankind. This is because of the prevalence of uncertainty in economic events. The problem with uncertainty is that, by its very nature, it can't be accounted for in any anticipatory sense. Things just happen that cannot be known beforehand. In such a world, people are bound to stumble upon monopoly market positions. In short, luck is bound to happen, and to the extent that luck is a fact of life, entrepreneurs can be counted on to count on luck in their investment decisions.

Are such monopoly positions a source of economic losses? We suggest not. Suppose that all prospects of monopoly positions were radically reduced, or wiped out, by antitrust policy and enforcement. The relevant question is, Would the world be a better place on balance? Identified markets might have less inefficiency and economic profits, as blackboard models suggest, but such a policy stance would do nothing but increase the prominence of failures in venture capitalists' portfolios. They would have to have higher rates of return—higher normal profits—for all nonmonopoly ventures. This would be the case because of the risk of greater net losses across all product or business lines, given that any prospects of making supranormal profits from monopolies that develop would have been eliminated. To undertake an array of ventures, without the prospect of monopoly profits in some of them, firms would have to have higher returns in the ventures undertaken just to keep the capital resources in the array of ventures.[26] Production costs in nonmonopoly endeavors would rise, resulting in a constriction of output levels sought in even perfectly competitive markets. The deadweight loss of monopoly must be weighed against these welfare losses, even though they might not be tagged by

economists (or policymakers who carry out the antitrust enforcement) as a
source of market inefficiency.

MARKET EFFICIENCY AND THE COUNT OF COMPETITORS

Before closing this chapter, we need to consider briefly what may be considered extraneous issues. We take them up because we seek to develop in this
book a fairly comprehensive review of conventional monopoly theory. Discussions of market efficiency never get more confused than when the specter of
the count of competitors, or the dominance of producers, is raised. The confusion is understandable, given the emphasis on the competitors' count embedded in the definition of the two market extremes, perfect competition and pure
monopoly. The former is defined as a market structure of *numerous* (or *innumerable*) competitors, whereas the latter is defined as a market structure with a
solitary producer. Given those definitions, it is all too easy to conclude that (1)
a market must operate with less than perfect efficiency if that market has fewer
than "numerous" competitors, and (2) a market is necessarily monopolized if
only one producer exists (or if one producer dominates any given market).[27]
The so-called natural monopoly is everywhere, supposedly, a monopoly.

In the case of perfect competition, the confusion, and resulting misunderstanding, are grounded in an often unrecognized goal of specifying the exact
market characteristics, including specification of "numerous producers": That
purpose is to spell out those market conditions that would *necessarily ensure*,
with mathematical certainty, the heralded market outcome of marginal cost
pricing along with perfect resource allocation and zero economic profits. That
is not to say that such a market outcome cannot be achieved with less stringent
specifications, for example, with fewer than "numerous producers" in the market. Far fewer competitors could prevail in a market with the outcome being
tolerably efficient, with price close to marginal cost, the idealized competitive
level.

Experimental economists have addressed the issue of how the count of
competitors affects the actual market outcome, in terms of price and quantity
traded, as compared with what is known to be the equilibrium price and quantity. Surprisingly, Charles Holt and his colleagues in experimental economics
have found that with as few as five traders on each side of the market, the equilibrium price and quantity realized over a sequence of trading periods will
come close to (but will not exactly match) the equilibrium price and quantity
predicted from the known supply and demand functions.[28] This line of experimental research suggests that just because real-world markets diverge from
the perfectly competitive markets in important ways—having a limited num-

ber of producers who provide differentiated goods behind entry barriers of some sort—it does not follow that the firms in real-world markets generate anything close to the level of deadweight losses that might be expected from textbook models.

In the case of monopoly, the supposed market power to destroy and transfer consumer surplus value to a single seller (or a few sellers) can be tightly constrained by *potential* competition, with the extent of potential competition affected by the ease of entry. This means that a natural monopoly, which in textbooks is shown to emerge as a single seller when economies of scale are rampant, is not *necessarily* the monopoly implied by its name. Granted, some natural monopolies are protected by barriers to entry. Municipal water systems can be just that, monopolies, because of their exclusive franchises or prohibitions against having more than one water main running under city streets. Other single sellers need not be accurately described as natural monopolies, because of the absence of entry barriers. Indeed, many natural monopolies may be more accurately labeled *natural single competitors* because they may be the only sellers in their markets but are unable to restrict production to set a monopoly price and garner monopoly rents. They can't do this because of the threat of potential competitors that can enter the market if the single producer tries to act like a monopoly to any significant extent, or else such single sellers may be able to price above marginal cost only to the extent they have production efficiencies that other firms are unable to develop. If that is the case, production is being carried on as efficiently as possible. This is doubly true when economists, courts, and policymakers don't possess the requisite knowledge and skills to reorganize markets on a more cost-effective basis. Just requiring natural monopolies to expand production or lower price can be no solution at all to the so-called inefficiency if such mandates are founded, as they must be, on cost information from the natural monopoly that is under the control of the natural monopoly, which means that regulations of the natural monopolist's production and pricing decision can give rise to costs that are greater than they have to be. The regulated natural monopoly might rightfully think, Why incur only minimal costs when revelation of those costs causes an expansion in production and a lower price? To put it another way, natural monopoly markets may not be perfectly efficient, using economists' standard notion of efficiency, but they can possess "competitive effectiveness," to use McGee's instructive turn of words (1971, 130).[29]

Schumpeter's "perennial gale" is of crucial importance to understanding the behavior of monopolies, even those who see their market positions as secure. They can see how the gale force has undermined a sequence of monopolies around them and through history, with many of the monopolies once thinking they were secure. Schumpeter must have chosen his words carefully, for *gale* has a connotation of persistence and force. Surely that means that not only must market systems be judged by history but also that history can affect just how insecure monopolies must feel and how forceful any continuing gale will be.

Admittedly, these points about natural monopoly and the importance of "potential competition" are not unrecognized and unacknowledged. However, we make them here for purposes of completeness of analysis, in case some readers have not encountered them. We also note them because of our larger purpose, that of suggesting that real-world market outcomes need not be constrained by the dictates of economists' specifications for their models of market structures.

CONCLUDING COMMENTS

Perfect competition (or some close approximation) is a fine model for static analysis of static markets. That is, addressing the question of what can happen to the static equilibrium price and output can be very useful when the product under analysis is assumed to exist and nobody is interested in taking the analysis further to, say, an exploration of how markets develop over time. A theme of this chapter is that one cannot infer from such a static market analysis anything about the emergence of a totally new product market or the dynamic development of a product or its market over time. The specified conditions of perfect competition simply will not allow for product development that is necessarily costly and that is, we'd like to think, the raison d'être of a real-world market economic system. Resource allocation for known goods and services through prices is important to markets, but hardly the whole story—not by a long shot, from Schumpeter's perspective.

Our purpose in this chapter has been to suggest anew that Schumpeter was right on one key and unheralded issue: Any system that is perfectly efficient at every point in time will likely lag behind any system that is *not* perfectly efficient at any point in time. (That is easy to say because a system of perfect efficiency implies no economic progress.) To have less than perfect efficiency, we emphasize, there needs to be at least some monopoly or market control over price. That means there need to be entry costs, or entry barriers of some sort and to some degree, in order that firms can anticipate the present discounted supranormal profits that motivate innovation and product development.

Hence, an important theme of this book is that for optimum economic development and growth in human welfare, some optimum amount of monopoly power must be present in a market economy. We would be the first to admit that we, at this point, have little idea of what that optimum amount would be, but we are convinced that the first step in coming to grips with the issue of the optimum monopoly presence is professional recognition that economic profits above absolute zero, along with some amount of static inefficiency, are prerequisites to the fluid functioning of a dynamic and developing market system. After we agree on that point, we can then debate what the optimum should be.

As odd as it might seem, our line of argument developed in this chapter and pursued in the remainder of the book does not imply that we wish to dispense altogether with the perfectly competitive model. We agree that the model has its classroom and textbook uses, for example, to explain how the price system works to aid in the allocation of resources and how it can adjust to changes in exogenous market conditions. The model is hardly perfect for doing that, but neither should we seek perfect pedagogical tools (for the same reason that we should not seek the development of perfect products or perfect competition in real-world markets). Tools are tools. We do with them what we can—until we can come up with better ones for the purposes at hand. In addition, as we have found in this chapter, the perfectly competitive model has been for us, oddly enough, a useful device for pointing to attributes of well-functioning real-world markets. We will continue to use the model in chapters that follow simply because it helps us highlight points that we could not make as clearly with other known devices at our disposal.

In the next chapter, we take up an issue not considered in most monopoly discussions: how *monopoly* is a coordination, or management, problem, a fact that imposes a necessary check on any monopoly's market power and therefore curbs the monopoly's ability to extract monopoly rents and impose inefficiency on its market. Anything that limits monopoly rents requires, of course, adjustments in rent-seeking theory, as we will show. Later, we will consider consumer switching costs, as a market counterpart on the consumer side to entry barriers on the producer side, which are widely seen to be a source of monopoly power, economic profits, reduction in consumer surplus, and market inefficiency. We will argue that some market conditions exist, well known to economists, under which switching costs can be welfare enhancing, not welfare destroying. Indeed, we will show why consumers would want to be locked in to certain types of products. That is to say, they would gain on balance from facing switching costs sufficiently high to permit the monopolist to impose monopoly prices.

Chapter 3

Monopoly as a
Coordination Problem

The traditional theory of monopoly leads to a set of theoretical deductions widely accepted by economists. As explained, a monopolist (no matter how imperfect), protected by external barriers to entry, will reduce output below the level achieved under idealized, perfectly competitive market conditions. The purpose of the output restriction is, of course, to raise the market price above competitive levels and to generate monopoly rents. The consequence is a deadweight loss resulting from the failure of the monopoly to produce units worth more to consumers than they cost the monopoly. Implicit in the graphical depiction of the extent of the deadweight loss is the assumption that the competitive supply curve is the same as the monopolist's marginal cost curve. This traditional view of a monopoly market is typically devoid of any consideration of the institutional setting of a monopolistically organized market as compared to a competitively organized market.

As explained in chapter 2, the potential social cost of a monopoly is now commonly accepted to be greater than indicated by the traditional theory. Monopolies, and the rents they create, are often the creations of government restrictions on entry. These monopoly rents are created and allocated in response to rent seeking, and the social cost of this rent seeking adds to the deadweight loss associated with monopoly restrictions on output, as explained in the last chapter. A guiding presumption in discussions of monopoly is that the only meaningful barriers to achieving monopoly price, output, and profit objectives are external to the monopoly.[1] This means that the only meaningful constraints on what a monopolist does are its competitors, those already in the market and potential competitors outside the market that could enter. Conventional takes on monopoly also mean that the extent of rent seeking relevant to the welfare costs of a monopoly position is unrelated to organizational and managerial problems within the monopoly firm.

In this chapter, we seek to extend our challenge to the conventional view of monopoly output and pricing behavior by taking account of the required institutional shift when a market is monopolized. Our point is a simple one: Aside from one-person firms, in which the residual claimant-principal and agent are one and the same, the achievement of monopoly rents is itself a coordination problem—that is, one of bringing about restrictions on output with agents (or employees) inside the firm whose incentives are imperfectly aligned with the interests of the principals (or owners). That is to say, as opposed to viewing a monopoly as a single-minded entity within which everyone is driven exclusively by the goal of maximum firm profits, a monopoly is best viewed as a group of individuals who are pursuing their own advantage through internal rent seeking that can reduce the monopoly profits below that implied by the standard monopoly model.[2]

We posit that achieving monopoly results is limited by both external *and* internal constraints, a fact that makes monopoly output restrictions less likely, and less severe, than the conventional theories of monopoly and rent seeking would indicate. This perspective on monopolies leads to conclusions that stand in sharp contrast with conventional implications: Even if production technology remains the same, the monopolist's marginal and average cost curves will not be the same as the competitive supply curve, contrary to textbook discussions. That is, contrary to what might be thought, the industry cost structure is bound to change. Indeed, the average cost faced by the monopolist will be higher than the average cost faced by independent competitors (again, assuming that production technology is the same), yet the monopolist's marginal cost curve is lower than the competitors' marginal cost curves. Because of the higher average cost, the monopoly profits will necessarily be smaller than is conventionally assumed at every output level. Because of the lower marginal cost, the monopoly output will be greater than in the conventional monopoly model. The reduced monopoly rents mean less political rent seeking to achieve monopoly ends and fewer government-protected monopolies than would be implied by conventional monopoly theory.

At the same time, following Schumpeter, innovation still can easily be higher under monopoly than under perfect competition, simply because, as argued in the last chapter, innovation that requires up-front costs is likely to be nil under perfect competition. Again, to repeat a theme of the book, maximum innovation requires some optimum degree of market power.

Our arguments lead to the conclusion that in seeking to achieve monopoly profits, the monopolist must be concerned not only with external entry barriers but also internal constraints in the form of agency costs that can reduce the degree to which output can be restricted and profits generated and retained by the monopoly firm. High agency costs can, in other words, have the same impact on monopoly production decisions as can low entry barriers. Improved systems of internal control of agents' behavior can lead to several outcomes not fully appreciated in the literature: greater restrictions on output and higher prices and profits in monopolized markets; more rent seeking; and more government-imposed restrictions on market entry.

THE CONVENTIONAL VIEW OF MONOPOLY

Figure 3.1 shows the usual way by which the efficiency of monopoly and competitive markets are compared (chap. 2, this vol.). In that illustration, for simplicity of exposition the long-run marginal (and average) cost curve for the monopolist is assumed to be horizontal. For purposes of making welfare comparisons between monopoly and competitive markets, we assume that standard production technology is the same for the monopolist as it would be if the industry were perfectly competitive. The underlying presumption of conventional theory is that the monopolist has as much incentive to minimize its production costs as do competitors, and that agency costs are unaffected by the market structure. After all, if the monopolist is intent on maximizing profits, then it has every incentive to hold costs down to the minimum. As is conventional, Michael Jensen and William Meckling (1976) have concluded that it is wrong to presume that monopolization of markets will lead to less "value maximization" than would be observed in competitive markets: "Since the owner of a monopoly has the same wealth incentives to minimize managerial costs as would the owner of a competitive firm, both will undertake that level of monitoring which equates the marginal cost of monitoring to the marginal wealth increment from reduced consumption of perquisites by the managers" (Jensen and Meckling 1976, 329–30).

As a consequence, a monopolist that takes over a once-competitive market will, according to the standard analysis, reduce output from Q_c to Q_m in order to raise the price from P_c to P_m and reap profits equal to the shaded rectangle P_cP_mac, which sets an upper limit on the amount of rent seeking to achieve the monopoly profits. As discussed in chapter 2, the inefficiency of the monopoly takeover is represented by the Harberger triangular area *abc* plus some portion, if not all, of the profit rectangle that is dissipated through political rent seeking.

Along much the same line, conventional analysis holds that competitors are unable to achieve monopoly results through the creation of a cartel because the profit incentives that might lead them to consider curbing output will undermine the curbs that are agreed upon. Once the cartel agreement is in place, each competitor can improve its individual profits by *not* restricting output. It can do even better by expanding output to make up for the curbs in output of

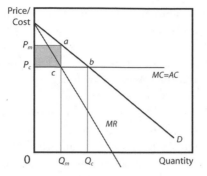

Figure 3.1. The standard monopoly model once again

other cartel members and in response to any price above the competitive level, if such ever occurs. The openness of competitive markets further destabilizes cartels simply because openness increases the number of competitors, actual and potential, who can enter and charge less than the cartel price.

AN UNCONVENTIONAL VIEW OF MONOPOLY

Clearly, conventional theory is asymmetrical in its conception of competitive and monopoly markets. The theory presumes that free riding (or the threat of it) is rampant in competitive markets, so much so that those competitors in perfectly competitive markets need not even try to cartelize their market. Yet, conventional theory presumes implicitly, if not explicitly, that once a monopoly firm has been established through the erection of barriers to entry, then the Prisoner's Dilemma and free-riding temptations are no longer problems worth analytical consideration (or, at least, standard analysis is silent on such matters). All that the monopolist needs, in order to achieve maximum monopoly rents, is the protection of entry barriers. The extent to which the market is closed to entry will determine the extent of the monopoly profits, given the minimum cost structure.

However, production, or lack thereof, is a coordination problem that necessarily involves the principals (owners) somehow getting the agents (managers and line workers) to do their bidding, which involves maximization of the principals' wealth through a maximization of the firm's long-run net income flow. As commonly recognized among economists, the principal-agent problem is a real problem simply because both the principals and the agents have conflicting personal objectives. The principals want to maximize their wealth from the firm, while the agents want to maximize some combination of their own wealth and security, perquisites, and prestige of their jobs with their firm. The conflict in the interests between principals and agents becomes acute because the principals, in any complex firm, must hand over to their agents at least some control over firm resources. The agents can, within limits, use the firm's resources to further their objectives at the expense of the principals.

The extent of the agency problem is typically assumed to grow with the size of the firm, following Ronald Coase (1937) and Mancur Olson (1965) (and graphically illustrated in Gurbaxani and Whang 1991). This is in part because with firm growth in terms of number of employees, the principals are less able to monitor the agents, which means that the agents can get away with more misuse of firm resources at lower (expected) personal cost. Growth in the size of a firm can also reduce the impact of the individual on the overall performance of the firm, which makes contributions of individual workers more difficult to assess. Besides, when an agent misuses firm resources, the costs are shared with—or are externalized to—other agents, as well as the principals (who can also be greater in number in a larger firm). Any common goal (of minimizing firm costs or maximizing firm profits) that the principals and agents might have shared becomes less controlling.

The solution to the principal-agent problem for the principals is straightforward: to align, in one way or another, the interests of the agents with their own. The alignment might come through monitoring and various payment and penalty schemes that make the agents' wealth dependent on the growth in the wealth of the principals.[3]

However, from the perspective of principal-agency theory, cost minimization, which is at the heart of competitive and monopoly models, is never assured for any given firm. Competitive markets can only pressure firms, and their principals and agents, to find cost-minimization strategies or else be run out of business by firms that do.

When tenets of principal-agency theory are applied to monopoly theory, the monopoly results are not likely to be achieved so costlessly as is conventionally posited. When a market is converted from being fully competitive to pure monopoly, the market participants within the production units change their economic roles rather dramatically as they shift from being principals/residual claimants of the individual competitive (relatively small) firms and become members of a much larger group of stockholders and/or become managers and line workers (agents).[4] Accordingly, the residual claimants have less of an incentive to devote themselves to the objective of profit maximization in the monopoly firm than they had when they were in independent competitor-firms.

If the formerly competitive market is assumed to be composed of idealized one-person firms, the principals and agents are one and the same, with no prospect of misalignment of incentives—and no incentive for efficiency-impairing shirking or misusing of firm resources, given that any costs incurred would be fully internalized.[5] However, when the industry is monopolized, many (of the potentially numerous) principals would surely become agents with the prospect of externalizing a share of the costs for their own actions. Alternatively, the principals would switch from being single proprietors to shareholders with minor stakes in their companies, and, again, with impaired incentives to monitor firm costs.

If the formerly competitive market were made up of firms with owners and agents separated into distinctly different groups, the problems of separation and control as well as agency costs would still be increased by the shift from a competitive to a monopoly market. Many former principals would become agents within a much larger organization, and the actions of each principal and agent would become less consequential in the context of the total monopoly.[6] They have more of an incentive to shirk and engage in opportunistic behavior because the costs of such behaviors are spread over a *larger* number of stock-holders.

Moreover, the pressure on both principals and agents to minimize agency costs will not be nearly so great in a monopoly firm, simply because the monopolist's position is less threatened (because of the entry barriers) than is the case in competitive markets. Perfectly competitive firms face imminent elimination when agency costs exceed minimum levels; monopoly firms do not. Those agents who absorb some of the monopoly rents through, for example, shirking and excessive salaries and perks, are more likely to survive, if for no other reason than that these activities would make survival absolutely impossible under perfect competition.[7]

The rent created by monopoly restrictions should be expected to give rise to efforts by the monopoly firm's employees to capture some of the rents—and the greater the monopoly rents, the greater the effort.[8] Clearly, firms devise policies and structures to reduce organizational rent seeking that reduces profits.[9] Such efforts imply that the more the monopoly firm restricts output back toward the idealized monopoly output level (Q_m), the greater the rents and the greater the attendant agency costs in the form of internal rent seeking and the firm's attempts to monitor and reduce rent seeking. Necessarily, therefore, the average cost curve facing firms in a perfectly competitive market and in a monopolist market cannot be one and the same even though the standard technology-based production function and costs remain the same. If the average cost curve looks like AC_1 (which equals MC_1) in figure 3.2 when the mar-

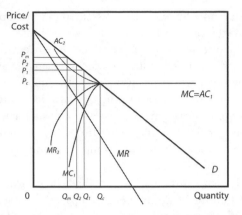

Figure 3.2. Monopoly as coordination problem

ket is competitive, it will look like, for example, AC_2 under monopoly. The exact position and shape of the new average cost curve will depend on exactly how monopoly profits change as output is restricted and on how agency and monitoring costs change with the monopolization of markets. That is, the new average cost curve will depend on the technology of monitoring and pay arrangements that align the interests of principals and agents.

The marginal cost curve also changes, but in an unexpected way. Rather than being identical to the higher average cost curve and diverging from the average cost curve in the conventional way, the marginal cost curve for the monopolist (with agency costs associated with restricted output) is below AC_2 and upward sloping, and asymptotic to the old AC_1 curve, as illustrated by MC_1 in figure 3.2. (Because the mathematics are relatively simple, proof of the shape of the curve is relegated to the appendix to this chapter.) The MC_1 curve is shaped the way it is because of the presence of agency costs that mount progressively with the *contraction* in output toward Q_m. This means that e*xpansion* of production from, say, Q_m toward Q_c implies, accordingly, a marginal cost that is now lower than the old marginal cost under competitive conditions without agency costs. This is the case because the new marginal cost is the same as the old marginal cost *minus* the agency costs that are no longer incurred when production is expanded by an additional unit. As the monopoly rents decrease with expanded output, the marginal *agency* costs go down, which implies an increase in the overall marginal cost until Q_c production level is achieved. In the case of figure 3.2, the new marginal cost curve MC_1 leads to the monopoly maximizing profit at output level Q_1, not Q_m.

Our discussion leads to the proposition that a monopolist that simply takes over a previously perfectly competitive market will necessarily face the problem of coordinating the activities of a number of previous competitors that may differ in size and be scattered geographically. The previous owners and residual claimants of the previous individual firms will then be agents of the monopolist, with the new agents taking on decidedly different roles with dramatically different incentives. Each agent will want to use discretion to maximize the agent's own welfare at the expense of the principal/monopolist. The central problem that the monopolist confronts is similar—but of course not identical—in structure to the problem faced by a cartel: overcoming the tendency of individual producing units to free ride and sacrifice potential collective gain for local or individual profits. The lack of independence of individual producing units within a monopoly no doubt mutes somewhat the free-riding problem, but the hierarchy itself superimposed over the various producing units within the monopoly to overcome free riding necessarily comes at a cost, mainly because the chain of command and control will be longer. The requisite incentive and monitoring systems will drain, to one extent or another, firm resources—and the firm's economic profit.

Admittedly, the hierarchical system's costliness cannot be determined conceptually and is actually irrelevant to the challenge to conventional theory mounted here. All we need note is that an effective monopoly replacement for an otherwise competitive market structure implies some system of cost monitoring, or else the restriction on output cannot be coordinated with any better profit results than would be expected under a truly competitive market made up of independent producers. The free riding within a cartel, if left unchecked, will cause the cartel to collapse; the free riding within a monopoly, if left unchecked, will drain the monopoly of all rents.

If free riding cannot be controlled at all, except at considerable cost (which is the case in perfectly competitive markets), restrictions on output through monopolization of the market would never be attempted. Hence, the extent of monopolization depends on more than external barriers to entry. It also depends on coordination or, what amounts to the same thing, agency costs.

Hence, the monopolist's economic profits will be something less than is conventionally believed for two reasons: First, the real resource costs associated with excessive perquisites and with monitoring will soak up some of the profits as well as divert production from Q_m. In this case, the waste of monopoly is larger than traditionally specified by the inefficiency triangle, with the added inefficiency equal to the value of the real resources soaked up in coordination of the output restrictions. Second, to achieve cost-effective coordination in restricting output, the monopolist will likely have to share some of the potential rents with the agents in the various producing units.

Although measured firm accounting costs may go up because of the agents' gains in the form of higher salaries or shirking, no necessary efficiency loss occurs because some of the rents are simply transferred from the pockets of the monopoly's owners to the pockets of the agents. Of course, even socially cost-less transfers are important because they signify the existence of less in the way of rents to be realized by the monopolist from rent seeking. Therefore, less political rent seeking (and the associated loss from the waste of resources involved in political rather than productive activity) should result than is commonly posited. Also, fewer monopoly restrictions should be achieved through government policies. Fewer monopoly profits will be transferred to those who can provide monopoly privileges. Hence, the prospect of rent absorption within a monopoly, once fortified, should reduce the prevalence of monopolies, given the lower return on rent-seeking investments.

CHANGES IN AGENCY COSTS

A major tenet of principal-agency theory is that agency costs retard efficiency in markets. Conversely, reductions in agency costs translate into improved efficiency. The view of monopoly presented in this chapter leads to a significantly different, more complicated conclusion: Firm agency costs can impair external rent seeking and reduce the monopolization of markets. They can also reduce the extent to which output is restricted and the extent to which the price is raised by monopolization. This implies that, given our revised per-spective, a *reduction* in agency costs, through, for example, technological devel-opments (such as computers and communication systems) that lead to more productive monitoring systems, can result in greater monopolization of mar-kets, lower outputs, and higher prices.[10] These results occur because the monopolist can more cost-effectively coordinate restrictions on output, moni-tor agents, and curb the costs imposed by the agents on the firm.

In terms of figure 3.2, a reduction in agency costs will lead to an upward shift in the monopolist's marginal cost curve. With the shift in the marginal cost curve from MC_1 to MC_2, the profit-maximizing output level falls (from Q_1 to Q_2) while the price rises (from P_1 to P_2). (At the same time, the average cost curve falls and monopoly rents grow because of the greater curb in production and the elimination of coordination and agency costs, which we omit from the figure to simplify the exposition.)

Whether the inefficiency loss goes up or down because of improved mon-itoring is uncertain. On the one hand, because of the improved monitoring, output is further restricted, increasing the size of the deadweight-loss triangle. On the other hand, the real waste from monitoring and excessive perquisites goes down. Nevertheless, the expected greater monopoly rents garnered by the firm can increase external rent seeking and result in more monopolized markets.

INNOVATION

The impact of prospective agency costs within a monopoly is hard to determine. If Schumpeter was right when he argued that monopoly profits can spur innovation, then agency costs that limit a monopoly's ability to restrict output and hike its price and profits can have a negative impact on innovation. The monopoly firm won't have the monopoly rents to put toward research and development. At the same time, with agency problems, the monopolist has a clear incentive to innovate in ways that better align principals' and agents' interests through better, more cost-effective monitoring and pay schemes, which can drive up monopoly profits and innovation, following Schumpeter's line of argument.

We noted in chapter 1 how firms in perfect competition have no incentive to innovate so long as the innovations require incurring up-front costs. Such costs cannot be recovered because of instantaneous duplication of successful products by existing firms and/or new entrants. It seems as though Adam Smith recognized the agency problems we have noted in this chapter and might have added that principals also lose their competitive drive as monopoly rents rise (see note 8, this chap.) . We see no reason that there could not also be a compromise position, that innovation might rise and then fall as an industry moves from a perfectly competitive structure to a fully monopolized one.

CONCLUDING COMMENTS

Conventional monopoly theory implicitly, if not explicitly, presumes that profit maximization of the monopoly firm is virtually automatic, that the mere existence of the firm implies that the agents will do what the stockholders tell them. Hence, it should be no surprise that discussions of incentives within the firm are totally absent in conventional analysis. However, this standard theory is sorely in need of correction. If monopoly is seen as a problem in coordinating the work of agents who do not "naturally" follow the dictates of the principals, the monopolist's marginal cost curve cannot be equivalent to the industry supply curve under competitive market conditions.

A central conclusion of this chapter is that more than external entry barriers count in the ability of monopolies to extract monopoly rents and, for that matter, for firms to seek monopoly positions. Agency costs, which necessarily arise because monopoly must be a coordination problem, also matter. Agency costs will impair the ability of a monopoly to profitably restrict output precisely because agency considerations change the cost structure of the monopoly and, therefore, the profit-maximizing output level.

Our line of analysis also leads to the conclusion that the inefficiency of monopoly can be, but is not necessarily, less than conventionally thought. Two consequences of market monopolization affect the market efficiency of monopoly in opposite ways: On the one hand, the prospects of monopoly agency costs that involve the use of real resources will add to the inefficiency of the monopolization process; on the other hand, the agency costs associated with restrictions on the monopoly output level will cause output to be higher than is conventionally thought. The rent available to shareholders will thereby be lower than conventionally thought, and the amount of rent seeking is likely to be lowered because of the agency costs.

Conventional principal-agency theory suggests, without qualification, that any improvement in the ability of firms to monitor their agents will increase productivity and efficiency. Our analysis introduces a major qualification. Although improvements in monitoring might reduce agency costs that are created in the process of monopolizing a market, the improvements also ease the coordinating and monitoring problems that the monopolist faces in curbing the output level. Reductions in monitoring and agency costs, in other words, can be expected to lead to a reduction in the output of the monopolist, an increase in monopoly rents, an increase in the inefficiency triangle, and an increase in rent seeking to obtain monopoly protection.

APPENDIX: AGENCY COSTS AND CARTELS

The implications of agency costs for a monopoly can be highlighted with a simple model. Let $P(Q)$ be the downward-sloping inverse demand curve facing the monopoly, where Q is the quantity of monopoly output. The cost that the monopoly incurs for each quantity of output is given by $C(Q, Q_C - Q)$, where Q_C is the competitive output—the quantity produced by the industry without monopoly restrictions. Based on our discussion in this chapter, we make the following plausible assumptions about this cost curve. Letting $C(Q)$ be the cost curve for the industry before formation of the monopoly, $C(Q, Q_C - Q) > C(Q)$ for all $Q < Q_C$. The total costs, and therefore the average costs, are higher for the monopoly than for the competitive industry at all output quantities less than Q_C. But at $Q_C = Q$, $C(Q, Q_C - Q) = C(Q, 0) = C(Q)$. Furthermore, as is standard, we impose the conditions that $C_1 > 0$ and $C_{11} > 0$, along with the just discussed condition that $C_2 > 0$ and the plausible condition $C_{22} > 0$.

We can now express the monopoly's objective as choosing the Q that maximizes the profit function

$$\prod = P(Q)Q - C(Q, Q_C - Q). \tag{1}$$

The maximizing Q, which we denote as Q^*, necessarily satisfies the condition

$$d\prod/dQ = P + (dP/dQ)Q - (C_1 - C_2) = 0, \tag{2}$$

or

$$P + (dP/dQ)Q = C_1 - C_2. \tag{2'}$$

Condition (2′) yields to the standard interpretation of the requirement for monopoly profit maximization: that marginal revenue equals marginal cost. The only difference is that in our case, marginal cost is lower than in the standard case because of the agency costs of reducing output: $C_1 - C_2 < C_1$. Although the agency costs increase the average cost, they reduce the marginal cost. When output is less than Q_C, an increase in production reduces the agency costs and therefore generates a partial offset to the increase in the standard costs of production. In the absence of agency costs, with $C_2 = 0$ for all Q, condition (2′) becomes the standard monopoly profit-maximizing condition and $Q^* = Q_M$. But, because of agency costs, $C_2 > 0$, and it follows from (2) that

$$P + (dP/dQ)Q < C_1, \tag{3}$$

or the cartel's marginal revenue is less than the standard marginal cost of production. If, as is almost always the case, the marginal revenue decreases in output, then (3) implies that $Q^* > Q_M$. The output that maximizes cartel profits is greater than the output that maximizes the profits of the standard monopoly.

On the other hand, if the monopoly is worth forming, its profit-maximizing output will be less than the competitive output level. At Q_C, if the monopoly marginally reduces output, it loses marginal revenue of $P + (dP/dQ)Q_C$, but it gains the marginal costs of $C_1 - C_2$. Since $P = C_1$ at Q_C, it follows that if $(dP/dQ)Q_C < -C_2$ (or $-(dP/dQ)Q_C > C_2$), then monopoly profits are increased by reducing output below Q_C. The possibility exists, of course, that $C_2 (Q_C, 0) >$ $-(dP/dQ)Q_C$.[11] If this is the case,

$$P + (dP/dQ)Q_C > C_1 - C_2 \tag{4}$$

at the competitive output level and the loss in revenue from a marginal reduction below Q_C is greater than the reduction in costs. Therefore, no motivation exists to reduce output, and nothing is to be gained from forming a monopoly.[12]

Chapter 4

Welfare-Enhancing Monopolies

The implications of the conventional textbook analysis of monopoly markets should be well established, given the attention they receive. As a consequence, consumers everywhere should be expected to oppose (if they had the requisite incentives to understand monopoly markets, which, of course, they don't) any effort on the part of the monopolist to enhance its protective barriers to entry, whatever their source. After all, such efforts could only raise the price that a profit-maximizing monopolist would charge and would lower consumers' surplus value. As a consequence, consumer support for the monopolist side of any antitrust case should seem paradoxical, and hard to explain if conventional monopoly theory is the last word on antitrust. Similarly, competitors' support of the government's side in an antitrust case should seem equally paradoxical, if the firm accused of violations of antitrust law has been acting like a monopolist. Restricted sales on the part of one (dominant) producer should open a larger share of the market for the competitors, who can then charge a higher price.

Our purpose in this chapter is to unravel this apparent paradox. To do that, we take up the issues of network effects and the peculiar characteristics of the growing markets for "digital goods," or those goods (such as software, e-books, e-music, and e-movies) that can be produced with 1s and 0s and can be distributed as electrons over wires and through the air. We refer often to the Microsoft antitrust case that was filed by the Justice Department and nineteen state attorneys general in the spring of 1998 and settled in 2002. We take up the Microsoft case because it vividly illustrates, to our way of thinking, how conventional monopoly theory can misguide discussions of a monopoly's supposed harm to consumers.[1] Moreover, as we will see, Microsoft's market rivals were the Justice Department's biggest boosters on the case in the United States and Europe, while consumers were largely supportive of Microsoft's side of the case. In addition, relatively new concepts to antitrust prosecutions such as "network effects" and consumer "lock-in" were at the foundation of the government's allegations of Microsoft's misdeeds in the operating system and browser market. Citing the monopoly issues in that case helps us make our more general point, that is, how and under what circumstances monopoly can be welfare enhancing for consumers.

THE PARADOX IN THE MICROSOFT ANTITRUST CASE

Following conventional monopoly wisdom, the existence of some identified barrier to entry, whether natural or artificial, necessarily translates into monopoly power. The higher the barrier, or the higher the cost that new entrants must incur to enter the market, the greater the monopoly power, and the greater the market inefficiency. The protected firm can be expected to exploit its favored market position just to maximize the wealth of the owners. An understandable presumption exists among economists and policymakers that a monopolist will fully exploit its market position. If a firm does not exploit its protected position, then the firm's stock price will suffer. Savvy investors can be expected to buy out the monopoly owners, hike the firm's product price to monopoly levels by curbing market supply, and then sell at a higher price reflecting the firm's monopoly rents.

If they *could* (at little or no cost), consumers would counter the monopolist's market power by colluding with the intent of taking one or some combination of the following collective actions.

- Buying off the monopolist, which would involve paying the monopolist more to expand output and sell at the competitive level than the monopolist would lose by not restricting production
- Setting a maximum price consumers would pay the monopolist exactly equal to the competitive level, which, as is easily shown, would induce the monopolist to expand production to the competitive output level
- Agreeing to suppress resale markets for the monopoly product in order that the monopolist might (perfectly) price-discriminate, leaving consumers with more output and, perhaps, greater consumer surplus

Barring their ability to collude (for collective decision-making reasons; see chap. 2, this vol.), we would expect consumers to favor antitrust prosecution against monopolists, but only if the costs of prosecution are not greater than the added consumer surplus resulting from greater competition, lower prices, and higher industry output. Consumers might understandably favor the regulation of monopoly, as long as the regulation were used to further the interests of consumers, not those of the regulated monopoly (which might be a political pipe dream)—all of which are points that should now be familiar to readers who have made their way through the first three chapters of this book.

A paradox therefore arises in the way that monopoly theory plays out in modern markets: Consumers continue to support monopolies that (supposedly or allegedly) utilize what appear to be the market restrictions of a monopolist (or any firm with market power). We say that because a federal district court in 2000 declared Microsoft to be an oppressive monopoly, protected by the so-called applications barrier to entry, which Microsoft had sought to fortify and to extend its market power by tying—or bolting—its Internet browser to its operating system. According to the district court, the company also engaged in predation against Netscape—which, at one time, was the most widely used Internet browser and which the court saw as a presumed critical component of a potential alternative computer platform to Windows—by giving away its Internet Explorer and by negotiating exclusive contracts for the distribution of Internet Explorer with an array of independent software developers, Internet access providers, computer manufacturers, and others.[2]

Although the appeals court reversed the lower court on several of Microsoft's alleged misdeeds, the appeals court did concur that Microsoft was a monopoly that had (in limited ways) abused its market position. Indeed, both the district court and the appeals court found that Microsoft (with an operating system market share found to be upward of 95 percent) was protected by the "applications barrier to entry" (made up, *supposedly*, of 70,000 Windows-based applications), which necessarily hikes entry costs for potential rivals. Accordingly, the appeals court unanimously upheld "the District Court's [that is, Judge Thomas Penfield Jackson's] finding of monopoly power in its entirety" (U.S. Court of Appeals for the District of Columbia 2001, 15), drawing that conclusion mainly on this determination.

> That barrier—the "applications barrier to entry"—stems from two characteristics of the software market: (1) most consumers prefer operating systems for which a large number of applications have already been written; and (2) most developers prefer to write for operating systems that already have a substantial consumer base. . . . This "chicken-and-egg" situation ensures that applications will continue to be written for the already dominant Windows, which in turn ensures that consumers will continue to prefer it over other operating systems. (20)[3]

On the other hand, survey after survey throughout the four-plus years of court proceedings found that a substantial number of computer users—upward of three-fourths—continued to favor the Microsoft side in the ongoing legal debate and would have liked nothing better than for the Justice Department and the nineteen state attorneys general pursuing the case to leave Microsoft alone. For example, Americans for Technology Leadership (van Lohuizen 2001), an advocacy trade association for a number of technology firms (but mainly financed by Microsoft), found just after the appeals court handed down its decision in late June 2001 that

- 84 percent of the 500 registered voters polled believed that Microsoft had benefited consumers, whereas only 8 percent believed that Microsoft had harmed consumers.
- 74 percent disapproved of preventing the shipment of Windows XP, which would, at the time of the poll, be shipped with additional inte-grated applications, and 57 percent of the respondents felt "strongly" about this point.
- 68 percent felt that Microsoft's competitors, not consumers, were benefiting most from the case.
- 78 percent said that Microsoft's competitors should spend more time on innovating and less time on litigating.

Moreover, 77 percent of those polled had a "very favorable" or "somewhat favorable" impression of Microsoft, whereas only 12 percent had a "somewhat unfavorable" or "very unfavorable" impression of Microsoft. Those ratings compare very favorably with the ratings received by AOL-Time Warner (58 percent to 21 percent), Sun Microsystems (31 percent to 3 percent), and Ora-cle (25 percent to 4 percent)—all firms that have never been legally tagged as monopolies. Only IBM—a firm that spent thirteen years defending itself in the courts against federal claims of antitrust violations—among the four alterna-tive firms covered in the survey had a better rating (80 percent to 5 percent).

Granted, these survey results might have been shaped by the people behind them, who surely were interested in making Microsoft look good and in hav-ing the antitrust case set aside. The Harris Poll found from a survey conducted in 1999 (a year and a half after the Microsoft antitrust case had been filed) that in spite of all the hostile commentaries on how the company had "bullied" practically everyone in the computer industry, Microsoft was rated number one in terms of overall reputation among the forty top technology companies, many of which—such as Dell, Amazon, and eBay—are in what might be deemed highly competitive markets (Alsop 1999).

The persistently high level of public support for the Microsoft side in the case seems to be all the more striking given how many hundreds of thousands of times Microsoft was tagged in the media (even before any court handed down a ruling) by respected policymakers, business people, journalists, and editorialists as a power-wielding "monopoly" that extracted its considerable cash reserves (in excess of $50 billion at this writing in mid-2006, after the company began setting aside long-standing private antitrust suits from a variety of companies with settlements in hundreds of millions, and billions, of dollars) from the hides of consumers.

Moreover, the survey findings on consumers' widely shared favorable view of Microsoft are all the more surprising when it is recognized that the so-called network effects that the Justice Department and others claim to be endemic to software markets can give rise to some unknown amount of consumer resentment toward Microsoft. If Microsoft is able to build its network for Windows through competitive means—for example, by charging relatively low prices—more people will buy Windows because more applications will be created (written by developers because of Microsoft's actual or expected market dominance). Consumers of Microsoft products will gain in the process. However, to the extent that Microsoft's market strategies and network success draw consumers away from alternative operating systems—say, Apple or Linux—Microsoft causes a collapse of the network effects for users of those alternative operating systems. Thus, those consumers should see themselves as harmed by Microsoft and, of course, might be expected to have an unfavorable, if not hostile, view of Microsoft.

There is, we agree, nothing in these (or other poll) findings that is conclusive. Understandably, economists take a dim view of what people report on surveys, since memories easily fade and the costs of giving distorted responses can be zero. However, the poll findings are worthy of serious reflection because if Microsoft were an abusive monopoly (at least in the conventional sense), you might expect consumers to do the opposite, that is, overwhelmingly favor the government's side, while Microsoft's competitors favor the Microsoft side. But again, the exact opposite has been the case, revealing a paradox important enough to demand an explanation. We are concerned here not so much with the particulars of the Microsoft case but rather with a more general question: Is it possible to conceive of a "monopolist" that has all the markers of a monopoly (that is, has a dominant market position with its market flanks protected by some entry barrier), acts like a monopolist (that is, seeks to price above marginal cost and to reinforce its entry barriers), and yet has consumers wanting it to retain its (supposed) market power? We submit that such a question would not be worth posing if we could not answer it in the affirmative.

UNRAVELING THE PARADOX

We see three possible ways of unraveling the paradox surrounding a so-called monopoly such as Microsoft that appears to have all the customer approval of a market-constrained competitor. First, perhaps computer users do not have the requisite information to judge Microsoft's behavior properly. If they did, so the argument might be developed, they would see Microsoft for what it *really* is, a monopolist that is, on balance, harmful to the vast majority of computer users. This explanation is hardly appealing to most economists, whose natural professional inclination is to go beyond popular commentaries that, in so many words, reduce to the refrain that "people are stupid." We economists tend to dismiss such explanations unless some reason compels the belief that consumers are uninformed. Maybe consumers are *rationally* ignorant when it comes to monopoly, as Gordon Tullock has explained (1967, chap. 7).[4]

Then again, if consumers are not aware that they have lost consumer surplus because of the monopoly behavior of a firm, can it be said that any harm has been done? The answer to that question is, at the very least, debatable, with no clear resolution—not to our minds at least. Continuing this avenue for reconciling the paradox appears to be no more productive than picking up on the proverbial debate over whether any sound occurs when a tree falls in the forest and no one is around to hear it.

The public choice and rent-seeking literature suggests another easy explanation for the observed paradox. Microsoft's competitors' support for the antitrust case, which contrasts with consumers' support for Microsoft's side, is prima facie evidence that the Justice Department has the case all wrong: Microsoft has been acting competitively, and the Justice Department has been out to protect Microsoft's competitors, not consumers, as several industrial organizations and legal scholars have stressed with eloquence.

Perhaps Milton Friedman was correct when he mused, indirectly providing his assessment of the Microsoft antitrust case,

> When I started in this business, as a believer in competition, I was a great supporter of antitrust laws; I thought enforcing them was one of the few desirable things the government could do to promote more competition. But as I watched what actually happened, I saw that, instead of promoting competition, antitrust laws tended to do exactly the opposite, because they tended, like so many government activities, to be taken over by the people they were supposed to regulate and control. And so, over time, I have gradually come to the conclusion that antitrust laws do far more harm than good, and that we would be better off if we didn't have them at all, if we could get rid of them. (1999)

William Baumol and Janusz Ordover have observed less kindly, "There is a specter that haunts our antitrust institutions. Its threat is that, far from serving as the bulwark of competition, these institutions will become the most powerful instrument in the hands of those who wish to subvert it. . . . We ignore it at our peril and would do well to take steps to exorcise it." They add later, "Paradoxically, then and only then, when the joint venture [or other market action] is beneficial [to consumers], can those rivals be relied upon to denounce the undertaking as 'anticompetitive'" (1985, 247, 257).

Former judge Robert Bork made the Baumol and Ordover point in the late 1970s even more strongly (two decades before he became a legal consultant on the Microsoft case for Microsoft's critics): "Modern antitrust has so decayed that the policy is no longer intellectually respectable. Some of it is not respectable as law; more of it is not respectable as economics; and now I wish to suggest that, because it pretends to one objective while frequently accomplishing its opposite, and because it too often forwards trends dangerous to our form of government and society, a great deal of antitrust is not even respectable as politics" (1978, 63).[5]

This explanation may be comforting both to antitrust experts with a public-choice bent and to Microsoft media supporters, such as the editors at the *Wall Street Journal*, but it hardly rings true for many of Microsoft's critics— including many lawyers in the Justice Department, as well as the eight judges (one at the district court level and seven at the appeals court level) who have heard the case—who seem to truly believe in it and have faith in their position that Microsoft is a protected dominant producer that has acted like a full-fledged, welfare-destroying monopoly. They posit that many consumers are, for all practical purposes, locked into the use of Windows by very high switching costs, attributable to network effects and the applications barrier to entry (another form of entry barrier taken up, with different twists in arguments, in the next chapter). Consumer lock-in supposedly gives Microsoft its predatory monopoly power against potential rivals and affords Microsoft the opportunity to exploit its market position in the future, if not before and during the trial.

Even if Microsoft had not immediately exploited its monopoly power, by the time of the trial, rational consumers should have felt the future harm that Microsoft was poised to inflict—the expected lost consumer surplus—as they, the consumers, developed present discounted estimates of the high price of using Microsoft products in the future. Nevertheless, many computer users do not seem to be particularly concerned that Microsoft may have precluded competitors from the market.

How might these reactions be explained without resorting to an explanation that posits consumer ignorance or a sinister political plot by the Justice

Department and Microsoft's competitors? More generally, and apart from the particulars of the Microsoft case, how can it be that a firm showing all the signs of being a protected monopoly is viewed by most consumers as benign, if not welfare enhancing? We can posit an even more intriguing question: Might there not be such a thing as a welfare-enhancing monopoly, contrary to what is suggested by practically all of the economic literature, with Joseph Schumpeter's (1942) and John McGee's (1971) works being the most prominent exceptions?

If we start with the standard monopoly model under which market demand is given and find that the marginal cost of producing additional units is positive, and possibly even increasing, then a protected, profit-maximizing monopoly cannot be welfare enhancing, at least not in a present-value sense. Consumers would clearly want the monopolist controlled. But perhaps the conventional hypothesized market conditions would not apply to all markets subject to monopolization. Perhaps we need a new perspective—or rather, we need to reconsider an old one.

In developing his view of markets as an evolutionary process of "creative destruction," Schumpeter (1942, chap. 8) reasoned that only by having monopolies, with their attendant negative consequences (as conventionally modeled by economists), can we count on growth reaching its full potential. Schumpeter suggests that monopolies established by market means play much the same role in markets that patents and contracts play, as barriers to entry with an array of provisions that allow firms to recover their up-front investments.[6]

We might quibble with Schumpeter's position, as have many economists (evident from the review of the literature in chap. 1). However, he seems to have a reasonable point: Before making their investments, entrepreneurs need to be able to at least *expect* to recover them. Patents, copyrights, regulatory regimes, and contracts are institutional means that have been developed to provide entrepreneurs with the requisite assurances and incentives to make their investments. We can conceive of market circumstances in which these other means of assurances don't work very well. For example, we can imagine circumstances that require more parties to sign contracts than is feasible. Further, some goods might be too cheaply copied to make patents and copyrights effective, and finally, governments might be too constrained constitutionally to permit regulatory regimes to create the required protection. However, in some subset of those cases, monopolies—with natural or artificial barriers erected— might provide the requisite entrepreneurial assurances for up-front investments to be made.

DIGITAL MARKETS

Schumpeter's view of what we might call welfare-enhancing monopolies might be more appropriate for our time than his own, mainly because of the advent of digital goods, or goods that basically consist of 1s and 0s. Two key attributes of such goods are their strong network effects and the low—close to zero, if not zero—marginal production cost.

Network Effects

Consider a market that has the attribute believed by the Justice Department to characterize the operating system market: network effects.[7] This term means that the value of the product to individual consumers escalates with the growth in the number of users. In the case of the operating system market, if more people use Windows, then more program developers will write applications for Windows. When more applications are written for Windows, then the demands of individual consumers for Windows will rise, mainly owing to the growth in the number of Windows users and the value of Windows to each user. There are, in other words, economies of scale in consumption that increase short-run market demand while potentially making the long-run demand for the network product highly elastic. As with scale economies on the production side, demand-side scale economies should be expected to lead to a concentration of sales among a few producers, if not a single producer.

To graphically see the impact of network effects, consider figure 4.1. In that figure, D_1 is the current short-run demand for a good that exhibits network effects of the sort just described, with future demand a function of the quantity currently bought. We can start with a high price of P_3, which will lead to a quantity bought of Q_1, which we assume, for simplicity's sake, is such a small quantity that no material network effects occur. However, if the price is lowered to P_2, the current consumption goes to Q_2, with the result that in the future, the short-run consumer demand rises to D_2—because the inframarginal values of all units rise with more people buying the good. Future consumption rises to Q_3 at price P_2. In the case of an operating system, the greater sales of the system lead to more programs being developed for the system. In the case of telephones, it means that all telephone subscribers have more people to call with more phone and service contract sales. If the current price is further lowered to P_1, consumption in the short-run expands along the short-run demand curve D_1 to Q_4. However, with time the short-run demand rises from D_1 to D_3. Consumption in the future at price P_1 rises to Q_5.

A couple of points emerge from this description of demand for a network

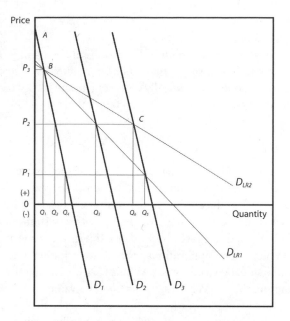

Figure 4.1. The lagged demand curve

good. First, the economist's old axiom that price doesn't affect demand as a functional relationship between price and quantity (but rather affects "quantity demanded") is no longer exactly right. Demand is affected by price (indirectly at least) via the quantity consumed by a larger pool of consumers. Price therefore affects value, which raises questions about the supposed antisocial nature of a monopolist's pricing strategy—because the standard static model is no longer representative of what a monopoly does and does not do.

Second, in standard demand analysis, the long-run elasticity of demand is affected by the length of the time period (because the time period affects the number of substitutes that can be sought out and considered by consumers). For a network good, the elasticity of demand is also affected by the *extent* of the network effects. The greater and more immediate the network effects, the greater the elasticity of the long-run demand and the greater the incentive the producer has to lower its initial price. In terms of figure 4.1 and the assumptions about the expansion of the short-run demand curves from D_1 to D_2 to D_3 when the price is lowered from P_3 to P_2 to P_1, respectively, the long-run demand is represented by the line D_{LR1}. However, if the network effects are so strong that the short-run demand expands with time from D_1 to D_3 when the price is lowered currently from P_3 to P_2, the long-run demand curve will be more elastic, D_{LR2} instead of D_{LR1}.

Third, network effects can give rise, beyond some point, to a tipping of the market toward a producer that appears to be winning any competitive battle. This means that consumers can be expected to move to the dominant producer because of that producer's increasing sales, which, again, must force up the values of all units bought. The firm that is the subject of the market tipping need not actually be the dominant producer at the time the market tips. All that is required is that consumers *think* or *expect* that the firm will be the dominant producer. Hence, all producers in the market should be expected to work to affect consumer expectations of their individual market dominance. One way for a producer to make believers of consumers is to price its product low, which can assure consumers that it will have lots of sales and that the market will tip its way. The up-front competition among would-be dominant producers can be expected to be intense, because the producers are competing not just for current sales but for a future stream of growing sales and market dominance, and the potential economic profits that can then come from market dominance.

Fourth, concerned with standard, non-network goods, economists understandably draw their blackboard demand curves fully contained within the first or positive quadrant. That is, the demand curve is never extended below the horizontal x-axis into the negative fourth quadrant (as done in fig. 4.1). This is because a (conventional textbook) firm never has a reason to charge a negative price (that is, the firm pays consumers to buy the good), even if the negative price would extend sales. Negative prices can never be profit maximizing for conventional goods because marginal cost is never negative, and no future benefit is to be derived from its negative prices. Network goods are categorically different. Zero and negative current prices are viable pricing options because of the network effects, or because the short-run demand in the future can be greater because of the current zero and below-zero prices, which suggest at least the potential for raising the price in the future. Zero or below-zero prices are not necessarily any more predatory for network goods than are positive prices for non-network goods.

Fifth, current (low) prices do not necessarily imply that consumers are better off than they will be in the future when the price is raised (if it is raised). The explanation hangs on the potential for an enlarged future network. Consumer surplus from the current low price can be lower than the consumer surplus realized when the then current demand in the future is higher and the price is higher. In terms of figure 4.1, the consumer surplus from a price of P_3, when the demand is D_1, is P_3AB. The consumer surplus from a price of P_2 in the future, when the demand is D_3, is off the chart, equal to the area above P_2C and below the demand curve D_3 (assuming that it is extended at the top to the vertical axis). Consequently, even if a producer of a network good comes to dominate totally its market (because of, say, the tipping process) and that producer charges (what are conventionally thought to be) monopoly prices (because at that point in the development of the market the price is above marginal cost and a deadweight-loss triangle and a rectangular economic profit box can be identified), consumers are not then necessarily worse off. Their net consumer surplus—the Dupuit triangle—can be greater at that future point in time when they pay monopoly prices. This is true even if consumers feel trapped by, or locked in to the purchase of, the network good. Indeed, consumers can find positive value in the *prospects* of being locked in to a network, meaning their demand for the good can be greater with the lock-in than without. With the potential for lock-in, consumers can be more willing to make their own up-front investments in adapting their behavior to the network good, with reduced fear that fellow consumers can easily move, unraveling the network and undercutting the value of consumers' up-front investments.

Sixth, any producer that comes to dominate its market because of network effects cannot be judged to be a monopolist solely by the economic profits that it is then making. Over the course of the relevant market periods, the monopolist might really have earnings that are far closer to normal profits. This is because it might have charged zero or negative prices (or more likely, below-cost prices) in early time periods. Its losses must be set against any future economic profits to determine the firm's true rate of return over time.

Low or Zero Marginal Cost

The marginal cost of reproducing units of the digital good can be close to zero, if not zero. At such cost, all (or practically all) production costs are up front—that is, sunk costs. In the case of Windows, Microsoft ships a master copy to computer manufacturers that they store on their central servers, and they, competing computer manufacturers, make copies electronically by transferring the code from their servers to the computers that are shipped, a process that makes the marginal cost of copies of Windows about as close to zero as can be imagined for Microsoft; and nothing suggests that marginal cost will ever rise, given the scant material and labor costs involved in the reproduction of copies from the master.

Graphically, the digital firm's cost structure is substantially different from the cost structure discussed in chapter 3 (fig. 3.1), in which the marginal cost and average cost curves are constant and identical. Assuming the limit of zero marginal cost, the long-run marginal cost curve lies along the horizontal axis in any constructed graph. The long-run average cost curve, however, starts out at one unit for which the average cost is equal to the up-front (fixed) cost. As more and more units are produced, the average cost descends, since the up-front costs are progressively prorated over a larger and larger quantity. The average cost curve will have a parabolic shape, with the curve becoming asymptotic to the horizontal axis. There are, indeed, virtually unlimited scale economies in supply in the case of the pure digital good.

Perhaps these economies of scale in supply and demand do not map perfectly to the Microsoft case. However, any lack of congruency should not distract us from the conceptual points that flow from a market beset by economies of scale on both sides of the market. If a number of producers were already in such a market, meaning that they have products and have incurred the up-front development costs, the up-front development costs would be ignored in their pricing decisions, as they should be. But this means that the price of the product can fall to zero in competitive markets in which the firms do not produce complements (and can possibly fall to below zero in competitive markets in which the firms produce complements, with negative prices translating into the producers paying buyers to take their products).[8] Even if the price were barely above zero, it would be in the interest of producers to lower their prices more, given the network effects and supply-side economies of scale. Clearly, the producers in such a market would agree that they made a big mistake in getting into the market in the first place. They would feel this way because they will not be able to cover their up-front costs. Their prior mistakes, however, will not deter them from pricing with only their marginal costs in mind (as we economists reverently teach our beginning students).

Dynamic Inefficiency

Recognizing the prospects of a zero price in markets with a zero marginal cost, producers will understandably look carefully at such markets before ever incurring the fixed development costs, a point that has been recognized in the economic literature for at least 150 years but that has been updated by a sequence of economists over the years.[9] In contemplating the creation of goods, producers will assess their chances of becoming the standard, or selling to the entire market, in the initial competitive struggle, but they will also assess the extent to which competitors can enter and capture their buyers after they have become the standard and incurred their up-front fixed development costs.

The situation faced by an aspiring monopolist of a network good is not unlike that of a rent-seeking firm attempting to secure a legal monopoly from Congress in competition with other firms. In the rent-seeking case, only one firm can succeed, and the money spent rent seeking is lost whether a firm wins or loses. The possibility exists, as shown by Tullock (1980), that the competition can result in more being spent on rent seeking than the legal monopoly is worth. In the case of firms taking losses on current sales of a network good as each attempts to become the dominant firm, Tullock's result establishes the possibility that the total current losses (which are gains to consumers) can be greater than the monopoly profits realized by the winning firm.[10] This is clearly a situation in which the consumers do very well even though they end up dealing with a monopolist (Tullock 1980).

One of the unrecognized problems with prices established in perfectly competitive markets, as stressed by Paul Romer (1994) in his contributions to the "neo-Schumpeterian growth theory," is that such prices reflect goods' marginal values only and, in turn, are equated only with producers' marginal costs of production. The disincentive that producers have to innovate under such circumstances is particularly acute in markets with high fixed costs (relative to marginal costs), as noted, but the incentive problems on the innovation front of perfectly competitive prices do not go away when fixed costs are relatively low. This is because the prices do not and cannot reflect the full inframarginal values of the goods that can be created.[11] In static analysis, this observation is of no consequence, because the goods are *given*, meaning they do not have to be created, but the observation can be critically important when the goods must first be created (or improved). With prices not reflecting the goods' full market value, entrepreneurs have an impaired incentive to innovate, that is, create the goods that can be then subjected to static analysis. While monopoly prices might give rise to the static deadweight loss, they also allow entrepreneurs to capture more of created goods' full market value, which can mean more goods than otherwise being created. Put another way, perfectly competitive prices can imply static Pareto efficiency but can also result in a form of dynamic inefficiency, or an underallocation of resources to the creation of new products and improvements in old ones. If created, such goods could enhance consumer welfare over time by far more than welfare is undercut by monopoly prices at any point in time, given the array of products that are then available.

As Romer (1994) suggests, static competitive analysis assumes away one of the more important problems any economy faces, the appropriate allocation of resources to the extraordinarily complex problem of selecting those goods that *will* in fact be created from a virtual infinite array of goods that *could* be created. In highly competitive markets, the high-fixed-cost problem will cause some goods that should be created (because their total value exceeds all costs) to go uncreated altogether, with development resources (mis)allocated toward the (over)creation of goods that do not confront the high-fixed-cost problem.

Competitive prices that allow for recovery of fixed costs can still lead to an underallocation of resources in the creation of the most highly valued new goods. And the problem of fixed costs, which are unavoidable when considering the *creation* of goods, is obviously of greater importance than economists have been willing to admit.

> Evidence that fixed costs are important comes from the observation that many services and goods are simply not available at any price in many parts of the world. If there were no fixed costs, one should find that all possible goods, services, and production processes and types of exchange are available to firms located everywhere in the world. (Romer 1994, 24–25)[12]

One of the totally unappreciated benefits of monopoly prices is that they allow for at least a partial correction of this dynamic resource allocation problem over time. Monopoly prices can capture more of the consumers' benefits and can, therefore, be better signals as to what entrepreneurs should do than competitive prices, which can capture few of those benefits (and the lower the marginal cost, the lower the benefits competitive prices capture).

THE RELEVANCE AND POTENTIAL WELFARE VALUE OF ENTRY BARRIERS

In the absence of entry barriers, a sole producer would be just that, a sole producer—but without market power. That entry barriers protect the sole producer's ability to curb its own production, and therefore market supply, can be surmised from William Landes and Richard Posner's (1981) supply-based formula for market power.[13] Indeed, it is altogether reasonable to deduce that a dominant firm's power to extract monopoly rents and impose deadweight losses is directly related to the height of the entry barriers. The higher the entry barriers, the greater the monopoly rents and deadweight losses, as conventionally argued.

Such a line of argument is fine as long as it is pursued for its own theoretical sake, because the conclusions drawn can be perfectly consistent with the underlying premises. The standard paradigm, however, can become problematic when it forms the basis of antitrust prosecution, mainly because it suggests that the primary task of antitrust enforcers is twofold: (1) to establish the firm's market dominance, and then (2) to establish the existence of entry barriers.

Accordingly, in the Microsoft case, the appeals court endorsed the district court's finding that Microsoft was an overwhelmingly dominant firm in the operating system market and that, in the absence of conventional entry barriers, an interesting new entry barrier had arisen in the operating systems market. This "applications barrier to entry" was justification enough for the district court to deduce that key Microsoft business strategies—such as giving away Internet Explorer or bolting Internet Explorer into Windows—were violations of antitrust laws, because they (and Microsoft's substantial expenditures supporting those strategies) could have no other conceivable justification than to maintain Microsoft's market dominance. Of course, the implications are that the barriers worked to lower consumer welfare, not so much in the usual way, through production restrictions, but through impairment of innovation (Jackson 1999, ¶ 412).

But are entry barriers always and everywhere destructive of welfare? Might they not advance welfare, at least sometimes? The answer to both questions is obviously confused as far as government policy is concerned. Governments everywhere have elaborated complex antitrust laws that focus on entry barriers as close to prima facie evidence of monopoly power. On the other hand, governments have equally complex copyright and patent laws that accomplish nothing if they do not erect entry barriers, all for the express purpose of providing the copyright and patent holders with an element of monopoly power, the presumed requisite incentive for holders to produce more new works than would otherwise be produced. This means that there is a presumption underlying copyright and patent laws that the added value to consumers from the additional works produced is greater than the lost value from all works having some monopoly privilege. Is there not some differential market condition that is driving the schism in the government's treatment of the different entry barriers?

Again, if the entry costs were zero, the producers would be understandably reluctant to enter the market. Indeed, they simply would not enter. They could anticipate being under constant threat of entry and would have to constantly fear that their prices would be pushed toward zero, if not *to* zero (and below). Producers of normal goods—those with positive and eventually rising marginal costs—do not have to worry nearly as much about market protections in the form of entry barriers because of the nature of their cost structure— namely, the positive and rising marginal cost of production. That marginal cost curve provides them with some protection against the price falling to zero and against their not being able to recoup their up-front investments. Indeed, the greater the marginal cost and the more steeply it rises, the greater protection such producers have and the less they have to be concerned about such auxiliary protections, most notably entry barriers.

Producers of goods with zero marginal costs, on the other hand, would naturally look for entry barriers to ensure that they can recover their development costs. They would also (more so than producers of goods with positive and rising marginal cost curves) critically assess a priori their market power—or monopoly position—after they become established in the market. The greater their prospect of recovering their development costs, the greater their willingness to produce the product, which converts to the proposition that the greater the entry barriers, the greater the producers' willingness to incur the development costs, with the end result being, potentially, greater consumer welfare.

Of course, products can vary along any number of dimensions, not the least of which are sophistication, usefulness, and reliability—what might be construed as quality—and the quality of a product can determine the required development costs. The greater the quality, the greater the required development costs, or so we might expect. Hence, we would rightfully anticipate that entry barriers can determine how much firms would be willing to incur in the way of development costs, which is to say, what quality they would seek in the products they develop. The greater the entry barriers, other things being equal, the greater the quality of the product.

As in the case of copyrights and patents, the added value from additional goods and higher quality goods being produced with entry barriers can exceed the monopoly efficiency losses on all monopoly goods.

Chicken-and-Egg Problem

As noted, some markets are said to harbor network effects. No doubt, some network effects are "natural," that is, they occur without any work on the part of the firms producing the products. However, many network effects require work and encouragement on the part of the firms that might benefit from them, if for no other reason than the widely acknowledged "chicken-and-egg-problems" that often are embedded in such network good markets. To encourage their customers to join their online banking networks, banks understood that they had to find ways to overcome many customers' resistance to incurring the initial costs of changing well-worn banking habits and learning new computer click sequences on the banks' Web sites. Hence, when it initiated its online bill-paying service, Citibank gave customers up to $25 for using its online system. Bank of America, Wells Fargo, Wachovia, and Washington Mutual offered the service free for at least two months and then priced the service below cost after the introductory free period. J. P. Morgan/Chase outdid them all by paying their customers $5 per transaction carried out online with the total payment per month limited to $50, with the offer period also limited to three months (Bayot 2003).

An operating system firm understands that an operating system is useless to most computer users without applications, and applications developers can reason that their applications are useless without an operating system. Accordingly, the applications developers' willingness to write for any given operating system will also be founded on their assessment of the operating system's chances of becoming the dominant producer.[14]

To overcome this classic chicken-and-egg problem and to improve its chances of being seen as the dominant producer, an operating system firm can be expected to work hard at improving its system *and*, just as important, easing the problems that developers face in writing for its operating system. The operating system firm also has two incentives to lower its initial price. First, a lower price will increase the copies sold and cause network effects to kick in. Second, a lower price can be expected to improve the chances that the applications developers will see the operating system as becoming the dominant producer, which can make for self-fulfilling expectations of the firm's market dominance.

Now, the extent of the entry barriers can affect how diligently—in terms of how many resources will be devoted and how fast they will be devoted—any firm will attempt to develop its potential network. The entry barriers will also determine how low a firm will push its initial price. It seems altogether reasonable to surmise that the greater the entry barriers, the lower the initial price and the faster the network will develop, because the prospective entry barrier for other potential entrants implies a greater reward for developing the network. In the case of the operating system firm, the lower the initial price, the greater the likelihood that it will have applications written for it, and if a barrier to entry exists in the form of an "applications barrier to entry," as the courts have affirmed is true of the Microsoft market, then the lower the initial price, the greater the applications barrier to entry.[15]

What makes the efforts by would-be monopolists to create and nurture entry barriers problematic is that any barrier, whatever its name, that is created and nurtured in the process of a firm taking advantage of network effects will be seen, by those who have adopted conventional monopoly theory, as inspiring monopoly behavior, or rather behavior that is, on balance, destructive of consumer welfare. If the firm charges anything above marginal cost (meaning above zero), the price will necessarily be seen as monopolistic, especially if the firm is dominant (because of the network effects). And if there is some entry barrier, the presumed monopoly (and harmful consequences of the firm's "restrictive practices" or its aggressive pricing and product development strategies to maintain its market dominance) will be fortified even more if the firm also makes a lot of money on current sales, as Microsoft does.

Interestingly, in the rebuttal phase of the Microsoft trial, the Justice Department's chief economic consultant, Franklin Fisher, argued that

Microsoft's monopoly position in operating systems is the reason that Microsoft can charge "superhigh prices" and earn "supernormal profits." Similarly, when the Computer and Communications Industry Association filed its antitrust complaint against Microsoft in early 2003, it argued that "Microsoft's extraordinary financial performance and pricing behaviour provide powerful evidence of its dominance. In particular, Microsoft's exceptional freedom from competition is apparent in its 80 percent profit margins for both its operating systems and personal productivity applications."[16] Conventional monopoly theory makes no allowance for the prospect that current monopoly rents, generated by above-marginal-cost pricing, may in some cases really be necessary, a form of payback for initial up-front, sunk expenditures and depressed prices, strategies the monopolist may have used to build its network, as well as build its requisite entry barriers. Moreover, the theory fails to consider that the existence and persistence of Microsoft-type monopolies can inspire a "perennial gale" of innovation throughout the economy, precisely because of the demonstrated monopoly rents garnered by the extant monopolies.

Entry barriers can seem on par with mountains: Once they exist, they never go away and never have to be fortified and maintained. However, that is not likely to be the case, except in instances in which the entry barriers are physical (as in exclusive control of a raw material). Even government regulatory entry barriers have to be maintained with continual lobbying to ensure that the ever-changing body of legislators sees the need to maintain the regulations as they are. In the case of an entry barrier such as the applications barrier to entry, the operating system firm may constantly have to assure the applications writers, through both the development and pricing of its operating system, that it will retain its dominant market position. The firm might even have to use whatever market power it has to keep competitors at bay. For example, it might integrate a browser into its operating system when faced with the prospects of a new personal computer platform emerging based in part on a browser.

Alternatively, the firm might figure that when faced with a market challenge, it can use the existing barrier to entry as a means of achieving contracts with computer manufacturers, independent software developers, and Internet access providers to use its browser over the browser of the rivals. The point is that the ability to fend off potential challengers will feed back into the firm's willingness to incur the up-front costs for developing its product and network effects, some of which occur by lowering the product's initial price (perhaps to zero or even below zero). The greater the ease with which potential rivals can be fended off, the greater the development costs incurred by the firm—and the greater the potential network benefits to consumers.

We can't stress enough that given the current antitrust thinking, which is grounded in conventional monopoly models, antitrust enforcers could easily interpret the efforts of the operating system firm to fend off rivals as anticompetitive and a violation of the country's antitrust laws. Indeed, as already noted, the district court declared Microsoft to be a monopoly because the company's substantial market share was protected by the applications barrier to entry. It then reasoned that Microsoft's efforts to zero-price its browser were predatory and that its restrictive contracts were exclusionary. Moreover, Microsoft had demonstrated a persistent "course of [monopoly] conduct" that justified a breakup of the company, or as Judge Thomas Penfield Jackson wrote in his Findings of Fact (1999, ¶ 412),

> Through its conduct toward Netscape, IBM, Compaq, Intel, and others, Microsoft has demonstrated that it will use its prodigious market power and immense profits to harm any firm that insists on pursuing initiatives that could intensify competition against one of Microsoft's core products. Microsoft's past success in hurting such companies and stifling innovation deters investment in technologies and businesses that exhibit the potential to threaten Microsoft. The ultimate result is that some innovations that would truly benefit consumers never occur for the sole reason that they do not coincide with Microsoft's self-interest.

With conventional monopoly theory as a reference, the normal assumption is that consumers would be against the monopolist preying against actual or potential market rivals—and the maintenance of its entry barriers. From the less static, evolutionary Schumpeterian perspective, the predation offers two sources of consumer gains that would cause consumers to support the firm's predation and its other efforts to maintain its entry barriers.

- First, consumers will understand that there are cases in which products might not be created and produced in the first place if the firm did not see the potential to maintain its protective entry barriers, by predation or otherwise.
- Second, if a firm fends off potential entrants, some consumers can gain from such predatory actions by the fact that the market might otherwise fragment, meaning that the network will unravel, leaving its consumers with fewer network effects and, beyond some point, the prospects of having to incur the costs of switching to another network.

In short, the Justice Department's and courts' view notwithstanding, a more consumer-friendly and developer-friendly explanation is possible for

Microsoft's actions that emerges from our discussion of how network effects influence pricing decisions *prior to* the evolutionary process by which any network emerges: *In a market beset by network effects, consumers and applications developers have an interest in some form of entry barrier, application or otherwise.* Consumers understand that the prospect of an applications entry barrier could be all the reason Microsoft needed to aggressively develop the network by lowering its up-front price and by encouraging developers to write applications for the Windows network, all to the benefit of the consumers. The network could have developed more rapidly and to a greater level of coverage, with a more sophisticated operating system and more sophisticated applications, than would have existed without the prospects of the applications barrier. Seeing the prospects of the applications barrier, the developers could have been all the more eager to join the network early on and to upgrade the quality of their programs, anticipating that their investment would not be voided by a later breakup of the network.

Similarly, applications developers and consumers have a good old-fashioned private interest in having the entry barriers maintained (even if the methods have to be predatory): If competitors move into the market, the network can be threatened. The applications developers' up-front investments can be undermined with a breakup of the network. The consumers' assessed value of the product can be undercut with the decline in available applications and reduction in the count of consumers.

THE PROBLEM OF DIGITAL PIRACY

Buyers of industrial-era goods—for example, cars—can replicate the goods they buy only at considerable cost, usually at a much higher cost than that of the producers of the bought copies. Consumers certainly cannot use their bought copies as a master. Hence, consumers are never imagined (in economists' models) to be producers. In sharp contrast with industrial-era goods, digital goods can be easily replicated by, potentially, nearly all buyers (with the actual cost of replication clearly on a downward trend, barring the creation of workable and cost-effective locks for electronic and digital goods). This means that buyers can become producers without having to incur any (or few) up-front development costs, and buyers certainly represent a credible threat when they have ready access to free and open distribution systems such as the Internet.

The fact that buyers can be producers gives rise to two prospects: (1) digital markets are far more open to entry than are other markets—unless auxiliary, artificial entry barriers are imposed; and (2) the marginal cost of production from all available producers of digital goods can remain at or close to zero for a much larger range of output than is the case for industrial-era goods, mainly because *if* marginal cost starts rising (which may not occur) for some producers (say, the developers), buyers can transform themselves, and have the incentive to transform themselves, into producers with an attendant marginal cost of production that is at or close to zero, drastically extending the production range before diminishing returns and scale diseconomies can be expected to set in. That is, the elasticity of supply is greatly increased, and the price is held close to zero. This set of circumstances can give rise to a virtually exponential explosion in potential producers, who can enter the digital markets at low purchase prices that have been suppressed by the price competition of the original producers with existing and potential buyers who become producers.

This issue of the potential for buyers morphing into producers is especially problematic for digital goods, given that the usual means of erecting entry barriers—policing and prosecuting pirates—might prove to be ineffective. Granted, Napster (which made a business out of making it easy for people to swap—that is, pirate—musical files) has been closed down, but as we developed this book, media reports began emerging on how new Internet sites were popping up overseas, giving away the music of top acts—for example, Bruce Springsteen—before they had been released by their labels (e.g., Healy 2002).

At any point in time in the real world, as opposed to the imagined static models economists employ, an array of goods must exist that can be produced. Without question, these goods will vary in the extent to which they can be profitably produced. Naturally, entrepreneurs will favor the more profitable goods as they pick and choose among the array of potential goods they can produce. Consequently, given the constraints of scarcity, some goods will not be produced, but it does not follow that the goods that are forgone are the goods with the least value to consumers. Some of the goods could be—and are likely to be—ones that have low or zero marginal costs and, because of low or a total absence of entry barriers, have little or no chance of being profitable (for long), precluding some artificially imposed entry barriers. Artificial barriers to entry, even when erected by the dominant producers, can in one sense lead to what might be construed as a "monopoly" (especially if monopolies are defined by observed entry barriers), with the presumption of a deadweight loss as output is restricted below competitive levels. However, no net inefficiency may occur, in spite of the price being above marginal cost: The entry barriers themselves help overcome another possible market inefficiency, or a misallocation: the overallocation of resources toward those goods that are protected by the usual, natural means, that is, by positive and rising marginal costs and by buyers not being able to easily replicate the goods they purchase.

The case for efficiency-enhancing entry barriers that we are seeking to make here is, as might have already been surmised, similar to the case for creating police- and court-enforced entry barriers that protect legitimate holders of copyrights and patents. Such barriers are created because the preponderance of the relevant costs in developing products that are subject to copyrights and patents are largely, if not totally, up-front, or sunk, costs. The holders are granted so-called monopoly positions (for what used to be limited, though increasingly lengthy, periods, but much less so today)[17] to enable them to recover their development costs.

The case for entry barriers that we are making also squares with the case for preventing piracy on digital and nondigital goods. The pirates do not have development costs, which means that if they are unconstrained, the producers of the original products will not be able to recover their development costs, or will have suppressed incentives to produce their products or to develop their products to higher-quality levels. And there is every reason to expect that the level of product development in terms of quality and sophistication will be related to the extent that all entry barriers protect markets sufficiently for original innovators to recover their quality-improvement costs.

When the goods at stake are digital, the pirates have a decided competitive advantage: They can buy a fully formed master for their products off the shelf, meaning, again, that they face virtually no barrier to entry on the product development side, and their replication costs can be inconsequential, just as might be true of the original producers, but they do not have to recover the type of development costs that the original producers have to recover.[18] Understandably, producers of many digital goods look to legal impediments—artificial entry barriers—to determine what, at what quality level, and how much they produce.

However, there is one important caveat to keep in mind: Some piracy is not all bad for the creators of all pirated goods, mainly those goods subject to network effects. This is because the pirated copies can increase the value consumers realize from buying copies. In the case of Microsoft's Windows operating system, pirated copies can increase the willingness of applications developers to write for Windows. The greater number of applications for Windows can spur the pirating of Windows, but they can also increase the number of bought copies of Windows (and, hence, bought copies of other Microsoft productivity applications like Word). In the case of music, pirated copies of music CDs can increase the number of people who buy the legitimate CDs because they want to listen to what other people are listening to (Becker 1991). To the extent that their products are copied, original producers may not have to lower their initial prices as much as otherwise to build their networks.

Indeed, because of piracy, at least some original producers *may* be able to charge higher prices in the future because of the buildup in demand over time with piracy and added purchases.[19]

ONCE AGAIN, WHY MONOPOLIES?

The lesson to be drawn from taking a Schumpeterian view of monopolies is that economists should not be surprised that monopolies with varying degrees of market power do exist and, at times, persist, at least long enough to allow the monopolies to recover their development costs. In an ideal world, the kind of monopolies that Schumpeter envisions would be unnecessary. Entrepreneurs would solve the need for recovering their development costs via contracts (if not patents and copyrights). However, entrepreneurs must make their way in a second-best world filled with limitations on institutional solutions such as contracts. As is widely recognized, developing contracts might not work at all under some conditions, for example, when the recovery of up-front investments requires a very long time, when enforcement mechanisms are uncertain, and when the groups of consumers and producers (e.g., developers) are in flux.

Monopolies might simply work better than competitive markets under some conditions, which could include situations that have high transaction costs. When high transaction costs are involved, we might expect firms to avoid working out the required contracts and to work within the market constraints determined by available protections afforded by extant entry barriers or by ones that can be erected. Alternatively, we might expect firms with high up-front investments and zero or close-to-zero marginal costs to gravitate toward the production of those goods that have natural entry barriers, as opposed to those goods that can be produced only with contracts that are costly to negotiate.

We should not be surprised that monopolies of the kind Schumpeter envisioned abound in markets for digital goods such as software. Given the zero, or just very low, marginal cost of production, the optimum firm size should be expected to be very large, which, given the number of consumers involved, could make transaction costs of negotiating the innumerable contracts quite high. Also, given the enormous potential for piracy in digital markets (which, again, emerges from the fact that each copy sold is a potential master for making other copies), the ability and temptation for customers to become producers is also high, which is all the more reason that a firm might not enter the market without some confidence that customers face entry barriers that the original producers don't face.

THE MICROSOFT PROBLEM FOR MICROSOFT'S COMPETITORS

Admittedly, the thrust of our arguments to this point relating to the Justice Department's antitrust case against Microsoft favors the Microsoft side. This bias exists not only because we see Microsoft as an example of our contention that firms with market power can benefit consumers but also because we see fundamental inconsistencies in the government's reasoning. Microsoft has been charged with being a monopoly but does not appear to have acted like one—at least in terms of its production and pricing decisions. The government's initial charge of "predatory" pricing suggests that Microsoft followed a market strategy that is opposite of what would be expected of a classic monopolist.

Granted, a firm might seek to destroy competition with low prices, only to charge monopoly prices in the future. However, the charge of predatory pricing against Microsoft was, at the time the case was settled in late 2002, at least a decade old, with no sign of Microsoft ever following through with a monopoly pricing strategy. In 1999, a year after the government filed its original complaint, the real price of Windows 98 was 58 percent below the real price of a much inferior version of Windows in the early 1990s. Moreover, Microsoft had increased its market share over the passing decade, not contracted it, as might have been expected of a true classic monopolist who reduces output and raises prices. Besides, the company's so-called predatory pricing for Internet Explorer is, as we have argued, perfectly consistent with the pricing strategy a firm would follow in a market beset with the conditions—network effects and close-to-zero marginal cost—on which the government founded its case.

Fortunately, in 2002, the appeals court set aside most of the government's claims of Microsoft's wrongdoing, with instructions that the case be reconsidered by a new judge at the district court level and that any remedy should focus on Microsoft's bullying of computer manufacturers and Internet service providers.

Nevertheless, Microsoft's competitors—including Sun Microsystems, Nokia, AOL/Time Warner, Kodak, Fujitsu, and Oracle—have not given up. In early 2003, through their trade organization, the Computer and Communications Industry Association (CCIA), Microsoft's competitors filed an antitrust complaint with the European Commission, arguing that Microsoft was using its "superdominant" monopoly position in the operating system, productivity applications, and browser market to muscle its way into adjacent software markets that it had not yet managed to but would soon dominate if left unchecked, according to the CCIA (2003).

The adjacent markets of concern to Microsoft's competitors are their markets for media players, e-mail client, instant messaging, server operating systems, e-mail and media servers, authentication, multimedia content and management, Internet advertising, handheld computing operating systems, smart phone, game consoles and set-top boxes, and Internet portal software. Microsoft's competitors argue that "Microsoft's anti-competitive behaviour exploits two key characteristics of software markets: (1) strong network effects and (2) strong interdependencies among software products, given that applications and the operating system must work together" (CCIA 2003, 2).

The European Commission bought Microsoft's competitors' argument, ruling in 2004 that Microsoft must provide competitors with its source code so that they could make their applications and server operating systems better operate with Windows, must provide a version of Windows without media player, and must pay a fine of $610 million for abusing its monopoly position. When the EC deemed Microsoft had stalled in opening its source code, it imposed another fine on Microsoft in mid-2006 of $358 million (Jacoby 2006).

From the perspective of standard microeconomic theory, it is hard to understand how Microsoft's efforts to move into adjacent markets can be seen as problems of *monopoly* per se, other than that Microsoft is a dominant producer in key markets and threatens to become dominant in adjacent markets. However, any market dominance achieved by Microsoft in adjacent markets means that Microsoft must extend its production, not contract it as would be expected in the case of a classic monopoly. Microsoft is also giving away several of the products identified—again, the exact opposite of what is expected of a classic monopoly. The antitrust complaint is also being filed by competitors, which suggests, from the perspective of standard theory, that they are being harmed by Microsoft's market strategies, but antitrust law is not supposed to be concerned with the prosperity of competitors, at least not directly. The complaint is not being filed by consumers, which suggests that most, if not all, consumers could be gaining by Microsoft's market strategies. Indeed, they could be gaining in three ways.

- First, consumers get the add-on software free (or at prices below the prices of Microsoft's competitors).
- Second, they benefit from the network that Microsoft proposes (or threatens, depending on perspective) to develop with its moves into the adjacent markets.
- Third, consumers get their add-on software from the same source as that of their operating system, productivity applications, and browser software, thereby reducing the risk of incompatibilities among programs. (If

the risk isn't reduced, consumers always have the option of going to alternative vendors.)

What is the competitors' true beef, then? We suggest that their complaint is not about monopoly or antitrust concerns, but the exact opposite: a firm—Microsoft—that is in a "supercompetitive" market position because of its ability to compete in adjacent markets. What the competitors are seeking in the way of remedy for the "Microsoft problem" are artificial barriers (in the form of product development prohibitions) to Microsoft's entry into their markets.[20]

The competitors' beef might be construed as identical with the problem we have already noted for competitors when marginal cost of production and entry costs are nil or small: They can't recoup their development costs (or, at the very least, have a seriously impaired chance of doing so). An add-on developer can incur the costs of identifying an unexploited market opportunity, developing a product for the identified market, and then incurring the costs of developing the market for the product. However, given that Windows is all but ubiquitous, with the cost of appending add-ons to Windows being very low, Microsoft has the equivalent of a twelve-lane, unobstructed freeway into any software market it wishes to enter. Microsoft can sit back and wait for others to incur all the initial development costs and then cherry pick, or as Bill Gates described his company's strategy in a 1995 meeting during which he made conquering the browser market the company's top priority, to quickly "embrace and extend" the successful add-ons, but only after the identified markets have reached critical mass, which will make Microsoft's entry into the market worthwhile.[21]

Of course, Gates and company might stand ready to buy out firms that have developed proven products, but the buyout price need not be any higher than Microsoft's development costs, because those are the only costs Microsoft has to incur after an identified market has reached critical mass. (And, because of its size, Microsoft's development costs could easily be much lower than the development costs of many upstart firms.) The buyout price also need not cover the costs that the developing firm had to incur in order to identify the market (which can include the development of many unsuccessful products or earlier versions of the successful product) and to develop the market for the identified product (including the costs associated with overcoming the initial chicken-and-egg problems mentioned earlier). If developing firms cannot recoup all their development costs, and have little or no chance of reaping economic profits, incentives to innovate can be impaired, resulting in less software development than would be the case if the developing firms could recoup their development costs and make a profit.

The restrictions that Microsoft's competitors have sought for Microsoft—including outright prohibition on what products Microsoft can include in Windows, not to mention the breakup of the company—*can be* (conceptually, at least) socially constructive, by encouraging other firms to be more innovative and welfare enhancing. We emphasize *can be* simply because the restrictions will have to be imposed through legislative, regulatory, or legal means, or all these ways. Our public choice backgrounds make us worry that although the restrictions actually imposed might be optimal, given the market circumstances, they could just as easily be excessive, resulting in the replacement of one less-than-optimal market condition by a worse one.

Regardless, we are inclined to believe that even if the theory of competition Microsoft's critics have articulated is valid in the Microsoft case (and we have our reservations), we don't see the issues raised as coming under the purview of antitrust law. To repeat, the market problems that are the source of the competitors' complaint do involve a dominant firm. However, that is as far as the association of the problem with monopoly goes, and the association is not tenable. The identified problems have nothing to do with the existence of entry barriers that allow a firm to restrict sales for the purpose of elevating market price and firm profits. If the identified problems have a legal home, that home would appear to be in the area of patent and copyright law under which the government-imposed market corrections have historically been in the form of market entry barriers. The beef that Microsoft's critics have with Microsoft could be that because of Microsoft's market dominance (and twelve-lane freeway into their market), Microsoft's competitors don't have the extent of monopoly privileges with their patents and copyrights that they might have thought they held. This is because *ideas* (as distinguished from the *expression of ideas*) cannot be patented or copyrighted. Ideas aren't provided legally enforced monopoly protection because such protection could stifle the development of more advanced ideas and innovations. Perhaps we need a whole new, yet-to-be-named subcategory of law for special cases such as Microsoft.

CONCLUDING COMMENTS

Monopoly theory has been grounded in the proposition that all entry barriers give rise to monopoly rents and net welfare losses. However, Schumpeter suggests that such a perspective is far too sweeping, because it is static and myopic, focusing too exclusively on the consequences of monopoly restrictions on production *when they are in place*. In effect, Schumpeter is suggesting that our standard monopoly diagrams do not capture all the benefits of monopolies. When *all* benefits are considered, including those from having products that would not arise at all were it not for so-called monopoly protections, much of what we describe as monopoly rent and deadweight loss evaporates.

Our intent is not to say that *all* monopolies are good. It is to say, however, that *some* monopolies have, on balance, beneficial effects for the particular markets they are in and for the economy taken as a whole over a long stretch of time. We might draw the demand and costs curves for such monopolies in the way economists always have, identifying the deadweight-loss triangle. Such a myopic perspective fails, however, to balance that deadweight loss with the even greater potential deadweight loss that could be imagined if the monopolies never existed. Perhaps we need a new name for this subset of monopolies. We might call them "welfare-enhancing monopolies." Then again, it might be better and more accurate to designate them "Schumpeterian monopolies" (mainly because Schumpeter made "welfare-enhancing monopolies" central to his view of the way capitalism advances through time).

At the very least, we need to be careful when we go from identifying market protections for firms (entry barriers and switching costs, for example) and observing that a firm's price is above marginal cost, to concluding that the firm is a welfare-destroying monopoly, as is so often done in antitrust cases. Breaking down all the market protections can be the policy equivalent of throwing out the baby with the bathwater.

Going against conventional wisdom, as we are doing in this volume, has a decided advantage. Doing so catches people's attention. By the same token, countervailing arguments also have a disadvantage. Listeners and readers may not understand the acknowledged limits of the argument that is posited. To be clear, our argument for entry barriers has its limits, just as arguments for copyrights and patents have their widely accepted limits. Indeed, the two sets of arguments for entry barriers and copyrights or patents are congruent, because the latter are founded on the necessity of limited entry barriers to spur innovation and economic development. Indeed, copyrights and patents are founded on an explicit trade, which is that the holders will receive highly circumscribed monopoly privileges for a limited period of time, allowing for the recovery of up-front development costs in exchange for the copyrighted and patented materials ultimately being transferred to the public domain.

Our arguments presented here actually add up to a call for a change in the way we think about entry barriers of all kinds. More specifically, our arguments call for thinking about the need *for* entry barriers—whether natural, firm cultivated, or government induced (e.g., through regulation)—in the same way that we think about the need for copyright and patent protections. In short, we should consider the need for some firms to create entry barriers as well as the need to ensure those barriers' demise.

Chapter 5

Locked-In Consumers

When incompatibilities exist between different variations of a product with network effects, it is possible for a producer of one of the variations to secure a competitive advantage over producers of other variations by being the first one to achieve a critical market share. The net result of such a market strategy can be that the market tips toward the dominant producer, causing its market share to expand as consumers receive increasing value from the producer's growing market dominance (Katz and Shapiro 1985, 1986, 1994).[1]

This chapter is concerned with how the tipping process in a market for network goods can give the producer of the network good monopoly power. However, the thrust of the analysis is directed toward explaining the limitations of the monopoly argument. We also explain how consumer lock-in and switching costs can benefit consumers. Indeed, consumers might want to be exploited (at least up to a degree) by a so-called monopoly producer of a network good.

CONSUMER LOCK-IN

With the retreat of other producers from the market as consumers move relentlessly toward one producer, consumers may find themselves locked in to the most widely used variation of the product simply because it is widely used, or so the argument has been developed (Arthur 1989). This is because, after the tipping process has run its course, no alternative source of supply may remain for the network good, at least not one providing the same level of network benefits. Even if an attractive alternative supplier exists, the cost of consumers actually switching to another technology or product can make switching impractical. Switching costs in the case of a computer operating system can include the costs of retraining, new equipment, and software, as well as the establishment of new office routines and, possibly, cultures.[2]

The result of the lock-in or (what amounts to the same thing) switching costs that can emerge in network markets is that the network producer has market power.[3] The greater the switching costs, the more inelastic the consumer demand for the network good. This implies the greater the market power for the firm toward which the market has tipped, a line of argument prominent in the Microsoft antitrust case.[4] The greater the market power, the greater the firm's monopoly earnings.[5]

In addition, locked-in consumers imply that new entrants will be locked out as surely as would be the case with any entry barrier protecting the borders of the market. This is because consumers' ability to move will be impaired by new entrants' inability to make sales. This also means that "superior" variations of the product can (supposedly) have a difficult time entering the market and attracting consumers. For example, Paul David (1985) has argued that the QWERTY keyboard continues to dominate the arrangement of keys on keyboards simply because QWERTY was adopted early on in the history of typewriters in order to minimize the extent to which keys would become entangled as they struck the paper. Even though the Dvorak keyboard is (supposedly) superior to the QWERTY keyboard in terms of achieved typing speed, the cost of retraining typists has locked in everyone—buyers and producers of typewriters and computer keyboards—and has prevented the adoption of the superior Dvorak keyboard.

The appeal of this line of argument was transparent in the Microsoft antitrust case, as we have already noted. However, virtually every element of the argument has been subject to scrutiny by economists and has been found wanting. At the forefront of this attack are Liebowitz and Margolis (1990, 1995), who argue on both empirical and theoretical grounds that little risk exists of inferior technologies and products becoming entrenched by lock-ins caused by network effects. For example, Liebowitz and Margolis question the inferiority of the QWERTY keyboard arrangement that supposedly remains the entrenched, dominant keyboard only because of the lock-in effect. They point out that the only researcher whose studies show that the Dvorak keyboard is superior was done by Mr. Dvorak, who designed the Dvorak keyboard, and his studies are suspect for other reasons as well.[6]

Of course, with constant technological improvements there are cases of existing technologies being widely used and benefiting from network effects and significant switching costs, despite being inferior to new technologies. But if the gains from switching are greater than the costs of doing so, incentives exist for entrepreneurs—so-called network sponsors—to overcome the built-in resistance to change. Each consumer may face the Prisoner's Dilemma of finding that it doesn't pay to give up the existing network benefits by switching to the new superior technology even though all would be better off if all (or most) did switch. The entrepreneur-owner of the new technology, however, can internalize this effect by sharing the gains of the efficiency improvements with customers through subsidies in the form of low, possibly negative, prices over some period of time. That said, not all network *effects* are necessarily network *externalities* (Liebowitz and Margolis 1995), which would lead to market inefficiencies.

Without such internalization of network effects it is hard to explain the large number of new products and technologies that overcame the network/switching cost advantage of previously dominant products and technologies. Examples of firms overcoming the problem of consumers being locked in have become common, including cellular phone companies (e.g., Cingular and Verizon) that have offered free or reduced-price phones for new customers; software companies (Microsoft) that have lowered the prices for users of competing applications; banks (Citibank) that have offered credits for customers' initial Internet transactions; and Internet retail sites (MotherNature.com) that have provided advertised discounts on customers' initial purchases.

The switching subsidies that new entrants have to pay consumers to switch need not be equal to the switching costs consumers have to incur. This is because if the established firm does try to exploit its market position, charging monopoly prices, there are "staying costs" for consumers equal to the present discounted value of the lost consumer welfare from the monopoly prices. The higher the prospective staying costs imposed on consumers, the lower the payments new entrants must make to entice consumers to switch.

Of course, a consumer subsidy to overcome the lock-in effect of an existing product is an investment on which sellers expect to generate positive returns with higher prices for their products after consumers get locked in again.[7] Obviously such investments are risky because the new products may not be sufficiently superior to replace existing products, or may have a short reign in the marketplace even if they do. We can think of the high prices temporarily realized from establishing a large and locked-in market share as an incentive for technological improvements and as a means by which consumers reimburse suppliers for helping them overcome their Prisoner's Dilemmas. Put another way, without the potential for some degree of lock-in, network firms might not have sufficient incentive to lower their initial prices (or to provide initial-use subsidies) for the purpose of creating the network and providing users with the attendant network benefits as the network expands. This situation suggests the need for caution in attempts to prevent firms from exploiting locked-in consumers with antitrust remedies. Even if a firm can exploit network effects and switching cost by locking in consumers indefinitely, preventing this "exploitation" by breaking up the firm to increase competition will do less to protect consumers than indicated by standard models, and may harm consumers.

Even then, if the market is subject to consumer turnover—with new consumers coming into the market all the time—the best pricing strategy for the entrenched producer can be one that encourages new entrants, a point developed at length by Joseph Farrell and Carl Shapiro (1998). To see their point, assume that the entrenched producer initially dominates the market with its consumer base benefiting from the network effects of the product they are consuming and that the network was developed by the entrenched producer by initially charging low prices. Suppose that the entrenched producer takes advantage of its consumer base, charging its customers a high monopoly price. Consumers might have little reason to object to the monopoly prices they are charged because they benefited from the low up-front prices and the network effects.

Now, suppose that new consumers start coming into the market. The entrenched producer can figure that the new consumers can be brought into the network with low prices (compensating the consumers for the expected higher monopoly prices in the future). But the entrenched producer can also figure that if it can't price-discriminate, it will have to charge everyone the low price, which means that it will have to give up on monopoly profits. With new consumers coming in all the time, a strategy of trying to bring all new consumers into the network can be a strategy that requires the entrenched producer to forgo monopoly profits perpetually. Seeing that prospect, the entrenched producer can reason that the wealth of the firm can be maximized only by leaving new consumers outside of the network. This means that the entrenched producer's strategy leaves a growing portion of the consumer base available to new entrants, which implies that switching costs faced by the entrenched producer's consumers can encourage entry. This also means that the total quantity sold by all producers and the efficiency of the market will be greater than is implied by the simple version of the switching-cost argument.[8]

In the next section we develop a model of a firm selling a product that generates network effects (not necessarily network externalities). Under the assumption that the firm is able to expand until it dominates the market and is able to fully exploit all network effects, we extend the analysis of others (e.g., Klemperer 1987, 1989; Katz and Shapiro 1985, 1994) and examine the effect of threatening to break up the firm into separate competing units (or in other ways that impair the ability of the firm to exploit locked-in consumers, which is what Microsoft's competitors recommended in dealing with the supposed entrapment of Windows users; see CCIA 2003). If a proposed breakup is ever made credible, we find that the effect of the breakup threat *can* be to increase the current price, and is certain to reduce the price by less than what the standard monopoly model would predict. Any increased efficiency that results is less than implied by the standard monopoly model, even when ignoring the very real possibility that the antitrust action reduces network benefits to consumers and retards the introduction of new technologies.

A PRODUCT WITH NETWORK EFFECTS: A MODEL

Consider a firm that is producing a product that generates a network effect. To capture this effect, we represent the price, P, in each time period as a negative function of the quantity sold currently and a nonnegative function of the cumulative quantity of all past sales, adjusted for decreases due to deterioration and discard. In period t, for example, the price, or inverse demand function, is given by

$$P^t\left(Q_t, \sum_{i=1}^{t-1} \lambda^{t-i}Q_i\right) \tag{1}$$

with $P_1^t < 0$ and $P_2^t \geq 0$, where the subscripts represent partial derivatives with respect to the indicated variable, Q_i is the quantity sold in period i, and $\lambda \in (0, 1)$ is the deterioration and discard rate each period. We assume that the marginal cost of production is zero in each period.

The firm's objective is to maximize the discounted present value of profits over some time horizon T, given by

$$\pi = P^1(Q_1,0) \, Q_1 + \sum_{t=2}^{T} P^t\left(Q_t, \sum_{i=1}^{t-1} \lambda^{t-i}Q_i\right) Q_t D^{t-1}, \tag{2}$$

where $D = 1/(1 + r)$, with r being the discount rate. We assume that the time horizon T is such that at time T the accumulated sales (net of deterioration and discard) are sufficiently large that the network effect is complete, or $P_2^T = 0$, with $P_2^t > 0$, for all $t < T$.

The Q_i's that maximize (2) necessarily satisfy

$$\frac{\partial \pi}{\partial Q_1} = \left[P^1 + Q_1 P_1^1\right] + \sum_{t=2}^{T} Q_t P_2^t \lambda^{t-1} D^{t-1} = 0, \tag{3.1}$$

$$\frac{\partial \pi}{\partial Q_t} = \left[P^t + Q_t P_1^t \right] D^{t-1} + \sum_{i=t+1}^{T} Q_i P_2^i \lambda^{i-t} D^{i-1} = 0,$$ (3.t)

$$\frac{\partial \pi}{\partial Q_1} = \left[P^T + Q_T P_1^T \right] D^{T-1} = 0.$$ (3.T)

These necessary conditions yield to a straightforward interpretation. The first term in each equation in (3) is the current period marginal revenue. The second term in the first $T - 1$ equation in (3) is the present value of future marginal revenue from current sales and is positive. Therefore, the current period marginal revenues are negative in the first $T - 1$ periods, and the quantities sold in periods 1 through $T - 1$ are increased until the marginal losses from current period sales are equal to the marginal gain from enhanced future demand through the network effect. In period T the marginal network effect is zero, and therefore the current period marginal revenue is also zero. There is no further advantage in expanding sales beyond the amount that maximizes current revenue. The negative marginal revenues in the earlier periods represent the investment mentioned in the introduction that begins yielding a return to the firm in period T when the firm begins behaving like a conventional monopolist—equating current period marginal revenue to marginal cost (zero in our model).

What do conditions (3) tell us about the effect of government action designed to prevent the firm from exploiting the monopoly position, beginning in period T, assuming that it achieves that position? Consider first the effect of a credible threat to prevent the future price from increasing to the monopoly level. Such a threat clearly reduces the return that the firm can expect to realize by investing in the network effect. By reducing the positive value of the second term in the first $T - 1$ equations in (3), a cap on future prices calls for a less negative current marginal value in the early periods. So, the attempt to protect consumers against high future prices results in higher current prices as the firm reduces output.[9] Not only are current prices increased, but also the value of the product is decreased as the reduction in output reduces the network advantage realized by consumers.[10]

Attempts to protect consumers against exploitation by a potentially successful network monopolist by breaking it up (or in any other way holding future prices and profits down) can also generate counterproductive results. If the breakup is anticipated, the result will be qualitatively the same as imposing a price cap on the future price. Not being able to capture the future monopoly benefits from subsidizing sales currently, the firm will respond by reducing sales (and network benefits) and charging higher prices in early periods.

But what if the firm is broken up at some point before the network monopoly is complete, say in period $j < T$? Such a breakup might cause a current increase in output and a lower price as several firms are now competing for market share—but it might not. And even if it does motivate more output and a lower price, the effect will be smaller than the standard monopoly model predicts. Being more precise, we rewrite the jth equation from the necessary conditions (3) as

$$\left[P^j + (1 - \delta)\, Q_j P_1^j \right] + (1 - \delta) \sum_{t=j+1}^{T} Q_t P_2^t \lambda^{t-1} D^{t-j} = 0 \tag{4}$$

with $\delta = 0$.

If the firm is broken up in period j, the parameter δ increases from zero, indicating that the firm no longer accounts for the entire market for the product. The question is, what is the effect of an increase in δ on the left-hand side of (4), the current and future marginal revenue in period j? Differentiating (4) with respect to δ, evaluated at $\delta = 0$, yields

$$-\left(Q_j P_1^j + \sum_{t=j+1}^{T} Q_t P_2^t \lambda^{t-1} D^{t-j} \right). \tag{5}$$

From (4) it follows that (5) = 0 when $P^j = 0$, (5) > 0 when $P^j > 0$, and (5) < 0 when $P^j < 0$. In the case in which $P^j > 0$, then breaking up the firm (assuming that production costs remain unaffected) results in an expansion of output to maintain a marginal revenue of zero. This is the standard result and is what one would hope for when combating monopoly influence. But, as we shall see, even in this case the effect is not as strong as the standard monopoly model leads us to expect. If $P^j = 0$, then breaking up the firm would have no effect on current output. And if $P^j < 0$, then breaking up the firm would have the effect of actually reducing current output and increasing price.

Considering the effect of a zero, or even a negative (or less than marginal *production* costs) price is not as far-fetched as it may seem. As argued earlier, with network effects, giving away a product, or even paying people to use it, can increase the present value of the product, and the present value of future revenues, sufficiently to make up for nonpositive prices in early periods. Indeed, the possibility of nonpositive prices is more likely than the present model indicates. In our model, the only positive spillover from current sales of the product is enhanced future demand. But commonly, the firm has several complementary products, and there are intratemporal, as well as intertemporal, positive spillovers from expanding the use of one of the products. Breaking up such a firm would not only reduce the intertemporal advantage of keeping the price of a product low but also could eliminate entirely the intratemporal motivations to do so, thereby increasing the likelihood that breaking up the firm will cause a price increase.

For example, Microsoft has an array of products that run from its chief operating system (Windows) to productivity applications (Word and Excel) to content sources (Encarta) to advertising on its Internet service site (MSN). When Microsoft holds down the price of Windows, it encourages the development of the Windows network as more computer users buy Windows, more programmers develop applications, and even more computer users buy Windows because more applications are available and more users are compatible. Microsoft also encourages the sale of personal computers and more software packages, more Internet use, and more advertising on the Web—with Microsoft garnering many of the benefits. By having this array of products, Microsoft has managed to internalize the benefits of holding the price of Windows in check, which adds to its incentives to do just that.

Breaking up a single firm into several competing firms has the well-known effect of increasing the marginal revenue of each firm over that of a single firm in the industry. By itself, the increase in marginal revenue provides a strong motivation for the firms to increase output and lower price. Because this motivation is unopposed in the standard model, the effect of breaking up a single firm is an unequivocal increase in output and reduction in price. With network effects the situation is complicated by the fact that breaking up a single firm reduces the internalization of the network effects. The ability of a single firm to capture the additional future revenue from increasing its current output is reduced as more firms are created. With several firms, the additional future demand that each firm's current sales create is captured in large measure by other firms. Therefore, breaking up a single firm reduces the future marginal revenue from current sales, which at least partially (and possibly more than) offsets the increase in the current marginal revenue from current sales.[11]

The analysis suggests an interesting possibility in the case of a cartel of firms producing a product generating a network effect. As opposed to the standard cartel model, each firm's marginal revenue (current and future combined) could be less than its marginal cost (zero in our model). Collectively the firms are better off if each takes into consideration the future benefits its sales are generating for the other firms and resists the temptation to adjust sales to bring its marginal revenue in line with its marginal cost. But if this temptation is not resisted, the cartel will, like most cartels, begin to break up. The striking difference in this case is that, as opposed to the standard cartel, this cartel will break up as a result of each firm reducing output and increasing price.

EFFICIENCY CONSIDERATIONS

Of primary interest when discussing the effect of actions to prevent a firm from exploiting a network effect to secure a monopoly position is how much, if any, efficiency is increased by the action. The standard of comparison is determined by maximizing the surplus from the product:

$$S = \int_0^{Q_1} P^1(\tau, 0)d\tau + \sum_{t=2}^T \int_0^{Q_t} P^2\left(\tau, \sum_{i=1}^{t-1} \lambda^{T-i}Q_i\right) d\tau D^{t-1} \tag{6}$$

with respect to each period's output. The Q_i's that maximize S necessarily satisfy the conditions

$$P^i + MFS_i = 0 \qquad i = 1, 2, \dots, T, \tag{7}$$

where MFS_i is the present value of the marginal future surplus from expanding output in period i. Because $MFS_i > 0$ for all $i < T$ (we continue to let T represent the period in which the marginal network effect is zero even though the time this occurs varies with the Q_i's), condition (7) requires that $P^i < 0$, $i = 1, 2, \dots, T - 1$.

The first thing to recognize is that it is not necessarily the case that, at least during the early periods, the firm, if left free to maximize profits through the creation of a network monopoly (conditions [3]), will underproduce and overcharge compared to the surplus-maximizing conditions given in (7). For any given Q_i and accumulated stock of the good in period i, P_i is greater than the single firm's current marginal revenue in period i, or $P^i + Q_i P_1^i$. But for any given sequence of Q's from period i to period T and any given accumulated stock in period i, the second term in (7), MFS_i, is also greater than the second term in the ith equation in (3), $\Sigma_{j=i+1}^T Q_t P_2^j \lambda^{j-1} D^{j-1}$. This follows from the fact that the second term in (7) captures all the future surplus from selling an additional unit in period i, whereas the second term in (3) captures only the additional revenue the firm receives from selling the additional unit in period i. So, the socially efficient output in period i may also be the one that satisfies the single-firm profit-maximizing condition in the same period. We are not suggesting that this is likely, just that it is possible. We also acknowledge that as time *T* is approached, the certainty increases that the single firm output will become smaller than the socially efficient output. The difference between P^i and current period marginal revenue in period *i* does not diminish in any systematic way as *T* is approached, but the difference between MFS_i and $\Sigma_{j=i+1}^{T} Q_t P_2^j \lambda^{j-1} D^{j-1}$ goes to zero as both vanish in period *T*. So, even though the single firm may produce close to, or even more than, the socially efficient quantity early on as it is attempting to establish a network monopoly, it will begin behaving more like a traditional monopolist as its monopoly position becomes established.

Given the eventual inefficiency of a potentially successful network monopolist, is it likely that public policy aimed at reducing the firm's exercise of monopoly power will improve efficiency? As discussed in the previous section, a credible commitment to preventing the firm from benefiting from a future network monopoly with a price ceiling or a future breakup has the effect of reducing the incentive to expand current output by reducing future marginal revenue with respect to that output. There is the interesting possibility that such a reduction in output can increase in-period efficiency because the firm may be selling more than the socially efficient amount in an early period. But the reason for the commitment to regulate is that the firm will eventually be producing too little, so a policy that reduces output will soon be reducing rather than increasing efficiency.

A policy of breaking up a firm into several competing firms before it has established a full network monopoly (or, again, by other means of holding down its future prices and profits) can also be counterproductive. If the breakup occurs when the firm's price is negative, we have seen that it will cause a decrease in current output by reducing the incentive effect of that output on future demand. Unless this occurs when the firm is producing more than called for by the conditions in (6), the effect will be the opposite of what efficiency requires, at least initially. Of course, later in time, when the single firm would have been charging a positive price, the effect of having broken it up will be to increase output and improve efficiency. Therefore, breaking up a potential network monopolist might improve overall efficiency. But the presence of network effects will severely limit the efficiency gains that can be generated by competing firms. Replacing a single firm with several competing firms will bring each firm's current marginal revenue more in line with the marginal social value of the product. But the greater the number of firms, the greater the discrepancy between each firm's future marginal revenue from current sales and the future marginal value of the social surplus generated by current sales. So although increasing the number of firms is promoting efficiency on one margin, it is undermining efficiency on another margin. The standard argument favoring numerous competing firms over one firm loses much of its force when network effects are present.

Of course, the efficiency gains from breaking up a firm creating a network monopoly are sure to turn positive and rise as the network becomes increasingly established, at least as indicated by a comparison of necessary conditions (3) and (7).[12] The smaller the marginal network effect from current sales, the more our analysis becomes a standard monopoly-versus-competition comparison and the greater the advantage of several competing firms over a monopoly supplier. Efficiency could no doubt be improved if a firm could be kept unaware of any antitrust threat until it had established a network monopoly and then was broken up. At least it could be improved in this one case. The problem is that any efficiency achieved in this one case will lead to expectations on the part of other firms whose products create network effects that will motivate inefficient responses. Once producers recognize the possibility that successful network monopolists will be broken up, new firms with new technologies will be less aggressive at cutting prices and expanding output to establish new, or replace existing, networks. The result could be to reduce not only the social value these firms create directly but also the indirect value they create through the discipline their existence exerts over the existing market power possessed by established network monopolists—a discipline more responsive to consumer preferences and consistent with dynamic efficiency than is realistically possible from antitrust action.

CREATING NETWORKS

Many discussions of networks presume that network effects are a part of nature, much as gravity or chemical reactions are. When an operating-system firm—the network sponsor—sells more copies of its operating system, applications firms are likely to write more applications, more or less naturally, without any encouragement from the operating system firm. That may sometimes be the case, but certainly not always. Developers may be reluctant to join the network for any number of reasons, not the least of which is that the network in question might not be the successful network. That is, as developers prepare to write applications for one network (Apple), the market could tip toward some other network (Windows). The developers' investments could then be worthless. The developers' investment risk costs are heightened by the fact that the size and durability of the network is outside their direct control and is controlled by the network sponsor, but this is a problem in risk allocation that can possibly be reduced by the sponsor with appropriate side payments.

As Katz and Shapiro (1985) have argued, given that much of the invest-ment in networks can be up front, the actual investment made by applications developers (and the network sponsor) will depend on their expectations about how the market will evolve over time, which can be influenced by how much the network sponsor is willing to spend up front to ensure that the market tips toward its network product and not toward some other firm's product. The network sponsor, in other words, may want to shoulder some of the applica-tions developers' risk costs just to manage expectations, that is, encourage the expectation among applications developers that the network sponsor's product will be the product toward which the market will tip. The greater the potential profits from the market tipping and lock-in, the more the network sponsor would be willing to spend up front to encourage the development of the net-work and of locked-in customers. This is a slightly different way of restating a central point of our argument, which is that even the customers need not mind being locked in securely, given that the network develops more rapidly and with greater consumer benefits when the network sponsor encourages the development of applications and lock-ins.

Understandably, if the market is prone to tip and to leave consumers and applications developers locked in, the applications developers also have to fear that the operating system firm/network sponsor will, after it has achieved its monopoly position, begin to extract monopoly rents, curbing its sales in the process, but also the sales of the developers' applications. The more they have to fear the monopoly practices of the network sponsor, the more reluctant they can be to write applications for the network. To overcome developers' reluc-tance, the firm sponsoring the network may either have to lower its up-front price or aid the developers by covering their development costs or providing outright payment to developers for writing for the network. Such payments can be viewed as prepayment of monopoly rents that the developers expect to be extracted later when the network sponsor achieves its monopoly position. This scenario leads to the interesting conclusion that the so-called monopoly, the dominant network sponsor, may have largely dissipated the expected monopoly rents among the developers and consumers prior to when the monopoly rents are extracted. Of course, the sponsor can invest in some of those writing applications, which will be seen as creating a strong motivation for it not to act like a textbook monopolist when (if) it achieves a dominant position. While this would reduce the likelihood of monopoly restrictions, it will likely be seen as a violation of antitrust laws supposedly designed to curb monopoly formation and maintenance.

The up-front payment problems of the network sponsor can be, as men-tioned earlier, a consequence of the fact that the network sponsor may not be able to make a credible commitment to avoid taking advantage of any monopoly position that is achieved in the future. The developers have to fear that the network sponsor will renege on its commitment, say, to hold its future prices to competitive levels. If it does achieve monopoly status but does not renege, then its stock price can be suppressed because of the absence of the potential monopoly profits that could be extracted. This means that savvy investors can take over the network firm and hike prices and profits. Seen from this perspective, the network sponsor/potential monopolist can favor antitrust enforcement. Antitrust enforcement can make the network sponsor's commitment to not charge monopoly prices in the future credible (or more credible than otherwise), which means that the network sponsor would not have to lower its price or increase its side payments to applications developers (by as much as otherwise).

Barring antitrust enforcement, the network sponsor can ease the fears of outside developers by licensing its network product to several producers. It can also develop complementary products, which, for an operating system firm, would mean creating productivity applications of its own (as Microsoft has done), which can, of course, be seen as heightening the network sponsor's market dominance and a violation of antitrust laws. The network sponsor would then have an incentive to hold down the price of its product, thereby easing the need to make side payments to outside developers. The greater the array of complements the network sponsor has, the greater the assurance that outside developers will have that the network sponsor will not in the future hike the price and curb the sales of the network good. Hence, a breakup of a horizontally integrated operating system/applications firm can, once again, reduce the incentive of the network firm to hold its prices down. It can thus reduce the incentive of the applications developers to stay with the network, possibly resulting in network contraction and lost consumer benefits.

Applications developers can also be concerned that the network sponsor will be timid about defending the network against takeover by some other network standard. The more durable they perceive the network to be, the more applications developers are willing to invest up front. Hence, it follows that the network sponsor can reduce its up-front payments to developers by showing them that it stands ready to compete ferociously to suppress any new competitive threat to its network standard, which, coincidentally, is precisely what Microsoft did when it was confronted with the prospects of its Windows standard being overrun by a new computing platform based in part on Netscape's Navigator. The judge in the Microsoft case interpreted Microsoft's zero and negative prices for Internet Explorer as "predation" with the obvious consequence of raising the "dangerous probability" that Microsoft would be able to act like a monopoly in the future (Jackson 2000a). Alternatively, Microsoft's zero and negative price could be interpreted as an effort to maintain the network and flow of gains to applications developers and, hence, to consumers.

CONCLUDING COMMENTS

Lock-in is not all bad. Nor are switching costs all bad. Switching costs might make it more difficult for new firms to attract customers from established producers. However, switching costs can also cause new firms with potentially superior products to incur substantial up-front development costs associated with many network goods (e.g., software). And for firms interested in developing a network, switching costs can make firms willing to underprice their product initially, which can have the benefit of helping to build the network at greater speed. In such network environments, threats to break up a successful network firm (because it is perceived to be the dominant producer and, hence, a monopolist, or because its pricing may appear predatory) or threats to limit such a firm's future price increases can have the effect of raising current prices, retarding the development of the network, and harming both current and future consumers. Such an outcome must be construed as perverse, given that the professed goal of antitrust enforcement is to improve consumer welfare.

Chapter 6

Monopoly Prices and the Client and Bonding Effects

       In conventional economic theory, monopoly prices (relative to lower competitive prices) are almost always viewed as destructive of consumer welfare. Monopoly prices are inefficient because they are above the marginal cost of production and they distort the distribution of income and consumer welfare. Under the conventional view of monopoly, monopoly prices have no offsetting benefits. In this chapter, we cover two unheralded ways by which monopoly prices can boost consumer welfare, which we dub the *client effect* and the *bonding effect*. The former changes the consumer welfare by changing the composition of consumers. The latter improves consumer welfare by increasing the confidence buyers have that producers will do what they say they will do.

THE CLIENT EFFECT

In some markets unregulated competition is supposed to drive prices down to ruinous levels. This is supposed to be the case in high-fixed-cost/low-marginal-cost industries (e.g., railroads). Interestingly, such ruinous price competition is not evident in other high-fixed-cost/low-marginal-cost industries (e.g., hotels). Indeed, many firms in such industries can rightfully be accused of charging monopoly prices, or prices above both marginal and average cost, enabling them to make nontrivial monopoly profits, at least for respectable stretches of time.

       Why the disparity in market outcomes? We argue that price competition is often moderated in high-fixed-cost/low-marginal-cost industries when the value one consumer realizes from the service is affected by the *characteristics* of other consumers. We develop a simple model of the client effect using the example of the demand for hotels and then generalize the implications of our model to other industries. Underlying our argument is a proposition that conventional analysis ignores: A high price (or a price above marginal cost) can make a good or service more valuable to consumers.

The most general and important point, which is consistent with the overall theme of this book, is one that squares with our analysis of the impact of network effects: Price can affect not just the amount demanded but also the market demand and how much value consumers derive from the purchase of a good. In the case of network goods, consumers' value is enhanced when the count of consumers goes up, enhancing further the effect of low prices on consumer surplus.[1] In the case of client-effect goods, the opposite can be the case: The surplus value of consumers who continue to buy the good when the price of the good price goes up can rise when the price affects the types, not just the quantity, of consumers who purchase the good. This is because in real-world markets (as distinct from economists' imaginary, blackboard worlds), the type and mix of consumers vary with the price being charged. When the price rises, the composition of consumers changes, mainly because consumers not willing to pay higher prices are pushed out of the market. This change in the composition of consumers can, at times, be expected to change the remaining consumers' demands. Granted, when consumers' demands fall with changing consumer composition due to the higher price, monopoly has a more pernicious, efficiency-destroying impact than conventional static models suggest. However, when the higher prices increase consumers' demands, the result can be a net increase in consumer welfare across consumers.

We focus on the market for hotels for two reasons: First, hotels are a concrete example to which readers can easily relate. Second, and more important, we want to move away from past discussions of network effects evident in modern technology markets and take up the problems of a market that was established long before the advent of personal computers. As we will explain, the client effect is decidedly different from network effects in terms of underlying character and in terms of how demand is affected by price.

By making the assumption that price can affect the composition of consumers and hence their consumer surplus, we can explain some observable characteristics of the hotel industry. For example, we observe patrons of different chains segmented by income and social characteristics. In addition, different hotel chains have established reputations for the level of services and the characteristics of the hotels' clientele. We would also expect, and in fact observe, that the parent companies of hotels—for example, Marriott—are holding companies for an array of chains that appeal to various clienteles. Marriott offers rooms in hotel chains that range from its low-end Fairfield Inns to its high-end Marriott Marquis Hotels. Even if you care to take issue with our example, our more important point—that monopoly pricing can be welfare enhancing for consumers who continue to consume the monopoly good in spite of the monopoly price they are required to pay—remains conceptually valid. It can help explain why many consumers do not lament above-marginal-cost prices as much as economists do. Our model of the client effect also explains why some high-fixed-cost/low-marginal cost industries such as hotels do not seem to have the problem of "ruinous price competition" that plagues other high-fixed-cost/low-marginal-cost industries.

Sources of "Ruinous Price Competition"

We begin our discussion by laying out the widely recognized problems of potentially ruinous price competition in industries with high fixed costs. It has long been argued that unregulated price competition, though desirable in most industries, is inappropriate in industries characterized by high fixed costs and low marginal costs. For example, the well-known business historian Alfred Chandler (1977, 134) writes:

> Competition between railroads bore little resemblance to competition between traditional small, single-unit commercial or industrial enterprises. . . . Never before . . . had competitors been saddled with such high fixed costs. . . . The relentless pressure of such costs quickly convinced railroad managers that uncontrolled competition . . . would be "ruinous." As long as a road had cars available to carry freight, the temptation to attract traffic by reducing rates was always there. Any rate that covered more than variable costs of transporting a shipment brought the road extra income. . . . To both the railroad managers and investors, the logic of such competition appeared to be bankruptcy for all.

Although most economists believe this argument can be overstated, few would deny that plausible models suggest that unrestrained competition between firms in a high-fixed-cost/low-marginal-cost industry can be inconsistent with maintaining a viable industry. For example, it has been argued in *U.S. v. Addyston Pipe Steel* (Bittlingmayer 1982, 203) "that explicit cartelization, tacit collusion, and horizontal merger can be viewed, in many instances, as the non-competitive arrangements that the firms in an industry must necessarily adopt."[2] Most economists also agree that the primary effect of government price regulation in high-fixed-cost industries (e.g., railroad shipping rates) has been to maintain those prices higher than they would have been under unregulated competition. And certainly firms in high-fixed-cost/low-marginal-cost industries, such as railroads and ocean shipping, have attempted, through cartel arrangements, to keep rates higher than would otherwise prevail.

However, in some industries characterized by high fixed costs and low marginal costs, intense competition exists with little if any attempt to cartelize or obtain government regulation to moderate it. The service provided by hotels, for example, requires very high fixed costs embodied in the physical facility but very low marginal costs. After a hotel has been built, very little cost is associated with accommodating an additional guest as long as any vacancy exists. Yet no one has seriously argued that competition among hotels is ruinous, with hotel rates likely being driven down to the cost of cleaning a room. Why not? If unregulated competition can supposedly drive the freight rates on railroads down to marginal cost (at least during periods of excess capacity), why shouldn't it do the same to hotel rates?

We argue here that the existence of a client effect in the demand for a service can explain differences in downward price pressures in the presence of excess capacity between some high-fixed-cost/low-marginal-cost industries and others. The client effect is clearly illustrated by comparing railroads and hotels. A person's demand for shipping freight on a railroad is not affected by who else is shipping freight or the type of other freight being shipped in the same train.[3] On the other hand, a person's demand for staying in a hotel is affected by the other people staying in the same hotel. There is no client effect in the demand for freight shipments on railroads, but there is in the demand for staying in hotels.

The Client Effect and Expensive Chocolate

The client effect exists when the value a consumer receives from consuming a good or service is influenced by the other consumers. Consider an extremely stylized example. Two hotels in the town you are visiting are identical except for their clientele. One is patronized by nonaffluent and poorly behaved rowdies who create loud disturbances all night, whereas the other is patronized by affluent, well-behaved folks who are careful not to disturb their neighbors. Which hotel would you prefer? Preferences differ, and no doubt some would prefer the action that is more likely available at the first hotel. But it is a safe bet that most affluent, well-behaved folks would prefer, and be willing to pay more for, the second hotel.

This client effect seems to suggest a profit opportunity for one of the hotel owners: Establish a reputation for catering to the affluent and well-behaved by refusing to rent to anyone else and then charge premium room rates. However, it is not easy to tell whether prospective guests are either affluent or well-behaved—particularly guests who make reservations by telephone. Also, even if unacceptable guests could be easily identified, refusing them a room could violate public-accommodation laws.

But another way—using price to screen out less desirable guests from desirable ones—has the advantage of being legal and of promoting the hotel owner's primary objective of high profits: Just charge higher room rates than the other hotel. The less desirable guests will tend to take their business to the low-priced hotel, making the high-priced hotel more valuable to those who can afford to pay extra to avoid guests who are unruly, less affluent, or both. This strategy won't work perfectly. It does not, for example, screen out rock bands, whose members may be affluent but unruly. But high prices can do a reasonable though imperfect job screening out less desirable guests.

Of course, all hotel owners would like to increase their profits by simply increasing their rates without having to spend more improving the quality of the service. Obviously, not everyone can succeed with this strategy. Because of competition, those who want to attract the well-to-do to their hotels with higher prices will find that they also have to provide nicer facilities and more services than are available at lower-priced hotels. So the higher fixed costs associated with a nicer facility and amenities will have to be incurred at high-priced hotels, along with some increase in the marginal cost. In equilibrium, these costs will be high enough to keep the rate of return on investment in high-priced hotels about the same as the rate of return on other investments, including investments in low-priced hotels (which because they are built to appeal to price-sensitive guests will likely have lower fixed costs relative to marginal costs). But because one benefit to guests at expensive hotels comes from associating with other guests who can afford to pay high rates, the frills at those hotels, when considered by themselves, won't necessarily be worth what they cost.[4]

Indeed, it is widely believed that people pay more for extras at expensive hotels than they are objectively worth. Just how much is it worth to have the bed turned down and a mint left on the pillow? A few years ago, one of the cut-rate hotel chains took advantage of the belief that some hotel amenities are overpriced by running a television commercial showing a hotel guest holding up a quarter-sized piece of chocolate wrapped nicely in gold foil and asking whether it was worth the extra $30 guests paid for it at a more expensive hotel. Viewers who thought not were urged to stay at the cut-rate hotel. It was a clever advertisement, but it ignored the fact that people are getting more for the extra $30 than the chocolate. They are getting a place to stay that screens out those who aren't willing or able to pay an extra $30 for a taste of chocolate.[5]

Hotel Demand and the Lack of Ruinous Competition

We now develop a simple model of the demand for a hotel that incorporates the client effect. To keep the presentation as simple as possible given the objectives of the chapter, we hold constant the quantity and quality of the physical facility and amenities that would be endogenously determined in a more complete analysis.[6]

Because the demand, as well as the amount demanded, depends on the room rate, the analysis begins with the consideration of a family of artificial demand curves, one for each rate. For example, demand curve D_{R1} in figure 6.1 shows the amount (number of rooms) demanded at each rate given the type of clientele resulting from room rate R_1.[7] If the only way to achieve that particular clientele is by actually charging R_1, demand curve D_{R1} is artificial in the sense that it is relevant only at rate R_1. With the somewhat improved clientele resulting from the higher rate R_2, the demand curve shifts out to D_{R2}. The demand curves associated with successively higher rates $R_3, R_4, R_5, \ldots, R_8, R_9,$ $R_{10},$ and R_{11} are also shown in figure 6.1, with a constant difference between each successive price. The varying distances shown between the successive demand curves reflect the assumptions that (1) the first few rate increases above the lowest rate, R_1, do little to improve the client mix and increase demand; (2) at some intermediate point, rate increases begin having a pronounced screening effect and significantly increase demand; and (3) the point is reached at which the screening effect of further rate increases diminishes and eventually does nothing to increase demand.[8]

Only one point is relevant on each of the rate-specific demand curves just discussed: the point determined by the rate assumed in the construction of the curve. The locus of these relevant points represents the equilibrium demand for the hotel.[9] As long as any upward demand shift occurs in response to a higher room rate, the equilibrium demand curve is steeper at each rate than is the relevant price-specific demand curve. In keeping with assumption (1) in the previous paragraph, over some initial range of low rates, the equilibrium demand curve will be only slightly steeper than the relevant rate-specific demand curves. Over some intermediate range of rates, however, assumption (2) implies that the steepness of the equilibrium demand curve increases relative to the relevant rate-specific demand curves, with the equilibrium demand curve possibly becoming very steep.[10] As the rate increases further, assumption (3) becomes operative and the slope of the equilibrium demand curve converges back toward the relevant rate-specific demand curves. The equilibrium demand curve is shown in figure 6.1 as D_E.

We have shown two equilibrium demand curves for a hotel in figure 6.2: D_P, representing the equilibrium demand during the peak season, and D_O, representing the equilibrium demand during the off-peak season. The number of rooms available in this hotel, or the capacity constraint, is given by the vertical line SS. The position of this capacity constraint reflects the trade-off

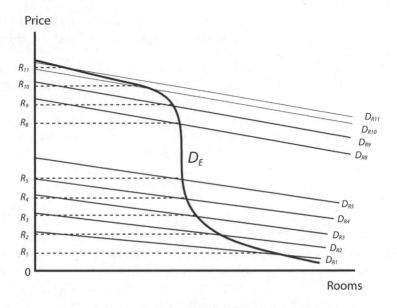

Figure 6.1. Rate specific and equilibrium demand curves

between having a hotel smaller than ideal during the peak-season demand and of having one larger than ideal during off-peak demand. With this trade-off in mind, we have positioned the capacity constraint so that it intersects the peak-season demand curve at the high rate R_P and intersects the off-peak demand at a low rate R_O. We assume that the marginal cost of accommodating a guest (renting another room) in the hotel is zero up to the capacity constraint, which means that the marginal cost curve is given by $0SS$ in figure 6.2.[11]

As the demand and cost conditions are constructed in figure 6.2, the marginal revenue curve to D_P (not shown) is positive at SS, and R_P is the profit-maximizing room rate during the peak period. At rate R_P, the market for this hotel clears; all its rooms are rented. But what if other hotels in the relevant market area have excess capacity at their rates, which are assumed constant when constructing the demand curve D_P? This could, of course, result in downward pressure on rates at these other hotels and cause a shift back in D_P, leading to a new equilibrium peak-period rate in figure 6.2 below R_P. But such downward pressure on prevailing hotel rates from excess capacity is not likely to push prices down very far, as becomes apparent when we consider the effect of moving to the off-peak demand situation in figure 6.2.

Under standard assumptions, if all hotels in the relevant market area faced

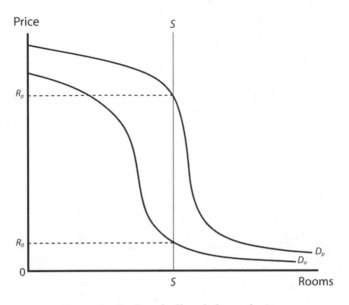

Figure 6.2. Peak and off-peak demand curves

demand curves that intersected their capacity constraints at positive rates and, as assumed, marginal costs are zero, competition is highly likely to drive down rates ruinously until excess capacity is eliminated. As the standard story is told, the marginal revenue of each individual hotel is greater than the collective marginal revenue of all hotels in the relevant market, so the temptation is to lower rates in a largely self-defeating effort to attract customers away from other hotels. But this competitive pressure for lower rates can be rendered inoperative, or quickly truncated, because of client effect influence on hotel demand curves.

For example, consider the off-peak demand curve D_O, which is now exhibited in figure 6.3, along with the capacity constraint SS. Because of the client effect, D_O is shown as becoming very inelastic over a range at rates lying somewhat below the profit-maximizing peak-season price R_p and then becoming quite elastic again as the rate approaches the off-peak market-clearing rate R_O. The marginal revenue curve associated with demand curve D_O is shown in figure 6.3 as MR_O and becomes negative under the inelastic region before becoming positively sloped, and possibly positive again, as the capacity constraint is approached. As constructed in figure 6.3, the profit-maximizing level of occupancy during the off-peak season occurs at Q_O (where MR_O equals zero)

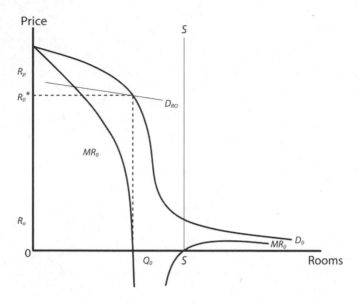

Figure 6.3. Off-peak profit maximization

at a room rate of R_O^*. As shown, R_O^* is a little less than R_P, the profit-maximizing peak-season rate, but far higher than R_O, the rate that would be predicted by the standard analysis of high-fixed-cost and low-marginal-cost situations.

So, as opposed to the standard analysis of ruinous competition, a hotel has little, if any, motivation to lower its rates to capture business from competitors or to protect its business against their rate reductions.[12] And even if competitors do reduce their rates, the effect will be to shift the hotel's demand curve back so that the highly inelastic portion remains operative over about the same range of rates as before, with little change in the profit-maximizing room rate.[13]

The argument here is that price competition can be greatly moderated in cases in which the client effect is important (such as hotel accommodation), even when fixed costs are high and marginal costs are low. But even with a strong client effect, there can still be downward pressure on prices in the face of excess capacity. An implication of the model, however, is that the price reductions will be limited and selective. Consider the rate-specific demand curve D_{RO} that intersects the demand curve D_O at rate R_O^* in figure 6.3. Cutting the rate below R_O^* would clearly be profitable if it could be done by moving out along D_{RO}, that is, done without altering the clientele mix. This is difficult to do. But hotels employ some pricing policies that can be understood as attempts to lower effective rates while minimizing adverse demand consequences from the client effect. Hotels often give room upgrades to selected customers at rates that typically apply to smaller, or less desirable, rooms. Preferred guest programs provide frequent customers with lower effective rates by allowing them to earn credits that can be redeemed for free stays, upgrades, or other awards. Convention rates can be considered a way of offering lower rates to people whose membership in a professional organization has prescreened them to some degree.[14] Weekend rates are typically explained as a profit-maximizing response to off-peak periods for hotels that cater to business travelers during the week. Without dismissing this explanation, it is also possible that the client effect is somewhat less important on the weekend when fewer people in the hotel are preoccupied with business pressures. Furthermore, as should be expected given the client effect, the number of rooms eligible for these discounts is typically limited.

A particularly interesting implication of the analysis is that we should predict more aggressive price competition between hotels located in remote and posh resort areas than between hotels located in large cities. The more remote and posh the area, the less the need to use high room rates to screen out undesirable clients. In downtown Chicago, Cleveland, or New York, the location does less to enhance the client effect, so price screening is relatively more important.[15] Assuming, then, the same shifts between peak and off-peak demand for both big city and remote resort hotels, we should expect rate fluctuations to maintain more uniform occupancy rates in the former hotels than in the latter. This is a highly speculative implication, however. Cheap airfares may have largely eliminated any such difference in rate fluctuations because remote resort hotels are no longer very remote. Also, if big city hotels can accommodate lower weekend rates without large client-effect concerns, then ski resorts may be able to protect against adverse client effects from summer rate reductions.

More General Observations

The previous discussion of the client effect has been confined to its implications for hotel pricing. But there are other services in which the client effect is important and has implications worth considering here, at least in a preliminary way.

Educational establishments can be characterized as having high fixed costs (especially when the salaries of tenured teachers and professors are appropriately treated as fixed costs) and low marginal costs. This suggests, according to the standard analysis, that competition between private colleges could easily be ruinous, thereby reducing their viability for a reason quite apart from the competition of state-supported colleges. Yet as a group, many private colleges are not financially threatened (some are struggling, of course, but others are doing very well), and they are certainly not engaged in ruinous price competition. Indeed, most of the discussion about private college tuition focuses on how high that tuition is. There are many explanations for the high tuition at private colleges, but the client effect has received little, if any attention.[16]

The client effect is obviously important in the demand for a college. The student who attends a college with intellectually capable and enthusiastic students will typically get a far better education than one who attends a college with intellectually weak and unmotivated students, even though both colleges are similar in terms of faculty and facilities.[17] Students learn not only from their professors but also from their interaction (both in and out of class) with other students. High tuition can give a private college more value by serving as a screening device, and this can moderate downward pressure on tuition even in the face of high fixed costs and low marginal cost. Private colleges do engage in some price discrimination by offering scholarships to some students. But scholarships are typically given to students who are expected (often for a variety of reasons) to enrich the student body, that is, not reduce demand through adverse client effects. As a consequence of merit scholarships, colleges can elevate even more their charges on those students who are not deemed meritorious but who draw value from having meritorious students on campus.

The pricing of airline travel (another high-fixed-cost/low-marginal-cost service) is consistent with the analysis of the client effect in some ways. The traditional high first-class fares are clearly consistent with the proposition that people will pay more to consume a service with others who have been screened by higher prices. First-class passengers receive better service, of course, but it is difficult to believe that the value of the improved service (in isolation of the client effect) can justify the additional fare. The wider seats, the cloth napkins (although the knives and forks are now plastic), and the help with coats have much in common with the turndown service and chocolate mint on the pillow in nice hotels.

Of course, under deregulation, airline consumers have become more price sensitive, with first-class service disappearing on many (relatively short) domestic flights and the fare differential between first-class and coach service becoming smaller.[18] But the decline in domestic first-class service is consistent with the client effect. As airline travel has become more commonplace (and therefore a less prestigious activity) and faster, the client effect has become less prevalent and important.[19] This situation contrasts with long international flights, for which the client effect can be expected to remain strong. And, consistent with our discussion, three different classes on international travel (economy class, business class, and first class) are often available, with steep fare differentials between them. Of course, the more comfortable seats and amenities are not insignificant advantages on long flights and clearly explain some of the fare differential. But just as clearly, businesspeople who want to work and sleep on a long overnight flight are willing to pay extra to increase the chances that their nearby fellow passengers want to do the same.[20]

Although the client effect will probably remain strong enough in airline travel to prevent the ruinous competition often associated with high-fixed-cost/low-marginal-cost services, the price competition that hampered airline profitability in the early 1990s and 2000s may be explained partly by a weaker client effect in the demand for air travel. But this explanation raises an interesting question. If the client effect in air travel demand was strong in the past, why did the airline industry feel the need to lobby so hard, and effectively, for a government cartel in the form of the Civil Aeronautics Board (CAB)? And why did the political influence of the airline industry wane, with the loss of its cartel, when the case for it became stronger (though not necessarily strong) with the decline in the client effect? These are largely political questions, and many factors are at work here besides the client effect. But the history of the CAB is not quite what the analysis of the client effect would predict.

In all cases in which the client effect is important, reputation plays an important role. High prices can both create and signal consumers on the presence of a reputation for quality. This chapter has emphasized the role of high prices in creating a reputation for quality by actually improving quality through the customers actually served (the client effect).[21] But a supplier who has a reputation for catering to less-than-desirable clients may find it difficult to alter that reputation. Such a supplier can attempt to develop a reputation for desirable clients by raising its price, but this may be making an investment that never pays off. The higher price may screen out the less desirable clients, but it will likely take a long time for others to become aware of that fact. And until they do, the supplier's reputation remains the same, and it has lost one set of clients without appealing to the other set.

An interesting example of the difficulty of improving a reputation related to the client effect by raising prices is Brazilian soccer. Soccer matches in Brazil, as elsewhere, have attracted large numbers of disruptive fans who often seem more interested in mob violence off the field than the game on the field. The result is that many real fans are fearful of attending soccer matches in Brazil. Significant numbers of these fans, however, flew to Dallas, Pasadena, and San Francisco and paid far higher ticket prices than in Brazil to see their team in action during the 1994 World Cup matches. The Brazilian authorities have responded by increasing ticket prices and stopping the sale of cheap blocks of tickets to supporter groups to price the hooligans out of the market. Unfortunately, the reputation that soccer matches in Brazil are dangerous has lingered, and the real fans have not returned. So the immediate effect has been large financial losses as soccer matches are being played before a few thousand fans in stadiums built for a hundred thousand or more. And those fans who do attend may find the experience less enjoyable than they expected because of the absence of a large number of other fans (Becker 1991). The attempt to improve the reputation of soccer in Brazil through higher prices and an improved client effect may prove profitable in the long run, but it is costly in the short run. It may be the case that the best strategy initially would have been, from the very beginning, high prices for soccer matches and a reputation for attracting respectable fans. However, once a reputation for spectator hooliganism has been established, the best policy may be to remain with that reputation, a policy that the British seem to have followed.[22]

In short, high up-front prices can hike demand and expand the size of the Dupuit triangle. The result can be higher profits and a larger Harberger triangle. At the same time, the increased size of the Dupuit triangle (and the gain it represents) can be larger than the increased size of the Harberger triangle (and the loss it represents), resulting in a net increase in consumer welfare.

THE BONDING EFFECT

Those familiar with principal-agency theory have often emphasized how businesses need to develop hostages or bonds that they, the businesses, can offer their customers as assurances that agreed-upon standards of contracted service will be met. The hostages and bonds are devices used by managers and firms to overcome any perceived opportunistic behavior and holdups.

Hostages and bonds enable managers and their firms to make so-called credible commitments.[23] To the extent that firms can do all these things, they can increase their prices and profits. To the extent that the reputational capital for credible commitments is attributable to managers, then the compensation packages of responsible managers can rise, which researchers have found to be the case (Jensen and Meckling 1976). Indeed, organizational economic theorists have argued that one very good reason for "overpaying" executives is that executives are in the best position to misuse and misdirect lots of firm resources. Hence, to ensure that executives seek to maximize the principals' (or stockholders') wealth, executives must be overpaid so that they suffer a real economic loss if caught engaging in behavior that maximizes their own wealth at the expense of the principals. Of course, this means that executives can't be paid merely an amount equal to their opportunity cost (Murphy 1986; Jensen and Murphy 1990; Lazear 1979, 2000).

The hostages or bonds are said to make the contracts self-enforcing, which can lower transaction costs, improving the overall efficiency of markets and increasing the array of goods and services available for consumption, since fewer resources will be needed to complete transactions and attendant contracts (written and unwritten) and to monitor businesspeople's commitments. Economic organizational theorists have pointed to how brand names and unnecessarily luxurious building façades can provide the needed assurances to buyers: If a firm that has invested in the brand names or luxurious facades fails to meet agreed-upon standards for the products that are delivered, the firm's reputation can suffer, nullifying in part or in total the firm's investment in its brand name and building facade.

Economic profit garnered by monopolies can similarly serve as a firm's hostage or bond—that profit can decline with poor performance or abrogation of contracts. Moreover, the economic profit can represent the deep pockets that attorneys need in order to pursue suits against a firm that fails to live up to its contracts. Hence, the economic profit that emerges as a monopoly raises its price can do more than curb production and give rise to deadweight loss; it can increase the value of the units that are purchased, in effect shifting up the demand, as the price is raised.[24] Once again, the Dupuit triangle can be expanded (and costs lowered), perhaps with the total expansion in surplus value more than offsetting the emergence of any deadweight loss that could be recovered if the competitive output level were sold at the competitive price.

Note that perfect competitors have zero economic profits to offer as a hostage or bond, but then the good in a perfectly competitive market is, by assumption, the same for all producers, so hostages and bonds are unnecessary in perfectly competitive markets to ensure quality. When we move away from such perfect markets, however, economic and monopoly profits can offer consumers some assurance that producers' commitments on the particulars of dissimilar products are credible. Producers then must lose something (over and above opportunity cost) for acting opportunistically and getting caught, which makes written and unwritten contracts closer to being self-enforcing. In effect, monopoly profits increase the present value of the penalty (discounted by time and the probability of getting caught) for wayward behavior.

CONCLUDING COMMENTS

The model developed here explains why product and service prices can be higher than predicted by standard models of competition in situations with high fixed cost and low marginal cost. Indeed, we have sought to explain two sources of advantages of monopoly pricing not touched on in conventional monopoly models, the client and bonding effects. In our discussion of the client effect, the high-price result obtained here adds some theoretical symmetry to models that explain why prices are often lower than standard economic models predict.

One such model is that a firm will not respond to excess demand by raising prices to the level needed to clear the market. The argument is that a firm's most loyal customers have invested in information on the price-quality characteristics of its product, and a sudden price increase renders that investment less valuable and can motivate those customers to seek new information, something the firm would prefer them not to do. Furthermore, a firm may be able to manage a queue so that its loyal customers have better access to the product than do transient consumers, something it cannot do if the queue is eliminated with a price increase. These arguments apply particularly to those cases in which the excess demand at the initial price is expected to be temporary.[25] It has also been argued that restaurants do not always raise prices to ration customers during periods of excess demand because the pleasure an individual derives from a restaurant meal may be positively related to the number of other people who want to eat in the same restaurant (Becker 1991). If so, an attempt to exploit excess demand by raising prices, even a little, can result in a precipitous drop in demand, as well as in amount demanded, and an increase in excess capacity.[26]

It could be that effects described by Becker (1991) and Haddock and McChesney (1994) are examples of the client effect helping to restrain a supplier from increasing prices during periods of excess demand, whereas the client effect discussed here operates to prevent the same supplier from lowering price by much during periods of excess capacity. An expensive hotel, for example, can benefit from the fact that it is known to be popular, which recommends against attempting to eliminate all excess demand during the peak season, while still recognizing that lowering prices by much during the off-peak season would adversely affect demand because of the client effect discussed in this chapter. So prices can be less flexible both upward and downward than the standard model indicates.

Also, the client effect discussed here can put downward pressure on prices as well as upward pressure, as is the case with our previous examples. The price of tickets to the concerts of popular rock groups is commonly less than the market-clearing price. Why would rock musicians sell tickets at a lower price when they could still fill the stadium at a higher price? A plausible explanation is the client effect. A higher price would do more to filter out young people than older folks because the latter typically have higher wage rates. On the other hand, with a less-than-market-clearing price the tickets will be rationed by waiting, and young people with relative lower wage rates are more likely to queue up by spending the night in a sleeping bag than an older person. And the more people in the audience who will yell, scream, and take off some of their clothes, the more exciting the concert. Furthermore, young fans are probably more likely to buy auxiliary products like CDs, DVDs, T-shirts, posters, and programs on offer. In this case, a better client mix results from a lower price rather than a higher price.[27]

We have taken up the bonding effect in this chapter because it along with the client effect reveal a glaring deficiency in standard monopoly theory, that price hikes can only be used by firms to curb sales. As we have argued, price hikes and the economic profits that arise from them can serve as a bond. Both the client and bonding effects can serve the function of increasing the value of the units bought, thus increasing the size of Dupuit triangles at the same time they give rise to Harberger triangles. When this central point is understood, it follows that some monopoly prices (or all prices that exceed marginal cost) do not reduce economic welfare. Indeed, such prices can at times be completely consistent with rigorous competition and increased consumer welfare.

Chapter 7

The Monopsony Problem

Monopsony is the buyer-side counterpart to monopoly. That is to say, a *monopsony*, in its pure form, is a single buyer of a resource, such as labor, that is protected from competition by barriers to entry facing potential buyers outside the monopsonist's market and also barriers making it very difficult for the resource (e.g., workers) from exiting the local market. In less pure or extreme form, a monopsony is any firm that has market power as a buyer of a resource. In this case, market power means that the firm can affect the resource price—or wage rate for labor—by adjusting its employment of the resource up or down. By altering its employment, the monopsony, by definition, affects the overall demand for the resource.

In this chapter, we will present the standard monopsony model, showing, as economists do in their classrooms and textbooks, how a monopsony underpays and underemploys the resources it buys. We focus on the market for labor because that is the resource market that seems to be the major concern to economists when they are discussing monopsony. That labor market is also likely to be of most concern to readers. Having developed the wage and employment effects of monopsony, the model is also used to show the extent to which a monopsony, like its seller-side counterpart, gives rise to market inefficiency and thus can be cited for being another source of market failure.

By now, readers might surmise, correctly, that our purpose in developing the conventional monopsony model is not to agree with the conventional view economists take on monopsony. Rather, it is to challenge that view. Like other economists, we can imagine the *existence* of a monopsonist, but, as we will argue, we are hard-pressed to believe any firm in the real workaday world would ever deliberately seek to rise sufficiently in prominence in its local labor markets to be able to significantly affect the wage it must pay its workers. We say this because, as we will argue, for a buyer to develop into a monopsonist in a resource market, it must pay above-competitive level prices for its resources.

This necessarily means that the monopsony can only underpay the resource (labor) in a peculiar sense: The monopsony pays less than economists can imagine it should pay, given the standard of perfectly competitive market conditions. However, such a pay level is very likely to impair, if not doom, the so-called monopsony in the product market, given its then way-above-market wages.

In chapter 8, we extend our discussion of monopsony by taking up a prominent widely presumed case of monopsony, the National Collegiate Athletics Association, that, supposedly, has cartelized college and university sports markets with the intent of exploiting budding athletes. We show there how the NCAA could not survive for long if it exploited athletes to the degree that the economist-critics of the NCAA have argued. Taking both this and the following chapters together, we conclude that monopsony, when it exists, can be welfare enhancing, as we believe is likely the case in the market for college athletes.

THE CONVENTIONAL MONOPSONY MODEL

Figure 7.1 captures the essence of the economist's textbook model of monopsony, which we can assume is for a pure monopsony, just for the sake of simplifying our demonstration. The downward-sloping demand curve D_1 is the monopsonist's demand for labor, which captures the underlying market value of what each additional worker (or each additional hour of labor) can produce and, therefore, what the monopsonist is willing to pay for each unit of labor laid out on the horizontal axis. Hence, D_1 illustrates the usual labor market relationship between the wage rate and the quantity of labor hired: the lower the wage rate, the greater the quantity of labor demanded. (Again, D_1 can be the demand for any resource, since all resource inputs can be expected to have declining marginal values within the range of production that is relevant to the buyer of the resource.)

The upward sloping supply curve S_1 captures the opportunity cost of each worker (or each hour of labor) and, therefore, the wage each worker must have before going to work for the monopsonist. The higher the worker's opportunity cost, the higher the wage rate required before the worker will go to work in the market. The higher the wage rate, the greater the number of workers who would be willing to work for the monopsonist.

The analysis of monopsony is developed by economists in much the same way that the monopoly is developed, by starting with the efficiency of a perfectly competitive market—in this case, the labor market. A perfectly competitive labor market has assumed conditions that mirror the conditions to a perfectly competitive product market: (1) all workers (and/or their units of labor) are identical, (2) numerous workers want to work, (3) numerous employers

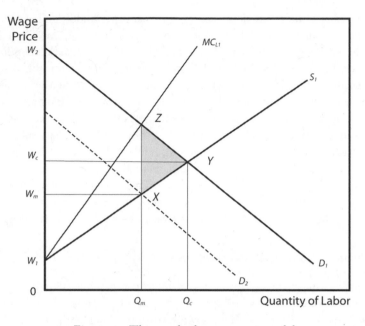

Figure 7.1. The standard monopsony model

want to hire workers (with no one employer large enough to affect the going market wage rate), (4) entry into or exit from the market is costless for workers and employers, (5) information on wages and employment opportunities across markets is zero, and (6) transaction costs are zero. Assuming perfect competition, the equilibrium wage would be the intersection of D_1 and S_1. The wage rate would be W_c and the quantity of labor employed would be Q_c.[1]

In addition to these wage and employment outcomes, we can observe that at equilibrium, all mutually beneficial trades between employers and workers would be exploited, given that the marginal value of the last worker hired, the Q_cth worker, would be exactly equal to that worker's opportunity cost and reservation wage. All workers before the Q_cth would contribute more in value than they would incur in cost, with the summation of their surplus value equal to the triangular area under the demand curve and above the supply curve, or W_1W_2Y. Any portion of this triangle not captured by the interaction of the two sides of the market is declared to be an inefficiency, or loss in surplus value—and an indication of a market failure.

How can an inefficiency arise in a monopsony market? A pure monopsony, by virtue of being the only employer in the market, can vary how much labor it demands in a search for the most profitable wage rate and employment level combination. Its task can be visualized in the graph by first noting that the monopsony (which, for simplification purposes, is assumed not to be able to discriminate among workers on the wages paid) must figure that as it increases the number of workers hired, it forces the wage rate that it must pay all workers up to the wage rate paid to the marginal worker. Therefore, if the monopsony hires one worker, it might have to pay that worker, say, $10 per hour. If it wishes to hire two workers, it might have to raise its wage for both workers from $10 to, say, $12 per hour. That means that the marginal cost of the second worker is not just $12 per hour, what the second worker is paid, but $14 per hour since the first worker has to be paid an additional $2. Put another way, the total wage bill for the monopsony goes from $10 an hour for one worker to $24 an hour for two workers, with the added cost of the second worker equal to the difference, $14 an hour.

From this example, we can deduce that the monopsony faces a marginal cost of labor curve, such as MC_{L1}, that starts at the wage rate for one worker and then is more steeply upward sloping than the monopsony's labor supply curve. The marginal cost of labor curve diverges further from the supply curve as more workers are hired because any increase in the wage rate needed to hire an additional worker has to be given to progressively more workers as the monopsony moves up its labor supply curve.[2]

In determining how many workers will be hired, and at what wage, the monopsony will weigh off the marginal value of each worker with each worker's marginal cost. This means it will compare the values on the demand curve, D_1, with the values on the MC_{L1} curve. It will extend its hiring of workers so long as the additional value of each worker exceeds the additional cost and will stop extending its hiring when the marginal value and marginal cost are equal, or up to Q_m. Beyond Q_m, firm profits are reduced with additional hiring because each additional worker then costs more than he or she is worth to the monopsony.

In settling on the wage rate it will pay, the monopsony looks to the labor supply curve, S_1, because that curve indicates what wage rate any quantity of labor would be willing to accept. The supply curve indicates that quantity of labor of Q_m would be willing to work for W_m.

This conventional analysis of monopsony leads to five key deductions.

- First, the monopsony effectively (and artificially) suppresses labor market demand (by suppressing its own demand), from the solid D_1 curve to dashed D_2 curve in figure 7.1.

- Second, the monopsony pays less than the competitive wage rate. As can be seen in figure 7.1, W_m is below W_c.
- Third, the monopsony employs fewer workers than would a competitive market. The quantity Q_m is below Q_c.
- Fourth, a monopsonized market leads to market inefficiency (in much the same manner as a monopolized market does, and for much the same reason, control over price). The monopolist hires too few workers when the marginal (opportunity) cost of hiring the last unit of labor is less than its marginal value. The monopsony also produces too little output with the marginal cost of the last unit of output less than its marginal value. In the illustration of figure 7.1, the inefficiency in the labor market is the triangular area *XYZ*. This also means that the final product would expected to be underproduced in most product markets dominated by monopsony employers.
- Fifth, some of the surplus value that would go to workers under a competitive labor market goes to the monopsony by virtue of the monopsony's management of its labor demand.

As can be seen, there is a presumption that workers are worse off because both their employment and income opportunities are constrained by the monopsony's management of labor market demand. Society at large also loses, from the perspective of this standard model, given that workers who could more valuably be employed in the monopsonized market are forced into unemployment or are forced to go elsewhere, to other competitive markets, where they are worth less.[3]

THE MYSTERIOUS EXISTENCE OF MONOPSONY

Our critique of monopsony theory begins with a reminder that the case against monopsony is made in terms of the efficiency standard associated with perfect competition, which is not likely to be relevant to any real-world market. The first and most important constraint on the achievement of any "perfect market outcome" is the fact of pervasive scarcity. Scarcity ensures that movement toward a more perfect market is, beyond some point, likely to become progressively more costly in an array of terms, not the least of which are the availability of information to buyers and sellers and the count of market participants.

We also point out that the monopsony outcome is often presumed to be the monopsony's fault alone, that is, a consequence directly and solely attributed to the monopsony's control of resource demand. The market outcome can also be said to be a consequence of the inability of the consumers of the final product to organize for the purpose of buying off the monopsony, that is, by paying the monopsony to hire more workers up to the idealized competitive level. When the consumers can't get together to do just that, we must assume that their organizational costs are greater than their gains to be had by buying off the monopsony. If that were the case, there would be no net efficiency improvement by achieving the competitive outcome. The costs of getting to that point could then be greater than the efficiency gain (or the triangle *XYZ*), making the competitive outcome less preferred than the monopsony outcome.[4]

Otherwise, we have no real complaint with the analysis of monopsony, *as far as it goes.* If a monopsony is brought magically into existence (by assumption) and then is superimposed on a labor market under the conditions specified, then the conventional monopsony model does tell us that welfare is destroyed as the monopsony transfers some of the undestroyed surplus value that would have gone to workers in competitive labor markets to itself. However, we have to wonder how a monopsony could ever emerge so magically in the real world. If it cannot magically appear on a labor market scene, we are left to wonder if a firm would ever want to do what it takes to become a monopsony, with the powers of demand management attributed to it in the standard monopsony model.

Our most important point is really very simple, which means our criticism of the monopsony model can be handled in far fewer words and pages than are typically devoted in textbooks to the development of the standard monopsony model. In elaborating our point we can't help but remember that at the start of the movie [Little Orphan] *Annie*, Ms. Hannigan—the decadent, boozing, sex-obsessed house mother of thirty or so little girls—wonders in obvious exasperation, "Why anyone would ever want to be an orphan beats me." She is right—no one in his right mind would ever choose to become an orphan (especially if they have the fabulously wealthy Daddy Warbucks as an alternative care option). The relevant issue is how Annie got to be in the orphanage and what her options were along the way. By the standard of where she came from (not where she went to live after her stint in the orphanage), the orphanage might be an improved form of child care. Indeed, it could have been her *best* care option, in spite of its obvious imperfections, made all the starker by the strained decadence of her Ms. Hannigan and the glitter of her adoptive home.

Similarly, monopsony might be seen as an improved state of markets if we first understand where the monopsony came from. In real-world markets, a monopsony doesn't just spring into existence fully capable of managing labor market demand. Large or dominant employers (not to mention single employers of any resource in a local market) almost always start out small. When successful at what they do, they grow. The more successful a firm is in satisfying consumers and in controlling principal-agency problems (and, therefore, controlling its production costs), and the more successful the firm is in developing its product and the product's market, the bigger the firm can become both in terms of market sales and workers employed. Seen from this perspective, the extant inefficiency attributed to the monopsony in figure 7.1 must be weighed against the unseen welfare gains in both the product and resource markets that were realized as the firm grew to become the sole or just dominant employer. There is no reason why a firm that can control the wage rate it pays is, on balance, any more of a net welfare loss to an economy than are other firms in other markets that do not grow to where they can affect the terms of worker employment.

It is important to note, again, that the only way a firm can grow is to hire more workers. Granted, it might initially grow without affecting the wage rate in its market. This is expected to be the usual case because its labor demand is initially (almost by definition of a new start-up firm) such a small part of the total labor demand in its relevant market(s). If the firm's demand for labor continues to grow because of its successes, it can, at some point, become so large that its demand begins to affect the wage rate. At such a point, it might be tagged as a monopsony by economists. However, at this point in its upward growth path, it can't just lower its wage rate below the prevailing wage rate, as might be expected of a monopsony (and as is certainly intimated in the presentation of the standard monopsony model). If the monopsony does lower its wage, it will contract, not grow, because workers will then go elsewhere to higher-paying opportunities.

The point is that a would-be monopsony's growth must add to the total demand for labor, which must put upward pressure on the wage rate, at least beyond some point. This means that a successful firm that grows to the position of market dominance of a monopsony must hike, not depress, workers' wage rate and employment level over and above what the wage rate and employment level would otherwise have been. In short, workers must be better off, not worse off, as is suggested by conventional monopsony analysis.

Almost surely, as the firm grew to dominate its labor market, it would have attracted at least some new workers into its labor market. If it was possible for labor to move in, then surely labor would then have sufficient mobility to move out were the monopoly to start suppressing wages below competitive levels that enable the dominant firm to expand in the first place. Economists can't have it both ways: assume that labor can enter a labor market in response to attractive pay bundles, but not move out in response to below-competitive pay bundles. But then, conventional monopsony theory implicitly assumes (wrongly, we argue) a Roach Motel view of labor markets: Labor can move in but is then forever trapped, subject to exploitation by a monopsony.

Granted, the monopsony might constrict employment below the point at which the marginal value of labor could be equal to the marginal cost, but such a matter is of no consequence. That idealized employment and wage rate level is not attainable, at least not by the usual welfare-enhancing negotiations between buyers and sellers.

Perhaps it could be attained if some federally mandated minimum wage (or, as some advocates of social justice propose, an even higher living wage) were imposed at W_c, a line of argument well worn in microeconomic theory, once the monopsony was in existence.[5] However, we have to ask whether such a minimum wage would actually be welfare enhancing, *on balance?* If the minimum wage were applied across all labor markets, both competitive and monopsonistic, then the welfare or efficiency gains in monopsony markets must be weighed against the welfare or efficiency losses in the competitive markets.

If the monopsony could expect the imposition of the minimum wage—before it started growing—then it is not at all clear that a minimum wage would be welfare enhancing even if the wage control were applicable only to monopsony markets. Surely, if the growth of the firm is predicated on paying less than the to-be-imposed minimum wage, then the anticipation of the minimum wage would affect the monopsony's future growth plans for product sales and employment, because the minimum wage would make it less profitable (in present discounted value terms).

Granted, in a riskless world in which producers didn't have to confront the prospects of product and firm failures, the anticipated minimum wage might have minimum impact, or have the effect economists argue it can have in monopsony markets. However, as noted in our discussion of problems with monopoly theory, scarcity practically mandates product and firm failures, and firms use the profitability (whether achieved from monopoly or monopsony pricing) of a few products to offset losses of failed products. Entrepreneurs often buy portfolios of firms, either directly through acquisitions of the firms or through the acquisition of their stock. Again, they do so assuming that the economic profit on the few profitable firms or stocks will offset or more than compensate them for the economic losses on the many. From the perspective being advanced here, minimum wages directed only at monopsonies, and the appropriation of monopsony rents, can be a surefire method of dampening investments across a range of labor markets, competitive and monopsonistic, the net effect of which can be a welfare loss from the development of new products, production processes, and product markets that can more than offset the welfare gain from the expansion of employment that is expected in any given monopsonized labor market.

But after dealing with this minimum-wage digression, we must come back to questioning why a monopsony would ever expand in any *given* or *local* labor market to where it began to materially hike the market wage that it would then have to pay—if it had other potential employment venues (which most firms have). If labor markets were fluid (or no less fluid as is normally assumed in conventional monopsony analysis), the wage rate in the yet-to-be-monopsony's *local* market should initially be more or less equal to the wage rate paid in other *local* labor markets.[6] If there is any difference in the wage rates among local labor markets, the difference should reflect the cost of firms and/or workers moving across the local labor market boundaries. This means that a growing firm, when it begins to push the wage in its local labor market upward, should begin to think about expanding elsewhere, where its expansion plans are sufficiently small that they no longer will result in the wage rate of that new local market being pushed up.

Granted, the conventional view of monopsony assumes that other viable labor markets don't exist (or that they are prohibitively costly to get to), both for the monopsony and the workers. However, here the source of the inefficiency is the (assumed) highly constrained options of the model, not the monopsony per se. People are basically trapped by the model's assumption of limited options—the presumed "state of nature"—not by the abuse of workers by an expanding firm. If the state of nature is so constrained, then we are hard-pressed to conclude that the monopsony is doing no more than what the workers are doing, which is the best that can be done under the circumstances. The presumption of inefficiency is illusory since competition is ruled out. Moreover, *exploitation* loses its pejorative connotation if workers have the option of morphing into producers. Of course, in the standard model, such morphing is precluded, but only by assumption (perhaps because the monopsony model was developed when such morphing was, understandably, considered infeasible, or less feasible than it is today in digital goods markets).

Our view of monopsony is founded on the more realistic view that both workers and firms have an array of employment options, which, naturally, means that the negative effects of monopsony, if they exist at all, are nowhere nearly as likely.

All of this leads us to draw a transparent conclusion. We should expect a would-be monopsony to do what many successful firms actually do: they expand by setting up production units in a growing array of labor market venues. They shift to new venues, both domestic and foreign, when conditions in any existing labor markets become so tight that their having the defining characteristic of being a monopsony is a real threat to their further expansion and profitability. Certainly those who are critical of firms that outsource jobs should at least acknowledge that those firms are reducing their real or potential monopsony power.

If a firm were to persist, blindly expanding in a given local labor market to where the firm acquired monopsony powers, you might think from standard analysis that the firm would be showered with the capital it needed for expansion. However, the exact opposite would likely be the case, which means *competitive* capital markets are effective means of disciplining would-be monopsonies that insisted on driving up labor costs, giving other producers in the final product market a decided market advantage. This suggests that in order for monopsonies to emerge with any frequency at all, there would have to be failures beyond those that are conceptualized for labor markets. The failures would have to extend to bizarre behavior on the part of investors in capital markets, which implies a form and level of systematic market inefficiencies (if not stupidity) not normally considered in monopsony analysis.

Seen from the perspective of this new view of monopsony, the only local labor market condition a firm would want to confront less than a market in which the market wage rate was rising because of the rise in the aggregate labor demand is a labor market in which it, individually, was the sole source of the rising wages. Hence, just like Annie might not want to become an orphan, so would a firm not want to become a monopsony, if it could help it.

Granted, the suggested desirability of being a monopsony comes from the implied assumption that a firm with a given demand curve for labor suddenly, and magically, finds itself with the same labor supply as before it became a monopsony, but with no competition for the labor supply and no way for the labor to move away from the monopsony. This would be nice from the firm's perspective, but so would a lot of other equally unrealistic market conditions we could assume.

THE MONOPSONISTIC "COMPANY TOWN"

We understand that historians have pointed to company towns as evidence of how a dominant employer—a monopsony—can exploit its workers. As the story could be, and is often, related, a mining company (as one of many potential examples) might set up a mine is some remote part of the Rockies. By virtue of its location, the firm is the only employer in the town (*town* used loosely) that it creates. It sets itself up, in other words, as a monopsony (a single buyer of labor and, for that matter, every other resource in the area), fully capable (supposedly) of exploiting its workers with below-competitive market wages.

Because the company owns all of the houses in town, it can further exploit its workers by its rental demands. Because it owns the only general store and bar (or whatever else) in the town, it can hike the prices for things its workers buy at the company's stores to the point that the workers' real incomes can be reduced (potentially) to a subsistence-level existence, which can be, in itself, a form of entrapment, because the worker must stay on, living from one paycheck to the next (as the story is developed). The implied economic logic of the story is captured by the lyrics to a song, "Sixteen Tons," that the late Tennessee Ernie Ford made widely popular in the 1960s.

> Sixteen tons and what do you get?
> Another day older and deeper in debt.
> Saint Peter don't you call me 'cause I can't go.
> I owe my soul to the company store.

The basic problem with this story is that it assumes an immense level of intelligence and clairvoyance on the part of the monopsonist and an immense level of irrationality or nonrationality, if not stupidity, and myopia on the part of the workers. In such a circumstance, we have to wonder if there is any market inefficiency in the company town scenario, because the workers' lack of awareness as to what they are getting themselves into should surely temper their own assessment of their own welfare loss from their own employment decisions that are made without much thought of the consequences. A question many economists seem to fail to entertain is whether there can be a material market inefficiency in a world in which choices are not made rationally. This question is particularly relevant when the adverse net consequences of worker exploitation in company towns are so blatantly obvious that even remote observers (economists and historians) can see them with clarity. Why can't the workers also see their own prospective exploitation, from afar, before they move to the company town?

In the case of the mining company, the workers would have to be willing to incur the substantial relocation costs of going to a remote location and to overlook obvious features of their new employment venues, not the least of which is that they would be facing a monopsony employer and a monopoly seller of housing and all other goods they would be buying. The workers who move to the remote location would also have to fail to recognize that the relocation costs of moving back would lock them into monopsony/monopoly exploitation. Often, they would also have to fall down in these regards and incur the relocation costs with an array of inattentive family members in tow, who are equally oblivious to what they are getting themselves into (and won't be able to get out of except at considerable cost).

Maybe some workers would be so deficient that they strike out for "them thar hills" without first investigating the consequences and taking account of the risks involved of being exploited beforehand that are supposed by the parameters of the company-town story. However, the mining company will have to figure that its expansion plans will be guided by those marginal workers who can appropriately assess the risks involved and will make wage demands based on their (more real worldly) assessments. And the greater the risks of being exploited either on the wage or product price ends can be expected to affect the workers' up-front willingness to move to the new location and, hence, the conditions of their employment. Of course, because worker willingness to move can affect employment costs for the monopsony, the monopsony has an interest in managing those risks, if it wants to grow and remain the type of employer that can continue to attract good workers—workers who, among other attributes, aren't completely stupid.

As economist Price Fishback (1992, chaps. 8, 9) has stressed, these market threats that workers face in going to remote company towns are precisely the reasons there are company towns in the first place. By virtue of its remote location, the company must pay a wage rate that is above what the workers would get where they are, say, back East. Otherwise, why else would they move to that remote spot, incurring the relocation and risk costs? The prospects of paying higher wages is all the more reason the mining company would want to minimize the risk workers perceive in relocating.

One strategy the company can use to minimize its workers' employment risk is for the company to pay the workers' moving expenses and to provide an up-front signing bonus that essentially compensates the workers for the risk costs of being exploited, contrary to the employment agreement that is written or even unwritten. The bonus can be seen as a bond that the workers can cash in the event the employer reneges on its agreement and "exploits" the workers by more than indicated or expected. Of course, the workers can use the signing bonus to move back where they came from, which is a means by which the monopsony tells workers in so many dollars, "I am increasing the elasticity of my labor supply, which is to say, I am limiting my own ability to exploit workers by suppressing their wages below competitive levels."

The company can also follow a strategy of building company houses it rents to its workers (as a means of lowering its signing bonuses or its wage bill). If it didn't provide the houses for workers and the workers had to sink their funds in their own houses, the workers would have to fear that they would indeed be locked in to (or would face high switching costs from) employment with the company—and would be far more open to exploitation. By providing the company housing, the company is basically saying to workers, "I am reducing your risk of coming to this remote spot. If I ever act like a monopsony, you can move on without putting up your housing investment at risk. I am, again, increasing the elasticity of worker supply. Moreover, if I ever act like a monopsony [to any substantial degree], I am putting the company's housing stock at risk. Moreover, I will be putting the company's investment in the general store, brothel, and bar at risk. I am not asking that you accept my word as my bond. You don't know me. As a consequence, I am asking you to accept my housing investment as my bond." The company's reason is, again, obvious: It can hire more workers at a lower wage (and a lower overall value of its payment bundles to its workers) than otherwise and can expand by more than it could if it didn't create the town, as they say, lock, stock, and barrel.

This all means, understandably, that the company has an incentive to develop a reputation for playing fair with its workers, for holding to its bargains, and for resisting the temptation to actually act like an exploitative monopsony—or opportunist or holdup artist. The monopsony also has an incentive to resist acting like a monopoly in its housing and general store markets. Otherwise, the higher the prices on the goods side of the company, the higher wage rate on the employment side. Indeed, by owning the entire town, the company internalizes the monopoly and monopsony consequences of its own actions, a factor that is bound to lead to an improvement in the overall efficiency of the market that it operates than would otherwise be possible. Ownership of the company town, in other words, is a substitute for a yet-to-be-earned reputation for fair dealing, or not acting like a monopsony. It is a source of welfare improvement.

Of course, the company's efforts to create its own town are costly. They can give rise to some later "exploitation," in the sense that the workers would be willing to endure what are then lower wage rates (that economists claim are below competitive). However, the point that can too easily get lost in monopsony wage payments is that workers could have earlier been compensated for any supposed exploitation by the initial, up-front signing bonus or by the offsetting subsidies embedded in the housing rentals.

In the name of efficiency, we might want to wish away the various bonding costs a company might have to incur on the grounds that the world would be a more efficient place without them. However, that is simply imagining efficiency by wishful thinking.

It's possible that the mining company could be paying less than economists imagine to be the wage rate of perfect competition. Again, if a criticism of markets is implied, we must wonder how a perfectly competitive market would ever be created in what are imagined to be remote places in the Rockies (or on South Seas desert islands). By the definition of the setting, such perfect markets are beyond realism, or amount to an imaginary world that only economists could construct. Ironically, in constructing their imaginary (labor market) worlds of monopsonies, economists might be the most consequential source of market distortions, or inefficiency, since their imaginary worlds form the intellectual foundations of policy recommendations that can be misguided.

FIRM AND WORKER MOBILITY AND MONOPSONY MARKET POWER

A monopsony's market power, and its effect on the market wage rate, must be functionally related to the mobility of resources, both its own ability to move about local labor markets and its workers' ability to do the same. The benefits of a firm's or would-be monopsony's own mobility is transparent. The greater its ability to move to other markets, the greater its potential profitability, because the would-be monopsony would then have a greater ability to avoid paying supra-local-market competitive wage rates (or wages paid elsewhere).

The benefits to the monopsony of worker mobility may be harder to see, given the economists' standard take on monopsony. Greater worker mobility under that model means that the monopsony would not be able to suppress worker wages below competitive levels. However, from our perspective, greater worker mobility, because it implies a greater elasticity of worker supply, lowers the increase in the wage rate that the monopsony would have to offer in order to expand production in any given local labor market. Whether or not greater worker mobility implies higher profits is uncertain. This is because other firms can benefit from worker mobility, with the market benefits of worker mobility being competed away through price competition on the product side of the market.

The fact of the matter is that resource mobility, especially labor mobility, has grown substantially over the last century as the cost of virtually all forms of transportation (and communication, which can enhance worker mobility) has steadily declined. Resource mobility has also grown with the development of computer and telecommunication technology. Where information once had to be transported in physical paper form via truck, plane, train, and/or boat for days or hours and at a cost that could easily run into the hundreds of dollars, it can now be sent around the world with a few keystrokes on a computer at virtually the speed of light and at the cost of cents (or fractions thereof). These improvements have surely reduced any inefficiency of whatever monopsony presence there is in any local, therefore isolated to one degree or another, economy. Workers can move to alternative local labor markets at far less cost than they once could, lowering the upper limit on the degree of labor exploitation. Firms' mobility has also improved dramatically, a fact that shows up in the willingness of firms to hopscotch among local labor markets on a world scale, thus reducing their need to pay above-market (albeit monopsony) wages.[7]

This increase in mobility of resources has directly increased the ability of firms to grow through a reduction in their out-of-pocket expenditures. It has also reduced the risk costs workers have had to incur. Accordingly, it has reduced firm costs by reducing their need for firms to provide such offsetting employment benefits as signing bonuses and houses. In short, because of the escalation in capital and worker mobility, company towns have become less prevalent in part because they have become a less necessary component of employment contracts as a means of attracting workers.

CONCLUDING COMMENTS

We must admit that with regard to the monopsony model, we are of two minds. In one sense we accept the standard monopsony analysis for what it is. *If* markets meet the specified conditions for monopsony that are set in the model, then the standard monopsony results follow. The model makes for at least one good lecture that may appeal to many students' predisposition to believe that market power on both the buyer's and seller's sides is everywhere evident in a market economy and, in all too many cases, in need of government remedy.

Our objection is with the specified resource market conditions, especially when the monopsony refers to a single seller and not to a cartel of employers. The most objectionable condition is that the monopsonist *exist* with no history of how the identified firm actually came to be a monopsony—that is, with no concern with the question of why a firm would, when it was small, ever want to grow so large in one particular location that its hiring drives up the prevailing wage, which is the key requirement in the monopsony model. The central point of this chapter is that if the analysis is changed to allow for the *emergence* of the monopsony through normal market success and growth processes, then it doesn't follow that the monopsony has all of the pernicious consequences that are attributed to it. Indeed, a growth-based, so-called monopsony can be, on balance, welfare enhancing. This means it can elevate the income and employment opportunities of workers, as well as all other stakeholders.

We can easily see how a governmental entity might emerge and continue to expand until it takes on the market prominence of a monopsony. This can be the case because it does not have to maximize stockholder equity. Government employment is all too often a political football and often, as such, a goal unto itself. In addition, governments are, by their very creation, landlocked. They are politically constrained from doing what a private firm can do, hopscotching among labor markets to take advantage of expansion opportunities without causing a hike in the wage rates it pays. Governments, understandably, often appear more than willing to expand in a given local labor market to the point that they begin to drive up resource prices above surrounding competitive levels.

We note that the wages of federal government workers in the District of Columbia are notoriously above the wages paid for comparable workers in the private sector. A part of the inflated wages can be attributed to the fact that members of Congress, whose political home bases are far removed from DC, do not have to worry about their constituencies objecting to the above-market wages paid in DC. Voters (especially those far beyond the Beltway) can be expected to be often rationally ignorant of such governmental details as worker pay. Also, members of Congress can shift the blame for overpayments to other members of Congress or on to Congress as a whole—or they can simply point out the obvious, that the preponderance of the federal government's work must be done in the district.

However, a part of the blame for the government's supracompetitive wage level is that the federal government has become, in staying within its political constraints, the closest thing to a monopsony in the DC area that we are likely to see. This observation, we suggest, corroborates our central thesis in this chapter, which is that a firm that develops to the stage of a monopsony must hike, not suppress, worker wage rates. If there is any inefficiency to be considered in the process, it is that the governmental services possibly could have been provided at lower cost had the federal government had the freedom to expand across local labor markets the way footloose private firms are able to do. But then, such a point can only be made by erring the same way a standard monopsony errs, by assuming, or wishing away, real-world economic constraints, which, in this case, have a political origin.

We concede that if a group of formerly competitive resource buyers conspire to manage their resource demand, then we have, potentially, another story, one of suppressed wages and employment opportunities and a market inefficiency, at least for a time. All that we would add is that the restrictions on employment, wage rates, and efficiency are not likely to be as great as the monopsony model suggests. This is because, as in the case of seller cartels, there are costs to coordinating and managing the buyer cartel. Those costs are likely to escalate with every decrease in labor market demand orchestrated by the cartel, and the escalation in the coordination cost will choke off further restrictions on the cartel's labor demand. Also, such a cartel would face out-migration from workers as the cartel attempted to use its monopsony power to reduce the wages that cartel members pay.

Having said that, not all firm organizations that have the look and feel of a monopsony cartel can be expected to have the supposed universally applicable oppressive market impact of a monopsony. We seek to drive that point home in the next chapter. There we critically examine the economic and legal roots of the NCAA, which is often held up as a grand, if not the grandest, example of an oppressive employment cartel designed to exploit college and university (mainly minority) athletes and to pad the pockets of NCAA members' coffers and their coaching staffs. With both this and the following chapters, we contend that economists have the monopsony problem wrong, both as a means of assessing labor market efficiency and, in general, as a foundation for critiquing the restrictive employment rules in college athletics.

Chapter 8

The NCAA: A Case Study of the Misuse of the Monopsony and Monopoly Models

The National Collegiate Athletic Association (NCAA) is under perennial attack from academic, sports, and media critics for its rules governing the recruitment and retention of athletes. Few people inside or outside colleges and universities are satisfied with the NCAA's rules, criticizing the NCAA for being both too strict and too lenient in the rules it makes and enforces. Cheating on NCAA rules appears to be widespread, if not rampant, as evidenced by the number and prestige of colleges and universities that have been penalized for rule infractions (Fleisher, Goff, and Tollison 1992, chap. 5). Few expect that rule infractions will ever be a thing of the past.

Many academic administrators and much of the general public appear to be worried that the NCAA has failed to adequately maintain the academic standards college athletes must meet to attend college. Concern also has been expressed about the payments, overt and covert, that member colleges and their supporters can make to athletes (Farrell 1985; Klein 1985).[1]

On the other hand, many members of the media and the economics profession appear convinced that existing NCAA rules represent an egregious, as well as inefficient, attempt by colleges and universities to cartelize the athletic labor markets for the purpose of facilitating a monopsony. As do all monopsonies (following conventional monopsony theory covered in chap. 7), the NCAA has, according to critics, suppressed the labor-market demand, in this case for student-athletes, thereby limiting their employment opportunities, wages, and fringe benefits. By restricting athletes' employment opportunities as well as restricting the number of games colleges and universities can play,

This chapter has its origins in a journal article that one of the authors (McKenzie) wrote with Thomas Sullivan (McKenzie and Sullivan 1987). We gratefully acknowledge Professor Sullivan's substantial contribution and willingness to allow us to extract and substantially revise at will this joint work for this volume.

and controlling collegiate games on television, the NCAA has imposed its collective will on the public with conventional monopoly consequences of a dominant "firm" with extensive monopoly power.

Economists Armen Alchian and William Allen popularized the cartel argument as applied to the NCAA within the economics profession in their introductory economics text first published more than four decades ago.[2] That argument has been adopted by others and continues to lie at the heart of professional critiques of the NCAA (Fleisher, Goff, and Tollison 1992; Koch 1973, 1983; McCormick 1985, 27). In their book-length investigation of the NCAA as a cartel, Arthur Fleisher, Brian Goff, and Robert Tollison insist,

> Economists generally view the NCAA as a cartel. They hold this view because the NCAA historically devised rules to restrict output (the number of games played and televised) and to restrict competition for inputs (student-athletes) . . . These points [all relating to the NCAA's cartel position] are well established in the literature, and, indeed, it could be observed that the NCAA has obtained much more durable returns on its cartel behavior than other, more notable cartels such as OPEC. (Fleisher, Goff, and Tollison 1992, 5)

Having assumed the NCAA's unquestionable cartel role, these authors go on to consider the only remaining issue that they consider worthy of investigation: "How is the cartel enforced? Who are the key regulators? Which schools are put on probation and why? How do member schools vote on rule changes? What is the nature of monopoly/monopsony rent distribution within the NCAA?" (5). After noting that in 1984 the U.S. Supreme Court had found the NCAA in violation of the nation's antitrust laws with its rules governing the televising of football games, Gary Becker stressed that "the NCAA's real monopoly power is over athletes" (1985, 18).[3]

Almost all critics detect significant hypocrisy in the NCAA's enforcement activity. Several have called for reform, including outright payments to student-athletes on the grounds that "maintenance of the present system can only continue to produce victims, not beneficiaries" (Howell 1985, 31).[4] The hypocrisy in the NCAA system is, according to proponents of the cartel thesis, patently evident in the differential treatment of a music student and a student-athlete. Both may have narrow academic goals, but only one—the student-athlete—is not permitted to sell his or her talents at market value (McCormick 1985, 27).[5]

With criticisms of the NCAA so widespread (and unrelenting), our purpose in this chapter is hardly to add to the array of critics. On the contrary, our central purpose is to reassess the conventional claims of economists that the NCAA is a welfare-destroying monopsonist and monopolist and, as a consequence, that wages of student-athletes are suppressed by the NCAA as evidenced by the existence of NCAA rules, the persistence of flagrant cheating, and the fact that ticket prices of collegiate athletic events have been moving toward monopoly limits. In so doing, we expect our assessment of the NCAA will fortify our critique of monopsony theory and show how following conventional monopsony/monopoly modeling can mislead policy discussions.

Our reassessment leads to strikingly unconventional conclusions. Most important, economists' cartel theory is hardly the only explanation for the NCAA behavior, contrary to what the critics have suggested with some zeal. The most notable explanation is that the NCAA devises rules for the types of games its members want to play and does so in a mutually beneficial way, a fact that appears to us to be self-evident in the growth of college athletics and NCAA membership over the past half century (and more), as well as the financial gains (economic profits) many member schools have realized. Moreover, we argue that athletes' wages are not generally and materially suppressed by the NCAA. Indeed, NCAA rules likely enhance the demand for student-athletes in general and increase their wages and employment opportunities in college athletics (a theme that emerged in our general treatment of monopsony in chap. 7). We conclude that overlooked but important market-based forces can be expected to contain any potentially ill-conceived and misused powers of the NCAA to exploit athletes that exist. This suggests that reoccurring moves to force the NCAA to permit its member colleges to pay athletes competitive wages are misguided. Athletes' wages can be expected to adjust over time in response to market forces without regulatory intervention.[6]

We begin by reviewing the conventional economic argument on how an employer, a monopsony cartel, which the NCAA is alleged to be, can suppress worker wages. This cartel theory relies on the uncritical acceptance of an unfounded presumption that more than a thousand colleges and universities can form through the NCAA an effective, workable cartel that can be maintained even without legal restrictions barring entry into the athletic labor markets by other sports associations that permit competitive wage payments to athletes.[7] We (with the considerable help of law professor Thomas Sullivan) find no legal and regulatory barriers to the emergence and entry of alternative sports associations into athletic labor markets.

In the absence of such barriers to entry, we argue further, the NCAA rules are, contrary to conventional wisdom, prudent measures by colleges to play the types of games they want to play and to increase the demand for intercollegiate athletics and college education. In short, the NCAA rules are a reasonably efficient contract among participants in a joint venture. They are similar in character and purpose to the rules that franchisors impose on their franchisees.

In fact, the observed cheating on NCAA rules is to be expected, as it is in franchise markets, because of the common benefits that the colleges' joint sports venture entails. Cheating by colleges can be construed (as we will show) as evidence of the public-goods character of the objectives of the NCAA rather than prima facie evidence of a cartelized labor market. Penalties on violators of NCAA rules are no less necessary, and no less expected, than penalties imposed by franchisors on wayward franchisees. Our review of antitrust law court decisions involving the NCAA directly, as well as decisions affecting a variety of other nonsports firms, suggests to us that economists, especially those who openly criticize the NCAA for being a monopsony, have much to learn from judges who have been willing to assess antitrust charges by not only considering the direct effects of market restrictions, given demand, on cooperative organizations such as the NCAA, but also by accounting for the impact of the restrictions on increasing market demand and, therefore, consumer surplus.

THE CONVENTIONAL CARTEL ARGUMENT AGAINST THE NCAA

Economists have leveled two sets of major charges against the NCAA. First, the NCAA operates as a seller cartel of athletic events, restricting the number of events its members can put on and have televised. In doing so, it transfers incomes from event attendees and television viewers to member colleges and universities (and their conferences and associations). While this is an important charge, we are not principally concerned with this set of charges in this chapter because we dealt with the monopoly issue in earlier chapters; we dedicate this chapter mainly to extending our understanding of monopsony (although we can't sidestep monopoly issues that have been intertwined with claims that the NCAA is a destructive monopsony). Here we mean only to remind readers that the cartel charges presume that market restrictions can affect the *nature* and *character* of the sports events offered and can, as a consequence, positively affect the long-run demand for college and university sporting events. Hence, buyers can be better off in spite of the higher prices that may (or may not) be charged and the monopoly, economic profits that are secured.

The second set of charges involves the claim that the NCAA acts as an employer cartel that suppresses athletes' wages: "A convincing prima facie case that the NCAA is a cartel can be derived from the explicit behavior of the NCAA" (Fleisher, Goff, and Tollison 1992, 7). This explicit behavior includes the NCAA's contract with a single television network, as well as other facts.

> While revenues to schools, coaches' salaries, and expenditures on athletic programs have exploded over the years since 1950, allowable compensation to athletes has remained essentially the same: a full grant-in-aid equal to tuition and fees, room and board, and books. Any athlete receiving more than a full grant-in-aid is automatically ineligible for NCAA participation. (Fleisher, Goff, and Tollison 1992, 7–8)

Through such restrictions (and many more), the NCAA creates market inefficiencies that ultimately have the effect of transferring income from athletes (a substantial percentage of whom in football and basketball are African American) to coaches (almost all of whom are Caucasian) and their colleges and universities (in much the same way that the pure monopsony did in chap. 7, through management of the aggregate labor market demand).[8] Also as a consequence, the NCAA breeds hypocrisy, given that the rules governing athlete recruitment and retention are founded on noble claims of encouraging fair play but also result in widespread cheating on rules. Implicit in these criticisms is the charge that temporary problems of underpayment to athletes are not subject to market self-correction. The presumed monopsony (and monopoly) power of the NCAA, therefore, must be corrected from outside the collegiate athletic market through, for example, antitrust enforcement or the passing of new laws that weaken, if not abolish, the NCAA's employment rules.

The NCAA as an Employer Cartel

The argument that the NCAA is a working cartel that suppresses athletes' wages (including fringe benefits) is grounded in the conventional microeconomic theory that labor-market competition among independent employers dissipates (quasi) rents that would otherwise go to employers. The wages paid to athletes by all colleges are raised by their bidding against one another in an effort to employ additional athletes when the wage is below the athletes' marginal value. Competition may help employ more athletes than otherwise would be employed, and the "efficient" employment level may be achieved. In the competitive process, however, revenue from sporting events is transferred from colleges (or, more precisely, their athletic departments) to athletes.[9]

For colleges contemplating the formation of a labor-market cartel, the competitive results are an unnecessary increase in the wage bill and an unnecessary reduction in the profits from college athletics. If they were not dissipated, the sports profits could be used to increase the salaries of coaches and athletic directors or could be transferred to nonathletic programs.

To keep the potential sports profits out of the hands of athletes, according to the NCAA's critics, colleges have an understandable desire to cartelize, or monopsonize, their labor market and suppress their intercollegiate athletic competition for labor. The NCAA's rules on the employment and payment of athletes are seen by some as workable devices for suppressing colleges' demand for college athletes and, thereby, labor-market competition and wages.[10]

Market Inefficiency and Income Transfers

The expected market consequences of the NCAA rules include reduced wages and employment opportunities for student-athletes, greater profits for colleges, market inefficiency, and a transfer of income from many low-income athletes to higher-income coaches and other members of athletic staffs.[11] Because of the suppressed labor-market demand, wages and employment opportunities for athletes will fall, and fewer athletes will be hired because fewer will be available for employment at the lower wages.

Because student-athletes are paid less than their market marginal value, monopsony rents will be collected by their colleges and universities. The intercollegiate athletic labor market exhibits inefficiency because the number of athletes actually hired is less than the competitive level, and the marginal value of additional athletes will exceed their opportunity costs. The gap between the marginal value and opportunity cost of athletes necessarily means that some athletes are forced to employ their talents where they are less valuable than in college athletics (Fleisher, Goff, and Tollison 1992, 8–9).

Cheating on NCAA Rules

If the NCAA is perceived as a cartel, cheating (or attempted cheating) on NCAA rules is fully anticipated. Each school can reason that because athletes' wages are below their market value, additional profits can be made by skirting the NCAA rules and paying more than the NCAA allows—attracting better athletes, higher rankings in national sports polls, larger attendance at events, more lucrative television contracts, and greater national publicity. Understanding its own incentives to cheat on the cartel rules allows each college to further conclude that other colleges will be induced to cheat and that it must cheat to remain competitive.

Indeed, the coaches who may benefit through higher-than-competitive-market salaries from the cartel rules will have a real, personal incentive to cheat or to allow cheating to persist by those around them. Premium players can contribute to winning records, with the result being increases in their coaches' salaries (Humphreys 2000). It follows that coaches who do not cheat or do not allow cheating may lose their salaries laden with economic rents to others who are willing to cheat and are, therefore, better able to attract larger crowds, television coverage, and national prominence.[12]

However, cheating is suppressed in two primary, cost-effective ways.

- First, when coaches, alumni, and other college and university constituents bid improperly for athletes and lose those bids, the NCAA can count on the losers to report the schools that must have been bidding improperly for those athletes.
- Second, as opposed to monitoring all athletic programs in any detail, the NCAA can spot-monitor by looking for and investigating in detail only schools that have sudden improvements in their win-loss records.

Both Fleisher, Goff, and Tollison (1992, chap. 5) and Humphreys and Ruseski (2001) have found that an improvement in a school's athletic performance can increase its likelihood of being investigated and put on probation.

Added Complexities

The foregoing standard but limited monopsony cartel argument has been refined and extended by Fleisher, Goff, and Tollison (1992). These economists argue that the NCAA's origins can be traced to 1873, when several universities—Columbia, Princeton, Rutgers, and Yale—met to standardize the rules for football (which amounted to varying combinations of the rules for soccer and rugby, plus a few rules not associated with either of those games). These universities formed what was called the Intercollegiate Football Association, which, in its short history, had an uneven record of retaining members and settling on uniform rules among member colleges.

Spurred by the growth in sports-related violence (which was reflected in 18 deaths and 159 serious injuries in 1905),[13] President Theodore Roosevelt brought together representatives from Harvard, Yale, and Princeton to discuss solutions to the violence problem. That initial meeting was followed later that year by a conference of 62 colleges and universities that gathered to deal more completely with football violence, forming the Intercollegiate Athletic Association, which in 1910 was renamed the National Collegiate Athletic Association (Fleisher, Goff, and Tollison 1992, 38–40).

Hence, Fleisher, Goff, and Tollison argued that the NCAA began and initially expanded with noble purposes in mind, to produce public goods in the form of rules standardization and the prevention of game-related violence. However, "while listing lofty goals and motivations," the constitution adopted by the members in 1906 "left ample room for the NCAA to expand from public-goods provider into cartel rules enforcer." In addition, given that the initial organizational costs of the NCAA had already been covered under the banner of producing public goods, it could readily expand into market restrictions at very little cost.[14] Accordingly, in the pursuit of cartel rents during the early part of the twentieth century, the members began to set player eligibility requirements, including the stipulation that student-athletes had to be (gasp!) full-time students. Moreover, "enticing students to stay in school through direct or indirect financial aid for the sole purpose of pursuing athletics was condemned" collectively by the members—more prima facie evidence of the suppression of labor-market competition, according to Fleisher, Goff, and Tollison (1992, 41).

Such restrictions are given a cartel intent by Fleisher, Goff, and Tollison because they obviously limit the resource input, both in terms of the number of people who could play and in terms of the quality of the players in games. By restricting inputs, the NCAA members could suppress their labor costs and enhance their monopsony rents. Their input restrictions also limited the members' collective output. With additional output restrictions in terms of the number of games that could be played and (after 1950) televised, the NCAA enabled its members to reap greater monopoly rents—which could be easily hidden by the members in "university general operating expenses, coaches' salaries, office facilities, and so on" in order to keep their real intent obscured from public scrutiny (1992, 21).

Given all the NCAA rules cited repeatedly by Fleisher, Goff, and Tollison as examples of labor-market restrictions—covering such details as how many times recruits can visit prospective campuses, what they can be provided while on their campus visit, the level of academic preparation of recruits, how many courses they must take, the minimum grade-point average players must maintain, how many years they can play—there appears to be nothing that the NCAA could have required of players and their member institutions during its formative years, and especially after it had become a well-oiled organization in the late 1940, that did not have a cartel-creation and maintenance interpretation. Of course, the growing array of input restrictions was part and parcel of an ongoing educational sham: "Member schools have successfully hidden cartel behavior behind the rhetoric of academic achievement and the nonproprietary setting of universities" (1992, 7).

A "cartel [labor-market monopsony] scheme" is also suggested by the fact that only student labor is singled out for competitive restrictions. The members' "brand names" and other capital assets (including, but hardly limited to, stadiums and training facilities) are not similarly restricted.

> If a quest for education, amateurism, and standardized rules were truly at the heart of NCAA behavior, these inputs would be regulated along with labor inputs. Indeed, if such purpose were a goal of the NCAA, then some schools would not be allowed to offer recruits a more attractive package than other schools, and student-athletes would not be allowed to choose schools freely. (1992, 8–9)

The resulting suppression of athletes' wages can be easily inferred from the fact that players such as Bo Jackson, Patrick Ewing, and Doug Flutie (their colleges' superstars of the 1980s, familiar to sports fans when Fleisher, Goff, and Tollison were writing their sweeping critique of the NCAA) could have earned millions if they had not taken their respective universities' athletic offers and instead had played for professional teams (1992, 8).

According to Fleisher, Goff, and Tollison, the ongoing increase in demand for NCAA member sporting events throughout the past hundred years is evi-

dent in the growth in game attendance and counts of radio and television viewers, along with the forty-six-fold growth in the (nominal dollar) value of
NCAA's television contracts (1992, chap. 4).[15] Total attendance at football
games across the country expanded from 19 million in 1948 to 36 million in
1989, the last year of available data to Fleisher, Goff, and Tollison before their
book went to press (1992, 54). With the growth in demand came a concomitant increase in NCAA rents, which gave rise to an increase in NCAA membership from 38 in 1906 to 1,017 in 1988 (the last year in the Fleisher, Goff,
and Tollison 1992 table, 67) to more than 1,250 in 2007—with 1,024 of the
members in 2007 being colleges and universities and with most of the remaining members being athletic associations (e.g., the American Football Coaches
Association) and athletic conferences (e.g., the Atlantic Coast Conference)
(NCAA Web home page 2007). With the growth in demand for the final product and rents, the demand for enforcement of cartel rules rose, according to
Fleisher, Goff, and Tollison.[16]

This growth in membership occurred throughout the century in spite of
the tightening restrictions on players and institutions and in spite of the fact
that the NCAA history consisted of an ongoing power struggle among the
established and nonestablished members over how the NCAA's monopoly/
monopsony rents would be divided. Fleisher, Goff, and Tollison see many
of the restrictions that have been adopted as devices by which the established members have been able to retain relatively dominant athletic positions and, hence, their relatively greater share of the rents. Indeed, the
established members have basically captured the NCAA's regulatory bodies,
using them for private rent-seeking purposes, the objects of which are
money, perquisites for everyone other than the athletes, and winning
records (which have feedback effects on the first two). The authors argue
that members with "substantial reputational and physical assets" have
advantages in recruiting athletes and in capturing the NCAA's enforcement
mechanisms. The existence of these advantages explains the oppressive rules
against the student-athletes: If nonestablished firms could compete by paying athletes in wages or benefits (and not forcing them to adhere to academic standards of any consequence), the established schools would lose
athletes and games—and rents.[17]

Why then don't the nonestablished powers break with the NCAA, set up
their own "NCAA-2," and agree to a whole new set of rules (including
allowance for paying athletes market wages) that will allow them to attract the
best athletes and secure a level of rents higher than the oppressed level they
receive as members of the NCAA? Fleisher, Goff, and Tollison have a ready-
made, two-part explanation.

One factor is the discontinuous, or "lumpy," entry condition in college athletics. One or even a few schools cannot produce a viable ten- or eleven-
game football season or a thirty-game basketball season. Coordination
among several schools would be necessary for a successful breakaway from
the NCAA. . . . In other words, there is a first-mover advantage. (1992,
10–11)[18]

The other factor is "the threat of sanctions against a school's *academic* programs" (1992, 11; emphasis in the original). Even though Fleisher, Goff, and
Tollison admit that the NCAA has no direct control over academic accreditation, they still claim (backed up by a single anecdote) that the NCAA "sanctions and pressures have influenced the process." Hence, the NCAA can
threaten the "brand-name capital" of institutions that do succeed, thus increasing the cost and likelihood of the succession and the establishment of viable
sports alternatives (1992, 11).

If the NCAA is the 800-pound sports gorilla that Fleisher, Goff, and Tollison make it out to be, then the inevitable perplexing puzzle surfaces (in the
words of the authors): "Why there is so little interest, in general, in market-
oriented reform of the NCAA, and, in particular, reform in the spirit of economic analysts, which would suggest paying players the value of their marginal
products" (1992, 3). But Fleisher, Goff, and Tollison have ready answers here
as well.

- In spite of fans' (supposedly) having to pay higher prices for sporting
  events (because of the NCAA's input and output restrictions), Fleisher,
  Goff, and Tollison posit that fans' interest in reform is "minimal"
  because they individually gain so little from organizing a reform movement (1992, 147, 148).
- Schools' faculties fail to support reform because they suffer under a
  "misconception" as to the substantial gains they receive from their
  schools' athletic programs.
- The media have shown little interest because they are on the take, given
  that their livelihoods are dependent on access to players and coaches and
  that they will suffer costs in terms of access if they wave reform banners
  (1992, 149–152). (Even so, aside from their self-acknowledged "speculative explanations," the media's lack of interest in reform remains something of a mystery to Fleisher, Goff, and Tollison).[19]
- Finally, the players don't press for reforms because they would have to
  endure the costs (in out-of-pocket expenditures and time) of organizing
  a unified reform movement, and they have very few resources and little
  time to mount the campaign.

The whole of the Fleisher, Goff, and Tollison argument ultimately rests on an interesting position: that their assessment of the NCAA is correct because absolutely no alternative, sensible explanation exists for what the NCAA has done. They make this point in their explanation of the media's lack of interest in the issue of the NCAA as an oppressive cartel.

> Given the evidence reviewed and presented in this book, if the NCAA is not a collusive organization of schools for economic benefit, then an indefensible alternative is left: the NCAA is filled with a majority of public-interested people who rarely recognize or understand the consequences of their own decisions. Given that people are generally self-interested and that NCAA policymakers are not dull-minded, this explanation seems inconceivable. (1992, 150)

Restrictions are restrictions, necessarily efficiency destroying, as well as oppressive to student-athletes, fans, reporters, and faculty, all of whom must have been co-opted in one way or another, to one extent or another. Otherwise, they suffer from delusions, or so it must seem. There is, supposedly, no way to imagine that restrictions for games or markets can be, on balance, welfare enhancing, or even Pareto efficient (or beneficial to everyone involved in college athletics—that is, to the NCAA's critics).

SCIENCE AS IDEOLOGY

Joseph Schumpeter titled his 1948 presidential address to the American Economic Association "Science and Ideology" (1949). By "ideology" he did not mean unflinching political or religious convictions. Rather, he meant the prescientific, original "Vision" (or "Intuition") that economists, as a matter of doing science, *must* take along with them into their analytical inquiries.[20] It is through this initial vision that we economists see and assess the world,[21] but the vision itself is hard to subject directly to scientific tests. This is because science, as a process for discovery and inventions, usually focuses exclusively on the test of the vision's implications (or hypotheses), with the whole testing process guided by professional biases in finding support of (or, rather, not finding fault with) the implications and therefore the underlying vision.[22] The problem with these initial visions or ideologies is that they, because of their success in an array of inquiries, can "become creeds which for the time being are impervious to argument" (1949, 358). In the end, however, science is an evolutionary process involving an "endless chain of give and take," with the original vision giving way to adjustments in findings and perceptions and then theories. Eventually, inferior original visions (which is obviously how Schumpeter viewed John Maynard Keynes's take on the macroeconomy) can lose their initial attraction and can be marginalized by the profession once their weaknesses are exposed (1949, 356).

Schumpeter was especially concerned with how economists' ideology with respect to monopoly enterprise has captured so much of economic discourse. Throughout this volume, we have stressed that he posited that it is very difficult for economists, captured by the monopoly model, to conceive of monopolies (or cartels) as having beneficial consequences.[23] Why? Because the models in the back of their minds exclusively focus on stationary cost and demand structures, which necessarily means that the only option available to the monopoly—restrictions on output to raise price—is necessarily detrimental, in the context of that model.

We submit here, as evident from the foregoing discussion, that the monopsony model has, in a similar way, captured the analytical skills of economists. When something can be labeled "restrictions" or "rules" for market players, and when an organization is formed to establish and openly promulgate and enforce "restrictions" and "rules" for its market, there can be, as Fleisher, Goff, and Tollison have concluded, only one analytical deduction, that the intent of the restrictions and rules is as oppressive, redistributive, or both as it is welfare destroying. Ergo, the promulgating organization, the NCAA in this instance, must collectively have an oppressive intent. Moreover, any explanation other than that of Fleisher, Goff, and Tollison for what the NCAA has done through its history is "inconceivable" (1992, 150).

The point of the following sections of this chapter is straightforward: Although a monopsony (or a dominant buyer cartel) clearly can, in the immediate period, restrict employment opportunities below what might be imagined for a perfectly competitive market and can suppress worker wages below some imagined (perfectly) competitive level, it is not self-evident that the NCAA is the kind of welfare-destroying monopsony, or employer cartel, that economists have in mind when parroting standard criticisms of any and all observed restrictions and rules. Under some market circumstances, restrictions and rules may do nothing other than curb immediate production, but they also can, at least in some other circumstances, define the nature of the product. In doing so, they can change an industry's dynamics over time, with the *long-term* consequences of the restrictions and rules being far more beneficial to expanded opportunities than any detriment from *short-run, passing* curbs on output and hikes in prices.

To repeat a Schumpeterian theme of this volume, a system of monopsony restrictions and rules that foster the appearance, if not the reality, of short-run inefficiencies may at times be necessary for maximum long-run growth of welfare. We treat the NCAA as a case study because the particulars of that organization's restrictions and rules can help us make a few evolutionary adjustments in the "vision" that undergirds the monopsony model.

If our perspective is right, then no mystery surrounds what Fleisher, Goff, and Tollison and other economists and NCAA critics see as a paradox, the widespread disinterest (or lack of interest) among various constituent groups in major reform of the NCAA-controlled athletic markets.[24] Using a different starting analytical vision, which allows them to distinguish among market circumstances, the courts have recognized as much in an array of decisions regarding the NCAA's monopsony powers, which Schumpeter would surely applaud. We suggest that economists can learn much about how to evaluate restrictions from the legal history we cover in a later section.

As we will demonstrate, the revisions in argumentation do not require (contrary to what Fleisher, Goff, and Tollison and others suggest) that we assume that NCAA policymakers are "dull-minded" or that they are "public spirited" (or are not motivated by self-interest).

THE MISTAKEN PRESUMPTION OF "UNDERPAID" ATHLETES

Proponents of the cartel theory of the NCAA implicitly, if not explicitly, conclude that resources are misallocated because athletes are "underpaid" for their services. As noted in the foregoing section, one representative and presumed piece of prima facie evidence is the NCAA rule that restricts colleges and universities from paying student-athletes more than the equivalent of room, board, tuition, and books. Using the pay of professional athletes as "shadow prices," the (approximate) extent of the underpayment becomes transparent, or so it is argued.

However, the critical pay variable determining the allocation of resources is the *expected*, not *actual*, pay of athletes. The expected pay of college athletes is typically greater than their actual pay by an amount equal to the present discounted value of the *anticipated* future income from future (especially professional sports) employment. Without doubt, the prospective pay in professional sports, if obtained, is a critical component of many (but not all) athletes' anticipated future income stream and their current calculation of the gains from playing college sports, but it is hardly the only variable, given that many athletes capable of playing at the college level couldn't even dream of professional play. For many athletes, their expected pay is rightly founded on combined estimates of their future employment in sports and nonsports areas. (Of course,

the fact that many athletes are willing to play their sports even without scholarships suggests that "joy of the game" cannot be totally dismissed as a non-
money form of payment for services rendered.)

This fact alone means that the value of the athletes' education, and the
effect that their degrees' reputation (and the contacts they make) has on their
future income streams (which can be bolstered by established industry-wide
rules), cannot be summarily dismissed. As most economists would attest, pay
restrictions can affect student-athletes' time allocations while in their universities. Because those restrictions apply to all players and schools, they can affect
what Fleisher, Goff, and Tollison call colleges' and universities' "reputational
capital"—which implies that pay restrictions can help athletes overcome a free-
rider problem. This also means that NCAA's rules can have the effect of placing on athletes' education the sports equivalent of a Good Housekeeping Seal
of Approval, especially if it is widely known that college and university presidents and faculty (with academic interests outside those in athletic departments) control the rules-making process, which is the case for the NCAA.[25]

Granted, few college athletes make professional teams. Many football and
basketball players, however, could turn professional before their college eligibility is finished.[26] The fact that many athletes—including most of the better
athletes (even those whom Fleisher, Goff, and Tollison consider to be examples of underpaid athletes [1992, 9])—voluntarily use years of their college eligibility before turning pro suggests that their extra year or years spent in college sports provide valuable on-the-job training and media exposure. The
result is an increase in their expected lifetime income (broadly defined) that
more than compensates for the loss of income during their college years.[27]

Clearly, because of the pay restrictions, some college and university athletes turn professional before they finish their years of eligibility. A handful of
high school graduates each year skip college altogether, choosing their
expected lifetime professional income streams over what they could have anticipated by first going to college and then into the pros. However, it must be
noted that the number of student-athletes who turn pro before the end of their
college eligibility is a very small part of the total count of athletes, even when
we restrict the count of total *viable* athletes (candidates for going pro) to those
in football and basketball at the 107 schools in the NCAA's Division I.[28] Even
if the percentage of athletes who don't avail themselves of their full college
sports experience were much larger than it is, it does not follow that the NCAA
pay restrictions can be judged to be oppressive in a monopsonistic sense. This
is because rules are rules, broadly applicable to people in widely varying circumstances. Few rules with any coverage at all are likely to fit all circumstances
equally, nor did anyone expect them to be designed to do so, mainly because of

the underlying economics of rule making. Making any given set of rules fully Pareto efficient can be as futile as trying to create a perfectly clean environment (or to develop a perfectly competitive market). The costs of trying to craft rules that are beneficial to everyone are likely to escalate with the rules' coverage. These economic considerations may be used to restrict the coverage of the rules.

However, why have such restrictions if the rules are generally beneficial and harmful to so few? The few student-athletes who turn professional obviously gain individually by their decisions, while the rules themselves can remain generally beneficial, on balance, to those athletes who remain in school. The fact that so many athletes stay in school suggests that the employment rules are hardly oppressive to them. Indeed, the fact that few athletes can and do make the shift to professional sports can be construed as good evidence that the exit costs of student-athletes going professional are hardly prohibitive, if athletes have the talent to make professional teams. That fact is also good evidence that the professional "shadow prices" grossly exaggerate the student-athletes' so-called underpayment. Indeed, the absence of an unchecked movement from college to professional sports could be construed as evidence that the student-athletes are as likely to be overpaid (given their opportunity cost) as underpaid. Then again, as will be argued later, the rules themselves could be defining college and university athletics in such ways that the student-athletes' expected incomes are higher than they would have been had the restrictions not been in place for so long and had the rules not allowed college and university athletes to call themselves student-athletes.

THE MISTAKEN INTERPRETATION OF CHEATING

Proponents of the cartel theory of college sports mistakenly conclude that the existence of cheating is prima facie evidence of an employer cartel that exploits athletes by materially depressing labor-market demand and athletes' wages. The existence of rules and the persistence of cheating, however, could be interpreted to be the products of voluntary collective efforts of member colleges to engage in a demand-enhancing joint venture. The joint venture may be characterized as the enhancement of the colleges' and universities' competitive athletics and internal and external support for nonathletic, as well as athletic, programs, which can be most effectively accomplished by ensuring that college athletics remains amateur. The members may believe quite correctly that the public's demand for college and university education may be significantly reduced by the creation of professional or semiprofessional college sporting events.[29]

The joint venture problem and the rules that emerge may be comparable to the quality-control problem faced by most sellers of brand names and franchises. The vertical restrictions are illustrative. For example, McDonald's restaurants collectively produce a joint product, that is, a reputation for fast-food service at a certain price and quality in reasonably clean facilities. Like the NCAA, the McDonald's Corporation also has detailed rules and restrictions for its franchisees to follow (and its rule book is at least as thick as the NCAA's). These restrictions cover such operational details as cleanliness of the kitchens and dining areas, the very exacting recipes for the products served, standards on employment, the parking facilities, and the amount of time customers should have to stand in line. Take note of an important attribute of the "restrictions": They define McDonald's products and, according to McDonald's, elevate the value that consumers ascribe to the company's products. The restrictions also establish uniformity in product and service with the intent of enhancing the reputation of McDonald's restaurants, increasing the predictability of McDonald's offerings and increasing the demand (and consumer value) for McDonald's products at all outlets—all with the intent of increasing the corporation's profits by way of enhancement of its customers' net value.[30]

The individual franchisees are willing to consent to the prospects of paying the penalties for violations because they understand that McDonald's overall institutional reputation across all franchises is important to their own individual franchise profits. The franchisees willingly accept the restrictions on their own behavior to ensure that limits are placed on the behavior of others, all to reduce free-rider problems.

At the same time, in the absence of monitoring and penalties, each franchisee at all times has an incentive to cheat on the restrictions. By cheating— for example, by not cleaning their bathrooms regularly or by adding soybean meal to hamburgers—individual franchisees can lower their *own* production costs and raise their *own* profits. Franchisees (especially those who have little repeat business from customers) also can rightfully reason that their individual reputation in general may be only marginally, if not inconsequentially, damaged by its own violations of McDonald's rules. Each franchisee understands, however, that all other franchisees have a similar incentive to cheat. If the benefits of improved market demand did not more than compensate for the added costs that franchisees incur to avoid penalties, the restrictions would presumably never be accepted. Moreover, franchises would not command such high prices.

Similarly, NCAA rules and regulations can be viewed as means to enhance the reputation of all those associated with college athletics—including athletes and nonathletes—by keeping college sports nonprofessional.[31] NCAA members will accept restrictions on payments to athletes to enhance the demand for college athletics, college enrollment, and contributions to athletic and non-athletic programs. Each NCAA member understands, however, that every other member has an incentive to cheat on the rules of the joint venture. From this perspective, penalties are required because, as in the case of McDonald's restaurants, cheating can be expected when the benefits from the joint venture are common to all participating members.[32]

To the extent that the demand for college athletics is enhanced by the NCAA's system of rules and penalties, the demand for athletes will increase, which means that the athletes will have more sports opportunities than would be the case without the restrictions. More college teams can survive and prosper.

In addition, more athletic talent at lower wages will be available for the professional ranks, which may explain professional teams' support of the NCAA system of rules and regulations. Proponents of the cartel theory of college sports have a difficult time explaining professional teams' support of the NCAA rules. If the NCAA were a cartel that suppressed wages *and* employment opportunities for athletes, the supply of athletes available for the professional ranks would be reduced, increasing the wages professional teams must pay. Also, when wages are suppressed by a cartel, we do not anticipate a surplus of labor that would spur nonprice competition in the form of talent improvement. If anything, a cartel that seriously suppressed wages would induce a reduction in athletic talent available to the college and professional ranks.

THE MISTAKEN PRESUMPTION OF MONOPSONY POWER

Proponents of the cartel theory mistakenly assume that because the NCAA includes more than a thousand members, it has substantial monopsony power that enables member colleges to suppress athletes' wages (e.g., below imagined perfectly competitive market conditions). The proponents acknowledge that colleges have substantial private incentives to cartelize their markets. They overlook, however, the critically important and patently obvious fact that the NCAA members are not a *single unified* firm but are a collection of many independent firms with different cost structures and different market demands. They have the same incentive to improve their profits by cheating on the cartel—even forming alternative collegiate or semiprofessional sports associations that permit explicit wage payments to athletes—as they do to form the cartel in the first place.[33] In other words, the proponents of the cartel theory fail to explain how any effective, exploitative sports cartel can be maintained in the long run, in the absence of forced membership or barriers to exit from the

NCAA by member colleges and barriers to entry into the sports market by alternative sports associations. Many economists who argue that the NCAA is an effective employer cartel would be the first to contend that it would be extremely difficult, if not impossible, for a collection of twenty-five or fifty firms in any other industry to maintain an effective cartel for long (without government backing, a point Schumpeter made, as readers may recall).

If the NCAA seriously depressed athletes' wages, the temptation of member colleges to drop their membership and form another association that permitted competitive wage payments would appear to be overwhelming. This is especially true because economists who have criticized the NCAA have also documented a symbiotic relationship between big-time athletic programs and the student demand for enrollment at those colleges and universities, which they found leads to higher SAT scores of entering students, other things being equal.[34] Schools that break with the NCAA could form their own sports network that allows for payments to athletes, as well as relaxed academic standards for athletes. As a consequence, the new sports network should be able to draw in the best athletes, which would allow breakaway members to develop much improved athletic programs and, at the same time, allow them to improve their academic standings (given that the demand for admission from higher-quality, nonathlete students should rise with the schools' athletic standing)—but only *if* the critics' case against the NCAA rules were solid. The incentive for schools to break away would be reinforced *if,* as calculated, the value (or marginal revenue product) of a "premium" college football player were a half million dollars annually to the school that gets him (Brown 1993) and *if* the breakaway teams could actually attract the premium payers through payments (that more than compensate them for any lost value from not being associated with nonpaying, NCAA-endorsed athletic programs), which the NCAA's critics presume would happen without fail but which is not assured by any means.

Proponents of the cartel theory cannot escape with the argument that the initial organizational costs have "lumpiness," founded on the proposition that in order to fill out their schedules, several teams must agree to form an alternative association, an argument made repeatedly by Fleisher, Goff, and Tollison (1992, 10–11 et passim). Their argument that the NCAA actually is now an effective cartel suggests that the creation of an alternative sports association is a viable possibility, or else an NCAA would not exist. Clearly, the NCAA overcame the lumpiness problem. In addition, regional and national conferences (e.g., the SEC and ACC) and the College Football Association (CFA), which are a part of the NCAA, are already well organized to secede from the NCAA as a unit and to establish alternative sports associations that would allow payments to athletes if the NCAA were not appropriately responsive to market forces and member schools. The existing associations—the National Association of Intercollegiate Athletics (NAIA) and the National Little College Athletic Association (NLCAA)—could take advantage of the NCAA's alleged exploitation of athletes and allow payment.

If athletes were *seriously* exploited under the NCAA, the seceding teams or conferences might reasonably expect that their exit would induce other teams and conferences to follow suit.[35] Because the seceding teams would be offering a better alternative, those that did secede would be the ones attracting the more sought-after athletes and presumably would benefit from larger attendances and television contracts to the detriment of the remaining NCAA colleges. In fact, entrepreneurs outside college athletic departments searching for sports profits should be willing to organize the necessary critical number of schools.[36] The openness of the association market is important because the emergence (or the threat of emergence) of alternative sports employment opportunities would cause wages of student-athletes to rise to something approximating competitive levels.

The logical extension of the proponents' own cartel premises leads to the inescapable conclusion that if colleges didn't see something intrinsically important in their efforts to maintain the pretense, if not the substance, of amateur athletics at the college level, the NCAA rules would not last long in the absence of significant barriers to exit from the NCAA or in the absence of significant barriers to entry into the sports association industry.[37] These barriers would have to be legal, and our review of the legal literature suggests a powerful point: *No legal impediments exist to the formation of alternative college and university sports associations, governed by a different set of employment rules.* And surely the NCAA's critics—most notably Fleisher, Goff, and Tollison—would never claim (or so we would think) that any legal or economic barriers (aside from cost and demand considerations) stand in the way of savvy entrepreneurs wishing to form an array of municipal, neighborhood, and company-based sports associations that could compete on more favorable terms (if they could be devised) for would-be student-athletes.

Fleisher, Goff, and Tollison point out that schools might suffer accreditation risks by seceding from the NCAA. In the absence of any more than the one anecdote the authors provide, we have to consider the claim baseless, more on the order of the pretense of documentation.[38]

We concede, but only for purposes of argument, that schools might initially lose some academic credibility, given the brand-name value of being associated with the NCAA relative to any new and necessarily untried association. However, if athletes are as seriously oppressed as the critics suggest (and the restrictions have no value apart from the direct labor-market rents they can generate), then any short-term credibility problems could be surely overcome in the long run. This is because the elimination of the labor-market restrictions can lead to an untold increase in market surplus value being garnered and shared by the seceding schools and their athletes. The schools' quality of play would (supposedly) improve dramatically as they secured the "best" athletes, which should give them more access to improved television contracts and lead to a greater demand from better students willing to pay higher prices, and more athletic and academic donations from private benefactors. The critics' suggestion that the oppression is so great, yet widespread secession does not appear to be in the offing, is more good evidence that the critics' case is made of straw.

SPORTS DEMAND AND NCAA MEMBERSHIP

We noted how the NCAA's critics have made much of the growth in the demand for college and university athletic events, as revealed by attendance figures and the dollar value of television contracts (Fleisher, Goff, and Tollison 1992, 51–56). According to the critics, such statistics indicate growth in NCAA rents, which, of course, is a cause for increased membership. The theory is relatively simple, as briefly noted earlier: The NCAA starts small, with the production of public goods as its original intention. After it has covered its organizational costs, it discovers that it can, at little added cost, increase its rents by imposing labor-market restrictions (as well as by imposing output restrictions). When the rents begin to pour in, other schools want their share, spurring an expansion in the NCAA's membership. The membership expansion becomes (at some undefined point) self-perpetuating, given that with the growth in NCAA membership, nonmember colleges and universities face growing problems in filling out their game schedules.

To review, the validity of this simple theory—or "vision," to use Schumpeter's word—is revealed, supposedly, by the growth in NCAA members (Fleisher, Goff, and Tollison 1992, table 4, 67).[39] The theory is further corroborated by a series of empirical studies that show the extent to which members have tried to influence NCAA control mechanisms to influence the distribution of the NCAA's total revenues among the members (chaps. 5–7). Any internal squabbling over rents implies the existence of rents, which implies the existence of monopsony (and monopoly), which must mean that the NCAA's restrictions are oppressive.

The unstated assumption in this scenario is that the growth in demand for athletics was unaffected in any positive way by the NCAA's restrictions and rules as well as its accompanying enforcement efforts. Confidence in a pure cartel theory of the NCAA's history must surely crack on the prospect that the reported demand dynamics over the past century could have been fueled, if only partially, by the expansion of NCAA restrictions and rules and the beneficial effects they have on the market value of the sporting events, as seen from the perspective of the relevant fan base. That is to say, the cited attendance figures through time could easily be interpreted as strong evidence against the applicability of the cartel theory. Surely, the raw figures do nothing to support the cartel theory and (in the absence of additional econometric work that is not provided) could undermine that theory. Cartels designed only to constrict both the input and output sides of the market are not market structures in which substantial ongoing growth should be a hallmark. Rather, an appropriate measure of the NCAA's impact should be how much growth has been impaired by the double-sided market restrictions and rules.

We also are very reluctant for two reasons to accept the claim that the growth in NCAA members indicates the success of the NCAA cartel. First, if rents were available to be gained by so many colleges and universities joining the NCAA cartel, then chances are that even more rents would be available for the would-be new members to form their own alternative NCAA cartel with different, and less oppressive, monopsony rules for their athletes, as argued. The would-be new members could also lower the price of tickets for fans, could attract more donors for their athletic *and* academic programs, and should be able to get more favorable publicity from the media (who could be given greater access to the country's best athletes whose performance in non-NCAA schools could be greater than in NCAA schools, because those athletes would have to spend little or no time in class or studying).

Our second reason for being reluctant to accept the critics' theory is that part and parcel of the theory is the presumed rampant discrimination in enforcement of cartel rules and in the allocation of cartel rents by the "established" schools against the nonestablished schools. In promulgating their argument, the critics must be assuming that institutional members in the NCAA are like lemmings, unable to see where their frantic march is taking them. Put another way, in joining the NCAA, the ever-growing count of non-establishment school members must have no capacity for self-directed, self-interested courses of action. If we accept the critics' argument in its entirety, we must wonder why similar cartels are not everywhere evident in markets, not just those in which the restrictions define the product and its value. After all, the NCAA is a cartel of over a thousand members with differing cost structures.

COLLEGE AND UNIVERSITY SPORTS AS GAMES

As economists have long argued, market-based exchanges are better viewed not so much as trades in *things* as trades in *rights*. More to the point of this chapter, trades almost always carry with them *restrictions* that can be publicly or privately enforced. The publicly enforced restrictions are often noted. People who buy pens or cars can't use them as weapons. In the case of pens, legal limits exist concerning what one can write with them. For example, pen owners cannot use them to make slanderous public comments. In the case of cars, the owners can't drive them (as a matter of course) on city sidewalks and, in many states, must get them inspected once a year. Clubs usually have physical facilities, the use of which by members is bounded in myriad ways by an extended set of restrictions, including restrictions on the development of inside markets (e.g., prohibitions on using the facilities to sell nonclub goods).

Indeed, it might be useful to think of goods that are bought and sold arrayed on an extended spectrum in terms of how much the goods are *defined* by or draw their *essential character*—and, hence, their market value—from the restrictions on how the goods can be used. On one end of the spectrum might be marshmallows, which are a good that is largely defined by and largely draws its market value from its physical attributes, including marshmallows' touch and taste (and calories). Marshmallows are, apparently, little affected by restrictions on use or any other matter, because relatively few such restrictions exist (that we can think of).

On the other hand, many board games are good examples of traded and experienced goods that are (typically) on the other end of the spectrum because their physical attributes are relatively inconsequential to their value. The board game Monopoly has only a few ounces of physical content, including a brightly marked piece of cardboard and bundles of play cash, all of which have in themselves little to no intrinsic value. The physical components are given value largely by the rules of play, or by the multitude of restrictions on what players can do during the course of play. Under Monopoly's restrictions, players can move only along prescribed paths, in accordance with counts of spaces from throws of the dice. Players must also buy (imagined) locations and houses at set prices and must use only their initial cash allotments and winnings to make purchases and pay fines. Players are expressly prohibited from using their own real money to make property and house purchases, and they can't use their own real money to enlist the cooperation of other players or to bribe the designated "banker" in an effort to win. We can only surmise that the makers of Monopoly ruled out the use of side payments in real money because that restriction enhanced the then perceived value of the game to potential players, with some (but clearly not all) of the added utility from the restrictions imposed on the play of the game being transferred to Parker Brothers, the game's producer, via a higher price for the game than otherwise. Everyone— players and owners alike—can be happier because of the highly detailed restrictions than they would otherwise be.

By their nature, field games (football and basketball, to name two) are much like board games, given that to be operational and to give value to the physical components of the game, they require rules that amount to restrictions on players' competitive impulses. Rules that require athletes to be students, and to maintain at least limited academic standards, share a common purpose with restrictions on the size of the playing field: Both sets of restrictions define the nature of the game that is to be played. Similarly, rules prohibiting college and university payments to athletes may be seen as materially the same as rules against changing the goal line or allowing for payments (or bribes) to referees intended to affect their calls during the game. Again, restrictions on payments of many kinds may be useful devices for increasing the perceived value of play, as well as increasing the extent to which competitive energies are directed toward improving player skills and the quality of competitive play.

In our view, the cartel case against the NCAA employment restrictions falters for a simple reason: The critics do not understand that the advocates and supporters of NCAA employment rules want to define the way they want the game played. The critics seem to want to play another game, which some might see as totally different from the one that the NCAA members (and a substantial majority of their various constituencies) want to play.

If the critics want to see their proposed games played—defined, in part, by allowing free-market payments to athletes and few or no academic restrictions on athletes—then by all means they should take the risks of developing such games. They really should not fall back on supposed problems of the lumpiness of organizational costs or on what amount to network effects, which are no less than natural costs many budding industries have to overcome. The critics should identify legal, externally imposed restrictions that would prevent the critics and others from developing alternative forms of play that they obviously dream of experiencing firsthand. If they are unwilling to incur the organization and lobbying costs of changing the constricting legal structure, then at least they could apprise us of exactly what legal or policy changes need to be made. Pointing to the absence of antitrust enforcement in college and university athletic markets is not sufficient for two reasons.

- First, critics of the NCAA are often critics of antitrust laws and have, at times, recommended their abandonment because their enforcement history is replete with instances of gross misuse.
- Second, as we will show, the courts have repeatedly refused to apply antitrust laws to college and university sports for very good reasons.

COLLEGE ATHLETICS AS AN OPEN MARKET:
A REVIEW OF THE LEGAL LITERATURE

Critics of the NCAA find it mysterious that the "NCAA can so successfully thumb its nose at the Sherman and Clayton acts . . . especially when one considers that the victims of this exploitation are predominately black" (McCormick and Meiners 1987, 235). The answer to their perplexity is not mysterious at all. Indeed, the answer is very clear. A review of antitrust law and attendant court decisions supports our central thesis that the NCAA acts not as a restrictive, welfare-destroying cartel but as a demand-enhancing joint venture that dominates college sports because of the mutual benefits it provides its members. Court rulings on collegiate athletic restrictions not only are compatible with our view of the function and purposes of the restrictions but also indicate that no legal barriers exist in antitrust or other areas of law to prevent entry of rival leagues, conferences, or associations of leagues and conferences. That colleges voluntarily enter conferences and join the NCAA as member colleges for the purpose of producing an entertainment product of a given kind and quality through joint control and regulation is evidenced by experience and legal approval (one of several points that judges have seen but that have been lost on the NCAA's critics who, held captive by their static models, fail to see that *restrictions* in themselves can be demand enhancing and that the demand increase can lead to welfare gains that overwhelm any deadweight loss embodied in a failure to achieve the competitive ideal).

The fact that colleges join the NCAA or combine in conferences to implement rules and regulations governing the production and marketing of college sports does not make the colleges per se "competitors in any economic sense," even though they "compete on the playing field."[40] Without cooperation and regulation, college sports might not exist at all or would not be as healthy an enterprise as it is. The courts have recognized that joint action is a precondition to the existence and success of the product, if for no other reason than that athletic games (e.g., football and basketball) require rules that define the boundaries within which competition will be allowed to prevail and that make the game interesting and mutually beneficial to the participants and fans.[41] The fact that restrictions on players are needed may only prove the existence of ancillary or incidental restraints necessary for the success of the joint venture.[42] Antitrust law has long sanctioned restraints that are ancillary or incidental to otherwise lawful combinations.

The ancillary restraint doctrine was established as early as 1898 as an accepted American rule of interpretation of the Sherman Act.[43] In *U.S. v. Addyston Pipe & Steel Co.*,[44] Judge Taft held that a contract or combination that produces an ancillary restraint is nevertheless reasonable and lawful as long as the main purpose of the contract, transaction, or combination is lawful and the restraint is limited in time, place, and manner of enforcement. The underlying rationale of the ancillary restraint doctrine is based on the premise that the incidental restraint enhances the efficiency of the main agreement (Bork 1978, 26–30). Throughout the history of the Sherman Act, the doctrine has enjoyed wide application and acceptance, including the sports market.

In *Smith v. Pro Football, Inc.*,[45] the District of Columbia Circuit applied the doctrine to its initial analysis of the National Football League (NFL) regulation of the player "draft." The court recognized that the NFL was a legal combination in the traditional antitrust sense. Joint cooperation was essential for the production of professional football. Normal market forces did not operate in the sports market because teams and leagues were not "interested in driving [other teams] out of business, whether in the counting-house or on the football field, for if the league fails, no one team can survive."[46] The joint venture produced a new product; it also produced restrictions on the actions of members of the league and players. A rule of reason was used to judge the legality of the regulations necessitated by joint venture.[47] Critical to the court's analysis was the characterization that sports leagues operate as joint ventures with the purpose of producing new products and increasing demand, not as a cartel that restricts output or supply.[48] The joint venture analysis of *Smith* was followed in the mid-1980s when the Supreme Court considered the restrictions of the NCAA on college sports.

In *NCAA v. Board of Regents*,[49] the Supreme Court, in a broad and sweeping decision, recognized the important role the NCAA plays in regulating collegiate sports.[50] Specifically noting the NCAA's regulation of "standards of amateurism, standards of academic eligibility, regulations concerning recruitment of athletes, and rules governing the size of the athletic squads and coaching staffs,"[51] the Court ruled that the NCAA is an association of colleges that compete against each other for athletes, fans, and television revenues.[52] But the Court was candid in recognizing that college sports is an "industry in which horizontal restraints on competition are essential if the product is to be available at all."[53] Quoting former appeals court judge Robert Bork, the Court said, "Some activities can only be carried out jointly."[54] The product marketed is "competition itself—contests between competing institutions."[55] Finding that incidental restraints are essential for the production and success of the product, the Court reasoned (showing a level of analytics about markets that is, in our view, more sophisticated than that of the NCAA's critics),

> Of course, this would be completely ineffective if there were no rules on which the competitors agreed to create and define the competition to be marketed. A myriad of rules affecting such matters as the size of the field, the number of players on a team, and the extent to which physical violence is to be encouraged or proscribed, all must be agreed upon, and all restrain the manner in which institutions compete.[56]

On college football, the Court was specific in approving the nontelevision regulations of the sport. The regulations enhance consumer demand and choice, including the choices available to athletes.[57] Because college football is a part of the academic tradition, the Court found that ancillary restraints produced by the NCAA joint venture are essential "in order to preserve the character and quality of the product."[58] Absent mutual agreement by colleges on the regulation, the "integrity" of the product would be compromised and "might otherwise be unavailable."[59]

The Court concluded that the integration produced by the NCAA joint venture, while placing some limited restraints on colleges and athletes, actually promotes increased competition and output by producing a product distinguished from other sports (professional) entertainment. The result enhances consumer and athlete choices. On balance, the joint venture's nontelevision regulation increases competitiveness. The restraints, which maintain the "competitive balance among amateur athletic teams,"[60] are a "justifiable means of fostering competition among amateur athletic teams and are therefore procompetitive because they enhance public interest in intercollegiate athletics."[61]

At bottom, the Supreme Court sanctioned many nontelevision regulations issued by the NCAA. Because the Court found that the "preservation of the student-athlete in higher education adds richness and diversity to intercollegiate athletics,"[62] it was willing to give the NCAA "ample latitude to play that role," a role "entirely consistent with the goals of the Sherman Act."[63] This conclusion was premised on the Court's implicit finding that amateurism and education are components of a market product, the promotion of which is procompetitive.[64] As long as the NCAA regulations have the design and the effect of enhancing the market product and preserving sports amateurism and education, they will receive favorable reviews from the Supreme Court.[65] Since *NCAA*, the antitrust outcome centers on the restraints' effect on output *and* consumer demand and preference (which, in our view, is how economists ought to always consider matters of monopoly).[66]

The review of legal cases presented here is not intended to suggest that the NCAA does not have some modicum of market power or that market power is a precondition to liability under section 1 of the Sherman Act. The Court in *NCAA* answered each of these concerns. First, the Court found that the NCAA does have market power in the regulation of television contracts.[67] Second, the Court explicitly said that market power is not a prerequisite for liability under a section 1 charge,[68] as is required under a section 2 claim. Although the Court did not decide whether the NCAA has market power over nontelevision aspects of the sports regulation, for our purposes the issue need not be debated. Even if the NCAA has monopsony power, which is debatable in markets for athletes, monopsony power alone is not illegal. The question is whether that power is exercised and, if so, whether the result is a predatory or exclusionary practice—one that deters entry of a potential competitor by raising the costs of entry, or one that discourages existing rivals from increasing output.[69] The focus is on whether the monopsony conduct is designed to destroy or smother competition. The exercise of monopsony power does not refer to monopsonistic pricing in the absence of entry barriers, but to the creation or preservation of market power by means that are anticompetitive (Sullivan and Hovenkamp 1984, 455).[70] On this point, the Supreme Court decision in *NCAA* is clear.

Again, the Court in *NCAA* recognized that certain market products cannot be produced without cooperation between competitors (Sullivan 1984; Easterbrook 1984). Specifically, the NCAA's nontelevision regulations over college sports were held to be lawful because they enhance output by increasing consumer *and* athlete demand.[71] Contrary to a finding of monopolization (e.g., market power plus exclusionary practices), the Court concluded that the NCAA's nontelevision regulations are ancillary but essential restraints that actually promote and more evenly distribute the market product of sports competition.

Implicit in this analysis is the finding that the NCAA did not act to reduce output or earn monopoly profits as is the case with a traditional cartel or single-firm monopolist. Indeed, the creation and success of the rival CFA, which has the purpose of promoting the interest of major football colleges,[72] belies the notion that the NCAA's conduct increased the cost or deferred the entry of a rival competitor. The nontelevision means used to achieve the integration of the NCAA's joint venture produced efficiencies, not anticompetitive consequences, through reduction of transaction costs. The result was an increased demand for amateur sports. As with other joint venture agreements, member colleges in the NCAA or CFA are able to obtain certain economies through lower costs that benefit not only the participating colleges but also consumers and athletes (Hovenkamp 1985, 111–13).[73] The result is the creation of a new product market.[74]

This same economic approach used in *NCAA* is evident as well in following Supreme Court antitrust jurisprudence. The one recurring theme is that economic efficiency is a valid business justification for conduct engaged in by a monopolist or joint venturers (Sullivan and Hovenkamp 1984).[75] During the same Court term in which *NCAA* was decided, the Court recognized in *Copperweld Corp. v. Independence Tube Corp.*[76] that integration and collective cooperation among related firms can produce efficiencies. Addressing the issue of whether a parent corporation and its wholly owned subsidiary would "conspire" within the meaning of the Sherman Act, Chief Justice Burger reasoned that

> Coordination within a firm is as likely to result from an effort to compete as from an effort to stifle competition. In the marketplace, such coordination may be necessary if a business enterprise is to compete effectively. . . . [To deny this reality] would serve no useful antitrust purpose but could well deprive consumers of the efficiencies.[77]

In *Northwest Wholesale Stationers, Inc. v. Pacific Stationery and Printing Co.*,[78] the Court unanimously ruled that per se illegality does not result from a horizontal concerted refusal to deal unless the defendant "possesses market power or exclusive access to an element essential to effective competition."[79] This relaxed standard of analysis was accepted in spite of a longstanding per se rule of illegality for horizontal concerted refusals to deal or group boycotts.[80] The justification for the changed legal standard was again an efficiency rationale— that the challenged practice might "enhance overall efficiency and make markets more competitive."[81] Speaking for the Court, Justice Brennan observed,

> Not every cooperative activity involving a restraint or exclusion will share . . . the likelihood of predominantly anticompetitive consequences. . . . Cooperative arrangements [may] seem to be "designed to increase economic efficiency and render markets more, rather than less, competitive." The [purchasing cooperative] arrangement permits the participating retailers to achieve economies of scale in both the purchase and warehousing of wholesale supplies, and also ensures ready access to a stock of goods that might otherwise be unavailable on short notice. The cost savings and order-filling guarantees enable smaller retailers to reduce prices and maintain their retail stock so as to compete more effectively with larger retailers.[82]

Finally, in *Aspen Skiing Co. v. Aspen Highlands Skiing Corp.*,[83] which was at the time (1985) the first monopolization case decided by the Court in nearly twenty years, the Court said a monopolist has "no general duty" to deal with a competitor. The right is not unqualified, however. As long as the conduct is not predatory or exclusionary, the monopolist can compete vigorously on the merits.[84] But the monopolist cannot deliberately refuse to deal with a competitor, whom it has dealt with before, when that refusal would change the "character of the market" and hurt the competitor and consumer, in the absence of an efficiency justification.[85]

In *Aspen Skiing*, the Court ruled against the monopolist because it failed to offer any business justification for the refusal to deal. From the lack of an efficiency defense, the Court concluded that the defendant had decided to forgo short-run profit for the long-run effect of weakening competition.[86] In characterizing the conduct, the Court decided, "If a firm has been 'attempting to exclude rivals on some basis other than efficiency,' it is fair to characterize its behavior as predatory."[87] Thus, it is clear from *Aspen Skiing* that had the monopolist engaged in the restraint for the purpose of promoting efficiency (reducing long-run costs, thereby increasing demand for the product), the Court might well have deemed the refusal to deal lawful.

Read together, *Copperweld, Northwest Wholesale Stationers*, and *Aspen Skiing* serve as authority for recognizing cooperation and integration as means of achieving cost-reducing efficiency objectives. Unlike raw cartels or single-firm monopolists, partially integrated associations, such as the NCAA joint venture, can increase output and consumer demand. The Court in *NCAA* found no less. Economic efficiency is sanctioned under the current antitrust laws, even when advanced by a horizontal agreement or a monopolist. Consequently, the NCAA's nontelevision regulations are inapposite to the traditional cartel goal of reducing output and increasing price. Allocative efficiency is promoted and, as the Supreme Court has held, the predisposing characteristics of cartelization are not present in the NCAA nontelevision regulations.

In short, legal barriers do not prevent the continuation of the present NCAA regulations or alternative competing leagues or associations from continuing or entering the market to compete against the NCAA for production and marketing of college sports. The emergence and presence of the CFA (or, for that matter, the National Association of Independent Colleges or the NLCAA) are substantial evidence of a lack of barriers to entry.[88] The current state of antitrust law encourages robust competition on the merits through efficiency-enhancing conduct. The present NCAA and CFA regulations are paradigms of this type of competition.

CONCLUDING COMMENTS

Our analysis leads inexorably to the conclusion that the conventional economic wisdom regarding the intent and consequences of NCAA restrictions on the recruitment and retention of athletes is hardly as solid, on conceptual grounds, as the NCAA critics assert, often without citing relevant court cases. We have argued that the conventional wisdom is wrong in suggesting that, as a general proposition,

- college athletes are materially "underpaid" and are "exploited";
- cheating on NCAA rules is prima facie evidence of a cartel intending to restrict employment and suppress athletes' wages;
- NCAA rules violate conventional antitrust doctrine;
- barriers to entry ensure the continuance of the NCAA's monopsony powers over athletes.

No such entry barriers (other than normal organizational costs, which need to be covered to meet any known efficiency test for new entrants) exist. In addition, the Supreme Court's decision in *NCAA* indicates that the NCAA would be unable to prevent through the courts the emergence of competing athletic associations. The actual existence of other athletic associations indicates that entry would be not only possible but also practical if athletes' wages were materially suppressed.

Conventional economic analysis of NCAA rules that we have challenged also is misleading in suggesting that collegiate sports would necessarily be improved if the NCAA were denied the authority to regulate the payment of athletes. Given the absence of legal barriers to entry into the athletic association market, it appears that if athletes' wages were materially suppressed (or as grossly suppressed as the critics claim), alternative sports associations would form or expand, and the NCAA would be unable to maintain its presumed monopsony market position. The incentive for colleges and universities to break with the NCAA would be overwhelming.

From our interpretation of NCAA rules, it does not follow necessarily that athletes should not receive any more compensation than they do currently. Clearly, market conditions change, and NCAA rules often must be adjusted to accommodate those changes.[89] In the absence of entry barriers, we can expect the NCAA to adjust, as it has adjusted, in a competitive manner its rules of play, recruitment, and retention of athletes (Farrell 1985, 29–32). Our central point is that contrary to the proponents of the monopsony thesis, the collegiate athletic market is subject to the self-correcting mechanism of market pressures. We have reason to believe that the proposed extension of the antitrust enforcement to the NCAA rules or proposed changes in sports law explicitly or implicitly recommended by the proponents of the cartel thesis would be not only unnecessary but also counterproductive.

Chapter 9

Monopoly as Entrepreneurship

Entrepreneurship plays an honorable, indispensable role in the evolution of market economies. It is the creative force that leads to the identification and development—through inventions and discoveries—of new products, improvements in old products, and the creation of new production technologies and refinements of old ones. The entrepreneur energizes the creative—and destructive—forces of markets by discovering profitable opportunities and then by taking advantage of those opportunities and/or by finding ways of motivating others to do so.

In this chapter, we suggest that one unrecognized reason monopolies are looked upon with disrepute among economists is that their economic models are empty of any role for entrepreneurship. In economists' models, monopolies are seen solely as static constrictors of production of already identified goods that, when the analysis is undertaken, have a fully developed market and cost structure (as represented by the demand and cost curves in graphical presentations). With such a single-purpose role, monopolies have no prior claim to any of the surplus value consumers receive from the goods and services that the monopolies produce. Hence, any consumer surplus the monopolist takes in the form of economic profits can, understandably, be disparaged as a form of unearned rent or, worse yet, as a form of theft. Any welfare loss that is destroyed in the process is viewed as worse than theft, on par with a burglar burning down the burglarized residence and running from the crime scene with the stolen loot.

We strive in this chapter to drive home three central points.

- First, monopolists as entrepreneurs have a claim on a portion of consumers' surplus value, given that they as entrepreneurs were responsible for the realization, if not the creation, of much of that surplus value.
- Second, entrepreneurs can be expected to seek out markets where

monopoly rents are a real possibility. This means that they will seek to develop goods and services in markets in which they have some realistic chance of earning supranormal profits, which in turn entails the prospect of being protected for a time by entry barriers that either exist in the nature of the markets or that the entrepreneurs can create.

- Third, instead of destroying value, given our take on monopolies, entry barriers are a source of added value, mainly because of their impact on monopoly rents and, concomitantly, entrepreneurial alertness. Hence, the creation of entry barriers can, once again, best be seen as part and parcel of the entrepreneurial process, as well as integral components (such as the color or accompanying features) of the goods and services that are produced.

We do not mean to suggest that all entry barriers and the monopolies they protect can be construed as welfare enhancing and hence can be judged as "good." We mean only to fortify with new twists a recurring theme of the book, which is that monopolies and their entry barriers are not all "bad" and that maximum economic advancement can be achieved only with some level of monopoly power evident in some markets within an economy.

THE ENTREPRENEURIAL ROLE IN FIRMS AND MARKETS

Economists Israel Kirzner (1973) and William Baumol (1968, 2002) see entrepreneurship as a category of human endeavor that stands apart from the important task of economizing—using given, known means of productions to maximize given, known ends. Entrepreneurship also stands apart from the actual exploitation of identified profitable opportunities. In its pure form, entrepreneurship is human action defined, according to Kirzner, by *alertness* to the existence of profitable opportunities: "Entrepreneurship does not consist of grasping a free ten-dollar bill which one has already discovered to be resting in one's hand; it consists in realizing that it [the ten-dollar bill] is in one's hand and that it is available for the grasping" (1973, 47).

This entrepreneurial process, in other words, has nothing to do with actually *making* a profit, which implies (given the use of "making") that costs must be incurred at some level. Rather, "the pure entrepreneur . . . proceeds by his alertness to discover and exploit situations in which he is able to sell for high prices that which he can buy for low prices. . . . The discovery of a profit opportunity *means the discovery of something obtainable for nothing at all*. No investment at all is required; the free ten-dollar bill is discovered to be already within one's grasp" (Kirzner 1973, 48; emphasis in the original).[1]

Similarly, Baumol argues that the entrepreneur's "job is to locate new ideas and to put them into effect. He must lead, perhaps even inspire; he cannot allow things to get into a rut and for him today's practice is never good enough for tomorrow. He is the individual who exercises what in the business literature is called 'leadership.' And it is he who is virtually absent from the received theory of the firm" (1968, 65).[2]

We like Kirzner's and Baumol's characterizations of the "pure entrepreneur," given that "alertness" (which is explicit in the Kirzner quote and implied in the Baumol quote) is an unheralded component of successful market processes. Without doubt, a whole subdiscipline could be developed around the factors that give rise to "alertness," and we don't propose to develop that subdiscipline here. However, it needs to be noted that real-world entrepreneurs, as distinct from pure ones, invariably do more than simply stand alert to profitable opportunities. They typically act on their discoveries, becoming investors and organizers of much new and improved economic activity. If real-world entrepreneurs didn't do more than remain alert to profitable opportunities, little new would get done. Their alertness would go nowhere but would remain a strictly mental phenomenon. Also, we clearly see that much real-world entrepreneurship is not as free as Kirzner's pure form (if not Baumol's also). Real-world entrepreneurship involves costs, mainly because alertness requires some devotion to task. It requires readiness to find and to act upon findings. And given the sophistication of modern goods and services, alertness must go hand in hand with investigations that can involve varying amounts of resources, including hard work on the part of entrepreneurs. An entrepreneur can't expect to stand idly by waiting for the concept of, for example, the integrated circuit or the plot for a best-selling novel to appear as if by magic. Some good ideas might come as flashes of insight, but that is hardly the case for most. That is to say, most entrepreneurs must work at being prepared to *see* or *realize* the opportunities that present themselves.

Alexander Fleming discovered, somewhat serendipitously, how a green mold, *Penicillium notatum*, could kill many bacteria that infect humans, but in making his discovery, he was clearly hard at work on another goal. Even then, it was left to others—Howard Florey and Ernst Chain, who were searching for ways to reduce battlefield infections in wounded soldiers—to recognize more than a decade later the medical value (and profit potential) of Fleming's discovery. Similarly, Xerox pioneered the development of the graphical user interface (GUI) for computer screens and the computer mouse. Xerox was alert to the GUI and mouse, or else these concepts would never have been made operational in the Xerox lab, but the "entrepreneurs" (if they can be called that) at Xerox did nothing with the company's inventions. It was left to

Steve Jobs and Stephen Wozniak to see how these technologies could be incorporated in personal computers and then make use of them. Without any doubt penicillin, the look and feel of our computer screens, and the way we navigate the Web owe their existence to entrepreneurial alertness, but Fleming, Florey, Chain, Jobs, and Wozniak were all working at being alert, or so it seems to us. Their alertness went beyond awareness. They stood ready to move resources (or move others to move resources for them).

Nevertheless, no matter exactly how entrepreneurship and entrepreneurs are perceived in their details, Baumol is right: Those constructs play little or no role in conventional microeconomic models. This is true largely because the products and production processes in those models are assumed to exist and because any improvements in products and technologies that are conceivable are assumed to already be conceived and adopted by producers in the identified markets. Microeconomic theory starts, in other words, with tenets that effectively assume away a great deal about what happens in market processes (which is why "price theory" is a more appropriate characterization of the models' intended use, to explain in large measure how prices are determined within different market structures). Those tenets unavoidably assume away any identifiable role for "entrepreneurs" that is functionally independent of resource owners, leaving the models' embedded actors (to the extent that there are any) solely concerned with a more mundane or uninspired single function, to maximize the production of *given* goods with *given* resources (Baumol 1968; Kirzner 1973, chap. 2). The analysis is thereby restricted to the problem of resource allocation to a narrow range of all that real-world firms do with the resources they marshal.[3]

Under perfect competition, individual competitors have no real choice about anything, not even about the prices they charge. We say that because perfect competitors *must* adopt the market price and respond to it in their production decisions, as if by rote, or be driven out of the market (Buchanan 1964). Absolutely no room exists in this model for error on any matter. But then, firm failures in such models are of no consequence to anything, because of the presumed costless fluidity of resources. In such a world, firms can't really fail, given that they can move their resources instantaneously, once the prospects of losses are detected, and can do so at zero cost. They always earn their opportunity costs, including normal profits by virtue of the ease of resource movement.

Under pure monopoly, the entrepreneurial function is limited (if it has any function at all) solely to that of "choosing" the price and output combination along its given market demand curve and is constrained by its given marginal cost function, with the curve being set by known production technologies (and with the monopolist's marginal cost curve assumed to be identical with the market supply curve of perfect competition).[4] We put "choosing" in quotation marks because price and output choices are actually dictated by the assumption of profit maximization, which eliminates all degrees of freedom, a point stressed by Buchanan (1964). The redeeming, albeit limited, value of the standard analytics is that the structure of the logic followed by the monopolist (or perfect competitor) in achieving profit maximization—weighing revenues and cost at the margin—can be inferred. This inferred logic of profit maximization can (possibly) inform real-world entrepreneurs who have a far more complex role than simply setting their production and price levels and who are not so constricted by the dictates of competition and profit maximization that the prospect of meaningful freedom is nonexistent—meaning that the profit-maximizing rule is not imposed on them.

When economists step outside of their formal modeling, they undoubtedly appreciate the role of the entrepreneur and entrepreneurship. After all, goods and services, which are sources of consumer value, don't descend as if from heaven for consumers to gather at will. Without entrepreneurs, goods and services would never be produced and distributed widely. Markets might operate efficiently, given the presence of people who could make optimal use of resources within the constraints of the available goods and services, resources, and technologies. But no room would exist for improvement beyond the status quo. We can't help but think that such a world would be dreadful because it would be hopelessly stuck in time.

MONOPOLY RENTS AS ENTREPRENEURIAL ENTITLEMENT

Entrepreneurs hold an honored role in economies because they do what consumers want and, presumably, can't do for themselves as cost effectively. The entrepreneurs identify, develop, produce, and distribute new goods and services that have value. At the same time, because new goods and services do not, by definition, initially have competitors, entrepreneurs who do create new goods are quickly chastised by economists for not doing *all* that consumers would like—expanding output to the competitive ideal level—a perspective that seems to be lacking completely in appreciation and gratitude for what has been done.

However, we don't treat all entrepreneurs the same. Consider, for example, artists (or composers and musicians) and manufacturers. Surely no one would fault Rembrandt and Picasso for what they accomplished as artists, mainly because these two artists imagined new and very great paintings and then brought them into existence. And their paintings have given people immense value for many years. Just as surely no one—not even their critics *or* economists—would now think to fault Rembrandt and Picasso for not having produced more paintings than they did during their lifetimes. This is the case in spite of the fact that Rembrandt and Picasso could have given more people more pleasure (surplus value) had they not restricted their painting (had they worked more of their waking hours than they did and sold the paintings that they completed at lower prices). We submit that few would find fault with Rembrandt and Picasso even if it were shown conclusively that they actively operated as the monopolists that they were, restricting their work (or just sales) to maximize (albeit imperfectly, but as best they could) their monopoly rents during the course of their lifetimes.

Indeed, to one extent or another, all highly creative people are monopolists. And we might stress that Rembrandt and Picasso didn't just happen to be monopolists (on par with monopolists who happen to exist within economists' models). They no doubt committed themselves early in their lives to becoming that which they became, exceptionally good artists who, because of the high quality of their works, achieved monopoly status, that is, control over market supply and, therefore, price. In short, they entrepreneured their respective monopoly market positions for their times. Should they not have had some legitimate claim on the consumer gains that could have been expected to flow from their monopoly-given work during their lifetimes? Of course they should.

But then, Rembrandt and Picasso are hardly in a league without equals through the ages. Art history books are replete with artists in a variety of fields who were monopolists for their times because they worked for what they became. Is the world a worse place today because so many artists intentionally worked to achieve a position of monopoly power? Could the world have been a better place had these artists been prevented from seeking and then garnering the rewards from their monopoly positions? Hardly not.

In more contemporary times, of the top-selling fifteen books published in the 1980s, twelve of them—representing an 80 percent market share—were written by just three authors, Stephen King, Tom Clancy, and Danielle Steel (Cowen 1998, 53). Now, with the publication of her Harry Potter fantasy adventure series, J. K. Rowling has pushed King's, Clancy's, and Steel's combined sales into the dustbins of publishing records, given that Rowling's first six Harry Potter books sold an astounding 300 million worldwide (in 62 languages) by the end of 2006 (and the seventh and final volume in the series was released shortly before this book went to press, with sales expectations on the seventh book exceeding the sales of all previous volumes.[5] These authors were hardly immune to the constraints of competition imposed by the tens of thousands of other books (and videos and other forms of entertainment) released each year, but just as surely, some portion of their current substantial fortunes was built from the monopoly rents they collected over the years as a consequence of their privileged market positions, achieved through hard work, as well as through the development of market protections, their pen names (which marketing scholars might deem "brands" when talking about soap or what Fleisher, Goff, and Tollison [1992] have called "reputational capital" when describing the market advantage of NCAA member schools). What is truly amazing is how Rowling, the monopoly holder of the Harry Potter storytelling brand, is revered by hundreds of millions of devoted readers who are not only willing to pay prices that must include substantial monopoly profits for both her and her publisher but are willing to wait hours, sometimes in inclement weather, to buy her books when they are released at midnight. You've got to believe that most Harry Potter readers think only of their Dupuit triangles and probably have never had even a passing thought about the welfare loss that might never have been generated (even if the concept has any relevance at all to assessing human welfare from what Rowling was able, in the span of ten years, to do).

Why then don't economists view, say, manufacturing monopolies in the same positive way creative people should be and are viewed, endowed with the acknowledged *right* to collect whatever monopoly rents they can create? We suggest that the explanation has (at least) two dimensions: First, manufacturing firms are all too often used as examples in economists' monopoly models, with the result being that economists' assessments of manufacturing monopolies are warped by what Joseph Schumpeter characterized as their "original Vision," grounded in static analysis. Under economists' model of monopoly, no place exists for the kind of creativity expressed by Rembrandt, Picasso, King, Clancy, Steel, and Rowling. We submit that this vacuum derives from the *goods* and *services* in the economists' model being the *given* as a starting point for analysis. No one talks about how or why the goods and services were created, or what the world (or consumer surplus value) would have been like had the goods and services never been *given*. Such talk is not needed, because the goods and services don't need to be created. They exist by assumption. Hence, the only issue of consequence in the analytics, subject to the control of the presumed monopolist, is what is *not* done, rather than what is created and then produced. Had the analysis started *before* the goods are *given*, the judgment imposed on manufacturing monopolists might be similar to the more positive valuation of monopoly artists and writers. The value generated from the goods that are *created* would then have to be weighed against any *lost* efficiency from the monopolists not producing as much as outside observers/economists might believe they should produce to achieve some idealized construction of efficiency (which, we remind you, can never be fully achieved in real-world markets).

A second reason that monopolists among artists and writers are treated more positively by economists is that all people's assessments of what others do or don't do must, we submit, be guided by larger and more compelling values than strict static market efficiency, as conceived by economists. One such value could be the *justice* of people's claims to streams of income or consumer surplus. And the justice of any person's claim to an income stream must be informed by the person's contribution to the generation of the income stream, a perspective adopted by no less than Adam Smith in his *Theory of Moral Sentiments* (1759). Where there is no effect on the generation of the income stream, there is no claim to it—or so one labor-based theory of the justice of ownership (or entitlement), founded on the work of John Locke, seems to suggest. Indeed, Locke started with the proposition that "natural law" dictated that each person owns himself, including his labor. This natural law necessarily implies that anything a person creates with labor alone becomes that person's private property (because the property does nothing more, according to Locke, than capture the value of what that person already owns, his labor).[6] Indeed, Locke went on to posit that a person is entitled to the ownership of the full product of whatever a person commingles with his labor with other previously unowned resources that are also used in the production of the product. Clearly, such a labor theory of just entitlement has problems, not the least of which is, according to the late philosopher Robert Nozick, that of setting the boundary for the property one owns when one mixes his labor with a previously unowned object in the natural world: "If a private astronaut clears a place on Mars, has he mixed his labor with (so he comes to own) the whole planet? Which plot does an act bring ownership?" (1974, 174).

Nozick goes on to suggest two principles of entitlement: (1) a person is entitled to a holding as long as the person has acquired the holding in a just manner, meaning that he has not stolen it, for example; and (2) he has acquired the holding from someone else who had acquired the holding in a just manner (1974, 150–53). That is to say, a person who acquires stolen property from someone else who stole the property would not be justly entitled to the ownership of the property.

We need not digress here into a full-fledged philosophical discussion of the justice of property rights. We simply point out that people's common assessments of what artists and writers do and how they take advantage of their market positions could be, and probably is, shaped by some crude variant of Locke's labor theory of entitlement. The artists and writers we identified clearly created (to the best of our knowledge) what they produced, both in concept and physical output. Had they not created what they did—had they not actually done the work on the paintings and books but instead had stolen them or had them fall like manna from heaven into their workplaces—the justice of their ownership claims to their holdings, including their works' future income streams, could and would surely be disputed on justice grounds, no matter what the assessed efficiency of the resulting market outcomes. But in some meaningful sense, from what we know, the artists and writers did create their works. From all accounts, they did not steal the materials they used, did not enslave anyone to get the paintings and books they produced, and did not buy the works they claimed as their own from known thieves. Their realized rewards for any given pieces were simply the incentive they imagined before they started work and provided incentive for their continued work.

The artists and writers acquired their works in accordance with what Nozick calls the "principle of justice in acquisition" and the "principle of justice in transfer." Accordingly, they possessed a just claim to exploit, if not all their future income stream—monopoly rents included—then surely a portion of it that goes beyond "normal profits." Indeed, most people would have no problem with the concept of the artists and writers receiving as much as possible of the resulting surplus value. The same can be said for the consumers. Indeed, the surplus value can be expected to be divided in whatever way the buyers and sellers can negotiate, as long as the negotiations themselves are done fairly, that is, in accordance with preconceived rules of exchange.

By way of contrast, monopolies of the abstract, textbook variety—not the usual kind in the real workaday world—have no such prior justification for a claim to the surplus value because they did not, within the restricted confines of formal models, create the goods and services subject to analysis. Those goods, to repeat for emphasis, are *given*, which means they are born devoid of any hint of prior claims of creation. The goods' producers simply make the decisions on how much of the *given* good should be produced and what price should be charged to maximize economic or monopoly rents. Under such analytics, the monopolist has no prior claim to the surplus value, but neither do consumers. Indeed, the legitimacy of any claim to the surplus value is left up in the air, unsettled in such models, which is why any economic rent garnered by the monopolist is treated by economists in their lectures as nothing more, nor less, than a redistribution of income with no negative welfare connotation (supposedly) imputed to the process.

However, matters are radically different, or should be, when the monopolist actually creates the good (or service) over which it has production control. This is true because a prior claim then exists to the surplus value, just as Picasso and Rowling have had claims to the surplus values of what they created. The argument can surely be made in this case that the product might not have been produced had the monopolist not been able to claim at least a portion, if not all, of the potential surplus value, which means some of the net gains from trade. In a world replete with failures, we remind you that it is hard to say whether "large monopoly profits" extracted on identified goods occur because of a firm's mere size or because of how much consumer surplus is left for consumers. This is the case because the critical concern to the monopolist-qua-entrepreneur is how much profit is made across an array of goods, some of which will likely be total market flops. When the good or service is *given*, any prior claim to the surplus value across an array of given goods is, we repeat, devoid of such justification.

The great redeeming value of markets, heralded since the days of Adam Smith, has been that welfare improvement emerges from mutually beneficial exchanges. What is peculiar about the way microeconomics is traditionally taught is how professors so often start their courses with David Ricardo's great demonstration, that there are mutual advantages from trades, resulting necessarily in an increase in aggregate income for the traders, even when one trader is absolutely more productive in all goods than all other traders. Gains can always emerge, students are shown, when trade occurs in line with the "law of comparative advantage." Indeed, in such demonstrations the increase in aggregate income cannot occur without trade being *mutually* beneficial, meaning the gains are truly greater than mere costs. However, as the course proceeds, professors eventually explain how the most efficient market structure conceivable—perfect competition, made up of numerous identical firms as well as numerous consumers—is one in which the gains are not *mutual* at all. Consumers get all the true net gains from the trades—that is, all the consumer surplus. Producers receive nothing other than coverage of their opportunity costs, which is no real gain in terms of what else could have been done.[7] This is truly an odd, and we believe ethically dubious, outcome when in fact the producers create the goods and then develop their markets from scratch while consumers have absolutely nothing to do with the creation and production of the goods they buy. The consumers' only contribution to the exchange process is the expression of their preferences for the goods they buy (and in real-world markets, even then the producers may have been responsible for stimulating, if not creating, consumer demand).

When microeconomics courses take up the issue of monopoly, they acknowledge what are clearly the mutual gains—consumers get some portion of the surplus value in the form of consumer surplus, the Dupuit triangle, while the monopolist receives some of the surplus value in the form of economic rents. But then while the gains of consumers are rarely noted, much less heralded, the gains going to the monopolist are everywhere condemned for the deadweight loss that results, as well as for their distorting influence on the income distribution. (And as we noted in an earlier chapter, consumers are never condemned for *not* paying the monopolist to extend its production.) Surely one can argue that the dictates of mutual gains from trades mitigate against the producers getting *all* the consumer surplus value from exchanges, but just as surely, those same dictates suggest to us (and to Schumpeter) that the producers have a claim to at least a portion of that which they created, especially if trades are expected to occur systematically. The producers' claim mandates, in our view, both the realization of monopoly rents for a time, as well as some (unspecified) degree of entry barriers for some (unspecified) time in order for the economic rents to emerge.

THE JUSTICE OF ENTRY BARRIERS RECONSIDERED

In standard textbook treatments of monopoly, entry barriers are, like the goods and services they protect, often assumed into existence, which means that they are not the consequence of anything producers do. Entry barriers are also independent of the goods and services they protect, are not in any way a source of independent value, and do not add value to the goods and services they protect. Entry barriers (other than copyrights and patents) have no socially redeeming purpose, according to the economists' model.

In addition, the privileged market position of standard textbook monopolies is often tainted by how the protective entry barriers arise. All too often, the entry barriers are assumed into existence, said to be "natural," or are a consequence of happenstance or of exclusive ownership of some strategically important resource. Worse yet, the entry barriers are assumed to be ordained, enforced, and maintained by the government. In such cases, the acquired economic rents in themselves may not be viewed as a market curse, but they surely cannot be seen as anything approaching just entitlement, given any reasonable and defensible philosophical foundation, such as the ones articulated by Locke or Nozick. As with income from land, the monopoly rents that "just happen" because of the fortuitous circumstances of nature can justifiably be viewed as the equivalent of pure rent on land, that is, as being unearned and with no trace of a claim of entitlement that is clearly above anyone else's claim. They can also be taxed away without damage to the allocation of resources or to anyone's sense of entitlement. When the monopoly rents are the consequence of entry barriers that the government (meaning politicians) erects in response to interest groups' rent-seeking payoffs, the monopoly rents can be construed as a form of theft, potentially no less destructive to social welfare than common burglaries and muggings, and violating Nozick's principles of justice in acquisition and transfer as well as an array of less sophisticated, commonsense understandings of entitlement.

However, there is no reason that such assumptions regarding the origins of entry barriers need be descriptive of *all* real-world markets. Indeed, we note that property rights in general often carry with them embedded entry barriers, and we hasten to add that economists sing the praises of how property rights contribute to economic efficiency by staving off "tragedies of the commons."

Patents and copyrights, which are nothing other than (limited) entry barriers, also represent a politically endorsed, contrary view of entry barriers. These legally established entry barriers provide their holders with some limited degree of monopoly power because they can add to the array of protected goods as well as add value to the individual goods produced. They do so because patents and copyrights provide people (producers) with an incentive to produce additional goods and services that might not otherwise be produced at all or, if produced, would be produced in lower quantities. These entry barriers also add value directly to the goods themselves because they give entrepreneurs an enhanced incentive to develop the qualities of their products by more than would otherwise be the case.[8]

When patent and copyright protections are achievable, we should expect, and do find, entrepreneurs seeking to obtain them, often at a modest cost in the case of copyrights but, at times, at considerable cost in the case of patents. This observation leads to a more general conclusion, which is that entrepreneurs should see other forms of entry barriers as part and parcel of the developmental process of the goods and services. Entrepreneurs can be expected to devote resources to the development of entry barriers at the same time that they develop the other various attributes of their products. How many resources they invest directly in the development of their products will, of course, depend upon the expected payoff. However, it needs to be stressed that the products' expected payoff is functionally related to how protective the entry barriers that are also under development can be expected to be, as well as to the value of the goods to consumers. It stands to reason that if entry barriers of any consequence are prohibitively expensive to develop, as is the case under perfect competition, then entrepreneurs have absolutely no reason to develop their product in the first place, because they could then expect no gain from product development. The reason for this is the unrecoverable development costs incurred on the product (and its market), as we noted earlier in the book. After the product (as well as the market for the product) is developed, other firms could enter the market and copy whatever product has been developed, thus causing the price to fall past the point at which the original developer or producer could recover its development costs.

Hence, we are led to a more benign, if not positive, view of many (but not all) entry barriers. Just how many products are developed will be functionally related to the cost of developing entry barriers: the lower the cost of entry-barrier development, the more the product will be developed and the greater the number of products on the market. This is because the cost of setting up (and maintaining) entry barriers can affect the confidence that firms have with respect to recovering their product and market development costs (especially in industries in which the marginal cost of reproduction is very low or minimal, e.g., digital goods). Some of the growth in consumer value from enhanced goods and more goods can, as a consequence, be seen as the productive contributions of entry barriers. Hence, both consumers and producer or monopolists can gain from entry barriers (as discussed earlier).

In traditional economics, any resources that a firm devotes to the erection of barriers to entry are necessarily destructive to social welfare because they allow the protected firms to restrict production and raise the price. Deadweight loss is created in two stages: Resources are allocated away from doing productive things to producing entry barriers. Then, behind the entry barriers, the protected firms can add to the deadweight loss by curbing production. Simultaneously, a portion of the consumer surplus derived from the good is transferred from consumers to producers (which can bother those economists who believe that consumers are more deserving of the consumer surplus than are the producers).

But is it always true that resources devoted to the production of entry barriers are destructive of welfare? Consider again the case of the good with high up-front costs in the form of expenditures on product and market development and low to zero marginal cost. Legally enforced copyright protection may provide little protection from pirates who understand that they have a slim chance of being caught, prosecuted, and convicted, with the expected penalties lower than the expected rewards from piracy. Presumably, the creation, development, and production of such goods would be curbed. Suppose that the producer were to develop a computer chip (or program) that, when embedded in the product, greatly increased the cost of the good being pirated. Might not the resources devoted to the creation of the chip—an entry barrier—enhance social welfare? In such cases, the entry barriers that are created serve the same function that deadbolt locks serve on apartments and stores (which are literal entry barriers). They redirect the use of misused resources of thieves. They also encourage production of more goods in greater quantities.

Brand names—Intel, Good Housekeeping, BMW—have frequently been cited as sources of monopoly power, given that once established, they can reduce the options that consumers will consider when purchasing, increase consumer switching costs, increase the inelasticity of consumer demand, and increase the entry costs for producers. The result is that the owners of the branded products can curb production and extract monopoly rents. The same line of argument can be applied to trade secrets that can provide firms with more durable entry barriers than copyrights and patents.

We have two reasons for not accepting this line of argument. First, with the establishment of identifiable brand names that carry marketing weight, we have to think that the demands for the branded products rise, which means that consumers' surplus value can rise along with any monopoly rents and any deadweight loss, as conceived by economists. If consumers become less responsive to price increases of the branded products, we believe it commonly happens for a reason: that the brand itself, apart from the product, carries some added value in itself. Of course, the consumers might be duped by producers, a prospect that seems to be the implied claim of the critics of branding. But if they are duped, who can say definitively that consumers are worse off from buying the branded products at monopoly prices? (If the consumers can be so duped, why can't people who see brands as having little value be duped as well, not just with respect to the branded products but also to the fact that other consumers have been duped?) Whether consumers are duped or not, if producers can acquire monopoly positions by branding their products, should we not expect more producers to create more products that are branded?

MONOPOLIES, PUBLIC GOODS, AND THE
GAINS FROM PRICE DISCRIMINATION

The monopolist in the standard monopoly model does produce less than is desirable, but we have to inject a point rarely mentioned. The monopolist does so because it is creating value over and above what it can capture. In the terminology of economics, the monopolist is creating a positive externality: The price of any addition unit of output (which reflects its value) is greater than the monopolist realizes from producing it.

For all practical purposes, the monopolist is in the same position as the person who creates a beautiful flower garden in a portion of his (or her) front yard, visible to those who drive by. This gardener is creating a positive externality that is analytically equivalent to the one created by the monopolist— because the motorists who enjoy the garden don't pay anything to the gardener for their enjoyment, the gardener is creating a value that is greater than he receives. It would be desirable if the gardener expanded the garden and made it even more beautiful and visible to passing motorists, but because the motorists won't pay for the additional value they would receive, the gardener has no motivation to do so.[9] No fair-minded person would criticize the gardener for not expanding his output as much as is socially desirable. Rather, most people would praise the gardener for providing more value to others than the gardener is receiving in return.

But the same argument can be made for a monopolist. The monopolist is providing more value to others than it is receiving in return (if not on the margin, then surely inframarginally and in total), even though it is not producing as much as consumers might ideally like. Criticizing someone who is producing something consumers value because the output is not as much as people want is tantamount to the preacher criticizing his congregation for being too small.

Again, the monopolist isn't necessarily as bad as typically depicted when the textbook model of monopoly is discussed. Whether a monopolist should be praised for making consumers better off than they would otherwise be, or pilloried for not making them as well off as it could, depends on why the firm has monopoly power in the first place.

The underproduction associated with positive externalities is possible only because of transaction costs. Whether we are talking about a gardener, a painter, or a monopoly firm, no problem would exist if it were costless for people to engage in transactions (as in perfect competition). A gardener could costlessly deny the visible benefit of the garden to passing motorists unless they paid him an amount equal to the marginal benefit they derived from it. In this case, the gardener would receive the information and motivation needed to increase the size of the garden until the marginal cost of doing so equaled the marginal value created. Similarly, without transaction costs, a monopolist and its customers would costlessly exchange additional output for a payment at least equal to its marginal cost until the price (value of the marginal unit) and marginal cost were equal.

One might wonder why we are even considering such an impossible situation as zero transaction costs. Of all people, economists—folks who try to make friends at parties by pointing out that there is a cost to everything—should know that there is no such thing as a free transaction. True enough. But even though transaction costs can never be eliminated, they can be reduced, and a consideration of zero transaction costs adds to our understanding of the efficiency implications of reducing them.[10]

Clearly, the monopolist and its customers (and potential customers) would like to reduce the transaction costs of doing business with each other. The deadweight loss in the standard monopoly model is wealth being left on the table, and some of that wealth could be appropriated and distributed in a way that made some better off and no one worse off, if only the costs of negotiating agreements and enforcing those agreements could be reduced. It would be difficult, if not impossible, for consumers to reduce those costs. They are too numerous to join forces and deal with a firm with monopoly power in a unified way. Consumers could individually approach the monopolist, of course, but two problems arise with that.

- First, the product is unlikely to be one that is important enough in a consumer's budget to justify trying to deal directly with the producer rather
  than just accept the quoted price. Your favorite band has monopoly
  power, but it certainly wouldn't pay you to try negotiating directly with
  the band's recording company. You just pay the listed price for the CD
  at the local store.[11]
- Second, even if the price being charged is high enough to make it worthwhile for some customers to try negotiating directly with the producer,
  the producer is unlikely to be interested in dealing with you. The only
  reason it would pay you to deal directly with the monopolist is to negotiate a lower price. But the monopolist is selling all it wants at the prevailing price. As widely acknowledged (see chap. 6), the monopolist
  might be willing to sell another unit to you at a lower price, but only if it
  can be sure that doing so won't result in lots of other consumers
  demanding a lower price also. Coordinating the cooperation of all the
  other consumers to provide that assurance would be impossible. Even if
  it weren't, what motivation would they have to allow you and a few others to get a lower price while they had to continue paying the high
  monopoly price?

The monopolist is in the best position to take the action necessary to
retrieve some of the wealth that would otherwise be lost. In other words, the
monopolist is in the best position to reduce the transaction costs that explain
the standard monopoly result, and it has a strong motivation to do so. A
monopoly increases its profits and the welfare of consumers by lowering transaction costs and converting the deadweight loss in the standard monopoly
model into wealth that is shared with consumers. The way a monopolist can
lower transaction costs is through price discrimination—or charging a different price for different units of the same good.

In most standard discussions of price discrimination, economists typically
assume that no transaction costs are associated with price discrimination with
two (or more) different prices. But although the monopolist can effectively
reduce the transaction costs associated with capturing some of the wealth lost
in the standard monopoly model, it obviously cannot eliminate the wealth loss.
Implementing even the simple two-price price discrimination encounters nontrivial transaction cost–type problems. The first problem is determining whom
to charge the high price and whom to charge the low price. If the higher price
is imposed on consumers who don't value the product very much and the lower
price is charged those who would buy just about as much at a much higher
price, then the price discrimination could reduce rather than increase the

amount sold. But even if the monopolist targets the different prices to the right consumers, a second problem arises: preventing those paying the lower price from reselling to those being charged the higher price. If that can be achieved, then the customers paying the lower price will out-compete the monopolist for the high-price customers, and the prices in the two markets will converge, eliminating the efficiency gains from price discrimination. Therefore, the two markets have to be separated by somehow increasing the costs of transacting with each other for the customers in the low-price and high-price markets. Somewhat paradoxically, to reduce the transaction costs between the monopolist and its customers enough to make price discrimination possible, the transaction costs among the customers have to be increased.

Many good examples exist of how firms with market power engage in imperfect price discrimination, the most important feature of which is that the firm is able to *segment* its markets so that different prices can be charged and, at the same time, those who buy the good at a low price can't resell what they buy to those customers who pay the higher prices.[12] What is not often noted in discussions of examples of price discrimination is how the monopolist, being the only producer (or one of a few producers), solves the transaction-cost problems that consumers face. Put differently, the monopolist effectively does for the consumers what they would do themselves, if their costs were not so high. In so doing, the monopolist produces a public good by internalizing the (consumer-side) externalities.

It might be comforting to think that the perfectly competitive output level *could be* achieved absent any firm with market power because of entry barriers. If such an output level were achievable, then the monopolist would indeed, through price discrimination, be doing nothing more for greater society than *recovering* the wealth lost from what the monopolist fails to do. However, readers should by now see the perfectly competitive standard as a conceptual pipe dream, founded on an assumption of an idealized world in which (among other things) transaction costs are nonexistent. From the perspective of a more realistic world, one in which transaction costs abound everywhere in the market, the monopolist doesn't just *recover* otherwise lost wealth, it *creates* wealth with the various methods it devises to segment markets, to erect barriers to entry and resales, and to engage in price discrimination. It creates the added wealth by finding ways to lower transaction costs (for itself but not for consumers) below not only what they would be for consumers but also below the net potential welfare gains from expanded production.

Moreover, price-discriminating monopolists can create wealth in a largely unheralded way, through improving on any dynamic efficiency achieved from nondiscriminatory monopoly pricing. We have noted that Romer (1994) has

stressed how competitive prices can be a poor indicator of the total value consumers place on various actual or potential products. This is because competitive prices tend to reflect only the marginal cost of production, and the problem of prices being poor signals of consumer value is especially acute under
perfect competition beset with high up-front development costs and very low
(to zero) marginal production costs. Actual or prospective price discrimination, which enables producers to capture more of the consumer surplus, can be
seen as giving improved signals on where and how entrepreneurs should focus
the resources at their command, thus improving dynamic, or long-run,
efficiency.

Economists have long understood that in order for a firm to engage in
price discrimination, the firm must have some degree of market power. Otherwise, the firm could not charge some consumers higher prices. Without market protection, those consumers paying the higher prices would soon be
offered lower prices by new market entrants. We have no problem with the
direction of this line of argument. However, we do suggest that economists all
too quickly reverse the direction of the argument: Price discrimination is
prima facie evidence of monopoly power. Hence, through price discrimination, the firm is, as noted previously, doing nothing more than *recovering* the
otherwise lost wealth that would have resulted from constricted production.
Any cost incurred to enable price discrimination is then seen to fall into a different (and destructive) category from costs that are incurred in the development of new goods and services. However, we suggest a different perspective:
Coming up with wealth-creating devices to cost-effectively segment the market can require the same kind of alertness to profitable opportunities that
entrepreneurs have been heralded for having in the development of new products and services. Indeed, the development of new goods and services by firms
can be profitable to firms because they lower the costs consumers would have
to incur in order to obtain the same goods and services. We are arguing that
methods of price discrimination (such as those economists frequently cite)
require no fewer entrepreneurial skills and do the same thing—create wealth
by lowering costs.

However, we should never forget that although methods of price discrimination can cause a monopolist's rents to rise, they can also enable the monopolist to go into business in the first place and to prevent its books from being
perennially covered in red ink. Firms with high fixed costs and low marginal
costs—for example, the nation's airlines—can see price discrimination as a survival tool. Because of the threats of war and terrorism after the collapse of the
World Trade Center on September 11, 2001, combined with a weak economy
(attributable in part to the negative wealth effect associated with the collapse of

the high-tech boom), demand for air travel dropped off, causing airlines to do what comes naturally: lowering their fares to fire-sale levels and, in the process, sending several airlines either into bankruptcy or to its brink. We can only imagine that more airlines would have continued to see their capital base erode by greater amounts had they not been able to price-discriminate, that is, find creative ways of charging practically every passenger (on some flights) a different fare.

THE EFFICIENCY OF MONOPOLY FAILURES

Joseph Schumpeter made "creative destruction" a centerpiece of his theory of how markets are constantly re-creating themselves, in spite of ever-present monopoly influences.

> The opening up of new markets, foreign or domestic, and the organizational development from the craft shop to such concerns as U.S. Steel illustrate the same process of industrial mutation—if I may use that biological term—that incessantly revolutionizes the economic structure *from within*, incessantly destroying the old one, incessantly creating a new one. This process of Creative Destruction is the essential fact about capitalism. It is what capitalism consists in and what every capitalist concern has got to live in. (1942, 83; emphasis in the original)

In a footnote, Schumpeter stresses that *incessant* is not exactly the right word for describing industrial revolutions from within, because the kind of revolutions he had in mind "occur in discrete rushes which are separated from each other by spans of comparative quiet," but he also adds that there is a meaningful sense in which the revolutions are "incessant," namely, "that there always is either revolution or absorption of the results of revolution, both together forming what are known as business cycles" (1942, 83, fn. 2).[13]

We have explained why Schumpeter was for several reasons not very concerned with monopoly elements in the economy. Monopolies were a destructive force in markets because they were also creative, contributing to the ongoing revolutions through the development of new products and services and new, more cost-effective methods of production.

Economists have spilled a great deal of ink on an implication of Schumpeter's third empirically testable point, that firm size and innovation go hand in hand (chap. 1, this vol.). They have paid far less attention to his more overarching point, albeit covered in a footnote, that industrial revolutions "occur in discrete rushes which are separated from each other by spans of comparative quiet." (The development process that occurs in spurts is now cited by academics in various disciplines from science to business as "punctuated equilibria.")[14] Many economists have not noticed an inherent paradox within Schumpeter's theory of creative destruction: Large firms with the kind of market power that comes with their domination of their markets lose their market dominance or fail altogether because of new market entrants with new and improved products and production methods. This is the case in spite of the fact that new entrants are often small (by virtue of their newness and limited access to capital because they lack proven records) and in spite of the fact that the old, established firms are supposed to be leaders in innovation, or so Schumpeter presumed.

Consider a short list of the dramatic cases of large-firm failures that have either failed, had to make market retreats, or had to reinvent themselves—Woolworth, Sears, LTV, U.S. Steel, K-Mart, General Motors, Wang Computers, Montgomery Ward, Eastern Airlines—all of which once dominated their market categories and have since either gone out of business or seen their market prominence collapse.

How can one reconcile what might be dubbed the "Schumpeter paradox"? The paradox has become more perplexing with recent scholarly revelations about the fate of so-called first movers in markets and their followers. In the 1990s, many business scholars and businesspeople resurrected the often-repeated but untested article of business faith that first movers (the first persons or companies to develop product lines) in any market had strong, strategic market advantages over following rivals.[15] First movers could establish brand names and could achieve economies of scale and lower their costs from "learning by doing," thus erecting formidable demand and costs entry barriers for followers. First movers could also create network effects, which could lead to the market's tipping toward the first mover, resulting in the first mover's market dominance building on itself.[16]

However, business professors Gerald Tellis and Peter Golder (2002) found that in sixty of the sixty-six manufacturing industries they studied, the first movers had, at the time of their study in the mid-1990s, long been eclipsed by second, third, and following movers. Moreover, the first movers, if they were still in business, generally did not then hold anything more than minor shares of their markets.[17]

Wal-Mart emerged in the 1960s, when Sears was being praised for creating an "extraordinary powerhouse of a company" (McDonald 1964) founded to a large extent on its development of "supply-chain managements"—an inventory maintenance strategy that Wal-Mart now seems to have radically advanced as a means of cutting costs and retail prices. Procter & Gamble and Gillette are current market leaders in key product lines—disposable diapers and safety razors, respectively—but they were hardly the pioneers in their market categories. P&G's Pampers were introduced in the 1960s, three decades after the first disposable diaper (Chux) was developed and sold. Similarly, Gillette introduced its first safety razor two decades after other firms had introduced theirs and more than a century after the first (Tellis and Golder 2002).

How could it be that first movers so often lose their market leadership? A complete list of the answers to that question is probably quite long. Schumpeter and many other economists could have been wrong on their initial, untested assessments of the relative innovativeness of established and large firms (which appears to be the case; see chap. 1, this vol.). Economists might point to the fact that markets are constantly being revolutionized and that dominant market positions cannot be held for long, given the rapidity of the ongoing technological advances in products and production processes—and especially if the first movers behave like monopolies, hiking their prices and profits and encouraging new entrants, or not concerning themselves with their costs because of their economic profit cushions. Schumpeter appears to have been right concerning another claim embedded in his theory, that "creative destruction" would tend to lead to what has in recent years been dubbed "serial monopolies," perhaps because monopolies couldn't resist behaving like monopolies.

It could well be that although first movers have certain advantages, second movers (or followers) have perhaps greater ones, not the least of which is not having to identify and prove the economic viability of the market for a product category. Second movers can refine what the first movers do, both in terms of product design and the cost of production (which appears to be how Wal-Mart, Procter & Gamble, Dell Computers, and Microsoft, among many companies, have been so successful).

We have no quibble with all these explanations, but we hasten to add another, often overlooked line of argument, namely, that the retrenchment or demise of firms, especially ones making monopoly profits, is often (but not always) built into their success (Christensen 1997; McKenzie and Galar 2003). This explanation has to do with what business professor Clayton Christensen calls the "innovator's dilemma." To see the market predicament of innovators, suppose that decades ago you owned the first firm to market a revolutionary new product—say, a mainframe computer—that quickly became very profitable because the product had considerable (cost-saving) value to buyers and because you could charge (within the constraints of limit pricing) monopoly prices. To maximize profits from the new technology, you would then need to develop a corporate culture and incentive system that direct the energies of line workers and managers toward gradually refining, upgrading, and exploiting the known technology. In defining your firm's internal control and development system, you determine not only what will be done in the firm but also what will not be done. In the case of your R&D work, you will likely limit the range of researchers' investigations, which can preclude research on other evolutionary new product categories, ones that do not rely directly on your firm's known technologies.

Of course, you could leave your business and R&D systems unconstrained, which means that employee energies can and will be directed in any number of directions. Your problem is that you have a known product and production technology that are producing profits. If you left your firm's R&D unfocused on your known product line, your employees could discover or invent the next big product breakthrough—what would be seen in retrospect as a "disruptive technology." However, you may have no more idea where the disruptive technology is coming from than anyone else does, and you can waste a lot of firm resources trying to find it. Furthermore, you can, in the process, divert resources from the exploitation of your known technology. The point of this discussion is that for many firms, the best option will be keeping the firm's focus on the known technology and having its workers refine and upgrade the known product with the intent of mining a fairly predictable profit stream. In the process of making that strategic decision, the firm can *intentionally* leave the discovery and development of new, disruptive technologies to other firms.

Now, it might be thought that the firm in an initial dominant market position can sit back and wait for the new technology to come on to the market and then either buy the firm that develops the product or simply copy the product. However, when disruptive technologies first appear, it is not always clear that they are indeed disruptive, or that they will cause the market retreat or demise of the established dominant firm and its products. After all, new products and technologies are *new*. This necessarily means they are untested in terms of initial profitability and long-run survivability. That is to say, no one can initially be sure that the new products and technologies will ever be able to achieve any profits, much less monopoly profits for as long as the dominant firm has achieved them with its existing products and technologies.

The established firm is also constrained in moving off into new markets and adopting new production technologies by its own internal culture and incentive systems. Although the corporate culture and incentive systems may be efficiently exploiting the known product and technology, those same systems might not work so effectively in the development and exploitation of the new products and technology. Of course, the established firm might frequently test its corporate flexibility, but such tests can be costly and, in themselves, disruptive in the sense that profits from known products and technologies can be lost in the process.

We suggested earlier that a good example of the type of innovator's dilemma we have in mind is mainframe computers. This example is appropriate because IBM was by far the most established, most prominent mainframe computer producer in the 1970s and before. When the personal computer emerged in the 1970s, no one—not Steve Jobs or the people at Big Blue— knew for sure whether the personal computer would actually challenge to any significant degree the market hegemony of the mainframe computer and IBM's total dominance of the mainframe market. IBM also had a tightly controlled corporate culture and incentive system, all directed toward further enhancing and selling mainframe computers and related services. IBM could have chosen early on to explore the personal computer market, but it also may have figured that the diversion of corporate talent was a waste, given that the personal computer might remain merely a sophisticated toy (as it was initially seen by many industry analysts) and never a significant challenge to mainframes in the market for business computing. IBM could also have reasoned, rightly (given the best but limited available information at the time) that it could sit back and wait for others to prove (or disprove) the viability of the personal computer market. Then, using its established position and brand name, it could quickly take over the then budding personal computer market. Needless to say, because of its wait-and-see strategy and because it made several crucial, mistaken market assessments, IBM was a fairly late mover in personal computers and has never achieved the prominence and profitability in that computer market that it had in 1970s and before in the mainframe market. With Dell and other personal computer companies selling circles around once indomitable IBM, IBM sold off its personal computer units to Lenovo, a Chinese personal computer manufacturer, in early 2005.

This is not to say that IBM made the wrong decision in the 1970s to hold its corporate focus on mainframe computers. In hindsight, one can say that *if* IBM had become a player in the personal computer market early on and *if* it could have avoided, concomitantly, taking up any number of other lines of new product development that could have proven to be financial dry holes (which a less focused corporate culture could have allowed), then it could have been a much stronger personal computer company in the 1980s and 1990s than it became (and at one time in the early 1990s, IBM looked as though it might not last the decade, partly because of the flow of red ink on its books from its personal computer business). However, those are really big ifs. Who's to say that IBM didn't, from the perspective of the 1970s, make decisions that maximized the then present value of the company's wealth, even if, by remaining inflexible, its decisions wound up causing the company's retreat in the personal computer market in the 1990s and early 2000s?

In other words, a company's ultimate market retreat, if not demise, can be part and parcel of a company's strategy for maximizing the company's wealth. And this point is especially applicable to firms that act like monopolies. A monopoly that restricts production to maximize profits can reason that it can maintain its market dominance only by trying to attract any new buyers that move into the market and fending off new rivals with a competitive pricing strategy. To do so, however, it might have to give up some of its economic profits in the market for its established products and technologies. The result could be that by always trying to survive, the company's stockholders suffer wealth losses.

CONCLUDING COMMENTS

Our central point in this chapter is that the creation and maintenance of monopoly market positions, along with the attendant entry barriers however privately devised, is as much an entrepreneurial endeavor as is the development of new products and technologies themselves. Furthermore, monopolists have a far greater claim of entitlement to monopoly rents (and hence consumer surplus) than is suggested by static model analysis, which assumes the goods under study into existence. This claim exists partially because, as Schumpeter recognized, monopolies "largely create what they exploit," referring to their market positions as well as the products they produce (1942, 101).

Our point goes beyond the observation that many business scholars and practitioners have failed to understand: firm retrenchment and even demise can be a wealth-maximizing strategy for stockholders. It is a broader point: that the persistence of constricted production and elevated prices by monopolies on known products and technologies, even in the face of their looming deaths, can contribute to overall economic and market efficiency. For monopolies to do otherwise—to remain flexible, without constraining business systems, and to be able to move rapidly into any and all potentially new and profitable product lines—carries with it notable costs and a threat to survival not recognized by popular business gurus who pound their lecterns for corporate flexibility, wanting corporations to always stand ready to reengineer themselves.

By restricting production and raising prices, monopolies "misallocate" resources, using the conventional standard of perfect competition. However, if they constantly try to survive and play the fully competitive game by always meeting new rivals on their terms—that is, by aping potential competitors on product development and prices—monopolies can also misallocate resources, perhaps to a greater extent, by sinking firm resources into a host of what we have called financial dry holes that more than offset any gains from new products that prove to be disruptive to their existing markets.

Market efficiency, in other words, can be enhanced in the way that Schumpeter suggested, by the "perennial gale of creative destruction." His key, unheralded message encapsulated in that compact phrase was, effectively, let monopolies be monopolies. Let the economic rents that monopolies garner be the requisite incentives they and their potential replacements need to create the goods and services that consumers want and that they, monopolies, exploit. In the process, monopolies not only add to the market efficiency of the moment but also give rise to their own retrenchment and demise. These results occur because monopoly rent, so long disparaged by economists, is simultaneously a creative and destructive force. Economists have long marveled at the market magic of Adam Smith's "invisible hand." But many don't seem to understand that the visible grip of monopolies on markets in the short run is an important source of the market's long-run magic.

Chapter 10

Property and Monopoly

For legal scholars, property rights is a muddled and, hence, highly contentious legal construct. For economists, private property is a far more straightforward concept: It is any bundle of limited (and incomplete) rights that define what a person can do with a physical thing (e.g., a car or an acre of land) or a nonphysical thing (e.g., a piece of copyrighted music, patented formula, or trademarked insignia).[1] Market exchanges are founded on trades that modern economists now readily see not so much as exchanges of things but as exchanges of the various bundles of rights that the trading parties have.

The exchange value of property, accordingly, will vary with the array of rights in the property bundle. If the use rights of land are obstructed by government regulation, the market value of the property can fall. If the copyright term for books is increased, the market value of many (but hardly all) books can be expected to rise.[2]

At the same time, one of the longer standing, more persistent claims and criticisms of markets, repeated frequently by economists and political theorists, is that property—especially landed and copyrighted property—amounts to a monopoly grant (albeit circumscribed to one degree or another) that is protected by state enforcement. This line of argument implies that, to one degree or another, property ownership gives rise to a market inefficiency as property owners exploit their monopoly rights to hike their prices and garner monopoly profits, indeed, for some, the equivalent of theft.

We argue that the presumption that a system of private property rights, including copyrights and patents, is tantamount to theft is founded on a confused understanding of monopoly. Indeed, as is well known among economists, private property rights have the effect, on balance, of expanding production and human welfare, which is hardly the expected outcome from a system of monopolies that emerges from a property rights regime. Clearly, property owners can often (but certainly not always) garner economic profits (or profits above competitive levels), but such above-competitive profits should be expected, as well as applauded, when markets are extended. We submit that a worthy distinction should and can be made between *economic profits* and *monopoly rents*. That is, not all economic profits should be construed as monopoly rents. The former emerges from an improvement in the allocation of resources that, in turn, emerges from expanded trade. The latter results from restricted trade. However, before these points can be developed, we need to revisit economists' and political philosophers' views on private property.

PROPERTY RENT AS MONOPOLY THEFT

The early founders of the discipline of economics—namely, Adam Smith, David Ricardo, and Thomas Malthus—viewed private property in land as a form of monopoly that invariably (in the words of Malthus) "bears a monopoly price" (1798, chap. 17, ¶ 10), which, in the thinking of Ricardo, "is at the very highest price at which the consumers are willing to purchase it" and "is nowhere regulated by the cost of production" (1817, chap. 17, ¶ 8; see also chap. 1, this vol.). The implication is clear: The return on land is a form of rent—more accurately, monopoly rent—that is unearned and derived from whatever god-given qualities the soil has and whatever market price landowners can extract for the natural qualities of the soil. That is to say, monopoly rent does not affect price but rather is a residual payment, meaning that which is left over from revenues after all market-determined payments to all inputs (other than the landed property) are deducted from firm revenues. Hence, taxing away the monopoly rents would leave the monopoly price unchanged, or in the words of Ricardo, "If all rent were relinquished by landlords, I am of the opinion, that the commodities produced on the land would be no cheaper, because there is always a portion of the same commodities produced on land, for which no rent is or can be paid, as the surplus produce is only sufficient to pay the profits of stock" (1821, chap. 20, ¶ 12).

During the first half of the nineteenth century, the tie between property and monopoly seemed to come often from reverse reasoning: Monopoly rent is any return to an input such as land that is unearned (not a consequence of a person's labor) and, therefore, is not morally or economically justified. Land earns rent. Accordingly, landed property amounts to a form of legalized "theft," according to socialist-anarchist Pierre-Joseph Proudhon (1809–65).[3] Any input that earns a return above opportunity cost—that is, earns a monopoly rent or economic profit—must be a monopoly (of some degree). Hence, monopoly is no less than a form of legalized theft, which justified various proposed plans to redistribute income from the "rich" (property owners) to the "poor" (workers).

John Ramsey McCulloch (1789–1864), British economist and author of *Principles of Political Economy*, wrote, "What is properly termed Rent is the sum paid for *the use of the natural and inherent powers of the soil*. It is entirely distinct from the sum paid for the use of buildings, enclosures, roads, or other improvements. *Rent is, then, always a monopoly*."[4] Clement Joseph Garnier (1813–81), a French economist and commentator on Adam Smith, clarified the distinction between monopoly rent and other forms of compensation.

> Rent paid to the landowner is fundamentally different from the payments made to the workman for his labor or to the entrepreneur as profit on the outlays made by him, in that these two types of payment represent compensation, to the one for pains taken, to the other for sacrifices or risks he has borne, whereas the landowner receives rent more *gratuitously* and *merely by virtue of a legal convention* that guarantees to certain individuals the right to landed property.[5]

The conceptual linkage between landed property and monopoly was widely believed to be so tight—a virtual truism—during the first half of the nineteenth century that French economic journalist Frédéric Bastiat (1801–50) devoted much ink to uncovering (if not ridiculing) what he thought were gross errors in the logic underlying the claims: "The theorists first characterized property so understood as a *necessary monopoly*, then merely as a *monopoly*, then as *injustice*, and finally as *theft*" (1850, chap. 9, ¶ 10; emphasis in the original). At the same time, Bastiat acknowledged that the "theorists" he quotes often and at length (1850, chap. 9) saw property-based monopolies as "necessary evils." Bastiat quoted Garnier (as well as others): "In short, it is apparently admitted by political economists [alas! yes, and herein lies the evil!] that property does not stem from divine rights, or rights of demesne, or from any other theoretical rights, but simply from its practical advantages. *It is merely a monopoly that is tolerated in the interest of all*, etc." (1850, chap. 9, ¶ 72;emphasis in the original, with interjection by Bastiat). Bastiat adds, "I believe that I have sufficiently proved that the economists, having started from the false assumption that *the forces of Nature possess or create value*, went on to the conclusion that private property (in so far as it appropriates and charges for this value that is independent of all human services) is a privilege, a monopoly, a usurpation, but a necessary privilege that must be maintained" (1850, chap. 9, ¶ 74).

Bastiat struggled to identify the inconsistency in claims surrounding private property. On the one hand, according to "socialists," landed property amounts to a "monopoly," which is socially "bad" because it allows the owners to usurp a part of a good's value without any justified claim of having created the value usurped. Private ownership of property is the moral equivalent of "cannibalism," "war," "slavery," "privilege," "fraud," and "plunder" (1850, chap. 8, ¶ 8). Nevertheless, the institution of landed property is maintained because property has a distinct economic advantage: It gives rise to an expansion of output beyond what could be had in the absence of assigned property rights. This gain outweighs any harm done by the monopoly's usurpation of a return above that which is required to keep the property employed where it is.

Bastiat attacked the inconsistency in two ways. First, he denied that nature is the source of value. Rather, he asserted:

> You [landed property owners] have not misappropriated the gifts of God. You have received them gratis from the hand of Nature, it is true; but you have also passed them on gratis to your fellow men and have withheld nothing. They have acted similarly toward you, and all that has passed between you has been *compensation* for mental or physical effort, for sweat and toil expended, for dangers faced, for skills contributed, for sacrifices made, for pains taken, for *services rendered and received.* You thought only of yourselves, perhaps, but even your own self-interest has become in the hands of an infinitely wise and all-seeing Providence an instrument for making greater abundance available to all men; for, had it not been for your efforts, all the *useful effects* that Nature at your command has transmitted without payment among men would have remained eternally dormant. I say, *without payment;* for the payment you received was only the simple return to you of the efforts you had expended, and not at all a price levied on the gifts of God. Live, then, in peace, without fear and without qualms. You have no other property in the world save your claim to services due you for services that you have fairly rendered, and that your fellow men have voluntarily accepted. This property of yours is legitimate, unassailable; no utopia can prevail against it, for it is part and parcel of our very nature. No new ideology will ever shake its foundations or wither its roots. (1850, chap. 8, ¶ 5)

A chapter later, Bastiat took on the particular claims that property and monopoly are much the same construct.

> Economists, you declare: "Rent is what is paid to the landowner for the use of the productive and indestructible powers of the soil."
>
> I answer: No. Rent is what is paid the water carrier for the pains he took to make his cart and his wheels, and the water would cost more if he carried it on his back. In the same manner, wheat, flax, wool, wood, meat, fruit

would cost us more if the landowner had not improved the instrument that produces them.

Socialists, you say: "Originally the masses enjoyed their right to the land subject to their labor. Now they are excluded and robbed of their natural heritage."
    I reply: No, they are not excluded or robbed; they do enjoy gratis the utility that the land has produced, subject to their labor, that is, on condition that they pay by their own labor those who spare them labor.

Egalitarians, you say: "The monopoly of the landowner consists in the fact that, while he did not make the means of production, he charges for its service."
    I answer: No, the land as a means of production, in so far as it is the work of God, produces *utility*, and this utility is gratuitous; it is not within the owner's power to charge for it. The land, as a means of production, in so far as the landowner has prepared it, worked on it, enclosed it, drained it, improved it, added other necessary implements to it, produces *value*, which represents human *services* made available, and this is the only thing he charges for. Either you must recognize the justice of this demand, or you must reject your own principle of *reciprocal services*. (1850, chap. 9, ¶¶ 106–11)

Second, Bastiat pointed out that competition among producers would eliminate any unearned return that is a "gratuitous gift" of Nature. He suggested that a part of the problem in understanding the social role of private property is that the gains to all, not just the property owners, are obscured by their ubiquity.

How many times, when considering the phenomena of the social order, have I not had cause to appreciate how profoundly right Rousseau was when he said, "It takes a great deal of scientific insight to observe what we see every day"! Thus it is that *habit*, that veil which is spread before the eyes of the ordinary man, which even the attentive observer does not always succeed in casting aside, prevents us from seeing the most marvelous of all social phenomena: real wealth constantly passing from the domain of private property into the communal domain. (1850, chap. 8, ¶ 40)

Later, Bastiat elaborates, "*Fortunately*, I maintain, the landowner can no more charge for the services of the land than for the wind's or the sun's," to which he adds in a paragraph that is inset in his text to add emphasis,

The earth is a wondrous chemical workshop wherein many materials and elements are mixed together and worked on, and finally come forth as grain, fruit, flax, etc. Nature has presented this vast workshop to man as a *gratuitous* gift, and has divided it into many compartments suitable for many different kinds of production. But certain men have come forth, have laid hands on these things, and have declared: This compartment belongs to me; that one also; all that comes from it will be my exclusive property. And, amazingly enough, *this usurpation of privilege*, far from being disastrous to society, has turned out to be advantageous. (1850, chap. 9, ¶ 57)

Third, Bastiat mocks those whose argument reduces to a syllogism built around the following embedded premises and conclusions.

- *Major Premise:* Landed property (and the contribution of land to output) is not created by people's labor. The value of property comes from God, not anything people do.
  Minor Premise: Monopoly, which is characterized by unearned income for owners, reduces to a form of theft.
  Minor Premise: The return on land, rent, is unearned, a "usurpation" of value that *should* go to all, not just the property owners.
- *Major Conclusion:* Landed property amounts to a monopoly.
  Minor Conclusion: Private property is a form of theft.
  Minor Conclusion: Private property is still good for all because there is no better way to ensure the efficient use of resources, which makes property a "necessary evil."
- *Major Conclusion:* The redistribution of monopoly rents is justified (with the implication that taxation of monopoly rents is not theft).

To this line of argument, Bastiat sarcastically quipped,

Taken literally, the famous formula, *property is theft*, is therefore absurdity raised to the nth degree. It would be no less outlandish to say that *theft is property;* that what is legal is illegal; that what is, is not, etc. It is probable that the author of this bizarre aphorism merely desired to catch people's attention with a striking paradox, and that what he really meant to state was this: Certain men succeed in getting paid not only for the work that they do but also for the work that they do not do, appropriating to themselves alone God's gifts, gratuitous utility, the common possession of all. But in that case it would first be necessary to prove the statement, and then to say: *Theft is theft.* (1850, chap. 8, ¶ 29)

THE PROPERTY-MONOPOLY EQUIVALENCE

We wish at this point that we could say that Bastiat got the best of the proponents of what we choose to dub the Proudhon view of property as a form of monopoly and theft. Unfortunately, that is hardly the case. Karl Marx (1818–83) founded the communist movement on the Proudhon view of property, which alone, apart from Marx's theory of the surplus value of production, served as a "just" foundation for the state's appropriation of all private property.

Moreover, the Proudhon view is seductive, even for more modern and contemporary economists who can, and have, extended its application beyond landed property to all capital, physical and nonphysical. Private property is a set of rights, including the right to vary the use of whatever is owned and to exclude others from its use. This means that private property owners can potentially vary market supply of whatever can be produced by the owned property. Because entry costs, to one extent or another, abound everywhere in real-world markets, property rights bestow on owners a measure of monopoly power that, in turn, can enable owners to extract some amount of monopoly rents from the products that are bought and sold.

Indeed, the economic and political case for copyrights and patents has historically been founded on the presumption that such property (nonphysical or intellectual) rights would provide people with sufficient monopoly powers that the creation of new things (books, pieces of music, movies, brands, and software) would be encouraged. Without monopoly protection, the development of new things (as well as the improvement of old things) could easily be suboptimal, given the ease with which innovations could be replicated by new firms that would not have to cover the cost of development. Hence, the price that could be charged by the innovator might, in the absence of copyrights and patents, not be sufficient to cover all costs, including the innovator's development costs.

The late economist Frank Knight (1885–1972) clearly understood that the classical economists (including Smith, Malthus, and Ricardo) had confused land rent, founded on the natural scarcity of a resource, with monopoly rent, founded on a firm's control of supply.

> Monopoly is usually defined as the control of the supply of a commodity. A common but disastrous error is the confusion of control with natural limitation of supply. We need not pause longer than to characterize as a serious misuse of words the denomination of land rent, for example, as a monopoly income. Even J. S. Mill fell into the error of defining monopoly as limitation, and it is exemplified in its extreme form by Mr. F. B. Hawley, who virtually calls all income due to the "scarcity" of any productive resource a monopoly return. Now, as all income, from the distributive standpoint, is dependent on the scarcity of the agents which produce it, and all in exactly the same way, the meaninglessness of such a description is apparent. And of

course the same applies to "scarcity income" in general, whether called monopoly gain or not. There is under free competition no other sort of income, qualitatively or quantitatively, and the designation neither distinguishes or in any significant way describes anything. (1921, pt. 2, chap. 6, ¶ 14)

At the same time, Knight accepted somewhat uneasily the monopoly case for copyrights and patents.

> The case of investment in invention is different again. Here, owing to the low cost of indefinitely multiplying an idea, it is usually difficult to capitalize an increase in productive power. Society generally permits an inventor or his assigns to keep his idea secret as long as possible or to safeguard it in any manner. But this is so commonly impracticable and the social value of new inventions so manifest that the patent system has come into general use establishing and protecting by law a *temporary*, and rather short-lived, property right in the improvement. (1921, pt. 3, chap. 12, ¶ 43)

Knight recognized that the copyright/patent systems were an "exceedingly crude" way of rewarding creators of new goods and services, partly because of the effects of the monopoly price, but also partly because the true innovators are not always the beneficiaries of the monopoly grants implied in copyrights and patents—points that the Austrian economist Ludwig von Mises also understood.[6]

COPYRIGHTS AS MONOPOLY ABUSE

A host of contemporary economic and legal scholars have adopted the monopoly case for copyrights and patents, all with a measure of reservation about providing such legal protection, which reveals an underlying philosophical conflict on the monopoly grants. On the one hand, copyrights (and patents) are viewed as being needed to spur innovations. Indeed, to spur innovations and new works, the U.S. Constitution gives Congress the authority to "promote the Progress of Science and useful Arts, by securing for *limited times* to Authors and Inventors the *exclusive* Right to their respective Writings and Discoveries" (article 1, section 8; emphasis added).

On the other hand, through the grant of "the exclusive Right," copyrights grant (so the argument is extended) a form of monopoly power, meaning the power to limit output and hike prices and economic profits. The presumption is that the grant curbs efficiency in the allocation of resources and goods. Supreme Court Justice Stephen Breyer starts his essay on the "uneasy case" for copyright (written before he was appointed to the Supreme Court) by quoting approvingly Thomas Babington Macaulay's often-quoted quip made in debate over a proposed increase in British copyright term before the House of Commons in 1841: Copyright is equivalent to "a tax on readers for the purpose of giving a bounty to writers" (Breyer 1970, 281).[7] Breyer then suggests that there are two possible foundations for copyright, moral and economic. The moral arguments, Breyer maintains, revolve around the claim that authors are due what they produce. As Breyer suggests, perhaps the moral foundation of a person's right to the income of that which the person creates is (and need be) no more sophisticated than the theory of property captured in the sixth century by King Diarmed of Ireland, who quipped, "To every cow its calf." Alternatively, a French lawyer reasoned in the sixteenth century, "The heavens and the earth belong to [God], because they are the work of his word. . . . So the author of a book is its complete master, and as such can dispose of it as he chooses" (Breyer 1970, 284–85). Breyer dismisses the moral case for copyright on (at least) five identified grounds.

- First, taking something of a Marxian position on the distribution of income, Breyer writes, "few workers receive salaries that approach the total value of what they produce," but no one is arguing that workers' labor should be restricted just so that workers can receive more of the surplus value they generate (285).
- Second, "it is not apparent that the producer has any stronger claim to the surplus than the consumer or that the author's claim is any stronger than that of other workers." He questions why the author's claim to above-competitive prices is stronger than a bookseller's (286).
- Third, copyright "rewards the wrong works," because it favors those that sell well, not those works that are "serious and important" (for example, scholarly books), that are "notoriously in need of funds" (287).
- Fourth, "intellectual creation" is a radically different thing than "land and chattels." The latter are subject to "congestion" (or are, in economists' jargon, *rivalrous* in consumption). Ideas, on the other hand, are infinitely divisible, which means they are nonrivalrous in consumption and are not subject to congestion (288–89).
- Fifth, as Immanuel Kant suggested, created works need protection because otherwise the works might be misinterpreted or garbled by "copiers." Breyer's response is, "One might quarrel with Kant's arguments, for the fact that unauthorized copying may *sometimes* interfere with an author's personal interests does not show that it *always* (or even *often*) will do so" (290; emphasis in the original).

Breyer concludes that because "none of the noneconomic goals served by copyright law seems an adequate justification for a copyright system," any justification for a copyright system must rest on economic arguments. An economic case for copyright protection must start with the cost advantage that copiers have over original publishers.[8] The case to be made for copyright must therefore rest on the claim that original publishers—and authors—need the legal entry barriers embedded in copyrights so that they can restrict sale and charge monopoly prices in order that they can cover their development costs. Still, Breyer maintains that the case for copyright remains "uneasy," because original publishers have the advantage of being first to market and can cover potential market sales before copiers have a chance to get their lower-priced copies to market (1970, 299–302). (Perhaps Breyer would revise his assessment somewhat today, given the advent of digital goods with pirated copies of music CDs and movie DVDs.)

Furthermore, Breyer notes, publishers have market solutions that don't involve copyrights available to them. In the absence of copyright, original publishers can negotiate with buyer groups (e.g., book clubs or major booksellers), with the buyer groups agreeing before a book is published to buy specified quantities of initial print runs. Through such prepublication orders, original publishers can cover their development costs without copyright protection.

Granted, as Breyer acknowledges, these negotiations can be costly. However, forcing publishers to incur such transaction costs can be an improvement over forcing consumers to pay monopoly prices. In addition, in the absence of copyrights, people who would like to use published works would not have to incur the transaction costs involved in obtaining permission to use copyrighted work (1970, 302–8).

We cover the particulars of Breyer's argument partly because they are interesting (and they represented, at the time his article was first published, new thinking on copyright laws). However, our main purpose in covering the particulars is to bring to light the economic foundation of his "uneasy case" for (but, really, mainly *against*) an extension of the copyright term: Copyrights, as a form of property right, endow holders with monopoly grants, meaning the market power to restrict sales and to charge higher-than-competitive prices to build authors' and publishers' monopoly rents. If the social consequences are, inevitably, an inefficiency in the allocation of scarce resources, any extension of the term will almost surely magnify the market inefficiency. This underlying theory of monopoly is self-evident in Breyer's central conclusion: "Removing copyright protection should induce competition in the production and sale of relatively high-volume titles" (1970, 313). The result would be, according to Breyer, lower prices and greater sales, maybe not in academic books, but certainly in trade books and textbooks that Breyer asserts (without reporting evidence or citing sources) garner monopoly returns. Hence, Breyer concludes that "the period of copyright protection is at present [1970] too long and should not be extended beyond fifty-six years" (although the copyright period was extended in 1976 to the author's life plus seventy years).

This common view of the monopoly consequences of copyright (and patents) captured with some scholarly force by Breyer has been picked up and extended more recently by Lawrence Lessig, who starts his analysis by making the tie between copyright and monopoly explicit: "The [copyright] law creates this 'exclusive right'—a.k.a. monopoly right—to help solve a problem that exists with creative information" (Lessig 2001, 58). He acknowledges (as did Breyer) that while copyright protection may be required to get works created, the protection should be limited because copyright represents a monopoly grant that can be counted to exact monopoly consequences drawn from static modeling. However, since the country was founded, the copyright term has been extended fifteen times, with eleven of the extensions being passed during the last four decades of the twentieth century (Lessig 2001).[9] The maximum copyright term in the United States was set at twenty-eight years (fourteen years for the original copyright with a fourteen-year renewal, provided that the author survived the first term) when the original copyright act was passed in 1790. The maximum term went to forty-two years in 1831, to fifty-six years in 1909, to seventy years in 1974, to life plus seventy years in 1976, to life plus ninety years in 1998 (Ochoa 2002, 26–51).

In addition, the coverage of copyright protection has been expanded in a variety of ways, most notably the following.

- Early in the history of the country (1790–99), only 4 percent of all book titles published were copyrighted. Now, all titles are copyrighted without the authors even having to go to the trouble of registering their works (Lessig 2001, 106–7).
- Before the turn of the twentieth century, all foreign books released in U.S. markets were not copyrighted. Now, they are (106).
- In the not-too-distant past, original artists could not control the use of *components* (for example, musical phrases) of their works. Now, because of a series of court cases favorable to the original artists and their heirs, use of components can require permission (109).
- When cable television began, cable companies could use the signals of the television network without charge. Now, the networks have rights of denial of use (109–10).

- Napster, the Internet company that facilitated peer-to-peer swapping of music files that emerged and rapidly expanded in the late 1990s, has been effectively shut down by the courts, which has reduced the ability of consumers to share their digital files with others without payment and has restricted the ability of many artists who don't care about royalty payments to have their works broadly disseminated (131).
- The "fair-use doctrine," which allows for personal (not commercial) reproductions of copyrighted works, has been constricted in several ways. For instance, copyrighted posters (and other reproduced art works) that buyers can display in their homes for others to see under the fair-use doctrine cannot be displayed on Web sites (181).
- The Digital Millennium Copyright Act of 1998 makes it illegal for programmers to crack the code included in digital recordings of books, music, movies, and software to prevent copying. This means that consumers are prevented from making copies for personal use, a further tightening of the domain of fair use (190).

The problem Lessig seeks to highlight is not only that copyright invariably translates into a monopoly right, giving rise to market inefficiencies due to constricted sales of the copyrighted works, but also to a more important constriction in the evolution of ideas, which, Lessig maintains, ultimately drives upward a country's economic, social, and political development through time. The evolution of ideas is dependent upon the growth in the "idea commons," or all of those ideas contained in works that fall into the public domain and that can be drawn on and employed productively, without permission or charge, by authors and artists who follow. However, with the greater coverage of copyright, the idea commons (whether communicated through books, scholarly research and articles, performances, or the Internet) can no longer grow freely and in unanticipated but innovative ways as it once could. Supposedly, the greater coverage of copyright hasn't totally prohibited the use of many created works, but, according to Lessig, the greater coverage certainly has increased the transaction costs involved in the use of many works, given the variety of permissions that must be sought and the copyright fees that must be paid. The trend in growth in control of intellectual property rights is clearly in the wrong direction, according to Lessig. Hence, he argues that many ideas that would have been advanced will likely not be advanced, mainly because of the greater transaction costs of making use of ideas that remain private property under an endlessly increasing copyright period.

In summary, Lessig begins his argument for curbs on the growth of control by acknowledging the potential validity of the "tragedy of the commons" as the foundation for the establishment of private property rights. When property is held in common, no one is able to prevent anyone else from using a given property—for example, a pasture—and the property will tend to be overused because the people who use it do not bear the full cost of use. In the case of the pasture, ranchers will continue to put cattle on the pasture until the grass is grazed to the nub and all cattle end up thinner than they could be. In the words of biologist Garrett Hardin, who paints the tragedy in bleak terms, popularizing the construct in the process.

> Therein is the tragedy. Each man is locked into a system that compels him to increase his herd without limit—in a world that is limited. Ruin is the destination toward which all men rush, each pursuing his own best interest in a society that believes in the freedom of the commons. Freedom in the commons brings ruin to all. (1968, 1243)

Lessig goes on to argue that academics and policymakers have become too enraptured by the eloquence of the logic underlying the tragedy of the commons and have, accordingly, sought the contraction, if not elimination, of all commons by expanding the range of private property rights, including copyrights—all without due recognition for having some property, those resources and products, such as ideas, that are nonrivalrous in consumption, held in common. He suggests that copyright (and patents) can be useful to bring creative works into existence, but that means that the rights under copyright need to be strictly limited both in length of term and of coverage so that copyrights do not allow for long-term monopoly rights. After all, anyone's use of an idea that has been created does not diminish the availability of that idea to anyone else. Ideas are categorically different from the grass on Hardin's pasture.

Drawing on the work of others (Heller 1998; Buchanan and Yoon 2000), Lessig then adds to the discussion of intellectual property rights an additional (potential) form of market inefficiency due to the extension of copyrights: the "tragedy of the innovation commons." More generally, this "tragedy" (which, strictly speaking, implies only a misallocation of resources) has been dubbed by Heller (1998) the "tragedy of the *anti*commons"—signaling a sharp contrast with the "tragedy of the commons"—because resources go underutilized attributable to the elevated transaction costs associated with privatization.[10] Lessig draws a variety of policy conclusions that condense to proposed curbs on copyrights to avert any emerging tragedy of the anticommons and to expand the competition of ideas, which can enhance market efficiency, both in the short and the long run.

PROPERTY IN PROPER CONTEXT

The discussion to this point reduces to the claim that private property in many, if not all, its various forms amounts to a monopoly grant, a claim that has significant consequences: Because of the monopoly grants, output is less than it could be. Prices are higher than they would otherwise be. And property owners are able to extract monopoly rents that are unearned and amount to a form of theft. The extensive literature on copyrights (and patents)—including the works that Breyer and Lessig covered—is replete with such empirical predictions regarding the consequences of copyright term extensions. Interestingly, this literature is equally devoid of empirical tests.[11] The empirical void in the copyright term literature should be of some concern to economic and legal scholars, if for no other reason than that casual empiricism raises doubts about the credibility of contentions that extending the copyright term necessarily has counterproductive effects.[12]

Filling the void of empirical work on the exact effects of changing the copyright law is not our purpose. Our purpose is limited to challenging the underlying conceptual framework for the monopoly predictions. In passing, however, we might note that our (casual) empirical evidence may be at odds with the predictions of the critics of copyright for several reasons, not the least of which could be that the growing copyright term and coverage over the last two hundred-plus years may not necessarily translate into an equivalent growth in the effective market protection of authors and publishers. Authors and publishers in 1790 were protected to a degree by the maximum twenty-eight-year copyright term, but they were also protected, perhaps to a much greater degree, from competition by the sheer cost that copiers had to incur to bring their copies to market. The costs of printing and distribution of books (especially in electronic form) in contemporary times is far lower than in colonial times. Hence, a copyright term of a hundred or more years today may (or may not) have any more of an incentive and wealth effect than did a copyright term of twenty-eight years at the turn of the nineteenth century. Understandably, critics of extending the copyright term rarely, if ever, acknowledge this point, and for good reason: It undermines their case for turning down any extension.

We fully understand that the length of the copyright term is only one of a number of key variables affecting the annual counts of book titles and copies sold, as well as the financial conditions of publishers. Our point is that the credibility of the claims of critics of copyright term extensions, founded as they are in static monopoly theory, is suspect. Perhaps copyrights in particular, and property rights in general, set up economic dynamics through time that result in net economic gains that are not captured by static models that are at the foundation of claims that property represents monopoly grants.

We suggest that claims about the monopoly consequences of property rights, including copyrights, reflect a fundamental confusion over the nature of a monopoly and the role of property in a market economy. At one level, the confusion has a political source: Opponents of markets, such as Proudhon, have had an interest in denigrating market institutions, one of the more prominent being private property. Monopoly is obviously "bad" because of its pernicious impact on prices, unearned rents, and allocative efficiency. By juxtaposing forms of property with discussions of monopoly as seen from static models, the supposed badness of monopoly is transferred to property, with the suggestion that private property and monopoly should be curbed for much the same reasons.

The confusion can also be traced to the inevitable choice of words in describing private property, which endows owners with varying degrees of *exclusivity* in *control* over the use of whatever physical or nonphysical thing is owned. The words "exclusivity" and "control" suggest that owners have an ability to restrict the use of the property, which in turn can affect the price and return that can be garnered from the property. Hence, "property" might understandably be equated with "monopoly," because "monopoly" also implies sole ownership of a market with the powers of manipulating the market price and return to the detriment of consumers. We noted how Lessig assumes that "exclusive control" necessarily implies "monopoly right."

We suggest, however, that the confusion has a more fundamental source in theorists' analytical tunnel vision. Analysts both past and present look at particular properties in the context of a functioning market economy, often without reference to the circumstances that gave rise to the *system* of property rights in the first place. In such a narrow context, ownership of land can understandably be seen as giving rise to restricted crops and higher prices and profits for landowners. A copyright means that no one other than the original publisher can print copies of copyrighted works. In the narrow context of a given published work for a given market, copyright can also lead to a constricted market with higher prices and profits for the given titles being treated as having separate markets. Both sets of property rights, land and copyrighted titles, can be destructive of welfare because they induce an inefficient allocation of resources—or so goes the thinking in such narrow analytical settings.

However, such deductions do not emerge from a less constricted perception of property rights. Consider again a state of common ownership. As Hardin (1968) correctly stressed, communal ownership can lead to its own tragedy, an overuse, misuse, and abuse of resources because of the absence of exclusivity, or, more to the point, the absence of owners' or users' ability to exclude all others. The case for private property is built on the presumption that when rights to exclude are assigned to individuals (or firms), there will be an improvement in the use of the resources. This follows because the owners will then bear a cost (in terms of the depreciation of the market value of the property) if the property is overused, misused, or abused. Because the property is treated with greater care, more resources will, in effect, be available to the extent that resources are not destroyed. This means there can be more, not fewer, goods on the market (and greater quantities of the greater count of goods).

With private control rights, owners have an enhanced incentive to utilize the local information at their disposal on how best to use and/or redeploy their assigned property. The value of the property can rise with the more effective employment of the property along with the value of the goods that are produced. This implies a greater *real* income for consumers in the form of greater goods production. Although the nominal prices of goods might or might not rise, their *real* prices are bound to fall with the more efficient employment of resources held as private property. This is especially true if property rights (particularly patents and copyrights) give rise to the creation, invention, or discovery of new things—new property—due to the incentives built in to the property regime. This is the case because people can capture the value of their efforts in the market value of the property that they create, invent, and discover. Today critically important new property can literally be created from a resource that amounts to thin air, 1s and 0s or electrons, and good ideas that, of course, often require alertness and due diligence.

Moreover, the assignment of property rights can give rise to trades, with the property assignments being reconfigured through trades so that the owners who can get the most value from the property will, after the trades have been consummated, have control of the relevant property rights. To the extent that markets expand, property can give rise to the benefits of greater specialization, much heralded by Adam Smith, which implies increasing returns to the scale (size and scope) of markets. If we give people property rights to that which they create, say, through copyrights, an expansion of property can occur beyond what would otherwise exist, and the greater property can expand the markets, and the benefits of markets, even further. Again, people's real incomes should be expected to expand.[13]

In summary, seen from this perspective, instead of constricting markets, property rights can expand them, with efficiency in the allocation of resources enhanced in the process. We find it difficult to appreciate how anyone can, under such outcomes, associate the "good" of property with the "bad" of monopoly, even if the association is purely semantic with due recognition to the prospects of "good monopolies," a mistake that can only extend the confusion of both the roles of property and monopolies in market economies.[14]

"GOOD" AND "BAD" MONOPOLIES

We would readily concede that property in general and copyright in particular may in given instances of the rights assignment lead to all the negative consequences of monopoly that critics stress. For example, for the sake of argument only, we might agree with critics of property rights and copyrights that the novelist John Grisham, the heirs of the late composer George Gershwin, and the software developer and chairman of Microsoft, Bill Gates, may be such dominant forces in their respective markets that they are capable of significantly curbing their sales and charging prices that are far removed from competitive levels and, hence, can impose a nontrivial degree of inefficiency on the economy. However, such isolated examples of true monopolies' consequences (if they are that) hardly make a case against property right and copyright institutions as critical components of a market system. The analytical mistake made is transparent: No system (designed to reduce the constraints of scarcity) will ever be perfect. There are often unavoidable problems or costs (or instances of inefficiency) with all institutions that are adopted because of their impact over a broad range of consequences. The critical question in judging property rights or copyright rights as institutions of markets is how those institutions perform *on balance*, given a full assessment of both the gains and the costs.

Even (supposedly) "bad" monopolies can be more than offset by a greater number and presence of "good" monopolies, as discussed earlier. Furthermore, we hasten to remind readers of a simple but crucial point: "Bad" monopolies can inspire the creation, invention, and discovery, as well as the development, of a plethora of other products in other markets that add more to consumer welfare than the "bad" monopolies deduct. This is because any monopoly rents garnered by the "bad" monopolies can be the requisite incentive that others need to take the risks of failure and to innovate in markets that are far-removed, as well as adjacent, to the markets that are monopolized. Indeed, in the absence of some property holders garnering monopoly rents, property rights and copyrights would lose their incentive advantage, which is their raison d'être.

Admittedly, the assignment of property rights and copyrights is a practical matter with practical (consumer and producer welfare) ends in mind. This means they can be taken too far. As Lessig explicitly argues, an unthinking effort to privatize all "commons," because of potential tragedies of the commons, can (conceptually, if not actually) give rise to tragedies of anticommons. The prospect of anticommons tragedies might suggest that the presence of commons tragedies could be optimal (given that worse problems from ubiquitous property can be imagined). As Breyer and Lessig implicitly suggest, there is some *optimum* copyright term. We readily make such concessions because we have a larger point in mind, one that is consistent with the Schumpeterian theme of this volume: Market institutions, whether property rights or copyrights (or patents), must be judged not by the prevalence of supposed "monopolies" (narrowly defined by their assigned exclusive rights to use physical and nonphysical things) but by what happens more broadly in the economy over time. These market institutions should be extended as long as they increase human welfare. Granted, Breyer and Lessig have tried to make the case that the copyright term and coverage should be curbed because the association of copyright with monopoly necessarily implies a loss of human welfare. Our point is that the association has been wrongly drawn. Even if the association is proper, the consequence could just as easily be an expansion of human welfare—because of the enacted potential for economic profits.

MONOPOLY PROFITS VERSUS ECONOMIC PROFITS

As a matter of analytical habit, economists associate any profits a firm makes over and above normal profits with monopoly rents or, which is assumed to be the same thing, economic profits. Reversing the analytics, evidence of economic profits or monopoly rents suggests the presence of firms with market power, or the ability of firms to restrict output to raise their prices above competitive levels. Economic profits are, accordingly, prima facie evidence of accompanying market failures.

From our perspective, a useful distinction needs to be drawn between economic profit and monopoly rent. The latter emerges when firms constrict their production due to a reduction in the competitiveness of their markets. The former emerges when firms find ways, through the deployment or redeployment of their property rights, to expand their production levels. The former—economic profits—are the carrots that cause firms to do more than they otherwise would. Economic profits are firms' part of the gains from mutually beneficial gains from greater trades that are associated with expanded markets (and that emerge because of the increasing returns to scale of markets). They give rise to more firms doing more, not less. The mere prospect, if not realization, of economic profits leads to more, not less, competition than would otherwise exist. Economic profits, because they emerge from expanded, mutually beneficial trades, also lead to mutual gains being received by consumers.

Unfortunately, economists continue to condemn the prevalence of economic profits as though their consequences were necessarily the same both in source and in effect as monopoly rents. Hence, they can't help but see (mistakenly) the visible hand of monopoly inefficiency in the most fundamental of market institutions, private property rights, as well as in copyrights (and patents). They fail to appreciate, paradoxically, the extent to which economic profits drive the much heralded invisible hand of markets.

Economists' traditional perspective is that economic profit, which equals monopoly rents, is always bad. We suggest a new perspective: Economic profits are always good. Our point, however, is that it is important to note a useful distinction because monopoly rents are markedly different in source and effect, but they are not always and everywhere bad. Monopoly rents received by some firms can lead to the realization of economic profits by other firms.

CONCLUDING COMMENTS

The debate over the monopoly consequences of private property rights in general and copyrights (and patents) in particular is loaded with hypotheses that are in desperate need of empirical testing by law and economics scholars. We have sidestepped such fact-based investigations partly because of the difficulty of undertaking the required tests under the auspices of this book but also partly because our purpose has been more narrowly focused on the conceptual foundation of widely accepted but misguided claims, most notably that property rights and copyrights amount to monopoly grants, with all the derisive effects monopoly connotes. We have argued that the easy association of a system of property rights and monopoly fails to recognize another important lesson that economists teach with conviction: A system of property rights is instituted for the purpose of expanding trade by increasing the productive value of the available property and by giving rise to new property. Monopoly, as represented in economists' static model, which is at the foundation of the association of property with monopoly, has the effect of constricting trade. Granted, private property rights make monopoly possible, but the view that property rights in general, and copyrights in particular, necessarily imply monopoly rights is as confused as the more general proposition that Joseph Schumpeter sought to correct, that monopoly is everywhere a drag on markets.

If economists could somehow differentiate between "monopoly rents" and "economic profits," we suspect that much confusion and awkward discussions could be eliminated from economic discussions. As it is, economists and legal scholars have to qualify their discussion of monopoly by conceding that "monopolies are not all bad" (Lessig 2001, 29) or "a monopoly, of the category described, is evidently 'productive'" (Knight 1921, pt. 2, chap. 6, ¶ 17). However, the phrase "good monopoly" (which seems to be the essence of what is meant in these quotations) appears to us to be the rhetorical equivalent of a "good bad" or "good inefficiency" or a "good market failure." All three phrases are not only internally contradictory, they just don't sound right.

We submit that the economics profession is in need of a new market category. Perhaps economists would be well served by talking about Schumpeterian firms, which seems to be far more descriptive of the intended kind of market model they have in mind. A Schumpeterian firm is a firm that has many of the major markings of a classic monopoly: It is dominant (or a single producer) in its market and makes above-normal profits by not producing the idealized competitive output level (or where price equals marginal cost). The main difference between a classic monopoly and a Schumpeterian firm is that the latter expands human welfare, its own and the welfare of consumers.

Chapter 11

Summing Up

We have pressed two themes throughout this book. First, conventional, static, microeconomic theory, as represented in contemporary textbooks, exaggerates the economic inefficiency of monopoly in market economies. The extent of the exaggeration is attributable in large measure to the use of perfect competition, an unachievable market state, as a standard of judgment.[1] Using a supposed state of market perfection, grounded in zero entry and exit costs, to assess the allocative efficiency of any real-world market is analytical folly. Assume any degree of entry and exit costs, and at least a portion of the supposed deadweight loss of the then imperfect market—as judged by the standard of the imagined idealized market—is no longer relevant, because no way then exists of improving on the efficiency with which resources are allocated. Hence, the true deadweight loss of monopoly is necessarily less than the Harberger triangle. On this score, our critique of monopoly theory affirms others' critiques of perfect competition as a standard for assessing real-world markets.

Second, in a world in which goods are not given—that is, they must be imagined, developed, produced, marketed, and distributed, with a significant probability of failure at each step—monopoly, and the prospects of it, can be expected in various ways to actually increase human welfare on both sides of the markets over time. This is the case not *in spite of*, but *because of* a monopoly's ability, for some period of time, to control market supply and to hike prices and economic profits above the level achievable in a perfectly competitive market. We repeated Paul Romer's (1994) crucially important but easily overlooked observation that perfectly competitive prices necessarily provide impaired signals and incentives in guiding entrepreneurs concerning which goods should be created, mainly because they do not and cannot capture the goods' full market values. Often, when the competitive price is very low, as it must be for low-marginal-cost goods—for example, digital goods—the price can capture little of the total consumer value. Monopoly prices can more fully capture the value of goods and can correct, albeit partially, what would be, with perfectly competitive prices, underutilization of resources toward the creation and development of some goods. That is, competitive prices can distort the allocation of resources across the goods that are developed, a distortion that can be corrected, at least partly, by so-called monopoly distortions.

Even if monopoly prices lead to static deadweight losses in the monopolized markets, the resulting monopoly profits can be a powerful incentive for entrepreneurs in both close-at-hand and far-removed markets to create and develop new products that have a chance of yielding above-competitive rates of return. Hence, the monopoly that impairs static efficiency can improve dynamic efficiency. A price-discriminating monopolist can improve dynamic efficiency even more (because more consumer surplus is extracted) at the same time, as conventionally argued, it improves static efficiency.

For sake of argument, we might concede that perfectly competitive prices can efficiently guide entrepreneurs when they don't have to create anything, and when all the other conditions of perfect competition are met. However, perfect competition, as we have argued, is a market recipe for economic stagnation simply because, as we noted, no incentive would exist in such markets for entrepreneurs to get off their proverbial dimes. They could never anticipate making anything more than normal profits, which implies no gains at all from improving what they produce, a reckless disregard for the first principle of market trades, which is that they must be mutually beneficial.

We understand that readers may be concerned that our line of argument leads to what, on first thought, is a paradoxical conclusion, that a form of meaningful, welfare-enhancing competition can be expected to emerge from firms that exercise market power. How can that be? We think the more problematic question is, How can meaningful *competition*, conceived of as a *process*, be conceptualized under the banner of "perfect competition"? First, *static* models are *static*, with all results determined instantaneously, or rather by specification of the model. No prospect exists of the kind of "process" that is required to allocate real resources over time in real-world markets. Second, with the conditions specified as "perfect," we can hardly imagine improvement, which is what real markets in a world of scarcity are supposed to foster, even if we could think in terms of the so-called price competition as a process. Last, under such a market setting, prices can alter the allocation of resources only in fairly minor ways, not in the fairly large ways that are likely to be involved when goods, and the markets for them, are not given but have to be imagined, created, and developed through time. At the very least, our perspective allows for the use of resources in ways that are truly crucial for human progress, the conception and development of new goods and of the markets for the goods (with the conception and development of *markets* for goods as important and perhaps no less challenging and resource demanding than the conception and development of the *goods* themselves).

We have indicated repeatedly how Joseph Schumpeter was far more on target in his treatment of monopoly, albeit limited and cursory, than are many contemporary economists, especially those who can't conceive of a "good monopoly" other than one that is held in check by way of antitrust prosecutions or, in other ways, is regulated into competitive submission. We have tried to explore and validate the subtle wisdom of the Schumpeter quote that we used as an epigraph.

> A system—any system, economic or other—that at *every* given point of time fully utilizes its possibilities to the best advantage may yet in the long run be inferior to a system that does so at *no* given point of time, because the latter's failure to do so may be a condition for the level or speed of long-run performance. (1942, 83; emphasis in the original)

Because our themes are stark and strike at the heart of what economists have taught for so long, we have to fear in closing that we will be misinterpreted, especially if we don't set out the required qualifications. To clarify our position, we have never claimed or meant to intimate in this book that *all* monopolies are good. Without question, beyond some point, there is some degree and persistence of monopoly power in given markets that would lead any economist or analyst to conclude that human welfare is, on balance, being reduced. We suggest that before the advent of private overnight delivery services and e-mail, the U.S. Postal Service, protected from the threat of competition by the legislated ban on private first-class mail delivery by private firms, was one such monopoly. Fortunately, communication technology has made first-class mail delivery an increasingly marginal service.

Our arguments lead us to the concept of *optimum monopoly*—a level of pervasiveness of monopoly and degree of market power of all monopolies that is "just right." Put in economic terms, optimum monopoly is that extent of monopoly presence in an economy that fully maximizes human welfare over time. The optimum level of monopoly may give rise to allocative inefficiencies in some markets at any (and perhaps every) point in time. However, those short-run inefficiencies are more than offset by the gains over time from the creativity inspired, or caused by the extent of, monopoly presence.

We don't pretend to know what that level of monopoly is, just as Schumpeter didn't know what the optimum was when he suggested the concept, albeit implicitly (and without using the phrase), in the preceding passage and throughout his classic work, *Capitalism, Socialism, and Democracy* (1942). Moreover, we don't need to know exactly what the optimum is any more than other economists need to know, exactly, what the efficient allocation of resources is (and, we insist, they have no idea what it is exactly). A concept such as *optimum monopoly* is useful only as an analytical construct that can inform positive and normative discussions of how a market economy operates and how it should be structured for the betterment of people.

But we are convinced, given all the arguments we have put forward, that an economy inundated with perfectly competitive markets is likely to be suboptimum, and an economy with nothing but oppressive pure monopolies is likely to be equally suboptimum. The optimum prevalence of monopoly is necessarily in between those two extremes. We also know that while optimum monopoly is difficult to define precisely as a standard for judging an economy, and far less subject to mathematical specification than is perfect competition, it is surely a better standard for judging the *efficiency* of an economy taken as a whole and over time than is perfect competition. Optimum monopoly is achievable. Perfect competition is not even conceivably achievable because of its presumption of perfect market conditions, including zero transaction and entry/exit costs and complete information, a blatant analytical sleight of hand that assumes away the bedrock cornerstone of economics, scarcity.

By the standard of optimum monopoly, a state of perfect competition throughout an economy and over time is necessarily less than perfect in terms of the standard we have in mind, maximization of human welfare over time (not just the more narrow concept of efficiency in the allocation of known and given resources in the production of known and given goods and services at a given point in time). That is to say, the level of human welfare achieved in a fully, perfectly competitive economy is subject to improvement by the introduction of some level of monopoly presence, or so we have argued at length. We see a movement away from a fully, perfectly competitive economy as leading to enhancement of human welfare in several key ways (all of which have been at the heart of discussions in foregoing chapters).

- "Normal profits," the minimum return required to keep capital in place in a static model, allow for no return for the discovery and creation of goods and services that are not given. This is because, in static analysis, no need exists for any reward for entrepreneurial alertness. The analysis is restricted to the goods and services that are given. The economic actors within firms in such analysis are limited in their role to that of managers or allocators or maximizers. They do not need to be alert to profitable opportunities that have theretofore gone unrecognized.

Hence, in a more dynamic, real-world economy in which *development* or *progress* is to be anticipated in some systematic way, some supranormal profits must occur, and this level of profitability must be above the level achievable in a perfectly competitive environment. This means, to our way of thinking, that there must be the reality or prospects of economic profits. If entrepreneurial alertness can be viewed as any other normal resource, we would expect that the extent and intensity of the alertness would be a function of the extent of economic profits. Therefore, entrepreneurial alertness, and the development it can spawn, can be functionally related to the extent of entry barriers, for without some barriers to entry at some level, there can be no economic profits.

- Economic profits may not be needed in a world in which the only variables subject to firm decisions are output and price for known goods and services for which the minimum production costs and demands are also known. However, in a world full of risk, economic profits are necessarily crucial. When products and services are created before markets for them are developed, product and firm failures are bound to occur, which means that economic losses are likely to abound. To achieve even normal profits across a portfolio of products and services and firms, the prospect of economic profits must exist that offset in present value terms the expected economic losses. The prospects of entry barriers (to some degree) in some entrepreneurial endeavors that allow for the required economic profits must therefore exist as well.

- As is usually done in narrow static analytics, economic profits drive firms to enter markets only where the economic profits were made. Hence, barriers to entry can undercut realizable economic gains because, in such narrow contexts, there is underproduction in the monopoly markets—and no thought is given to offsetting gains elsewhere in the economy. However, the reality or just the prospects of economic profits in some protected market can energize entrepreneurs to create goods and services—and the markets for those goods and services—that are far removed in product category from the monopolized market. The economic gains from product and service discovery and creation in these far-removed markets can easily swamp in value any short-run efficiency losses in the monopolized markets. We can only surmise that at least up to some point, the greater the reality of economic profits in monopolized markets, the more entrepreneurs will be energized to discover and create products and services in far-removed markets.

- Zero economic profits that characterize perfectly competitive markets, because of no entry barriers and zero transactions costs, create a situation that does not allow for firms to engage in strategic pricing behavior across time that can ultimately work to the betterment of consumers as well as the monopolies. We noted how network effects can encourage firms to charge low, zero, or negative prices initially in order to build their networks, which can lead to an enhancement in consumer demand as the networks grow through time. If economic profits were precluded from building such network markets, producers would have an impaired incentive to lower their prices initially. The networks, if they are built, might then grow more slowly, be less pervasive, and be less beneficial than they would be if network firms were able to achieve monopoly profits (because of, say, the presence of switching costs) when the network is developed.

- We noted in our discussion of the client effect and bonding effect that monopoly price increases can actually increase inframarginal consumer welfare when the value that consumers place on goods is a function of who consumes the good or service. And price increases are bound to affect exactly who will do the consuming and, hence, can create consumer mixes that increase consumer welfare.

- We also noted in our discussion of the bonding effect that monopoly prices and profits ensure that monopolies can suffer a true economic loss for misbehavior and, hence, can add to the value consumers get from buying the good, because contracts then have a self-enforcing dimension.

- Clearly, not all monopoly prices are antisocial. We posit that few people, including economists, would argue that a monopolized hit-man market would be socially inferior to a competitive one, mainly because there would then be fewer hits under the monopolized market condition (which the people subject to the hits would likely appreciate, even if economists don't).[2] This leads us to the more general point that the monopolization of markets for "bads" (as distinguished from "goods") could yield social value apart from any welfare gains the consumers might expect.[3]

- Finally, if all economic gains (above costs, including normal profits) were realized solely by consumers, as is the case in perfectly competitive markets, we have argued that the justice of such outcomes would be deemed dubious even by consumers. This, of course, would clearly be the case if such a distribution of gains adversely affected the flow of new and improved products that are available for consumption. Consumers would want to share the gains—some of their consumer surplus—with producers just to heighten the flow of new and improved products. However, we suggest that even independent of any enhanced flow of new and improved products, many consumers would find some sense of improved justice in the distribution of gains if at least some portion of the gains flowed to the firms that created them. Even economists should want gains from trade to be *mutually* beneficial, which to us means that firms creating added consumer surplus should be able to share, at least to some extent, in the added value the firms create.

These points lead us to the view that, at least for purposes of argumentation, we can think of starting with an economy in which perfectly competitive markets are fully pervasive. At this end of the competitive spectrum for the economy, the introduction of some minimum degree of monopolization could immediately improve people's assessments of their present discounted evaluation of their welfare. Over time, the monopoly profits—those generated currently and those expected in the future—could inspire the development of more new and improved goods and services through time. We can imagine that as the monopolization of markets is extended, additional gains could occur.

Having said that, however, we can also imagine that *beyond some point* as the monopolization of markets is extended, human welfare could begin to decline. This is because the inefficiencies generated from the allocative inefficiencies in a sequence of short runs begin to more than offset any potential gains to be had from additional incentives for entrepreneurs to discover, innovate, and heighten the "perennial gale of creative destruction" through time. At that extent of competitiveness (or monopolization), the economy would have reached the level of *optimum monopoly*.

How much is too much monopolization? Frankly, we confess again that we don't know, and the matter is of little concern to us, mainly because the optimum (as is true of all optimums) is bound to differ from economy to economy and across time. Also, the optimum we have in mind could not be represented with a scalar measure, but would be represented by a mix of monopoly powers that varied from industry to industry. Our main focus in this book has been on positing the existence of such an optimum that could be far removed from economists' idealized competitive economy. Beyond making that conceptual point, we suggest that the conventional view of monopoly has warped policy discussions and practices, perhaps leading to too much emphasis on identifying the "evils of monopoly" at every bend in the economy and not recognizing monopolies' offsetting merits. Our concern here is evident in public policy discussions of how brand names, switching costs, network effects, market dominance, and tacit (as well as explicit) collusions have practically everywhere contributed to the creation and maintenance of market power that, in itself, is prima facie evidence of consumer welfare losses and by the virtual absence of public recognition (aside from the arguments pressed by neo-Schumpeterian economists) that some level of monopoly presence in the economy could foster economic development over time. And we hasten to add that although we may not know the point of optimum monopoly, the economists at the Federal Trade Commission and in the Antitrust Division of the Justice Department have no firmer idea of what the optimum is than do we. Indeed, we suspect our position on the issue is superior to that of legions of policymakers and competition enforcers because we have at least considered carefully that the optimum can be something significantly less perfect than perfect competition.

We acknowledge that our perspective on monopoly could lead to the view that because some monopoly presence is "good," it should be promoted with (renewed) government-dictated regulations intended to restrict market entry and price competition. For example, our line of argument could be used to justify the resurrection of now defunct government agencies, for example, the Civil Aeronautics Board (which regulated plane fares and routes) and the Interstate Commerce Commission (which regulated the entry, rates, and routes for the trucking industry). The problem with such an extension of our argument is not that it would be incorrect in a few identified cases *if* properly done—a very big *if*.[4] The problem is, as Schumpeter recognized explicitly, "There is no general case for indiscriminate 'trust-busting' or for the prosecution of everything that qualifies as a restraint of trade. Rational as distinguished from vindictive regulation by public authority turns out to be an extremely delicate problem which not every government agency, particularly when in full cry against big business, can be trusted to solve" (1942, 95). Moreover, the politics of the moment can lead to the misuse and abuse of any argument that "monopoly is good" by industry interest groups that would like nothing better than to increase their stockholders' wealth (above that implied by our arguments for optimum monopoly) through the legislation of their own protection from competition. The argument could also be easily misused and abused by politicians who would like nothing better than to pad the pockets of the industry interest groups that, in turn, pad the politicians' campaign coffers, if not pockets. We would be the first among economists to fear that our argument's wide acceptance could weaken the case against destructive rent seeking in Washington and state capitals and thereby could lead to too much monopoly.

What can and should be done? Our purpose in this volume has not been to improve policy by listing concrete reform proposals. Our purpose has been mainly to change the orientation of professional discussions of monopoly in the economy; therefore, any answer to the question we pose must be limited. Nevertheless, because so much of antitrust policy has been founded on the standard perfect competition/pure monopoly dichotomy in economics, we think that a total review of antitrust law and practice is in order. Perhaps that body of law and practice should be reconstituted with more liberties given to at least *privately engineered* monopolies, to allow them to be monopolies without so much fear of being prosecuted for antitrust violations. We emphasize *privately engineered* because we share Schumpeter's predisposition that monopolies that are not supported by public authorities are likely to be temporary, that is, have a tendency to eventually sow the seeds of their own market retrenchment and demise. Even enduring monopolies should not, from our perspective, necessarily be candidates for antitrust busting. The problem is that such an assault on successful and enduring monopolies can undermine the creative energies of a host of entrepreneurs, ones that also seek to become successful and enduring monopolies. As we have said, monopolies, and their profits, are an unheralded source of energy for Adam Smith's "invisible hand" that works its wonder through markets.

It probably comes as no surprise that we have a healthy skepticism about the long-run efficacy of antitrust policy, given that the record of antitrust prosecution has been full of episodes of its misuse and abuse, with the government's enforcement resources too easily captured by firms seeking to use antitrust law to protect themselves against market competition from more efficient firms.[5] This skepticism has been built on the observed *practice* of antitrust enforcement, not on perceived problems with the underlying monopoly theory. The arguments put forth in this volume should heighten skepticism over whether antitrust enforcement will in practice lead to social improvement since the underlying theory is in key ways defective and can misguide enforcement even when the enforcers believe they have the best of intentions.

The truly worrisome monopolies are those that are government engineered and maintained. We are too steeped in the rent-seeking literature to not worry about opening wider the gates to government-established and government-maintained monopolies. We can only hope that our arguments are not misused.

Notes

Preface

1. Developed in the mid-1930s, more than two hundred million copies of Monopoly have been sold in twenty-six languages and in eighty countries (as reported on the Parker Brothers Web site for its Monopoly board game, http://monopoly.com).

2. Strictly speaking, economists recognize three market structures in which firms have monopoly or market power: pure monopoly (a market with a single producer that has no close substitutes and that is protected by prohibitive barrier to entry), oligopoly (a market in which a handful of producers' production and pricing decisions are interdependent), and monopolistic competition (a market in which a number of producers' production and pricing decisions are not interdependent). The key unifying features of all three market structures is that the demand curves of individual firms are downward sloping, which makes the firms price searchers (as opposed to price takers under perfect competition). The fact that all firms in these three market structures can search for the profit-maximizing price by restricting their production below competitive levels necessarily implies that the markets will not be optimally efficient.

3. In chapters 4 and 5, we cover the various court rulings that Microsoft is a monopoly. Here we can point out that when the *Wall Street Journal* reported Microsoft's growth in sales and profits during the first quarter of 2003, the reporter couldn't resist adding, "Still, the overall results showed Microsoft—at least for now—continues to weather the technology downturn better than its competitors, owing to its *monopoly* position in personal-computer software. The company is milking the benefits of a new licensing program introduced in July that created an unprecedented surge in deferred revenue" (Guth 2003, n.p., emphasis added).

4. This is a theme that William Baumol develops at length in *The Free-Market Innovation Machine* (2002), with citations to a number of theoretical and empirical studies, most notably Lucas 1988, Romer 1994, and Solow 1957.

5. Standard Oil in 1910 and Microsoft in 1998 were accused of establishing their monopolies through predatory practices that, once successful, enabled them to capture substantial monopoly profits. The arguments of the antitrust authorities have been critiqued in the two cases by McGee (1958) and McKenzie (2000).

6. Schumpeter wrote, "The fundamental impulse that sets and keeps the capitalist engine in motion comes from the new consumers' goods, the new methods of production or transportation, and the new markets, the new forms of industrial organization that capitalist enterprises create" (1942, 83). Schumpeter's point, and our central theme, has been echoed more recently, and supported with an array of

empirical studies, by William Baumol: "The static efficiency properties that are stressed by standard welfare economics are emphatically *not* the most important qualities of capitalist economies" (2002, viii; emphasis in the original).

7. Romer's exact words are, referring to an example Dupuit used to illustrate the problem of how market prices would not lead to some public goods being produced, "The bridge that is not built is as easy to overlook as the dog that did not bark" (1994, 26).

Chapter 1

1. Kenneth Boulding (1945), in a defense of monopoly that focused on monopoly as a societal means of alleviating more serious societal problems associated with "deflationary spirals," noted the failures of economists in attracting the attention of policymakers: "Ever since Adam Smith let off the first thunderous broadside, the attack on Monopoly has been a favorite occupation of economists," only to quickly add that "it cannot be claimed, however, that the attack has been particularly successful; indeed, it seems to have produced more smoke than shot," given the extent to which governments everywhere have been in the business of granting monopoly favors across the business landscape (1945, 524).

2. The resource "misallocation" occurs because of the presumption that the units of the goods not produced in the monopolized industries, because of the monopolies' restrictions on market supply, are more valuable to consumers than the units of the goods actually produced with the freed resources in the competitive markets. The misallocation problem will be discussed in some detail in chapter 2.

3. Of course, economists, scholars, and judges would agree that the government's cost of imposing a solution for monopoly must not be greater than the gains from dissolving the monopoly.

4. Smith writes, "All the original sources of revenue, the wages of labour, the rent of land, and the profits of stock, the monopoly renders much less abundant than they otherwise would be. To promote the little interest of one little order of men in one country, it hurts the interest of all other orders of men in that country, and of all men in all other countries" (1776, bk. 4, chap. 7, ¶ 146).

5. From Smith's perspective,

> Good roads, canals, and navigable rivers, by diminishing the expence of carriage, put the remote parts of the country more nearly upon a level with those in the neighbourhood of the town. They are upon that account the greatest of all improvements. They encourage the cultivation of the remote, which must always be the most extensive circle of the country. They are advantageous to the town, by breaking down the monopoly of the country in its neighbourhood. They are advantageous even to that part of the country. Though they introduce some rival commodities into the old market, they open many new markets to its produce. (1776, bk. 1, chap. 11, ¶ 14)

6. Smith writes, "That this monopoly of the home-market frequently gives great encouragement to that particular species of industry which enjoys it, and frequently turns towards that employment a greater share of both the labour and stock

of the society than would otherwise have gone to it, cannot be doubted. But whether it tends either to increase the general industry of the society, or to give it the most advantageous direction, is not, perhaps, altogether so evident" (1776, bk. 4, chap. 2, ¶ 2).

7. Smith noted that "the cruellest of our revenue laws, I will venture to affirm, are mild and gentle in comparison of some of those which the clamour of our merchants and manufacturers has extorted from the legislature for the support of their own absurd and oppressive monopolies. Like the laws of Draco, these laws may be said to be all written in blood" (1776, bk. 4, chap. 8, ¶ 17).

8. Smith explained,

> The high duties which have been imposed upon the importation of many different sorts of foreign goods, in order to discourage their consumption in Great Britain, have in many cases served only to encourage smuggling, and in all cases have reduced the revenue of the customs below what more moderate duties would have afforded. The saying of Dr. Swift, that in the arithmetic of the customs two and two, instead of making four, make sometimes only one, holds perfectly true with regard to such heavy duties which never could have been imposed had not the mercantile system taught us, in many cases, to employ taxation as an instrument, not of revenue, but of monopoly. (1776, bk. 5, chap. 2, ¶ 172)

9. In Smith's words, "Merchants and manufacturers are not contented with the monopoly of the home market, but desire likewise the most extensive foreign sale for their goods. Their country has no jurisdiction in foreign nations, and therefore can seldom procure them any monopoly there. They are generally obliged, therefore, to content themselves with petitioning for certain encouragements to exportation" (1776, bk. 4, chap. 4, ¶ 1).

10. Malthus maintained that by more equally distributing land, there would be a more equal distribution of monopoly rent. However, such an outcome from a more equal distribution of land would do little to deny his pessimistic view of the impact on human suffering from the press of population growth.

> While from the law of primogeniture, and other European customs, land bears a monopoly price, a capital can never be employed in it with much advantage to the individual; and, therefore, it is not probable that the soil should be properly cultivated. And, though in every civilized state, a class of proprietors and a class of labourers must exist; yet one permanent advantage would always result from a nearer equalization of property. The greater the number of proprietors, the smaller must be the number of labourers: a greater part of society would be in the happy state of possessing property; and a smaller part in the unhappy state of possessing no other property than their labour. But the best directed exertions, though they may alleviate, can never remove the pressure of want; and it will be difficult for any person who contemplates the genuine situation of man on earth, and the general laws of nature, to suppose it possible that any, but the most enlightened efforts, could place mankind in a state where "few would die without measuring out the

whole period of present existence allotted to them; where pain and distemper would be unknown among them; and death would come upon them like a sleep, in consequence of no other cause than gradual and unavoidable decay." (1798, chap. 17, ¶ 10)

11. In Ricardo's words, "But how can they permanently support the market price of their goods above the natural price, when every one of their fellow citizens is free to enter into the trade? They are guaranteed against foreign, but not against home competition. The real evil arising to the country from such monopolies, if they can be called by that name, lies, not in raising the market price of such goods, but in raising their real and natural price. By increasing the cost of production, a portion of the labour of the country is less productively employed" (1817, n. 54).

12. In *Economic Sophisms*, Bastiat wrote in his petition,

We are suffering from the ruinous competition of a foreign rival who apparently works under conditions so far superior to our own for the production of light that he is *flooding* the *domestic market* with it at an incredibly low price; for the moment he appears, our sales cease, all the consumers turn to him, and a branch of French industry whose ramifications are innumerable is all at once reduced to complete stagnation. This rival, which is none other than the sun, is waging war on us so mercilessly that we suspect he is being stirred up against us by perfidious Albion (excellent diplomacy nowadays!), particularly because he has for that haughty island a respect that he does not show for us.

We ask you to be so good as to pass a law requiring the closing of all windows, dormers, skylights, inside and outside shutters, curtains, casements, bull's-eyes, deadlights, and blinds—in short, all openings, holes, chinks, and fissures through which the light of the sun is wont to enter houses, to the detriment of the fair industries with which, we are proud to say, we have endowed the country, a country that cannot, without betraying ingratitude, abandon us today to so unequal a combat. (1845, ser. 1, chap. 7, ¶¶ 6, 7)

13. Bastiat wrote in *Economic Harmonies*,

But, make no mistake about it, to affirm this is to affirm that man's tendencies are inherently evil, evil in their nature, evil in their essence; it is to affirm that his natural bent is toward his deterioration and that his mind is attracted irresistibly toward error. What good, then, are our schools, our study, our research, our discussions, except to add momentum to our descent down the fatal slope; since, for man, to learn to choose is to learn to commit suicide? And if man's tendencies are perverse, where will the social planners seek to place their fulcrum? According to their premises, it will have to be outside of humanity. Will they seek it within themselves, in their own intelligence, in their own hearts? But they are not yet gods: they too are men and hence, along with all humanity, careening down toward the fatal abyss. Will they call upon the state to intervene? But the state is composed of men; and we should have to prove that the men who form the state constitute a class apart, to whom the general laws of society are not applicable, since they are called upon to make the laws. Unless this be proved, the facing of the dilemma is not even postponed. (1850, chap. 1, ¶ 87)

In *Selected Essays on Political Economy*, Bastiat lampooned the argument that "competition leads to monopoly" by suggesting if that were, "*For the same reason, low costs lead to high prices? That competition tends to exhaust the sources of consumption and pushes production into a destructive activity? That competition forces production to increase and consumption to decrease?* Whence it follows that free peoples produce in order not to consume—that liberty *means both oppression and madness,* and that M. Louis Blanc simply must step in and set matters straight?" (1848, chap. 2, ¶ 200).

14. Bastiat wrote, "I do not mean here a tendency to desire equality, but a tendency to achieve it. Nevertheless, equality has not been achieved or else is being achieved so slowly that when we compare two widely separated ages we can hardly discern that any forward steps have been taken at all" (1850, chap. 16, ¶ 110).

15. For example, Bastiat writes,

The earth is a wondrous chemical workshop wherein many materials and elements are mixed together and worked on, and finally come forth as grain, fruit, flax, etc. Nature has presented this vast workshop to man as a *gratuitous* gift, and has divided it into many compartments suitable for many different kinds of production. But certain men have come forth, have laid hands on these things, and have declared: This compartment belongs to me; that one also; all that comes from it will be my exclusive property. And, amazingly enough, *this usurpation of privilege,* far from being disastrous to society, has turned out to be advantageous. (1850, chap. 9, ¶ 57)

16. Bastiat obviously enjoyed his retort to people who equated property rights with monopoly power.

After he had invested the rest of his dollars in buildings, fences, clearings, trenchings, drainage, preparations, etc., after he had dug, plowed, harrowed, sowed, and harvested, came the moment for selling the crop. "Now at last I'll know," cried Jonathan, still obsessed with the problem of value, "whether in becoming a landowner I have turned into a monopolist, a privileged aristocrat, a despoiler of my fellow men, or a usurper of the divine bounty." (1850, chap. 9, ¶ 122)

17. Bastiat wrote, "There is, then, between the favors bestowed by Nature and artificial monopoly this profound difference: the former are the result of pre-existent and inevitable scarcity; the latter is the cause of artificial and unnatural scarcity" (1850, n. 13).

18. A Prisoner's Dilemma is a game-theoretic predicament in which all parties, acting individually and rationally, can end up worse off by their actions. Each person driving to work can reason that exhaust from his car does little to nothing, by itself, to degrade air quality, but the exhaust of *all* drivers can cause an environmental mess and health problems for all drivers and everyone else in the area.

19. The word *monopoly* or *monopolist* is nowhere found in Marx's principal work, *Capital.*

20. Alfred Marshall wrote,

Again, markets vary with regard to the period of time which is allowed to the forces of demand and supply to bring themselves into equilibrium with one another, as well as with regard to the area over which they extend. And this element of Time requires more careful attention just now than does that of Space. For the nature of the equilibrium itself, and that of the causes by which it is determined, depend on the length of the period over which the market is taken to extend. We shall find that if the period is short, the supply is limited to the stores which happen to be at hand: if the period is longer, the supply will be influenced, more or less, by the cost of producing the commodity in question; and if the period is very long, this cost will in its turn be influenced, more or less, by the cost of producing the labour and the material things required for producing the commodity. These three classes of course merge into one another by imperceptible degrees. We will begin with the first class; and consider in the next chapter those temporary equilibria of demand and supply, in which "supply" means in effect merely the stock available at the time for sale in the market; so that it cannot be directly influenced by the cost of production. (1890, bk. 5, chap. 1, ¶ 20)

21. With regard to a change in the monopolist's fixed cost, Marshall wrote,

First let this increase or diminution of the expenses be a fixed sum, bearing on the undertaking as one undivided whole and not varying with the amount of the commodity produced. Then, whatever be the price charged and the amount of the commodity sold, the monopoly revenue will be increased or diminished, as the case may be, by this sum; and therefore that selling price which afforded the maximum monopoly revenue before the change will afford it afterwards; the change therefore will not offer to the monopolist any inducement to alter his course of action. (1890, bk. 5, chap. 14, ¶ 11)

To this Marshall adds, "The same is true of a tax or a bounty proportioned not to the gross receipts of the undertaking, but to its monopoly revenue" (1890, bk. 5, chap. 14, ¶ 12).

22. Marshall wrote,

On the other hand a tax proportional to the amount produced gives an inducement to the monopolist to lessen his output and raise his price. For by so doing he diminishes his expenses. And the excess of total receipts over total outlay may therefore be now increased by a diminution of output; though before the imposition of the tax it would have been lessened. Further, if before the imposition of the tax the net revenue was only a little greater than that which would have been afforded by much smaller sales, then the monopolist would gain by reducing his production very greatly; and hence in such cases as this, the change is likely to cause a very great diminution of production and rise of price. The opposite effects will be caused by a change which diminishes the expense of working the monopoly by a sum that varies directly with the amount produced under it. (1890, bk. 5, chap. 14, ¶ 13)

23. In Marshall's words,

The following general results are capable of exact proof; but on a little consideration they will appear so manifestly true as hardly to require proof. Firstly, the amount which the monopolist will offer for sale will be greater (and the price at which he will sell it will be less) if he is to any extent desirous to promote the interests of consumers than if his sole aim is to obtain the greatest possible monopoly revenue; and secondly, the amount produced will be greater (and the selling price will be less) the greater be the desire of the monopolist to promote the interests of consumers; *i.e.* the larger be the percentage of its actual value at which he counts in consumers' surplus with his own revenue. (1890, bk. 5, chap. 14, ¶ 5)

24. Bain wrote,

The value of the condition of entry may be positive and there may be *"effectively impeded" entry* in the following sense: The most favored established firms could raise their prices . . . enough above their competitive level without attracting entry to make their long-run profits at the best entry-forestalling price greater than if they charged higher prices and induced entry (thus sharing the market with further sellers. At the same time, the best entry-forestalling price *is below that which would maximize their profits were there no threat of entry*. This implies that the entry-forestalling price is moderately above costs, but not as high as a "monopolistic" price would be in the absence of any threat of entry. (1956, 22; emphasis in the original)

The theory of entry-forestalling or limit pricing has been severely criticized by Osborne (1964), Stigler (1968, 67–70), Pashigian (1968), and McGee (1971, 72–75).

25. According to *Merriam-Webster's Unabridged Dictionary*, monopoloid means "of, relating to, or resembling a monopoly, implying 'gigantism.'"

26. Schumpeter's predilection to assess economists' professional "vision" of perfect competition as an "ideology" resulting everywhere in the denunciation of monopoly was evident in Schumpeter's American Economic Association presidential address. In that address, he takes on what he saw as the absence of an "ideology" underlying the work of Adam Smith, but a pervasive ideology underlying the work of Karl Marx and John Maynard Keynes. He concludes by pointing to how economists' vision of "pure competition" warps inappropriately economists' thinking on monopoly at the same time that such a vision was necessary for the advance of economics as a "science."

A majority of economists would subscribe to Molina's dictum: *monopolium est injustum et rei publicae injuriosum* [a monopoly is an injustice and a real public injury]. But it is not this value judgment which is relevant to my argument—one may dislike modern largest-scale business exactly as one may dislike many other features of modern civilization—but the analysis that leads up to it, and the ideological influence this analysis displays. Anyone who has read Marshall's *Principles* . . . should know that among the innumerable patterns that are covered by those terms are many of which benefit and not injury to economic efficiency and the consumer's interest ought to be predicated. More modern analysis permits to show still more clearly that no sweeping or unqualified statement can be true for all of them; and that the mere fact of size, single-sellership, discrimination, and cooperative price setting are in themselves inadequate for asserting that the resulting performance is, in any relevant sense of the word, inferior to the one which could be expected under pure competition in conditions attainable under pure competition—in other words, that the analysis offers no material in support of *indiscriminate* "trust busting" and that such material must be looked for in the particular circumstances of each individual case. Nevertheless, many economists support *indiscriminate* "trust busting" and the interesting point is that enthusiastic sponsors of the private-enterprise system are particularly prominent among them. Theirs is the ideology of a capitalist economy that would fill its social functions admirably by virtue of the magic of pure competition were it not for the monster of monopoly or oligopoly that casts a shadow on an otherwise bright scene. No argument avails about the performance of largest-scale business, about the inevitability of its emergence, about the social costs involved in destroying existing structures, about the futility of the hallowed ideal of pure competition—or in fact ever elicits any response other than most obviously sincere indignation. (1949, 357–58; emphasis in the original)

Schumpeter concludes his address by noting an inherent irony in science, that of how the "prescientific cognitive act" of devising a "vision" of markets captured in pure competition that is a source of economists' ideology with regard to monopoly is also "a prerequisite of our scientific work": "No new departure in any science is possible without it. Our stock of facts and tools grows and rejuvenates itself in the process. And so—though we proceed slowly because of our ideologies, we might not proceed at all without them" (1949, 359). In a real sense, Schumpeter saw the "perennial gale of creative destruction" to be as critical to the advancement of science as it was for the advancement of whole economies, and for much the same reasons: "There is more comfort in the observation that no economic ideology lasts forever and that, with a likelihood that approximates certainty, we eventually grow out of each" (1949, 359).

27. Schumpeter gave greater importance in terms of motivating firms to the threat of nonprice competition over actual nonprice competition.

It is hardly necessary to point out that competition of this kind we now have in mind [from new products, technologies, and organizational forms] acts not only when in being but also when it is merely an ever-present threat. It disciplines before it attacks. The businessman feels himself to be in a competitive situation even if he is alone in his field or if, though not alone, he holds a position such that investigating government experts fail to see any effective competition between him and any other firms in the same or a neighboring field and in consequence conclude that his talk, under examination, about his competitive sorrows is all make-believe. In many cases, though not in all, this will in the long-run enforce behavior very similar to the perfectly competitive pattern. (1942, 85)

28. Innovations are the ultimate source of economic profits in the Schumpeterian system, mainly because at the instant they occur, there can be no direct competitors: "Since the entrepreneur has no competitors when the new product first appears, the determination of price proceeds wholly, or within certain limits, according to the principles of monopoly price. Thus there is a monopoly element in profit in a capitalist economy" (1934, 152). However, the profit is not likely to be long-lived, since there is a "tendency" built in to capitalism for industry to be "reorganized" that "will finally restore the rule of the law of cost" (1934, 135). Schumpeter points to how a trading company might make a profit by setting up trade in "glass beads to a negro tribe" for the first time, but that "an appropriate organization would soon come into existence and trade in glass beads would very soon no longer yield a profit" (1934, 135).

29. In his *Theory of Economic Development* (1934), Schumpeter gave "profit" a more critical role in capitalism than a mere "incentive": "Without development there is no profit, without profit no development. For the capitalist system it must be added further that without profit there would be no accumulation of wealth. At least there would not be the great social phenomenon which we have viewed—this is certainly a consequence of development and indeed of profit" (154). To Schumpeter, "profit" was not the equivalent of "saving," meaning nonconsumption, "in the proper sense." This is because profit, which springs from the work of entrepreneurs and feeds the buildup of "most fortunes," "is not an encroachment upon the customary standard of life" (154).

30. As Oakley (1990, 140) has pointed out, profit was not simply the residual, what is left over from revenues after all claimants other than the entrepreneur are paid. Schumpeter wrote, "We want finally to emphasize that profit is also not wages, although the analogy is tempting. It is certainly not a residuum; it is the expression of the value of what the entrepreneur contributes to production in exactly the same sense that wages are the value expression of what the worker 'produces'" (1934, 153). Schumpeter seems to suggest here that profit is the entrepreneur's incentive to innovate, an especially appealing interpretation given the extent to which Schumpeter viewed innovation as endogenous to the economic system. However, he confused the interpretation when he wrote that "it cannot be said of . . . [profit] that it just suffices to call forth precisely the 'quantity of entrepreneurial services required.' Such a quantity, theoretically determined, does not exist. And the total amount of profit actually obtained in a given time, as well as the profit

realised by an individual entrepreneur, may be much greater than that necessary to call forth the entrepreneurial services which were actually operative" (1934, 154–55).

31. Schumpeter wrote,

Practically any investment entails, as a necessary complement of entrepreneurial action, certain safeguarding activities such as insuring or hedging. Long-range investing under rapidly changing conditions, especially under conditions that change or may change at any moment under the impact of new commodities and technologies, is like shooting at a target that is not only indistinct but moving—and moving jerkily at that. Hence it becomes necessary to resort to such protective devices as patents and temporary secrecy of processes or, in some cases, long-period contracts secured in advance. But these protective devices which most economists accept as normal elements of rational management are only special cases of a larger class comprising many others which most economists condemn although they do not differ fundamentally from the recognized ones. (1942, 88)

32. Schumpeter adds,

What we have got to accept is that it ["large scale establishment or unit of control"] has come to be the most powerful engine of that progress and in particular long-term expansion of total output not only in spite of, but to a considerable extent through, this strategy which looks so restrictive when viewed in the individual case and from the individual point in time. In this respect, perfect competition is not only impossible, but inferior, and has no title to being set up as a model of ideal efficiency. (1942, 106)

33. Schumpeter adds later, "Especially in manufacturing, a monopoly position is in general no cushion to sleep on. As it [a monopoly position] can be gained, so it can be retained only by alertness and energy" (1942, 102).

34. At the same time that Schumpeter defended "bigness" in business, as well as marveled at capitalism's accomplishments, he saw a potential dark side to the growth and efficiency of business: The growth would be a source of capitalism's undoing, leading to a replacement by a socialist state. He reasoned that technological progress was "increasingly becoming the business of teams of trained specialists who turn out what is required and make it work in predictable ways" (1942, 132), a process that eliminates the "romantic" role of the entrepreneurial ventures and "expropriates the bourgeoisie as a class" (1942, 134). He concludes that with the entrepreneur displaced, "dematerialized, defunctionalized, and absentee ownership" cannot possibly "call forth moral allegiance," the net result of which is that there will be no one left to defend capitalism (1942, 142). The state can then do what large private firms once did, clearly a deduction that represents an echo of Marx (Gintis 1991).

35. Early in his *Recent Economic Changes*, Wells makes the same point, that "nothing marks more clearly the rate of material progress than the rapidity with

which that which is old and has been considered wealth is destroyed by new inventions and discoveries" (1889, 30–31).

36. Wells pointed out that Standard Oil had used its "millions of capital . . . most skillfully in promoting consumption, and in devising and adopting a great number of ingenious methods whereby the cost of production has been reduced to an extent that, at the outset, would not have seemed possible" (1889, 132).

37. For example, Nelson and Winter (1982, 114) have restated it this way: "A market structure involving large firms with considerable degree of market power is the price that society must pay for rapid technological advance." Adams and Dirlam (1966, 167) in their examination of the steel industry interpreted the hypothesis to mean "that large firms with substantial market power have both greater incentive and more resources for research and development." Mansfield argues that Schumpeter meant "that in recent times innovations have been carried out primarily by very large firms" (1968, 84) and that "such firms are needed to produce the technical achievements on which economic progress depends" (6).

38. For example, Worley (1961) found that for firms in six out of eight two-digit industries studied, R&D personnel as a percentage of total employment fell with firm size. Rosenberg drew much the same conclusion (1976). Hamberg (1964) found that within the twelve industries he studied, R&D expenditures increased with firm sales and with industry concentration ratios. However, only 30 percent of the variance in R&D could be explained by industry concentration. Horowitz (1962) found a similar but weak relationship between R&D expenditures and industry concentration.

39. For example, Scherer (1965) found that "inventive output" (measured by patents issued in 1959 to 448 of the 500 firms on *Fortune*'s list of the 500 largest industrial firms) increased with firm sales, but at a less than proportional rate. He also found that inventive output was not found to be related to firms' market power, profitability, liquidity, or product diversification. Markham (1965) found that the R&D expenditures-to-sales ration rose "markedly" until the firm reached an annual sales level of $100 million, only to decline slightly thereafter. Markham also found that the differences in the ratios of R&D to sales between different size firms declined "substantially" as smaller firms increased their research activities, mainly as "imitators."

40. For example, Mansfield (1964) found that the relative R&D expenditures as a percentage of sales for the "largest" and "somewhat smaller firms" varied by industry. In the petroleum, drugs, and glass industries, the largest firms' expenditures on R&D were a smaller percentage of sales than their "somewhat smaller" industry counterparts. However, the largest firms spent more in the chemical industry and less in the steel industry.

41. For a more recent review of the literature, see Sanjay 1988.

42. Then there are other researchers who concede that firm size could very well lead to constricted innovativeness and inventiveness. After all, large firms have long chains of command and impaired incentives for managers and workers to be innovative. Nevertheless, the revolution in information technology can be expected to

correct these organizational and incentive problems, thus giving new life to Schumpeter's hypothesis (Nolan and Croson 1995), a subject to which we will return in later chapters.

43. Successful companies can be thought of as often being on the horns of a nontrivial R&D dilemma, whether further to refine and exploit known and successful technologies that they have or break with their current product line (or way of doing business) and assume the added risks of developing breakthrough technologies. Their dilemma is made more troublesome and problematic for them because the benefits of developing their known products are better known than are the benefits of developing new products and production processes, which suggests that following the second course can lead to more failed products, as well as added costs of redirecting the firms' organizational structure and culture. By choosing (rationally) to leave the development of breakthrough products to other firms, successful firms can give rise to their own demise because of outside firms that develop the breakthrough products. Established firms can offset some of these risks by having outside firms develop the breakthrough products and then by buying the outside firms, or the products they develop, that prove successful. For more on this line of argument on the "innovator's dilemma," see Christensen 1997 and McKenzie and Galar 2003.

44. The full text of the passage in which he spells out his hypothesis is, "As soon as we go into the details and inquire into the individual items in which progress has been most conspicuous, the trail leads not to the doors of those firms that work under conditions of comparatively free competition but precisely to the doors of the large concerns—which, as in the case of agricultural machinery, also account for much of the progress in the competitive sector—*and a shocking suspicion dawns on us that big business may have had more to do with creating that standard of life than with keeping it down*" (1942, 82; emphasis added).

45. McNulty (1974, 629) points out that in *Business Cycles*, Schumpeter wrote, "Even in the world of giant firms, new ones arise and others fall into the background. Innovations still emerge primarily with the 'young' ones, and the 'old' ones display as a rule symptoms of what is euphemistically called conservatism" (1939, vol. 1, 96). In addition, Schumpeter wrote in a footnote, "There would then be some justification for treating innovations—excepting, perhaps, 'revolutionary' ones—as a function of the size of firms (possibly, as measured by output) and for arriving at a descending cost curve after all which would include such changes of the production function as presuppose a certain size and are easier to carry to effect for big firms. But we see now that this means stressing the secondary element and obscuring the essential one" (1939, vol. 1, 97, n. 1).

46. Schumpeter wrote, "Disregarding the effects of lumpiness or smoothing them [the short-run cost curves from expanded scale] out by drawing a monotonic curve through the alternating stretches of rising and falling average costs, we should, strictly speaking, get a curve which would for a small individual firm, be parallel to the quantity axis" (1939, 90), only to add that "our impression of a prevalence of decreasing cost . . . is innovation, the intrusion into the system of new production functions which incessantly shift existing cost curves" (1939, 91).

47. Specifically, Schumpeter writes, "Pure cases of long-run monopoly must be of the rarest occurrence—and that even tolerable approximations to the requirements of the concept must be still rarer than are the cases of perfect competition. The power to exploit at pleasure a given pattern of demand . . . can under the conditions of intact capitalism hardly persist for a period long enough to matter for the analysis of total output, unless buttressed by public authority, in the case of fiscal monopolies" (99).

48. Schumpeter wrote, "It is the cheap cloth, the cheap cotton and rayon fabric, boots, motorcars and so on that are the typical achievements of capitalist production, and not as a rule improvements that would mean much to the rich man. Queen Elizabeth owned silk stockings. The capitalist achievement does not typically consist in providing more silk stockings for queens but in bringing them within the reach of factory girls in return for steadily decreasing amounts of effort" (1942, 67).

49. According to Allen Oakley (1990, chaps. 1, 2), Schumpeter recognized two stages of economic development. The first stage involved the playing out of markets that approximated the requirements of highly (if not perfectly) competitive markets in which price competition dominated competition. The second stage was something of a take-off stage. In this stage firms began to grow with the success of their products, and their growth afforded them control over price.

50. Perhaps surprisingly, Schumpeter was of two minds on "perfect competition." On the one hand he denounced the market model as irrelevant. On the other hand, in his review of Joan Robinson's (1933) book on imperfect competition, he recognized the importance of the perfectly competitive model to the progress of economic science.

> It cannot be repeated too often that the case of perfect competition owes the fundamental importance which it always had and still has in economic theory to certain properties characteristic of it and neither to any tendency in the facts to conform to it nor any "desirability" of the state of the things it depicts. . . . For by virtue of those properties the theory of perfect competition still remains useful and almost indispensable background with which to compare, and therefore by which to understand, any other situation, however far removed it may be from it. (1951, 125)

51. Of course, economists often note that policies that engender monopolies should not be abolished when the costs of changing the policies are greater than the deadweight loss that can be recouped from the elimination of monopoly pricing.

52. Although Schumpeter never used the term *optimum monopoly*, the need for a balance among firms of varying size and differing market power comes through in this statement: "Economic evolution or 'progress' would differ substantially from the picture we are about to draw, if that form of organization prevailed throughout the economic organism. Giant concerns still have to react to each other's innovations, of course, but they do so in other and less predictable ways than firms which are drops in a competitive sea, and many details—in some points, more than details—would then have to be altered in our model" (1939, 96).

53. Schumpeter writes, "It [his construction of monopoly] does show that there is no general case against indiscriminate 'trust-busting' or for the prosecution of everything that qualifies as a restraint of trade. Rational as distinguished from vindictive regulation by public authority turns out to be an extremely delicate problem which not every government agency, particularly when in full cry against big business, can be trusted to solve" (1942, 91).

54. Many economists fortify the claim we intend to challenge by asking their students to repeat the refrain, "Price affects the quantity demanded, not the demand. Because of the way the demand curve is constructed as a functional relationship between price and quantity, price cannot affect demand. Something other than price must affect the demand." Our point is not that the rule economists press with their students is wrong everywhere, but rather there are important cases that violate economists' conventional position that price changes do not affect the position of the demand curve. We identify these cases as we move through the book.

Chapter 2

1. For a complete theoretical discussion of the conditions of perfect competition, see Graaff 1971.

2. Alternatively, although the *market* demand for a product might have its standard downward slope (meaning that the quantity consumers are willing and able to buy varies inversely with market price), the firms will each face a demand that is infinitely (or perfectly) elastic.

3. If the price is above the intersection, a market surplus (equal to the amount by which the amount offered on the market exceeds the amount demanded) will appear, the result of which is price competition among the sellers. The price will fall all the way *to* the intersection, and not just move *toward* the intersection. That is, the price will not hold steady at some point above the intersection, or equilibrium, price, because each producer is so small relative to the market that no one producer can withhold a part or even all of its output and keep the price from falling all the way *to* the intersection. If any firm were able to withhold its output, and hold the price above the equilibrium price, the price would be above marginal cost, and some firm or firms would move into the market, all without entry costs, to grab the unexploited profit on those last sales. The new entrants would ensure that the quantity provided in the market would match the equilibrium quantity, which means the market would not clear until the price falls to the equilibrium or intersection level.

4. We rush to note in passing that if there truly were zero transaction costs everywhere, then bargaining between buyers and sellers would also be pervasive, which means that buyers could pay sellers not to collude and sellers could pay buyers not to collude, if not colluding were wealth maximizing.

5. It's worth noting here that economists often parrot the refrain, "There is no such thing as a free lunch." That adage has merit when it is intended to convey the prevalence of cost in all matters. The Q_e units produced in figure 2.1 do have costs, as indicated by the supply curve. At the same time, in a meaningful sense there is a

gain to the market process, equal to the triangular area *ABC*, that is, in a sense, free for the taking.

6. The inefficiency is limited to the triangular area *EDC*, and not the entire area underneath the demand curve, because a presumption exists that when production is restricted in this market, the resources are released to be used elsewhere. The value of the goods in this market not produced is lost, but that loss is partially offset by the value of goods produced in other markets by the released resources.

7. We go through the development of the monopoly model here only for the benefit of those readers who might not remember their introduction to monopoly theory.

8. The pure monopolist need not make a profit in the short run. Consumers might value the monopolist's product so little that the firm can't find a price at which it can cover its costs. However, if it doesn't make a profit, or doesn't expect to make one in the long run, then it will not stay in the market, a fact that encourages the frequently heard comment, "All monopolies are (very) profitable."

9. Normal profit is that minimum level of payment that capital owners would require in order not to shift their investment elsewhere. Firms receiving a book profit equal to normal profit would be receiving an economic profit of zero.

10. The monopolist's marginal revenue curve (*MR*) is below and pivots away from its demand because it must lower its price to sell more units. If it charges $10 and sells only one unit, and if it has to lower its price to $9 to sell two units, the monopolist's marginal revenue on the second unit is $8. This is because while it sells the second unit for $9, it has to lower the price of the first unit to $9, or by a dollar, in order to sell the second. Hence, the monopolist adds only $8 ($9 – $1) to its total revenues. If the monopolist sells seven units at $7, and has to lower the price to $6 to sell eight, its marginal revenue on the eighth unit is –$1 [$6 (the selling price) – $7, the reduction in revenue from the first seven units].

11. We add "beyond some point" in parentheses to acknowledge that the level of inefficiency varies up and down as the demand curve moves from being perfectly inelastic, where there is no market inefficiency, to perfectly elastic, where there is (again) no market inefficiency. As the demand elasticity rises from zero to anything above zero, initially the inefficiency of monopoly rises. Beyond some point, however, the inefficiency must fall off, just to get back down to zero.

12. See any standard textbook in microeconomic theory, for example, Pindyck and Rubinfeld 2005, chap. 12.

13. For details of this point, see Pindyck and Rubinfeld 2005, chap. 12.

14. Of course, this argument has to be carefully circumscribed, as Buchanan recognized (1973). This is because when the monopoly restricts output of "bads," street drugs, for example, it can drive up total expenditures that consumers' drugs must make for whatever quantity of the bads is made available. Hence, while the Mafia can reduce the sale of criminalized goods, the Mafia can induce consumers to commit more crimes (muggings and bank robberies) in order to fund their purchases of criminalized goods.

15. However, it needs to be noted that estimates of the harm done by monopoly

from production restricted below competitive levels and from prices above competitive levels in the U.S. economy have been minor. Harberger (1954) estimated the summation of Harberger triangles across all industries in the United States at .1 percent of GDP. By including advertising expenditures as a part of monopoly waste generated from efforts of producers to differentiate their products, Cowling and Mueller (1978) came up with a larger estimate of the deadweight loss from monopoly power in the U.S. economy. Ferguson (1988) put the estimated deadweight loss at 1 percent of GDP by including price distortions from regulations and trade protection that give rise to market power and transfers of market surplus value from consumers to producers.

16. At the same time, firms such as Costco and Sam's Club can have a profit incentive to organize and effectively operate on behalf of consumers interested in a larger quantity through a cartel-like collective agreement. Such stores can build memberships and negotiate with wholesalers that have market pricing power on extended sales that are restricted to their members, who must pay an annual membership fee to remain among the eligible "cartel" of buyers.

17. The best, most efficient outcome is for the rent seeking to take the form of political campaign contributions that end up as cash transfers to those people who are in a position to grant the monopoly privileges. The cash transfers mean that real resources aren't wasted. However, the cash transfers can give those in power all the more incentive to grant additional monopoly privileges.

18. In his own words, Robbins defined economics this way: "Economics, as we have seen, is concerned with that aspect of behaviour which arises because of scarcity of means to achieve given means" (1946, 24).

19. In trying to explain his point about the absence of choice in much economic analysis, and to suggest how much "economics" is really applied mathematics, Buchanan asks how a beginning economics student might be expected to respond to the question, "What is the difference between an economic and a technological problem?" Buchanan suggests the student would likely be given a good grade from most principles teachers with this answer: "An economic problem arises when mutually conflicting ends are present, and when choices must be made among them. A technological problem, by comparison, is characterized by the fact that there is only one end to be maximized. There is a single best or optimal solution." He would improve his grade with this example: "When the consumer finds that she has only $10 to spend in the supermarket, she confronts an economic problem in choosing among the many competing products that are available for meeting diverse ends and objectives. By contrast, the construction engineer has $1,000,000 allotted to build the dam to certain specifications. There is only one best way to do this; locating this way constitutes the technological problem." Buchanan suggests rightly that there is no difference in the two settings or, if there is a difference, it is a difference of degree, not kind (1964, 24–25).

20. It should be noted that Robbins himself was quite emphatic about restricting his conception of the discipline to the ways in which people use exchanges to solve their scarcity problems (1946, chap. 1).

21. Our analysis extends McGee's critique of monopoly theory. McGee

explained how the rate of output and total size of a market over time can affect industry concentration and monopoly prices and profits. He then explained how the conventional presumption that industry concentration achieved because of scale economies or mergers is inefficient because the dominant (monopoly) firm faces a downward-sloping demand curve can be found wanting because of its possibly wrongheaded policy solution.

> The dissolution of such firms would be a disservice to consumers and to national strength. When firms grow to sizes that create concentration or when such structure is created by mergers and persists for many years, there is a very strong prima facie case that the firms' sizes are related to efficiency. By efficiency I mean "competitive effectiveness" within the bounds of the law, and competitive effectiveness means service to consumers. If the leading firms in a concentrated industry are restricting their output in order to obtain prices above the competitive level, their efficiency must be sufficiently superior to that of all actual and potential rivals to offset that behavior. Were this not the case, rivals would be enabled to expand their market shares because of the abnormally high prices and would thus deconcentrate the industry. (1971, 130)

While McGee is willing to admit that markets are not always perfect and that monopolies might cause some market damage, he raises "grave doubt that economists, lawyers, courts, and regulators" can actually improve, on balance, on the efficiency level achieved by markets "freed of legal barriers" (1971, 130).

22. As pointed out in chapter 1, Schumpeter recognized the point we are stressing here (1942, 104–5).

23. McGee makes much the same point this way.

> If discovery is not costless, literally no one in the industry would bother himself with it. Its private cost is positive; but its private yield is zero. It yields nothing, because emulation is costless and instantaneous. No discovery, however valuable to consumers, would get made except by pure accident—which does not happen with perfect knowledge—since no one could profit by making it. A single-firm monopolist, on the other hand, faces better pay-off prospects for research and invention, as would atomistic competitors under conditions of frictions and long lags, and inventors facing a patent system that gives monopoly rights to discovery. (1971, 101)

24. We assume that the demand rises by more than the cost curve because the product improvement would not be instituted were that not the case.

25. The argument made here is similar to one made in organization economics, which posits that the pay and benefits of higher top executives of corporations must be far higher than the pay of lower managers in order to properly incentivize the lower managers to work hard in hopes of reaching the top management level (Milgrom and Roberts 1992; Murphy 1986; Jensen and Murphy 1990).

26. Put another way, entrepreneurs will look at the rate of return across their portfolio of investments to determine whether to keep their resources where they

are. The profits for their entire portfolios may be at a minimum level, given the prospects of monopoly profits of some investments. If the prospect of monopoly profits is wiped out at the same time that nothing is done to relieve the prospects of failures, the entrepreneurs would have to generate higher returns from their non-monopoly positions just to make up for the ventures that no longer can generate lost monopoly profits. The normal profits on their nonmonopoly ventures can be expected to rise because in the absence of higher normal profits, investment will be constricted, which can be expected to lead to higher prices and higher normal profits.

27. As Chamberlin made the point, "If sellers have regard to their total influence upon price, the price will be the monopoly one. Independence of the producers and the pursuit of their self-interest are not sufficient to lower it. Only if the number is large enough to render negligible the effect of an adjustment by any one upon each of the others is the equilibrium price the purely competitive one. If the market is imperfect, however, true self-interest requires the neglect of the indirect influence to a degree depending upon the degree of imperfection" (1933, 54).

28. Holt (2003) reviews key articles in experimental economics that evaluate how competitive markets in laboratory and classroom settings move toward equilibrium with only several rounds of bidding. When the subjects are few in number (say, five or six), and individuals within the markets have the capacity to withhold their assigned product from the market with the result that they can drive up prices, the market prices may also start high, but will also quickly move toward the competitive price, staying just slightly above the competitive price. See also Smith 1982.

29. McGee also shows that a market can be highly concentrated—even under a single "natural monopoly"—even with upward sloping marginal and average cost curves for production during a specified time, which is usually assumed for standard modeling. This can be the case when total sales *over time* can be limited, so much so that no other, or few, producers are induced to enter the market, in spite of the profits made by firms in the market during the limited periods (1971, esp. chap. 3). Similarly, Phillip Nelson (1970) argues that an industry can be monopolized, or highly concentrated, because of the costs of searching for and assessing the value of goods he identifies as "experience goods." If the cost of searching for goods and then experiencing them is relatively high, then consumers can be expected to restrict their searches and test consumptions among the variety of available goods. McGee explicitly asks, while Nelson implicitly questions, whether the monopoly power exerted by firms who operate under conditions of a limited total market over time or who have downward sloping demand curves because of the limited searches of consumers are truly "inefficient" in the sense described by the standard monopoly model. To make such firms more efficient in the limited sense of the monopoly model would require a greater inefficiency that would come by expanding the array of producers at greater costs than the benefits that can be reaped.

Chapter 3

Chapter 3 is a significantly revised version of the authors' chapter in a book in honor of Gordon Tullock (McKenzie and Lee 2000).

1. See Browning and Zupan (1996, chap. 12).

2. Our analysis is grounded in Coase's classic work on the theory of the firm (1937) and in the considerable literature on institutional-organization economics spawned by Coase's work, a literature that, despite the date of Coase's original contribution, didn't truly begin flourishing until the late 1970s.

3. The authors have covered principal-agent theory, along with various solutions, in some detail in their 1998 book. See also Roberts 2004.

4. For discussions of the impact of group size on incentives, see Tullock 1965, Olson 1965, and Radner 1987. For example, Tullock (1965, 132) states, "Yet most of the members of the hierarchy may be doing things that are either opposed to [the principal's] desires or, at best, neutral. The difficulty here arises because in a large hierarchy, the persons within it will be doing far more things than can be ordered by any one man, regardless of his rank, diligence, and ability. Those orders that he directly issues will represent only a very small part of the total 'output' of the organization, which must, by necessity, operate on the basis of established decision rules."

5. See Tullock 1965, Alchian and Demsetz 1972, and Fama 1980 for a discussion of the role of shirking and other forms of agency costs in organizational theory.

6. Granted, in imperfectly competitive markets, agency costs might exist. Still, we would expect agency costs to rise with the monopolization of the market, given that the agency problems become more severe with more people in the firm and with a shift in the roles that are played by firm members.

7. Johnson and Libecap (1989) evaluate the issue of salary growth in protected markets in the context of highly protected government monopolies.

8. Jensen (1986) recognizes the efficiency problems that are bound to arise as monopoly profits (which will be realized in the form of free cash flow) emerge with curbs in production. We also noted in chapter 1 how Adam Smith seems to have recognized our point that we make in the language of modern principal-agent theory. Smith saw monopoly as "a great enemy to good management" (1776, bk. 1, chap. 11, ¶ 14), noting elsewhere, "The high rate of profit seems every where to destroy that parsimony which in other circumstances is natural to the character of the merchant. When profits are high that sober virtue seems to be superfluous and expensive luxury to suit better the affluence of his situation" (1776, bk. 4, chap. 7, ¶ 147).

9. Pay rules that tie pay in law firms to years of seniority, not to the market or productivity (Gilson and Mnookin 1985), or that reduce the dispersion of pay among academic workers have been explained as a means of reducing internal organizational rent seeking (Pfeffer and Langton 1988).

10. Gurbaxani and Whang (1991) discuss the various ways in which computers and communication systems have improved monitoring and reduced agency and monitoring costs.

11. This possibility is remote when the competitive output occurs in the inelastic portion of the market demand curve. In such cases, since the marginal revenue curve is negative at Q_C, the marginal agency cost would have to be large enough to

cause the cartel's marginal cost also to be negative (less than the negative marginal revenue) at Q_C. Marginal agency cost is unlikely to be this large for the first little bit of output reduction below Q_C.

12. The condition in (4) appears to suggest that profits could be increased by expanding output above the competitive level. But this is not the case. The inequality in (4) holds in only one direction: for reductions in output. In the other direction (an increase in output), there is no marginal agency cost ($C_2 = 0$), and the inequality in (4) is reversed.

Chapter 4

1. Also, one of the authors (McKenzie) has written a book on the Microsoft case (2000).

2. For a detailed discussion of the Microsoft antitrust case, see McKenzie 2000.

3. One of the authors, McKenzie (2000), has challenged the presumed availability of 70,000 Windows applications, mainly on the grounds that the applications count was noted in passing at a trial by a former head of Compaq as the count of applications developed *since the first days MS-DOS became available.* In addition, the count includes large numbers of applications that are better characterized as "applets" rather than full-fledged "applications," such as Word, that the term *applications* commonly connotes. McKenzie has also noted that most computer users use only a handful of applications, which suggests that the operating system market is far more open to challenge than supposed by the judge and the Justice Department, *if* Microsoft acted like a monopolist. The key point addressed here is that the presumed existence of a substantial applications entry barrier led many on the prosecution's side in the case to deduce that Microsoft's business practices could have only had an anticompetitive intent and effect, which means they were necessarily detrimental to consumers.

4. Tullock (1972) was mainly concerned with "rationally ignorant voters" who remained largely uninformed about political candidates' positions on relevant policy issues in elections. He attributed voters' ignorance to the fact that voters might anticipate few benefits to seeing one political candidate win the election over any other and to the fact that any individual's vote was unlikely to influence the outcome of any election. Hence, the costs to voters of becoming informed typically far exceeded their expected personal payoff. Similarly, consumers might reason that there is no expected payoff to their becoming informed about Microsoft's monopoly position, since individual consumers cannot influence Microsoft's pricing and output policies.

5. It needs to be noted that at the time Bork published his book, the available evidence on the relative size of the deadweight loss from monopolies in the United States was minor, no more than 1 percent, and possibly as low as .1 percent (see Harberger 1954; Cowling and Mueller 1981). Moreover, the measured social benefits of antitrust enforcement were hard to identify. See Winston 2006 for a review of this literature.

6. Schumpeter might agree that such "market means" could include (but are not limited to) ownership of key resources (including both material resources and

human capital), branding, superior products and organizations that cannot be easily duplicated, network effects, lock-ins, economies of scale and scope, and trade secrets.

7. For theoretical discussions of network effects, see Arthur 1989, 1990, 1996. Also, our discussion of how network goods force a rethinking of monopoly theory applies, in varying degrees, to discussions of experience goods (Nelson 1970), additive goods (Becker and Murphy 1988), and lagged-demand goods (Lee and Kreutzer 1982), all of which presume a tie between current and future consumption levels, or the consumption of the good today and the demand in later periods.

8. In addition, if firms produce complementary goods, then they might understandably think of the marginal cost of the good in question as negative, following the analysis of Benjamin Klein (1999). This is because the additional revenue on the additional copies of complementary goods sold, when more copies of the good in question are sold, can be construed as a reduction in the marginal cost of the good in question. When Microsoft lowers the price of Windows to sell more copies, then it can expect to sell more copies of Office (and a host of other back-office software programs). In pricing Windows, Microsoft could understandably see the revenue received from additional copies of Office as a reduction in the marginal cost of Windows. There are, in other words, (extreme) economies of scale on the supply side.

9. See Dupuit 1844, Hotelling 1938, and Romer 1994.

10. Indeed, Tullock (1980) writes that it is even possible for the winning rent seeker (or aspiring network sponsor) to spend (lose) more acquiring the monopoly position than it is worth in higher profits.

11. In Romer's words, "In competitive markets, prices work at the margin. If good Z already existed, then prices that are equal to marginal cost give the right signals about how much of Z to use in this production process. But these prices do not attach the correct overall value to the associated bundle of goods, and cannot be used as a guide in the decision about whether or not to incur a cost and invent good Z" (1994, 16).

12. Romer (1994, 25) then points out that direct evidence of the importance of fixed cost is available from Teece 1977.

13. The Landes and Posner formula for monopoly power is

$$(P_m - P_c) = S_i/(e_m^d + e_j^s(1 - S_j)).$$

Where:

P_m = monopoly price, P_c = competitive price (marginal cost), S_j = firm's market share, e_m^d = market elasticity of demand, and e_j^s = elasticity of supply of competing or fringe firms

14. As the district court found, after noting that new operating systems might survive in narrow market segments, "Still, while a niche operating system might turn a profit, the chicken-and-egg problem (hereinafter referred to as the 'applica-

tions barrier to entry') would make it prohibitively expensive for a new Intel-compatible operating system to attract enough developers and consumers to become a viable alternative to a dominant incumbent in less than a few years" (Jackson 1999, ¶ 31). This is because the available Windows applications would discourage investors from trying to secure the necessary funding to develop the requisite (large) number of applications and because consumers would encounter switching costs, to which we will return later.

15. We need to make note here of another paradox. A firm in a market with a zero marginal cost structure would seek out markets with entry costs. But if there are entry costs that bar other firms from entry, how is the first firm going to get in the market in the first place? The answer to the riddle is that the first entrant must be able to create and nurture barriers to entry *after* entry. This is basically what is done in the case of patents or copyrights. The patent or copyright holder obtains what is nothing more than artificial, government-enforced market protection that is, we might add, not challengeable by antitrust enforcers. Those firms that have to create and nurture their own barriers to entry are, of course, open to antitrust prosecution.

16. At the time of this writing, the actual complaint document was sealed for legal reasons. The quotation was taken from the "summary of the complaint" (CCIA 2003, n.p.).

17. Several scholars have expressed concern that over the last fifty or more years, the limited monopoly rights of copyrights especially have been made unlimited, for all practical purposes, or have at least extended the implied monopoly privileges beyond what is required to provide adequate incentives for product development. See Lessig 2001 and Vaidhyanathan 2001.

18. Granted, pirates cannot escape some development costs, given that they do have to establish Web sites and other distributional systems, as well as make the pirated copies look, sound, and feel like the originals.

19. Piracy can cause the original producers' demand and, hence, prices to rise or fall over time, depending on the relative magnitude of obvious offsetting effects. One study of the word processing market in England found that between 1987 and 1992, researchers for a software developer found that 85 percent of the growth in one firm's copies in use were pirated, but they also found that 80 percent of the copies sold were attributable to the network effects of the pirated copies (Givon, Mahajan, and Muller 1999). In another study of piracy of music, researchers found from regression analysis that while the music industry lamented billions of dollars in lost revenues from nearly two billion pirated copies of music, the actual losses were much less due primarily to the fact that, as they found, one pirated copy reduced world sales of CDs in 1998 by .42 units. The worldwide falloff in industry revenues attributable to piracy (after adjusting for other factors) was no more than 6.6 percent (Hui and Png 2002).

20. Among the proposed remedies, the CCIA seeks "a requirement to unbundle illegally bundled products and to refrain from future bundling," plus a breakup of Microsoft (CCIA 2003, 19).

21. Bill Gates started his keynote address in on December 7, 1995, with these words.

Well, good morning. I was realizing this morning that December 7th is kind of a famous day. [*Laughter.*] Fifty-four years ago or something. And I was trying to think if there were any parallels to what was going on here. And I really couldn't come up with any. The only connection I could think of at all was that probably the most intelligent comment that was made on that day wasn't made on Wall Street, or even by any type of that analyst; it was actually Admiral Yamomoto, who observed that he feared they had awakened a sleeping giant. [*Laughter.*]

Well, the Internet is a very exciting development. It's sort of the beginning of a world of electronic communications. In any phenomenon like this you get long periods of time where people anticipate it, and yet there isn't critical mass. There's not enough users, so there isn't enough content; there's not enough content, so there isn't enough users. (1)

He continued later in his talk,

So the Internet, the competition will be kind of, once again, embrace and extend, and we will embrace all the popular Internet protocols. Anything that a significant number of publishers are using and taking advantage of we will support. We will do some extensions to those things. (5)

Chapter 5

A version of this paper was published by the authors in the *Hastings Law Journal* (Lee and McKenzie 2001).

1. Fax machines and computer operating systems are two of the more obvious examples of goods with network effects, which we have cited in prior chapters. However, it has been pointed out that many other products—for example, some books—also exhibit network effects, given that readers gain the added benefits of being able to discuss the book when many others read the same one (Frank and Cook 1995).

2. District Court Judge Thomas Penfield Jackson described the switching costs involved in the operating system market this way (1999, ¶ 20).

Since only Intel-compatible PC operating systems will work with Intel-compatible PCs, a consumer cannot opt for a non-Intel-compatible PC operating system without obtaining a non-Intel-compatible PC. Thus, for consumers who already own an Intel-compatible PC system, the cost of switching to a non-Intel compatible PC operating system includes the price of not only a new operating system, but also a new PC and new peripheral devices. It also includes the effort of learning to use the new system, the cost of acquiring a new set of compatible applications, and the work of replacing files and documents that were associated with the old applications. Very few consumers would incur these costs in response to the trivial increase in the price of an Intel-compatible PC system that would result from even a substantial increase in the price of an Intel-compatible PC operating system. For example, users of Intel-compatible PC operating systems would not switch in large numbers to the Mac OS in response to even a substantial, sustained increase in the price of an Intel-compatible PC operating system.

3. Michael Porter (1980, 10) simply asserts that a "barrier to entry is created by switching costs," while Joseph Farrell and Carl Shapiro add details on how switching costs translate into an entry barrier: "The relationship-specific assets [associated with finding and establishing a working tie with a new supplier] create *switching costs* for a buyer changing from one supplier to another. Evidently, such brand loyalty gives the seller some monopoly power: in the absence of effective long-term contracts a buyer is open to exploitation by an opportunistic seller who could raise the price above competitors' by an amount almost equal to the buyer's switching costs" (1998, 123; emphasis in the original).

4. MIT economist Frederick Warren-Bolton, one of the Justice Department's chief economists on the Microsoft antitrust case, described the switching costs involved in the operating system market this way.

A second barrier both to entry [in addition to the barrier created by the development costs of a new operating system] and to expansion by an existing competitor is that users tend to become "locked in" to a particular operating system. As discussed above, users are reluctant to switch from Windows to another operating system, even another PC operating system, because to do so requires them to replace application software, to convert files, and to learn how to operate the new software. Often, switching operating systems also means replacing or modifying hardware. Businesses can face even greater switching costs, as they must integrate PCs using the new operating systems and application software within their PC networks and train their employees to use the new software. Accordingly, both personal and corporate consumers are extremely reluctant to change PC operating systems. The software "lock-in" phenomenon creates a barrier to entry for new PC operating systems to the extent that consumers' estimate of the switching costs is large relative to the perceived incremental value of the new operating system.

Additional switching costs arise from the fact that, for most users, operating systems are only a means to an end—it is the application software that was designed to work with the operating system that users want. Once they have purchased an operating system, users are naturally reluctant to consider a different operating system. Unless their current operating system product prevents them from using new applications or hardware, they are likely to continue to use that operating system; for operating systems, unlike other goods, do not wear out. (2000, ¶¶ 49, 50)

5. One study found that a quarter of the additional profit Norwegian banks made from additional borrowers could be attributed to their customers' switching costs.

6. Liebowitz and Margolis (1990, 1995) also argue that contrary to widely repeated conventional wisdom, VHS tape-recording format did not win out over

the Beta format in spite of its (VHS's) inferiority, but did so because the VHS format was able to capture entire movies on a single tape. See also Liebowitz and Margolis 1994; Rohlfs 2001, chap. 6.

7. Klemperer (1989) has argued that with switching costs, price wars are likely. Indeed, the intensity of the price wars can be a function of the switching costs.

8. Of course, as has been noted by Farrell and Shapiro (1998) and Klemperer (1988), the entrenched producer's pricing strategy can result in the entry of new producers that have higher production costs than the entrenched producer, which can give rise to another form of inefficiency, offsetting partially the efficiency gains from the expanded number of producers and expanded sales.

9. The analysis here, which suggests that network effects lead to suppressed initial prices, is similar to the work of Lee and Kreutzer (1982), who developed a theory of lagged demand, and Becker and Murphy (1988), who were concerned with the development of a theory of rational addiction.

10. The effect of the threat is particularly detrimental to consumer welfare when all or most costs of production are up-front costs, that is, the marginal cost of production is zero, or close to zero (which is presumed to be the case in many lines of software, especially operating systems, given that copies of an operating system can be loaded on new computers by original equipment manufacturers by simply copying files from one computer to the next with few material resources and little time involved). In the absence of lock-ins, or switching costs, potential network sponsors would be reluctant to make the up-front investment in the development of their products for fear that their investments would rightfully be treated as sunk costs in ongoing competitive struggles with other firms in which the price would be pushed toward marginal cost, which is close or equal to zero (Klemperer 1989; Katz and Shapiro 1985).

11. Benjamin Klein (1999) has developed a similar line of argument, but using graphical techniques, to explain why a firm with complementary products might charge subzero prices, which leads to the conclusion that a breakup of the firm can lead to positive prices.

12. It should be pointed out that the efficiency conditions in (7) are not practically possible since they call for prices to be less than marginal cost (zero) and average cost until period T.

Chapter 6

This chapter is a substantially revised and extended discussion of the authors' work published in the *Southern Economic Journal* (Lee and McKenzie 1998).

1. Of course, as noted in the last chapter, a producer of a network good might lower its current price in order to boost future demand and charge a higher, even monopoly price in the future. The higher future monopoly price can be welfare enhancing because it can induce network good producers to lower their current prices by more than otherwise and can give rise to a faster-than-otherwise development of the network.

2. It has also been argued (Bittlingmayer 1985) that the necessity for some

cooperation between firms in high-fixed-cost/low-marginal-cost industries explains why enforcement of the Sherman Antitrust Act (in particular court decisions against price fixing) led to the merger wave of 1898 through 1902.

3. We ignore concerns such as those that the shipment of unstable explosives or deadly poisons might arouse in the owners of other cargo.

4. The Juniper Island Club, a private club located off the Florida coast, illustrates the value people can place on associating with what they consider a preferred set of people while at leisure. The club is one of the country's most exclusive resorts, and although this exclusivity has been achieved primarily by a highly restrictive admissions policy, it is reinforced with a steep admissions charge. And although the club's amenities are nice, the *Wall Street Journal* (Parcelle 1995, A7) pointed out that "the lure of the club has never been swank facilities. Its chief appeal is in its exclusivity."

5. We don't want to overemphasize the difference between the cost of providing a package of extras (or frills) at expensive hotels and the value of those extras to guests. Because of competition, hotels are strongly motivated to provide those extras that, for any given cost, provide as much real value to their guests as possible. But this is consistent with a hotel being able to realize a competitive advantage by increasing the supply of extras into the range where the extras themselves are worth less to the guests than they are paying for them because of the screening benefit provided by the extra charge.

6. The quantity and quality of the facility and amenities obviously influence the demand (and therefore the average revenue, with respect to the number of guests, the hotel can generate) and the average cost of accommodating guests (which in equilibrium equals average revenue). A hotel with a facility of a given physical quantity and quality may not be able to generate enough revenues to cover costs in an existing location, regardless of how well it responds to higher-income clients. Such a hotel may, however, become viable by letting its facility decline in quality, for example, and appealing to a different type of client.

7. As drawn, these demand curves are assumed to be quite price elastic, suggesting a significant degree of competition between hotels, competition of the type commonly thought to drive prices down to marginal cost in periods of excess capacity.

8. Obviously the price intervals associated with these three client-effect responses to price vary with the quality of the hotel. Even for a very low-quality hotel, some positive client (demand) effect exists as price increases above zero and the facility ceases to be an unrationed homeless shelter. But at quite low prices, the positive client effect from price increases at such hotels will cease because low-quality hotels aren't demanded by those able and willing to pay high rates to stay in luxury hotels with other guests with similar preferences.

9. The approach here is identical to that employed by Leibenstein (1950) in his development of a demand curve reflecting what he called the Veblen effect (an effect caused by a perceived prestige in consuming higher-priced goods that is independent of the inherent quality of the good). Though the construction of the

demand curve is formally the same in the case of both the Veblen and client effects, it should be emphasized that the client effect has a very real influence on the inherent quality of the good or service being demanded.

10. Indeed, it is possible that the equilibrium demand curve becomes positively sloped over some price range. This possibility is developed and discussed by Leibenstein (1950) in his analysis of the Veblen effect and is an interesting curiosity. A positively sloped demand curve is not necessary to the primary conclusion of this chapter, however, and we note it only in passing.

11. A zero marginal cost up to the hotel's capacity is obviously unrealistic, but it strengthens the primary conclusion of the chapter by assuming a cost situation that makes the temptation to engage in ruinous competition during periods of off-peak demand as large as possible.

12. This is completely consistent with hotels facing highly elastic demand curves for any given mix of clienteles. Attempts to capture customers from other hotels by lowering the room rate aren't very effective because they alter the clientele mix adversely.

13. Although this chapter is not concerned with optimal hotel capacity, the moderating influence of the client effect on price competition is relevant to the consideration of capacity. If the peak-demand curve applied year round, capacity would be increased to the level that allowed the maximum profits to be realized with this peak demand. Let this level be represented by C_p. But if an off-peak demand curve applies for part of the year, the optimal capacity is less than C_p. At some point before capacity C_p is reached, the increase in profits during the peak season from a marginal increase in capacity will be less than the resulting decrease in profits during the off-peak season. This point will obviously be reached sooner, if excess capacity results in price competition driving rates down to ruinous levels, than it will be in the situation described here. Therefore, another implication of the moderating influence of the client effect on hotel rates is that hotel capacity will be greater than would otherwise be the case.

14. Such screening is far from perfect, as anyone who has attended a convention knows. Also, lower convention rates may reflect cost considerations that come from dealing with a large group through one contact person, the advantages of more demand certainty, and the extra profits conventions generate from the use of conference facilities.

15. We want to thank Don Boudreaux for suggesting this implication of the analysis. It should be noted that some of the Ivy League colleges have been accused of conspiring to fix maximum financial aid payments (tuition reductions) to students. Whether such a conspiracy had a significant effect on tuition revenues is subject to some controversy, but it does suggest another explanation for high tuition payments. We believe, however, that the client effect is a more important factor behind high tuition payments and one that has received far less attention.

16. What we are calling the *client effect* is commonly referred to as the *peer group effect* when applied to education. Some economists (Summers and Wolfe 1977; Henderson, Mieskowski, and Sauvageau 1978) have found significant peer group

effects in education. Others (Evans, Oates, and Schwab 1992) are more cautious in their conclusions, while being careful not to deny the existence of peer-group effects.

17. Epple and Romano (1998) have developed a model of competition between private and public schools that incorporates positive peer-group effects.

18. According to one article (Jennings 1994), passengers can actually find themselves paying more for a full-fare coach ticket than they would for a first-class ticket on the same flight.

19. The major airlines have attempted to counter price sensitivity with frequent-flyer programs and special promotions for their elite customers. Of course, these programs have been a factor in reducing the price differential between first-class and coach service.

20. The importance of the client effect on international flights was brought home to one of the authors a few years ago when he was flying economy class to Europe on a flight containing a large number of very excited and, soon, quite intoxicated college students.

21. Klein and Leffler (1981) developed a model that considers a variety of ways, including high prices, that suppliers can provide a credible signal on the quality of products. But their model does not consider the client effect nor how high prices can improve the quality of a product (or service) through that effect.

22. We are grateful to David Haddock for suggesting the soccer example and providing us with the information just discussed.

23. For reviews of the extensive principal-agent literature, see Milgrom and Roberts 1992, chap. 5; Rubin 1990; and Roberts 2004, chaps. 3–5.

24. Alternatively put, the profits reduce the need for firms to incur other costs of developing bonds or hostages, which means that some of the monopoly profits can be seen as cost reductions.

25. For the development of these and other arguments in an underpricing model, with illustrative examples, see Haddock and McChesney 1994.

26. Becker (1991) also uses his analysis to explain why excess demand for sporting events, plays, concerts, and books is often increased by price increases.

27. This example comes from Landsburg 1993, 12–13.

Chapter 7

1. For those readers new to supply-and-demand curve models, the quantity of labor supplied would just match the quantity of labor demanded, meaning the market would clear. The wage rate goes to W_c because if the wage rate were above W_c in a competitive market, there would be more labor available than there would be workers hired, with the resulting labor-market surplus pushing the wage rate down to W_c. If the wage rate were below W_c, the quantity of workers demanded would be greater than the quantity of workers available, the effect of which would be to push the wage rate upward toward W_c.

2. For more details on the development of the monopsony model in graphical form, see McKenzie and Lee 2006, chap. 13.

3. The workers who are forced to go elsewhere would earn more than the wage offered by the monopsony, but their contribution to the value of production (or their marginal revenue product) would be worth less than their value working for the monopsony. One has to wonder, however, how the monopsony could get by without paying the competitive wage if workers are able to move freely among markets. If the marginal workers could go elsewhere and earn more than the monopsony wage, then the workers the monopsony hires could, presumably, do the same, which would force the wages in the alternative markets to fall and the monopsony wage to rise.

4. Also, the monopsony can do better than the monopsony employment level by wage discrimination, paying workers hired beyond Q_m a wage equal to the competitive wage W_c. Wage discrimination requires, of course, that the wage differences among workers are kept quiet and/or that workers hired at the monopsony wage rate cannot leave and be rehired at the higher competitive wage rate.

5. A minimum wage imposed on a monopsony market can actually lead to an expansion of the monopsony's employment. Consider a minimum wage imposed at the intersection of the supply and demand for labor W_c (fig. 7.1). Because the monopsony has no control over the wage, W_c is the marginal cost of labor up to Q_c. This means monopsony's then profit maximization employment will be Q_c, and the marginal value of each additional unit of labor up to Q_c will be greater than the marginal cost of labor, or the minimum wage. Hence, a minimum wage set at W_c can raise employment from Q_m to Q_c.

6. We consider monopsonies only in local labor markets because we frankly can't imagine private firms that could or would ever be a monopsony in the national market.

7. For documentation and extensive discussion on the growth in the mobility of resources on a world scale, see McKenzie and Lee 1991.

Chapter 8

1. Two bills were introduced in the House of Representatives in the 99th Congress to establish a joint congressional committee to advise the Congress on "the balance between athletics and academics . . . in particular the need for establishing stricter eligibility and academic requirements for athletes, and less frequent and fewer competitive events to allow for greater pursuit of academic goals by athletes, and the role of regulation and enforcement in the areas of athletic recruiting, financing, and scheduling." H.R. 5213, 5484, 99th Cong., 2d Sess. (1986); see 132 *Cong. Rec.* H4690 (daily ed. July 22, 1986) (statement of Rep. Luken).

2. See Alchian and Allen 1977, 210–12.

3. Becker concludes, "The NCAA's efforts to justify its restrictions on competition for athletes should be viewed with suspicion because of the financial benefits colleges receive from football, basketball, and other sports. I would have expected greater hostility from Congress and the courts to a policy that lowers earnings of young African-Americans and other athletes with limited opportunities" (1985, 18). We suggest that the critics' (including Becker's) case against the NCAA's

restrictions should be viewed with suspicion because of the absence of hostility toward the restrictions by Congress and the courts. One might think that the courts and Congress would be predisposed to favor the critics' case, given that minorities are supposedly harmed most by the restrictions. For additional ways economists have traditionally criticized the NCAA, see also Becker 1987; Koch 1973, 1983; Fleisher, Goff, Shughart, and Tollison 1988.

4. See also Editorial, *New York Times* 1985, 22.

5. See also Yoder 1985, A4.

6. Nothing in our argument suggests that the NCAA member colleges should not make payments over and above tuition as well as room and board. Our thesis is simply that market forces can be expected to determine the extent of payment. (At the time the journal article on which this chapter is based was being completed in the mid-1980s, the NCAA was preparing to consider at its annual meeting a proposal to allow Division 1-A colleges to make modest payments of $50 to $100 a month to their athletes to cover laundry and similar expenses.) A requirement that the NCAA be forced to allow payments of any particular amount, or through the abolition of rules against bidding for athletes, is misguided.

7. To be more precise, in 2004, the United States had over 4,200 degree-granting institutions, 2,500 of which were four-year colleges and universities and 1,700 of which were two-year granting institutions (U.S. Bureau of the Census 2007, table 267). Many of the colleges and universities did not have major sports programs. Only 1,250 of the total colleges and universities are members of the NCAA. However, they all would be *potential* competitors for athletes, given that all of them could develop sports programs if athletes were materially underpaid.

8. For example, Becker (1987) writes, "The NCAA's efforts to justify its restrictions on competition for athletes should be viewed with suspicion because they increase the financial benefits colleges receive from football, basketball, and other sports. I would have expected greater hostility from Congress and the courts to a policy that lowers the earnings of young blacks and other athletes with limited opportunities." McCormick (1985, 27) notes: "Some student athletes, especially blacks, come from very poor families. The NCAA only allows school scholarships to pay for tuition, room and board, and books, and prohibits students from working during the school year. One would think that administrators would be ashamed to prevent these students from being given small sums that would allow them to dress and socialize like the more well-heeled students. Perhaps it salves the consciences of some university presidents to deplore the plight of black workers in South Africa because of the exploitation they promote on their campuses."

9. In technical terms, the labor-market competition results in reciprocal "pecuniary externalities" imposed by colleges on each other.

10. See Fleisher, Shughart, and Tollison 1989.

11. Nonathletic members of the colleges' administrations and faculties are thought to support the NCAA wages rules because of the presumed transfer of rents from the athletic programs to the nonathletic programs.

12. Although it may be true that coaches' winning records affect their salaries, it

is not at all obvious that a cartelized market for student-athletes should be expected to lead to compensation packages for coaches that are higher overall than they would be in absence of the cartelized markets. This is because, presumably, the cartel checks how many student-athletes are hired. We can only surmise that such a curb on employment will curb the demand for coaches, because fewer players and perhaps fewer games would be available to coach. The concomitant decrease in the demand for coaches could be expected to translate into lower compensation packages for coaches. The NCAA critics have never argued, to our knowledge, that the coaches have responded by monopolizing their market, although such an argument could be implicit in their presumption that coaches' compensation packages are elevated by the restrictions on the student-athletes' labor market. However, what happens to coaches' compensation packages is not clear. We suppose that the NCAA critics could argue that the coaches have control over the distribution of their universities' share of the NCAA's cartel rents. Perhaps. But maybe not. University presidents and faculties, as a matter of organizational structure of the NCAA, have ultimate control over what the NCAA does, which, according to the NCAA critics, explains the widespread support of university presidents and faculties for the NCAA rules. *If* presidents and faculty have ultimate control, the critics have to expand their arguments to include an explanation for why presidents and faculty would be more inclined to share their rents with coaches whose overall labor-market demand is suppressed by NCAA rules. Such a line of argument has not been made.

13. Fleisher, Goff, and Tollison write only about the "violence" prevalent in football. They do not say whether the deaths and injuries in 1905 were the results of on-the-field or off-the-field fights, the use of approved or unapproved weapons in games, or the consequences of poorly constructed equipment (1992, 38–39).

14. Fleisher, Goff, and Tollison write, "Once an association is organized, given that the initial organizational costs are borne, the marginal costs of agreeing to extend the scale and scope of the association are low" (1992, 21). Perhaps this is true of the "marginal costs of *agreeing* to extend the scale and scope" (emphasis added). However, Fleisher, Goff, and Tollison explain at some length how the expansion of any organization designed to restrict output and increase rents leads to an increase in the incentive of members to cheat and the actual occurrences of cheating. The increase in the potential for cheating can dramatically increase the enforcement costs (1992, chap. 5).

15. See also Greenspan 1988, nn. 125, 158, 199, 308, the source of much of the Fleisher, Goff, and Tollison data on sports attendance and television contracts.

16. Fleisher, Goff, and Tollison write, "As cartel theory suggests, the return to producers from collusion on inputs and outputs is greater as the demand for the final product grows. The demand growth for college sports over this period increased the benefits of an effective enforcement mechanism across institutions" (1992, 51).

17. Fleisher, Goff, and Tollison write, "In effect, these schools grandfathered themselves into control of the enforcement apparatus and over time have remained

in control of NCAA committees." This means that enforcement actions will "generally be directed against schools which show an improvement in winning percentage and thereby threaten the status and rents of the traditional football powers" (1992, 133).

18. The presumption of a first-mover advantage in collegiate athletics may be no more correct than was the presumption of a first-mover advantage in a host of other industries. Tellis and Golder (2002) found in their study of sixty-six industries that the first movers in sixty-two industries had been long replaced by second and third movers. That is to say, being a first mover does not provide firms with secured locks on their markets.

19. Fleisher, Goff, and Tollison write that in spite of all the oppression they cite in college athletics, "yet the NCAA as a cartel does not receive any air or press time. Without a theory of media behavior, we simply must conclude that the answer to the media's paradoxical behavior in the case of the NCAA lies elsewhere" (1992, 152). As an aside, if the analysis in the Fleisher, Goff, and Tollison book is truly meant to be exclusively "positive," as opposed to "normative" (1992, 144), we must wonder how the media behavior can be deemed "paradoxical."

20. Schumpeter explained what he meant by the original "Vision," "Though prescientific, it [the perception of a set of related phenomena] is not preanalytic. It does not simply consist of perceiving facts by one of our senses. These facts must be recognized as having some meaning or relevance that justifies our interest in them and they must be recognized as related—so that we might separate them from others—which involves some analytic work by our fancy or common sense" (1949, 350). This "mixture" of perceptions and prescientific separation of related from unrelated observations is what he meant by "Vision" (350).

21. In the case of Adam Smith and his immediate followers, the original "vision" was more or less informal. In the case of modern economics extending from Schumpeter's time to the present, the original vision has been captured in more formal "model building," which "consists in picking out certain facts rather than others, in pinning them down by labeling them, in accumulating further facts in order not only to supplement but in part also to replace those originally fastened upon, in formulating and improving the relations perceived—briefly, in 'factual' and 'theoretical' research that go on in an endless chain of give and take, the facts suggesting new analytic instruments (theories) and these in turn carrying us toward the recognition of new facts" (1949, 350).

22. In Schumpeter's words, "*For ideologies are not simply lies;* they are truthful statements about what a man thinks he sees. Just as the medieval knight saw himself as he wished to see himself and just as the modern bureaucrat does the same and just as both fail to see whatever may be adduced against their seeing themselves as defenders of the weak and innocent and the sponsors of the Common Good, so every other social group develops a protective ideology which is nothing if not sincere. *Ex hypothesi* we are not aware of our rationalizations—how then is it possible to recognize and guard against them?" (1949, 349; emphasis in the original).

23. For the purpose of emphasizing here Schumpeter's concern over the alle-

giance economists show monopoly as a theoretical construct, we repeat one of our favorite passages from Schumpeter's "Science and Ideology."

A majority of economists would subscribe to Molina's dictum: *monopolium est injustum et rei publicae injuriosum* [a monopoly is an injustice and a real public injury]. But it is not this value judgment which is relevant to my argument—one may dislike modern largest-scale business exactly as one may dislike many other features of modern civilization—but the analysis that leads up to it, and the ideological influence this analysis displays. Anyone who has read Marshall's *Principles* . . . should know that among the innumerable patterns that are covered by those terms are many of which benefit and not injury to economic efficiency and the consumer's interest ought to be predicated. More modern analysis permits to show still more clearly that no sweeping or unqualified statement can be true for all of them; and that the mere fact of size, single-sellership, discrimination, and cooperative price setting are in themselves inadequate for asserting that the resulting performance is, in any relevant sense of the word, inferior to the one which could be expected under pure competition in conditions attainable under pure competition—in other words, that the analysis offers no material in support of *indiscriminate* "trust busting" and that such material must be looked for in the particular circumstances of each individual case. Nevertheless, many economists support *indiscriminate* "trust busting" and the interesting point is that enthusiastic sponsors of the private-enterprise system are particularly prominent among them. Theirs is the ideology of a capitalist economy that would fill its social functions admirably by virtue of the magic of pure competition were it not for the monster of monopoly or oligopoly that casts a shadow on an otherwise bright scene. No argument avails about the performance of largest-scale business, about the inevitability of its emergence, about the social costs involved in destroying existing structures, about the futility of the hallowed ideal of pure competition—or in fact ever elicits any response other than most obviously sincere indignation. (1949, 357–58; emphasis in the original)

24. Clearly, an ongoing interest remains among NCAA members in marginal, if not substantive, revisions in NCAA restrictions and rules, given a variety of social, economic, and academic forces afoot over time. However, the disinterest that Fleisher, Goff, and Tollison cite as paradoxical really pertains to their obvious interest in seeing practically all, if not in fact all, labor market results in college and university sports markets be market driven, with little or no guidance from meta-market NCAA restrictions and rules.

25. We can grant that the reputation of the education that many, if not most, athletes at the majority of NCAA schools now get suffers from the generally low admissions requirements for athletes and from many media and gossip-based stories of the weaknesses in athletes' courses of study and the easy grading accorded them by professors all too eager to further the interests of their schools' athletic conquests. However, our purpose here is to talk about the theoretical foundation of

what the NCAA *seeks* to accomplish with its pay restrictions and academic require-ments, not the problems it has in accomplishing those objectives. Our point is that, in spite of the problems encountered, the NCAA's requirements could elevate the reputations of the athletes' education over and above what it could be in the absences of the established requirements, or in the explicit pursuit of what are offered as (and presumed to be) alternative, market-based educational require-ments. We can only imagine that the "reputational capital" of athletes could very well suffer generally and substantially if athletes were allowed to major in football and basketball (concentrations in their sports specialties, e.g., field goals or free-throw shots, as one economist-critic of the NCAA has wholeheartedly advocated) (Shughart 1990b).

26. Indeed, the value of college experience to athletes is clearly indicated by the number of high school athletes who could follow the lead of basketball player Moses Malone and try out for the professional ranks directly out of high school. Admittedly, there are few high school athletes who could successfully make the transition, but that is, again, only a way of asserting the value of college athletics.

27. Herschel Walker, for example, played his junior year at the University of Georgia when he could have turned professional and earned several hundred thou-sand dollars, if not more than a million. Because he stayed at Georgia his junior year, he must have expected the nonmonetary benefits of an extra year in college (including the prospects of receiving the Heisman Trophy, which he did receive) and the added lifetime income from the greater experience to exceed the profes-sional salary he would have received had he turned professional.

For athletes with less talent than Herschel Walker, the years of college experi-ence may be more valuable because they offer more opportunities for improvement of skills, media exposure, and education. The increase in the present discounted value of the less-talented athletes' future income may be greater than for many of the more talented athletes.

28. Assuming a limit of 95 football players and 12 basketball players on college teams, the total number of athletes at the 107 Division I schools at any point in time is 11,449. The one or two dozen athletes who go into professional sports without going to college or finishing their years of eligibility is a minor fraction of 1 per-cent.

29. Granted, we are making an unsubstantiated claim here about the impact of the restrictions on demand. However, this hardly makes our analytics inferior to the analytics of the NCAA's critics, given that underlying their static analysis of monopsony is an equally unsubstantiated claim, that the restrictions have no effect on demand for either the final sports products or the demand for athletes. At least our argument is supported by what the critics see as mysterious widespread support for the restrictions among virtually all constituencies of colleges and universities, fans, donors, faculty, administrators inside and outside of sports departments, media, as well as possibly many (if not most) student-athletes.

30. Admittedly, McDonald's does not restrict wage payments made by fran-chisees to their employees. However, it may influence the prices charged.

31. Exactly why the member colleges believe that the NCAA will further the

interests of the colleges through a joint venture is of no consequence to the argument. Different schools may actually receive various types of benefits, just as the different McDonald's franchises receive various types of benefits. The critical requirement is that benefits from a joint venture are perceived.

32. As would be true of all ventures in which joint action results in benefits to all that have some durability (e.g., through the creation of a "reputation" for amateur sports), individual participants—for example, players—have an additional short-term incentive to a free ride by cheating. Athletes can reason that if they accept side payments, such payments may never be uncovered and, even if they are uncovered, may have no detectable effect on athletes' own expected income over the expected relatively short time involved in a college education. The reputation benefits for amateur sports in college may evaporate with rampant cheating; athletes can reason, however, that they will have long completed their college career when the joint venture benefits do evaporate. Tensions inevitably exist between the short-term interests of athletes (and coaches and, for that matter, all others whose stay at colleges is perceived to be short term) and the long-term interests of colleges as institutions. This is not to say, however, that the athletes themselves don't have good reasons to want the NCAA rules in place, as we will explain.

33. Even Gary Becker (1971, 99–100) acknowledges the legitimacy of the incentive to cheat on cartels: "Since collusion, even if by merger, is the only way to internalize and thus incorporate these effects, one might expect every industry to evolve into an effectively monopolized one. But just as all firms together have a strong incentive to depart from the competitive solution, each separately has an equally strong incentive to depart from monopoly solution. . . . Since all firms want to expand output, collusion has a tendency to break down because of 'chiseling' by the members. Each firm, in effect, hopes that all others act monopolistically while it acts competitively." Becker recognizes that the effectiveness of a cartel depends on the costs imposed on violators for departing from the cartel agreement. In the sports market, this means that the NCAA would have to have a means of imposing sufficient costs on colleges for seceding from the NCAA and setting up their own sports association that would allow for payment of athletes to more than cover the benefits of secession.

34. Economists Robert McCormick and Maurice Tinsley (1987) included 150 schools in their study. In 1971, 63 of these schools were declared to have "big-time athletic programs" by virtue of their membership in "big-time athletic conferences: Atlantic Coast Conference, Southwest Conference, Southeastern Conference, Big Ten, Big Eight, Pacific Athletic Conference, and major independents." In various regression equations with the schools' 1971 SAT scores as the independent variable, their dummy variable for "big-time athletic programs" was always statistically significant and positive, after adjusting for such factors as faculty pay, tuition, age of the schools, faculty/student ratios, schools' endowments, and the size of the student bodies (1105). McCormick and Tinsley determined that having a big-time program increased schools' SAT scores by an average of 3 percent (1106, n. 5).

35. The NAIA and the NLCAA could, of course, expand their sports programs considerably by allowing for payments.

36. It would appear that officials of the NCAA or athletic associations in other countries would also take advantage of their experience with running sports associations and understanding of the exploitative rules of the NCAA and seek to organize alternative sports associations by enlisting the support of colleges, if not their conferences.

37. Proponents of the cartel thesis might reply, as they have replied in private conversations with the authors, that if member colleges are capable of cohering over the long run within the NCAA to produce a joint product, they are every bit as capable of cohering within the NCAA to cartelize the market for the purpose of suppressing athletes' wages. This argument doesn't necessarily follow, mainly because of the brand-name benefits of being associated with the NCAA. Membership in the NCAA would collapse if no brand-name benefits—no demand-enhancing benefits—were associated with membership. Few schools would long endure the penalties, which run into the millions of dollars, imposed by the NCAA for infraction of rules.

38. Of course, Fleisher, Goff, and Tollison never entertain the prospect that restrictions can improve the quality of the product, which means they might never concede that the elimination of the restrictions could have a detrimental impact on schools' reputations.

39. Much of the growth in the count of NCAA members can be chalked up to factors such as the growth in population and the count and size of colleges and universities, growth factors not considered by Fleisher, Goff, and Tollison.

40. *Smith v. Pro Football, Inc.*, 593 F2d 1173, 1179 (D.C. Cir. 1978).

41. Id. at 1179.

42. The very fact that critics of NCAA payment restrictions on athletes have never, to our knowledge, advocated allowing coaches to tender bribes to referees in the middle of games to change calls suggests that they understand the validity of the legal point made here, including that some payment restrictions are necessary (or just beneficial) to create the type of game that they want to play.

43. *United States v. Addyston Pipe & Steel Co.*, 85 F 271 (6th Cir. 1898), aff'd, 175 U.S. 211 (1899).

44. 85 F. 271 (6th Cir. 1898), aff'd, 175 U.S. 211 (1899).

45. 29 593 F.2d 1173 (D.C. Cir. 1978).

46. 30 Id. at 1179.

47. The court ultimately held that the player draft was an unreasonable restraint of trade because of its anticompetitive impact on the market for players' services. Id. at 1189. See also *Mackey v. National Football League*, 543 F.2d 606 (8th Cir. 1976); Weistart and Lowell (1979, 114–18; and supp. 1985, 128); and Robinson 1980.

48. Even though employment may be restricted to some level below the idealized competitive level, the employment level and the payments the employees receive can be greater than they otherwise would have been. Moreover, consumer surplus on the product end can be enhanced by the restrictions.

49. 104 S. Ct. 2948 (1984).

50. Id. at 2954.

51. Id.

52. Id. at 2959.

53. Id. at 2961, 2959. See also *Broadcast Music, Inc. v. CBS*, 441 U.S. 1 (1979); *Continental TV. Inc. v. GTE Sylvania Inc.*, 433 U.S. 36 (1977).

54. 104 S. Ct. at 2969 (citing Bork 1978, 278).

55. 104 S. Ct. at 2961.

56. Id.

57. Id. The Court struck down the NCAA's television contracts, finding that they restricted output and demand without producing offsetting procompetitive benefits. For an analysis of output as the key factor in balancing the competitive effects, see Sullivan 1984, 771.

58. 104 S. Ct. at 2961.

59. Id.

60. Id. at 2969.

61. Id. The Court rejected Justices White and Rehnquist's argument that the NCAA regulations were noneconomic in nature (nonmarket goods) that produced a social benefit in promoting amateur athletics. Instead, the majority said antitrust laws permit an examination only into the competitive impact of the restraints, not into whether those restraints promote public interest or other values. See *National Society of Professional Engineers v. U.S.*, 435 U.S. 679 (1978); Sullivan 1982.

62. 104 S. Ct. at 2971.

63. Id. See also *Gunter Hartz Sports, Inc. v. U.S. Tennis Assoc., Inc.*, 665 F.2d 222, 223 (8th Cir. 1981); *Neeld v. NHL*, 594 F.2d 1297, 1298–1300 (9th Cir. 1979); Weistart and Lowell 1979, 757.

64. See, e.g., *Hennessey v. NCAA*, 564 F.2d 1136, 1151–53 (5th Cir. 1977); see Note, Antitrust and Nonmarket Goods, The Supreme Court Fumbles Again, 60 *Wash. L. Rev.* 721, 729 (1985); Note, Antitrust and Nonprofit Entities, 94 *Harv. L. Rev.* 802 (1981); Haveman and Knopf 1966, 209.

65. This might include more severe collective restraints if the NCAA were faced with "intrabrand competition from other products, produced by another association or league as may be developing with the College Football Association (CFA) whose purpose is to promote the interest of major college football schools." 104 S. Ct. at 2968 n.55. See generally Weistart and Lowell 1979, 760–62, 768–69.

66. 104 S. Ct. at 2963–64; Sullivan 1984.

67. 104 S. Ct. at 2966.

68. Id. at 2965. See also *FTC v. Indiana Federation of Dentists*, 106 S. Ct. 2009 (1986).

69. See, e.g., *U.S. v. Griffith*, 334 U.S. 100 (1948); *Berkey Photo, Inc. v. Eastman Kodak Co.*, 603 F.2d 263 (2d Cir. 1979), cert. denied, 444 U.S. 1093 (1980); *U.S. v. Machinery Corp.*, 110 F. Supp. 295 (D. Mass. 1953), aff'd, 347 U.S. 521 (1954); Sullivan and Hovenkamp 1984; Hovenkamp 1985.

70. See also Areeda and Turner 1978, 271 (reduced output by the monopolist will be offset by expanded output by other competitors); *Berkey Photo, Inc. v. Eastman Kodak Co.*, 603 F.2d 263 (2d Cir. 1979), cert. denied, 444 U.S. 1093 (1980). The analysis should not differ for monopsony as compared with monopoly. A

monopoly buyer, a monopsonist, is one who has the ability to reduce demand by forcing the seller to sell at a lower price. The contention is that the NCAA is a monopsonist that forces the athlete to sell his or her service at a lower wage than that prevailing in a competitive market, resulting in a deadweight loss similar to that achieved by a monopoly seller (H. Hovenkamp 1985, 17–18). For reasons discussed herein, the monopsony theory is contrary to actual practice found by the Supreme Court in NCAA. Questions also exist as to whether the Sherman Act covers buyer cartels or monopsony power. During the debates, Senator Sherman said: "There is nothing in the bill to prevent a refusal by anyone to buy something. All that it says is that people producing or selling a particular article shall not make combinations to advance the price of the necessaries of life." 20 *Cong. Rec.* 1458 (1889), quoted in Hovenkamp 1985, 18. More recent authority is to the contrary. See, e.g., In re Beef Industry Antitrust Litigations, 600 F.2d 1148 (5th Cir. 1979), *cert. denied*, 449 U.S. 905 (1980).

71. 104 S. Ct. at 2969.

72. Id. at 2954. The CFA was formed during the same period that the NCAA's power to regulate was on the increase. To be sure, the CFA, made up of five major conferences that emphasize football, was created to increase the influence of the major football colleges within the NCAA structure.

73. The economies might include (1) operation at an efficient scale, (2) avoiding high market costs, (3) reducing market costs or improving market opportunities, and (4) avoiding the free-rider problems such as in the advertising of the product.

74. See, e.g., *Broadcast Music, Inc. v. CBS*, 441 U.S. 1 (1979); *Appalachian Coals, Inc. v. U.S.*, 268 U.S. 344 (1933); *Chicago Board of Trade v. U.S.*, 246 U.S. 231 (1918); *Buffalo Broadcasting Co., Inc. v. American Society of Composers*, 744 F.2d 917 (2d Cir. 1984).

75. See also *Northwest Wholesale Stationers, Inc. v. Pacific Stationery and Printing Co.*, 105 S. Ct. 2613 (1985); *Aspen Skiing Co. v. Aspen Highlands Skiing Corp.*, 105 S. Ct. 2847 (1985); *Copperweld Corp. v. Independence Tube Corp.*, 104 S. Ct. 2731 (1984).

76. 104 S. Ct. 2731, 2740–43 (1984).

77. Id. at 2741. The Court held that a parent corporation is incapable of conspiring with its wholly owned subsidiary under section 1 of the Sherman Act.

78. 105 S. Ct. 2613 (1985).

79. Id. at 2621.

80. See, e.g., *Kior's, Inc. v. Broadway-Hale Stores, Inc.*, 359 U.S. 207 (1959); *Fashion Originators Guild of America, Inc. v. FTC*, 312 U.S. 457 (1941).

81. 105 S. Ct. at 2620–22.

82. Id. at 2620.

83. 105 S. Ct. 2847 (1985). See also *Lorain Journal v. United States*, 342 U.S. 143 (1951) (the right to refuse to deal not unqualified).

84. See generally *Transamerica Computer Co. v. IBM*, 698 F.2d 1337 (9th Cir.), cert. denied, 104 S. Ct. 370 (1983); *Berkey Photo, Inc. v. Eastman Kodak Co.*, 603 F.2d 263 (2d Cir. 1979), *cert. denied*, 444 U.S. 1093 (1980); *Telex Corp. v. IBM*, 510 F.2d 894 (10th Cir.), *cert. denied*, 423 U.S. 802 (1975).

85. 105 S. Ct. at 2857.60.

86. Id. at 2860. See also Sullivan and Hovenkamp 1984, 85.

87. 105 S. Ct. at 2859. The Court accepted the Areeda and Turner analysis that "'exclusionary' [conduct] 'comprehends at the most behavior that not only 1) tends to impair the opportunities of rivals, but also 2) either does not further competition on the merits or does so in an unnecessarily restrictive way.'" Id. at 2859 n.32.

88. Defenders of the cartel thesis seem to imagine that the NCAA has been able to maintain its monopsony stranglehold over member colleges through academic accreditation controls that require NCAA approval of the member colleges' athletic programs. For example, Alchian and Allen (1977) write, "The answer [to the question of how the NCAA maintains control] is that any college violating the athletic 'code' could find its academic credentials threatened." Suffice it to say that the imagined controls simply do not exist.

89. Indeed, to the extent that the NCAA is successful in increasing the demand for college athletics, we would expect athletes' wages to rise. Given the increase in the price of attending college relative to the prices of other goods, the wages of athletes have effectively risen over time.

Chapter 9

1. By taking this position on the role of the entrepreneur, Kirzner is clearly denying the validity of the sweeping, unqualified claim of the economist, "there's no such thing as a free lunch." Perhaps the dictum applies to nonentrepreneurs, but certainly not to entrepreneurs (as Kirzner's "pure entrepreneurs"). Providing free lunches is the restricted role of the entrepreneur in Kirzner's view of the economic world.

2. As does Kirzner, Baumol recognizes the prominent role of the manager in the theory of the firm.

> We may define the manager to be the individual who oversees the ongoing efficiency of continuing processes. It is his task to see that the available processes and techniques are combined in proportions appropriate for current output levels and for the future outputs that are already in prospect. He sees to it that inputs are not wasted, that schedules and contracts are met, he makes routine pricing and advertising outlay decisions, etc., etc. In sum, he takes charge of the activities and decisions encompassed in our traditional models. (1968, 64–65)

3. The absence of an entrepreneurial role in standard monopolist models precludes any return in such models for entrepreneurial alertness, thereby implying that "normal profits" are insufficient to provide adequate incentive to encourage the alertness that is so crucial to the development of a truly dynamic and progress-filled market economy. Real-world firms must therefore earn more than the normal profits of economic models, which in turn means that not all monopoly rents (usually identified as earnings above normal profits) are the unproductive income transfers they have been made out to be.

4. The monopolist's marginal cost curve is assumed to be the same as the mar-

ket supply curve, if the market is organized as a perfectly competitive market, even though the incentive structure of operatives within a monopoly can be radically different from the incentives of operatives within perfectly competitive markets. As argued in chapter 3, perfect competition's market supply curve cannot be identical to the monopolist's marginal cost curve, simply because the assumption of incentives remaining the same under both market structures is untenable.

5. In the first twenty-four hours after it was released, the sixth volume of the Harry Potter series sold 6.9 million copies in the United States alone, as reported by Reuters (July 18, 2005).

6. Accordingly, Locke argued in the *Second Treatise* that private property had a moral as well as practical foundation: "'tis labour indeed that puts the difference of value on every thing; and let anyone consider, what the difference is between an acre of land planted with tobacco, or sugar, sown with wheat or barley; and an acre of the same land lying in common, without husbandry upon it, and he will find, that the improvement of the labour makes the far greater part of the value" (1953, 314). Karen Vaughn, a Locke scholar, maintains that "the implication [of the preceding quote] is that unassisted nature provides little that is useful to mankind" (1980, 85). Indeed, she points out that Locke himself estimates that 90 percent of all that is "useful to the life of man" is the result of labor (85).

7. Granted, Ricardo and all following economists have recognized that resources differ in their productivity, which means that perfect competitors need not be identical in their production costs and that "Ricardian (inframarginal) rents" can be captured by producers who have access to the exceptionally productive or well-placed resources. Even then, it must be acknowledged that at the margin, a producer realizes no net gains under such a construction of perfect competition. In addition, if there are identifiable units of resources that are exceptionally productive or well placed, then their Ricardian rents will be capitalized in their prices, which suggests that the perfect competitors that use those specialized resources will have the exact same overall cost structure as the marginal cost producer. They will either have to buy those specialized resources at prices inflated by their Ricardian rents, or they will incur the opportunity cost of not selling their resources at prices inflated by the Ricardian rents.

8. Trade secrets can be no less of an entry barrier than patents and copyright. Indeed, trade secrets can be more formidable entry barriers than legal protections since they do not have to be on file for inspection in public agencies and can, potentially, last longer, which, of course, means that monopoly rents can be garnered for a longer time.

9. This statement has to be qualified to recognize that we are talking about a positive externality on the marginal unit. In other words, the additional unit provided has to provide a benefit that is not completely captured by those providing it. There could be positive externalities, but unless they are positive at the margin, there is no inefficiency. For example, even though the passersby place a positive value on the garden as it is, they might not benefit further if it were expanded or improved in some other way. In this case the gardener provides the efficient amount of garden in response to his or her own enjoyment. But this is never the

case with a textbook-case monopoly. Because the price is always greater than the marginal revenue, the positive externality created by the textbook monopolist is always positive at the margin. Our discussion continues under the assumption that the externality created by the gardener is also positive at the margin.

10. Probably the most famous article by Nobel Prize–winning economist Ronald Coase (1960) considers the implications of zero transaction costs. It provided important insight into the implications of the positive transaction costs of the real world for the efficiency of law and public policy over a wide range of issues. Many readers of this article conclude that Coase was arguing that transaction costs could be ignored. Quite the opposite. Coase wrote his article to explain the importance of transaction costs.

11. Of course, you might just download your favorite band's music into your computer and pay nothing. This possibility has some profound and interesting implications for monopoly pricing that we discuss later.

12. Methods by which firms price-discriminate abound in a variety of industries. Grocery stores are well known for their price discrimination through the distribution of coupons. Those customers who redeem coupons can be thought to have more elastic demands than other customers. Movie theaters charge moviegoers in various age groups different prices for their tickets. Fast-food restaurants discriminate on the prices of different quantities of sodas by selling sodas in different size cups. Computer chip manufacturers discriminate with chips of different speeds. Colleges and universities price-discriminate through the use of scholarships. Airlines sell different priced seats with first-class ticket holders not only getting meals, they are treated to shorter check-in lines and security check lines. Similarly, Disneyland sells "premium" passes for rides that allow holders to effectively break line. Many producers of electronic gadgets and appliances introduce their products at relatively high prices, only to gradually lower their prices over time, only after the consumers with inelastic demands (because of their interest in having the "latest and greatest" version of gadgets and appliances) have bought all they want at high prices.

13. We have indicated Schumpeter's main three reasons: First, monopoly profits were a source of investment funds essential to the development of new products and technologies (1942, 88), as well as necessary to offset inevitable losses on failed products and business ventures (89–90). In making this point, Schumpeter argued, "Enterprise would in most cases be impossible if it were not known at the outset that exceptionally favorable situations are likely to arise which if exploited by price, quality and quantity manipulation will produce profits adequate to tide over exceptionally unfavorable situations provided these are similarly managed. Again this requires strategy that in the short run is often restrictive" (89–90).

Second, monopolies that act like restrictive monopolies would likely be short-lived precisely because they attract competitors and can't long survive "unless buttressed by public authority" (99). The pressure from the advent of new producers with new products and production technologies would likely cause many existing monopolies to innovate as well as hold their prices and short-run profits in check, leading any existing monopolist to shift its production "optimum toward or beyond the competitive cost price . . . , thus doing the work—partly, wholly, or more than wholly—of the competitive mechanism" (101).

Third, as an empirical matter, when economists have assessed the sources of economic progress over stretches of time, "the trail leads not to the doors of those firms that work under conditions of comparatively free competition but precisely to the doors of the large concerns," which necessarily leads to the "shocking suspicion" (contrary to economic "ideology") that "big business may have had more to do with creating that standard of life than with keeping it down" (82).

14. See Gould and Eldridge 1977; Kuhn 1970; Gersick 1991; Tushman and Romanelli 1985; Tushman, Newman, and Romanelli 1986.

15. For example, in the early 1980s, *Advertising Age* reported that of the twenty-five market leaders of identified markets (e.g., in toothpaste, chewing gum, and bacon) in 1923, nineteen were market leaders in the year the study was published (1983).

16. The tipping argument is endemic to the work of several scholars, including Carpenter and Nakamoto 1989, Bass and Pilon 1980, and Lal and Padmanabhan 1995.

17. Tellis and Golder use a large number of case studies to debunk the first-mover advantage argument. They also present summary statistics. For example, as of 2000, the failure rate of first movers in the sixty-six industries they studied was high: 64 percent. The failure rate for high-tech industries was 50 percent, whereas that for traditional industries was 71 percent (with first movers in traditional industries having more time to fail). The market share of first movers in all sixty-six industries was a mere 6 percent (2002, 43, table 3.1, 44, table 3.2). Tellis and Golder conclude, "Market pioneers rarely endure as leaders. Most of them have low market share or fail completely. Actually, market pioneering is neither necessary nor sufficient for enduring success" (41).

Chapter 10

1. We recognize that the definition of *property* is subject to considerable debate among legal scholars and has varied over time. For example, see Underkuffler 2003 and Penner 1997 to appreciate the fullness of the legal debate over the conception of property. This debate revolves around the nature of things and rights, as well as the exact relationship of people to things. However, because the intricacies of this debate are not relevant to the purpose of this chapter, we adopt here a commonly understood definition of property that has been repeated among legal scholars. C. B. Macpherson argues that "in law and in the writers, property is . . . *rights*, rights in or to things" (1978, 2). Similarly, the American Law Institute defines property as establishing "legal relations between persons with respect to . . . things" (2001, 2).

2. Just about everything written in property right theory has to be qualified. We write that faced with new regulation, the market value of land can fall for a good reason: Whether the market value actually does fall depends on whether the regulations were *anticipated* before they were enacted and imposed on the landowners. If the regulations were anticipated, the consequences of the regulations would

have already been capitalized into the value of the property by the time the regulations are enacted and/or enforced. Then again, what happens to the value of the land depends upon the exact nature of the regulation. If the regulation prevents all landowners from externalizing their use costs and imposing the costs on surrounding landowners (that is, the regulation forces, for example, pollution abatement), the regulations can force all landowners to internalize their own costs and seek a more efficient use of their land, causing their property values for the more limited array of use rights to rise. In a similar manner, an extension of the copyright term for a book can be expected to affect the market value of only those books that are expected to be in demand beyond the previous term limits. Also, an extension of the term limit beyond some here-unspecified limit can cause the present discounted value of any greater income stream received in some remote future period to be so low that the current market value of the copyrighted work is affected very little or is unaffected.

3. Proudhon's first published work in 1840 carried the question *What Is Property?* as its title. His answer was sharp: "Property is theft."

4. As quoted (with emphasis) by Bastiat (1850, chap. 9, ¶ 35).

5. As quoted (with emphasis) by Bastiat (1850, chap. 9, ¶ 68).

6. Knight continued,

It is manifest that this is an exceedingly crude way of rewarding invention. Not merely do the consumers of the product pay, which is doubtless fair, but large numbers of other persons suffer who are prevented from using the commodity by the artificially high price. And as the thing works out, it is undoubtedly a very rare and exceptional case where the really deserving inventor gets anything like a fair reward. If any one gains, it is some purchaser of the invention or at best an inventor who adds a detail or finishing touch that makes an idea practicable where the real work of pioneering and exploration has been done by others. It would seem to be a matter of political intelligence and administrative capacity to replace artificial monopoly with some direct method of stimulating and rewarding research. (1921, pt. 3, chap. 12, ¶ 43)

Von Mises wrote in his *Human Action*,

Patents and copyrights are results of the legal evolution of the last centuries. Their place in the traditional body of property rights is still controversial. People look askance at them and deem them irregular. They are considered privileges, a vestige of the rudimentary period of their evolution when legal protection was accorded to authors and inventors only by virtue of an exceptional privilege granted by the authorities. They are suspect, as they are lucrative only if they make it possible to sell at monopoly prices. Moreover, the fairness of patent laws is contested on the ground that they reward only those who put the finishing touch leading to practical utilization of achievements of many predecessors. These precursors go empty-handed although their contribution to the final result was often much more weighty than that of the patentee. (1949, pt. 4, chap. 23, ¶ 4)

7. The extended passage of Macaulay's remarks on the then proposed extension of the copyright term in Britain from twenty-eight years to the life of the author plus sixty years (1841) follows.

> The tax is an exceedingly bad one; it is a tax on one of the most innocent and most salutary of human pleasures; and never let us forget, that a tax on innocent pleasures is a premium on vicious pleasures. I admit, however, the necessity of giving a bounty to genius and learning. In order to give such a bounty, I willingly submit even to this severe and burdensome tax. Nay, I am ready to increase the tax, if it can be shown that by so doing I should proportionally increase the bounty. My complaint is, that my honorable and learned friend doubles, triples, quadruples, the tax, and makes scarcely a perceptible addition to the bounty. Why, Sir, what is the additional amount of taxation which would have been levied on the public for Dr. Johnson's works alone, if my honorable and learned friend's bill had been the law of the land? I have not data sufficient to form an opinion. But I am confident that the taxation on his Dictionary alone would have amounted to many thousands of pounds. In reckoning the whole additional sum which the holders of his copyrights would have taken out of the pockets of the public during the last half century at twenty thousand pounds, I feel satisfied that I very greatly underrate it. Now, I again say that I think it but fair that we should pay twenty thousand pounds in consideration of twenty thousand pounds worth of pleasure and encouragement received by Dr. Johnson. But I think it very hard that we should pay twenty thousand pounds for what he would not have valued at five shillings.

Deriding the extension of the copyright beyond the life of the author, Macaulay observed,

> The evil effects of the monopoly are proportioned to the length of its duration. But the good effects for the sake of which we bear with the evil effects are by no means proportioned to the length of its duration. A monopoly of sixty years produces twice as much evil as a monopoly of thirty years, and thrice as much evil as a monopoly of twenty years. But it is by no means the fact that a posthumous monopoly of sixty years gives to an author thrice as much pleasure and thrice as strong a motive as a posthumous monopoly of twenty years. (1841)

Macaulay actually favored an extension of the copyright term. He felt that the 1841 bill made too great an extension. In 1842, he proposed an extension of the copyright term to forty-two years, or an increase of fourteen years (1842).

8. Through what he considered to be illustrative costs in book publication for a print run of five thousand copies of a book, Breyer roughly estimates that copiers have a 24 percent cost advantage of the "first publisher" (1970, 294–95).

9. However, it needs to be said that of the eleven extensions of the copyright term passed between 1962 and 1998, seven extensions were for one- and two-year periods to allow Congress more time to devise a copyright bill that could pass both Houses.

10. For the first discussion of the "tragedy of the anticommons," see Heller 1998. See also Buchanan and Yoon 2000.

11. For example, when the Copyright Term Extension Act, which extended the copyright term of all copyrighted works another twenty years, was signed into law in late 1998, Richard Epstein opined in the *Wall Street Journal*, "This was no Mickey Mouse extension but a gift of billions of dollars in future revenues. Thanks to Congress's giveaway, its happy gang of cartoon characters—Mickey, Donald, Goofy, and Snow White—won't soon slip into the public domain" (1998). However, in his review of the literature on copyright term extensions, Yeshiva University law professor Marci Hamilton found, "There is an embarrassing lack of empirical research on the issue of the *mechanism* by which copyright law furthers the end of the public welfare designated in the Constitution. There is much talk in the literature and the cases of the 'incentive' nature of copyright law. But there is no factual study that shows how much incentive is enough to further creative activity, or what kinds of incentives work: money, control, or time. The fact is that we do not really know what difference twenty extra years would make. A survey of the testimony before Congress on duration extension reveals no support for the many factual claims made about extension [Karjala 1994]. Rather, conclusions are based on hypotheses built on hypotheses" (1996).

12. Over the last two centuries, book sales have risen exponentially with the relative price of books falling. The book industry has all the signs of being a highly competitive, robust industry, not exactly what you would expect if copyright laws created harmful monopoly power. Moreover, when the Library of Congress was first established, it had no books in its collection. It bought Thomas Jefferson's collection of 6,500 books in 1815. In 1851, it had only 55,000 volumes. In 2007, it boasts more than 29 million books (and more than 100 million other items) in its collection, covering 530 miles of bookshelves. Its collection has clearly grown at a far faster pace than has the population.

13. James Buchanan and Yong Yoon (1994) revisit Adam Smith's treatment of economies of specialization in his classic example, the nail factory (Smith 1776, bk. 1, chap. 1). They argue that he was trying to make a little-appreciated point, that an expansion of markets (via the elimination of tariffs and lower transportation costs) permits greater specialization within and across local markets, thus giving rise to increasing returns to the scale of markets.

14. Even Frank Knight, a legendary proponent of markets, adds to the confusion of the role of monopolies.

> A monopoly, of the category described, is evidently "productive" in the economic or mechanical causality sense. It may be viewed either as a separate productive element, in which case it is property in perfectly good business standing, and may be exchanged for other property on an income basis. Allowance will be made for the security of the income, but this allowance is perhaps as likely to be in favor of the monopoly as against it. Or we may take the view that the monopoly of a consumption good confers superior productivity on the agencies producing it, above physically identical agencies in other uses. As

long as these are debarred in any way from producing the monopolized good the effect is the same as that of a physical incapacity to do so, and they are, like the branded article, economically differentiated, however similar physically. If the monopoly is of the character of a patent, and freely salable separately from the plant producing the goods, it is better to treat it as a productive agency on its own account. (1921, pt. 2, chap. 6, ¶ 17)

Chapter 11

1. We understand that some economists might develop in class versions of monopoly theory that represent improvements over conventional treatments (perhaps containing one or more points developed in this book). However, we have consistently directed our criticisms at conventional or textbook versions of monopoly theory because of its pervasiveness in theoretical and policy discussions and because it is the version most in error and in need of revision.

2. We noted in chapter 2 Buchanan's argument (1973) that organized crime, which can cartelize, if not monopolize, the hit-man market, can be socially beneficial to the extent that the count of hits would be reduced by the centralized control of the market.

3. We need to insert a caveat here. If heroin is considered a "bad," then it follows that monopolization of the heroin market can lead to fewer sales of heroin, which can be construed as good. However, if the monopoly heroin seller causes total expenditures on heroin to rise with the price hike, then heroin addicts might have to commit more crimes (muggings) in order to feed their habits. Whether there is social improvement with lower sales of heroin and higher other crimes is, of course, debatable.

4. We concede that faced with the threats that came with worldwide terrorism, the plight of the American airline industry in the early part of the twenty-first century looks ominous without some form of lower limit to price competition. But whether this can be done properly is a serious concern, and one that likely makes the attempt ill conceived.

5. The problem of past uses of antitrust laws to further the interests of competitors has been discussed at length by Bork (1978); Baxter (1980); Fisher, McGowan, and Greenwood (1983); Baumol and Ordover (1985); Shughart (1990a); Armentano (1990); Friedman (1999); Crandall and Winston (2003); and Winston (2006). McKenzie (2000, chaps. 7–9) has reviewed this literature.

Bibliography

Ackerman, Bruce A., and William T. Hassler. 1981. *Clean air/dirty air; or, How the Clean Air Act became a multibillion dollar bailout to high-sulfur coal producers and what should be done about it.* New Haven: Yale University Press.

Adams, Walter, and Joel B. Dirlam. 1966. Big steel, invention, and innovation. *Quarterly Journal of Economics* 80 (May): 167–89.

Advertising Age. 1983. Study: Majority of 25 leaders in 1923 still on top—"Old standbys" hold their own. September 19, 32.

Alchian, Armen A., and William R. Allen. 1977. *Exchange and production: Competition, coordination, and control.* 2d ed. Belmont, CA: Wadsworth.

Alchian, Armen A., and H. Demsetz. 1972. Production, information costs, and economic organization. *American Economic Review* 62:777–95.

Alsop, Ronald. 1999. The best reputations in high tech. *Wall Street Journal,* November 18, B1.

American Law Institute. 2001. *A concise restatement of property.* St. Paul, MN: American Law Institute.

Areeda, Phillip, and Donald F. Turner. 1978. *Antitrust law: An analysis of antitrust principles and their application.* 11 vols. Boston: Little, Brown.

Armentano, Dominick T. 1990. *Antitrust and monopoly: Anatomy of a policy failure.* Oakland, CA: Independent Institute.

Arthur, W. Brian. 1989. Competing technologies, increasing returns, and lock-in by historical events. *Economic Journal* 99:116–31.

Arthur, W. Brian. 1996. Increasing returns and the new world of business. *Harvard Business Review* (July–August): 100–109.

Bain, Joe S. 1949. A note on pricing in monopoly and oligopoly. *American Economic Review* 39 (March): 448–69.

Bain, Joe S. 1956. *Barriers to new competition: Their character and consequences in manufacturing industries.* Cambridge, MA: Harvard University Press.

Bain, Joe S. 1990. Positive feedbacks in the economy. *Scientific American* 262:92–99.

Bass, Frank M., and T. L. Pilon. 1980. A stochastic brand choice framework for econometric modeling of time series market share behavior. *Journal of Marketing Research* 17 (November): 486–97.

Bastiat, Frédéric. 1845. *Economic sophisms.* Trans. and ed. Arthur Goddard. Irvington-on-Hudson, NY: Foundation for Economic Education, 1996. Library of Economics and Liberty. http: //www.econlib.org/library/Bastiat/basSoph3 .html (accessed January 17, 2003).

Bastiat, Frédéric. 1848. *Selected essays on political economy.* Ed. George B. de Huszar. Trans. Seymour Cain. Irvington-on-Hudson, NY: Foundation for Economic

Education, 1995. Library of Economics and Liberty. http: //www.econlib.org/library/Bastiat/basEss1.html (accessed January 17, 2003).

Bastiat, Frédéric.1850. *Economic harmonies.* Ed. George B. de Huszar. Trans. W. Hayden Boyers. Irvington-on-Hudson, NY: Foundation for Economic Education, 1996. Library of Economics and Liberty. http://www.econlib.org /library/Bastiat/ basHar1.html. (accessed January 17, 2003).

Baumol, William J. 1968. Entrepreneurship in economic theory. *American Economic Review* 58 (May): 64–71.

Baumol, William J. 1990. Entrepreneurship: Productive, unproductive, and destructive. *Journal of Political Economy* 98:893–921.

Baumol, William J. 2002. *The free-market innovation machine: Analyzing the growth miracle of capitalism.* Princeton: Princeton University Press.

Baumol, William J., and Janusz Ordover. 1985. Use of antitrust to subvert competition. *Journal of Law and Economics* 28 (2): 247–65.

Baxter, William F. 1980. The political economy of antitrust. In *The political economy of antitrust: Principal papers by William Baxter*, ed. Robert D. Tollison, 3–49. Lexington, MA: Lexington Books.

Bayot, Jennifer. 2003. Banks offer sweeteners to paying bills online. *New York Times*, April 21, sec. C.

Becker, Gary S. 1971. *Economic theory.* Chicago: University of Chicago Press.

Becker, Gary S. 1985. College athletes should get paid what they are worth. *Business Week*, September 30, 18.

Becker, Gary S. 1987. The NCAA: A cartel in sheepskin clothing. *Business Week*, September 14, 24.

Becker, Gary S. 1991. A note on restaurant pricing and other examples of social influence on price. *Journal of Political Economy* 99 (5): 1109–16.

Becker, Gary S., and Kevin Murphy. 1988. A theory of rational addiction. *Journal of Political Economy* 96 (August): 675–700.

Bentham, Jeremy. 1787. *Defence of usury.* 4th ed. London: Payne and Foss, 1818. Library of Economics and Liberty. http://www.econlib.org/library/Bentham/bnthUs3.html (accessed January 14, 2003).

Bittlingmayer, George. 1982. Decreasing average cost and competition: A new look at the Addyston Pipe case. *Journal of Law and Economics* 25:201–29.

Bittlingmayer, George. 1985. Did antitrust policy cause the great merger wave? *Journal of Law and Economics* 28:77–118.

Blackstone, William. 1925. *Commentaries on the law in England.* London: Butterworth and Son.

Blais, Jacqueline. 2005. Harry Potter casts successful spell over J. K. Rowling. *USA Today*, July 18. http://www.usatoday.com/life/books/news/2003-06-22-potter-main_x.htm (accessed July 18, 2005).

Bork, Robert H. 1978. *The antitrust paradox: A policy at war with itself.* New York: Basic Books.

Boulding, K. E. 1945. In defense of monopoly. *Quarterly Journal of Economics* 59 (4): 524–42.

Breyer, Stephen. 1970. The uneasy case for copyright: A study of copyright of books, photographs, and computer programs. *Harvard Law Review* 84 (2): 281–353.

Brown, Robert W. 1993. An estimate of the rent generated by a premium college football player. *Economic Inquiry* 31 (4): 671–84.

Browning, Edgar K., and Mark A. Zupan. 1996. *Microeconomic theory and applications.* 5th ed. New York: HarperCollins.

Buchanan, James M. 1964. What should economists do? *Southern Economic Journal* 30 (3): 213–22.

Buchanan, James M. 1967. *Public finance in democratic process: Fiscal institutions and individual choice.* Chapel Hill: University of North Carolina Press.

Buchanan, James M. 1973. A defense of organized crime. In *The economics of crime and punishment,* ed. Simon Rottenberg, 119–32. Washington, DC: American Enterprise Institute.

Buchanan, James M. 1975. *The limits of liberty.* Chicago: University of Chicago Press.

Buchanan, James M. 1979. What should economists do? In *What should economists do?* 17–38. Indianapolis: Liberty Press.

Buchanan, James M. 1988. Market failure and political failure. *Cato Journal* 8 (Spring/Summer): 1–13.

Buchanan, James M. 2000. Symmetric tragedies: Commons and anticommons. *Journal of Law and Economics* 43 (April): 1–14.

Buchanan, James M., Robert D. Tollison, and Gordon Tullock, eds. 1980. *Toward a theory of the rent-seeking society.* College Station: Texas A&M University Press.

Buchanan, James M., and Gordon Tullock. 1962. *The calculus of consent.* Ann Arbor: University of Michigan Press.

Buchanan, James M., and Gordon Tullock. 1975. Polluters' profits and political response: Direct controls versus taxes. *American Economic Review* 65:39–47.

Buchanan, James M., and Yong J. Yoon. 1994. *The return to increasing returns.* Ann Arbor: University of Michigan Press.

Buchanan, James M., and Yong J. Yoon. 2000. Symmetric tragedies: Commons and anticommons. *Journal of Law and Economics* 43 (1): 1–13.

Business Software Alliance. 2003. *Eighth annual BSA global software piracy study: Trends in software piracy, 1994–2002.* West Chester, PA: International Planning and Research Corporation. http: //global.bsa.org/globalstudy/2003_GSPS.pdf (accessed February 6, 2004).

Carpenter, Gregory S., and Kent Nakamoto. 1989. Consumer preference formation and pioneering advantage. *Journal of Marketing Research* 26 (August): 285–98.

CCIA (Computer and Communications Industry Association). 2003. Summary of Complaint. *CCIA v. Microsoft Corporation,* http://www.ccianet.org/ms_eu.php3 (accessed February 21, 2003).

Chamberlin, Edward H. 1933. *The theory of monopolistic competition: A re-orientation of the theory of value.* Cambridge, MA: Harvard University Press.

Chamberlin, Edward H. 1951. The impact of recent monopoly theory on the Schumpeterian system. *Revew of Economics and Statistics* 33 (2): 133–38.

Chandler, Alfred D. 1977. *The visible hand: The managerial revolution in American business.* Cambridge, MA: Harvard University Press.

Christensen, Clayton M. 1997. *The innovator's dilemma: When new technologies cause great firms to fail.* Cambridge, MA: Harvard Business School Press.

Coase, Ronald H. 1937. The nature of the firm. *Economica* 4:1–44.

Coase, Ronald H. 1960. The problem of social cost. *Journal of Law and Economics* 3 (1): 1–44.

Cohen, W. M., and R. C. Levin. 1989. Empirical studies of innovation and market structure. In *Handbook of industrial organization,* ed. Richard Schmalensee and R. D. Willig, 1060–1107. Amsterdam: New Holland Press.

Cowen, Tyler. 1998. *In praise of commercial society.* Cambridge, MA: Harvard University Press.

Cowen, Tyler, and Dwight R. Lee. 1992. The usefulness of inefficient procurement. *Defense Economics* 3:219–27.

Cowling, Keith, and Dennis Mueller. 1981. The social costs of monopoly. *Economic Journal* 91 (363): 721–25.

Crandall, Robert W., and Clifford Winston. 2003. Does antitrust policy improve consumer welfare? Assessing the evidence. *Journal of Economic Perspective* 17 (Fall): 3–26.

David, Paul A. 1985. Clio and the economics of QWERTY. *American Economic Review* 75:332–37.

Dewey, Donald. 1959. *Monopoly in economics and law.* Chicago: Greenwood Press, 1976.

Downs, Anthony. 1957. *An economic theory of democracy.* New York: Harper and Row.

Dupuit, Jules. 1844. On the measurement of the utility of public works. Trans. R. H. Barback, 1952. *International Economic Papers* 2:83–110.

Easterbrook, Frank H. 1984. The limits of antitrust. *Texas Law Review* 63 (1): 1–14.

Economist. 1996. Violent and irrational—And that's just the policy. June 8, 23–25.

Elzinga, Kenneth G., and David E. Mills. 1997. The distribution and pricing of prescription drugs. *International Journal of the Economics of Business* 4:287–99.

Epple, Dennis, and Richard E. Romano. 1998. Competition between private and public schools, vouchers, and peer group effects. *American Economic Review* 88 (March): 33–62.

Epstein, Richard A. 1998. Congress's copyright giveaway. *Wall Street Journal,* December 21. http://www.law.asu.edu/HomePages/Karjala/OpposingCopy rightExtension/commentary/jhornAP.html (accessed April 22, 2003).

Evans, William N., Wallace E. Oates, and Robert M. Schwab. 1992. Measuring peer group effects: A study of teenage behavior. *Journal of Political Economy* 100:966–91.

Fama, Eugene F. 1980. Agency problems and the theory of the firm. *Journal of Political Economy* 88:288–307.

Farrell, Joseph. 1985. NCAA members to vote on 110 proposals to change governing rules covering college sports. *Chronicle of Higher Education,* November 20, 29–32.

Farrell, Joseph, and Carl Shapiro. 1998. Dynamic competition with switching costs. *Rand Journal of Economics* 19 (Spring): 123–37.

Ferguson, Paul R. 1988. *Industrial economics: Issues and perspective.* London: Macmillan.

Ferleger, Herbert Ronald. 1977. *David A. Wells and the American revenue system, 1865–1870.* Philadelphia: Porcupine Press.

Fishback, Price V. 1992. *Soft coal, hard choices: The economic welfare of bituminous coal, 1890–1930.* New York: Oxford University Press.

Fisher, Franklin M., John J. McGowan, and Joen E. Greenwood. 1983. *Folded, spindled, and mutilated: Economic analysis and the U.S. v. IBM.* Cambridge, MA: MIT Press.

Fisher, Franklin M., and Peter Temin. 1965. Research and technical change in the pharmaceutical industry. *Review of Economics and Statistics* 47:182–90.

Fleisher, Arthur A., Brian L. Goff, William F. Shughart II, and Robert D. Tollison. 1988. Crime and punishment: Enforcement of the NCAA football cartel. *Journal of Economic Behavior and Organization* 10 (4): 433–51.

Fleisher, Arthur A., Brian L. Goff, and Robert D. Tollison. 1992. *The national collegiate athletic association: A study in cartel behavior.* Chicago: University of Chicago Press.

Fleisher, Arthur, William F. Shughart II, and Robert D. Tollison. 1989. Ownership structure of professional sports. *Research in Law and Economics,* ed. R. O. Zerbe, 12:71–76.

Frank, Robert H., and Philip J. Cook. 1995. *The winner-take-all society: Why the few at the top get so much more than the rest of us.* New York: Penguin Books.

Friedman, Milton. 1953. *Essays on positive economics.* Chicago: University of Chicago Press.

Friedman, Milton. 1999. The risky road to regulation. *National Post,* July 5, sec. C.

Gates, Bill. 1995. Internet strategy workshop. Keynote address, Microsoft Corporation, Seattle. http://www.microsoft.com/presspass/trial/exhibits/feb99/341/sld001.asp?Fimg=img005.gif (accessed February 21, 2003).

Gersick, Connie J. G. 1991. Revolutionary change theories: A multilevel exploration of the punctuated equilibrium paradigm. *Academy of Management Journal* 37 (5): 10–36.

Gilson, Ronald, and Robert Mnookin. 1985. Sharing among human capitalists: An economic inquiry into the corporate law firms and how partners split profits. *Stanford Law Review* 37 (January): 313–92.

Gintis, Herbert. 1991. Where did Schumpeter go wrong? *Challenge* (January–February): 27–33.

Givon, M., V. Mahajan, and E. Muller. 1999. Software piracy: Estimation of lost sales and the impact of software diffusion. *Journal of Marketing* 59:29–37.

Goff, Brian L., William F. Shughart II, and Robert D. Tollison. 1988. Disqualification by decree: Amateur rules as barriers to entry. *Journal of Institutional and Theoretical Economics* 144 (June): 515–23.

Gould, Stephen Jay, and Niles Eldridge. 1977. Punctuated equilibria: The tempo and mode of evolution reconsidered. *Paleobiologist* 3:115–51.

Graaff, J. de V. 1971. *Theoretical welfare economics.* Cambridge, UK: Cambridge University Press.

Greenspan, David. 1988. College football's biggest fumble: The economic impact of the Supreme Court's decision in National Collegiate Athletic Association v. Board of Regents of the University of Oklahoma. *Antitrust Bulletin* 33 (Spring): 1–65.

Gurbaxani, Vijay, and Seungjin Whang. 1991. The impact of information systems on organizations and markets. *Communication of the ACM* (January): 59–73.

Guth, Robert A. 2003. Microsoft posts strong profit, helped by licensing program. *Wall Street Journal,* April 16. http: //online.wsj.com/article/ 0,,SB105034592 667619000-search,00.html?collection=wsjie%2F30day&vql_string=intel+ and+ monopoly%3Cin%3E%28article%2Dbody%29 (accessed May 9, 2003).

Haddock, David D., and Fred S. McChesney. 1994. Why do firms contrive shortages? The economics of intentional mispricing. *Economic Inquiry* 32:562–81.

Hamberg, Dan. 1964. Size of firm, oligopoly, and research: The evidence. *Canadian Journal of Economics and Political Science* (February): 62–75.

Hamilton, Marci A. 1996. Copyright duration extension and the dark heart of copyright. *Cardoza Arts and Entertainment Law Journal* 14 (3): 655–60. http: //www.law.asu.edu/HomePages/Karjala/OpposingCopyrightExtension/com mentary/hamilton-art.html (accessed April 22, 2003).

Harberger, Arnold C. 1954. Monopoly and resource allocation. *American Economic Review* 44 (September): 77–87.

Hardin, Garrett. 1968. The tragedy of the commons. *Science* 62 (December): 1243–54.

Haveman, Robert H. 1988. *Starting even: An equal opportunity program to combat the nation's new poverty.* New York: Simon and Schuster.

Haveman, Robert H., and Kenyon Knopf. 1966. *The market system.* New York: John Wiley and Sons.

Hayek, Frederick A. 1944. *The road to serfdom.* Chicago: University of Chicago Press.

Hayek, Frederick A. 1945. The use of knowledge in society. *American Economic Review* 35 (September): 519–30.

Healy, Jon. 2002. Forthcoming CDs pirated on Web. *Los Angeles Times,* July 26, sec. C.

Heller, Michael A. 1998. The tragedy of the anticommons: Property in transition. *Harvard Law Review* 111:621–88.

Henderson, Vernon, Peter Mieszkowski, and Yvon Sauvageau. 1978. Peer group effects in education production function. *Journal of Public Economics* 10 (1): 97–106.

Holcombe, Randall G. 1994. *The economic foundations of government.* New York: New York University Press.

Holt, Charles A. 2003. Economic science: An experimental approach for teaching and research. *Southern Economic Journal* 69 (Spring): 755–71.

Horowitz, Ira. 1962. Firm size and research activity. *Southern Economic Journal* 30 (January): 298–301.

Hotelling, Harold. 1938. The general welfare in relation to problems of taxation and railway and utility rates. *Econometrica* 6 (3): 242–69.

Hovenkamp, Herbert J. 1985. *Economics and federal antitrust law*. St. Paul, MN: West.

Howell, Jeremy. 1985. Letter to the Editor. College athletes are underpaid. *Wall Street Journal*, October 29, B31.

Hui, Kai-Lung, and I. P. L. Png. 2002. Piracy and the legitimate demand for recorded music. Faculty Working Paper, School of Computing, National University of Singapore. http: //papers.ssrn.com/sol3/papers.cfm?abstract_id= 262651 (accessed May 28, 2003).

Humphreys, Brad R. 2000. Equal pay on the hardwood: The earnings gap between male and female NCAA Division I basketball coaches. *Journal of Sports Economics* 1 (August): 299–307.

Humphreys, Brad R., and Jane E. Ruseski. 2001. Monitoring cartel behavior and stability: Evidence from NCAA Football. Faculty Working Paper. Doctoral Studies in Economics, Research in Transition Economies, CERGE-EI. http: //www.cerge-ei.cz/pdf/events/papers/011029_t.pdf (accessed March 19, 2003).

Jackson, Thomas Penfield. 1999. Findings of fact. *United States v. Microsoft Corporation*. First District Court, civil action no. 98–1232 (D.C. Cir.). http: //www.usdoj.gov/atr/cases/f3800/msjudgex.htm (accessed February 23, 2003).

Jackson, Thomas Penfield. 2000a. Conclusions of Law. *United States v. Microsoft Corporation*. First District Court, civil action no. 98–1232 (D.C. Cir.). http: //www.usdoj.gov/atr/cases/f4400/4469.htm (accessed February 22, 2003).

Jackson, Thomas Penfield. 2000b. Final Judgment. *United States v. Microsoft Corporation*. First District Court, civil action no. 98–1232 (D.C. Cir.). http: //www.microsoft.com/presspass/trial/nov02/11-12FinalJudgment.asp (accessed February 22, 2003).

Jacoby, Mary. 2006. EU hits Microsoft with $358.3 million penalty. *Wall Street Journal*, July 13, A6.

Jennings, Daniel F. 1995. Entrepreneurial activity and firm size: Re-examining Schumpeter's hypothesis. Faculty Working Paper. Baylor University. http: //www.sbaer.uca.edu/Research/1996/USASBE/96usa195.txt (accessed February 17, 2003).

Jennings, Daniel F., and J. R. Lumpkin. 1989. Functionally modeling corporate entrepreneurship: An empirical integrative analysis. *Journal of Management* 15:485–502.

Jennings, Mead. 1994. Pricing: Still juggling American Airline prices. *Airline Business* (August): 42–44.

Jensen, Michael C. 1986. Agency costs of free cash flow, corporate finance, and takeovers. *American Economic Review* 76:323–29.

Jensen, Michael C., and William H. Meckling. 1976. Theory of the firm: Managerial behavior, agency costs, and ownership structure. *Journal of Financial Economics* 3 (October): 305–60.

Jensen, Michael C., and Kevin J. Murphy. 1990. Performance pay and top-management incentives. *Journal of Political Economy* 98 (2): 225–63.

Johnson, Ronald N., and Gary D. Libecap. 1989. Agency growth, salaries, and the protected bureaucrat. *Economic Inquiry* 27 (July): 431–51.

Kamien, M. I., and N. L. Schwartz. 1975. Market structure and innovation: A survey. *Journal of Economic Literature* 13 (1): 1–37.

Karjala, Dennis S. 1994. Comment of U.S. copyright law professors on the Copyright Office term of protection study. *European Intellectual Property Review* 16:531.

Katz, Michael L. 1986. Technology adoption in the presence of network externalities. *Journal of Political Economy* 94:822–41.

Katz, Michael L., and Carl Shapiro. 1985. Network externalities, competition, and compatibility. *American Economic Review* 75:424–40.

Katz, Michael L., and C. Shapiro. 1994. Systems competition and network effects. *Journal of Economic Perspectives* 8:93–115.

Kirzner, Israel S. 1973. *Competition and entrepreneurship.* Chicago: University of Chicago Press.

Klein, Benjamin. 1999. Microsoft's use of zero price bundling to fight the "browser wars." In *Competition, innovation, and the Microsoft monopoly: Antitrust in the digital marketplace,* 217–54. Boston: Kluwer Academic.

Klein, Benjamin, and Keith B. Leffler. 1981. The role of market forces in assuring contractual performance. *Journal of Political Economy* 89:615–41.

Klein, Frederick. 1985. Designated villains. *Wall Street Journal,* October 16, 28.

Klein, Joel I., et al. 1998. Complaint. *United States v. Microsoft Corporation.* First District Court, civil action no. 98–1232. http://www.usdoj.gov/atr/cases/f1700/ 1763.htm (accessed February 22, 2003).

Klemperer, Paul. 1987. Entry deterrence in markets with consumer switching costs. *Economic Journal* 97:99–117.

Klemperer, Paul. 1988. Welfare effects of entry into markets with switching costs. *Journal of Industrial Economics* 37 (December): 159–65.

Klemperer, Paul. 1989. Price wars caused by switching costs. *Review of Economic Studies* 56:405–20.

Knight, Frank H. 1921. *Risk, uncertainty, and profit.* Boston: Hart, Schaffner, and Marx / Houghton Mifflin. Library of Economics and Liberty. http://www.econlib.org/library/Knight/knRUP5.html (accessed April 18, 2003).

Koch, James V. 1973. A troubled cartel: The NCAA. *Law and Contemporary Problems* 38 (Winter/Spring): 39–69.

Koch, James V. 1983. Intercollegiate athletics: An economic explanation. *Social Science Quarterly* 64 (2): 360–74.

Krueger, Anne O. 1974. The political economy of the rent-seeking society. *American Economic Review* 64:291–303.

Kuhn, Thomas S. 1970. *The structure of scientific revolutions.* 2d ed. Chicago: University of Chicago Press.

Lal, Rajiv, and V. Padmanabhan. 1995. Competitive response and equilibria. *Marketing Science* 14 (3): G101–G108.

Landes, William M., and Richard A. Posner. 1981. Market power in antitrust cases. *Harvard Law Review* 94 (March): 937–64.

Landsburg, Steven E. 1993. *The armchair economists: Economics and everyday life.* New York: Free Press.

Lazear, Edward. 1979. Why is there mandatory retirement? *Journal of Political Economy* 87 (December): 1261–84.

Lazear, Edward. 2000. Performance pay and productivity. *American Economic Review* 90:1346–61.

Lee, Dwight R. 1989. The impossibility of a desirable minimal state. *Public Choice* 61 (June): 277–84.

Lee, Dwight R. 1998. How the client effect moderates price competition. *Southern Economic Journal* 64 (3): 741–52.

Lee, Dwight R. 2001. A case for letting firms take advantage of "locked-in" customers. *Hastings Law Journal* 52 (April): 795–812.

Lee, Dwight R., and David Kreutzer. 1982. Lagged demand and a perverse response to threatened property rights. *Economic Inquiry* 20 (October): 579–88.

Lee, Dwight R., and Richard B. McKenzie. 1987. *Regulating government: A preface to constitutional economics.* Lexington, MA: Lexington Books.

Leibenstein, Harvey. 1950. Bandwagon, snob, and Veblen effects in the theory of consumers' demand. *Quarterly Journal of Economics* 64:183–207.

Lessig, Lawrence. 2001. *The future of ideas: The fate of the commons in a connected world.* New York: Random House.

Liebowitz, Stan J. 1994. Network externality: An uncommon tragedy. *Journal of Economic Perspectives* 8 (Spring): 133–50.

Liebowitz, Stan J. 1995. Path dependence, lock-in, and history. *Journal of Law, Economics, and Organization* 11:205–26.

Liebowitz, Stan J. 1999. *Winners, losers, and Microsoft.* Oakland, CA: Independence Institute.

Liebowitz, Stan J., and Steven E. Margolis. 1990. The fable of the keys. *Journal of Law and Economics* 3:1–26.

Link, Albert N. 1980. Firm size and efficient entrepreneurial activity: A reformulation of the Schumpeter Hypothesis. *Journal of Political Economy* 88 (August): 771–82.

Little, Charles E. 1886. *Historical lights: Six thousand quotations from standard histories and biographies.* Toronto: Funk and Wagnalls.

Locke, John. 1953. *Two treatises on government.* 2d ed. Ed. Peter Laslett. Cambridge, UK: Cambridge University Press.

Lucas, Robert E., Jr. 1988. On the mechanics of economic development. *Journal of Monetary Economics* 22 (July): 3–42.

Macaulay, Thomas Babington. 1841. Opposing proposed life + 60 copyright term. Speech to House of Commons. http://www.law.asu.edu/HomePages/Kar jala/OpposingCopyrightExtension/commentary/MacaulaySpeeches.html (accessed April 21, 2003).

Macaulay, Thomas Babington. 1842. Speech to a Committee of the House of

Commons. http: //www.law.asu.edu/HomePages/Karjala/OpposingCopyright Extension/commentary/MacaulaySpeeches.html (accessed April 21, 2003).

Macpherson, C. B. 1978. The meaning of property. In *Property: Mainstream and critical positions.* Ed. C. B. Macpherson, 1–13. Toronto: University of Toronto Press.

Malthus, Thomas Robert. 1798. *An essay on the principle of population.* London: J. Johnson. Library of Economics and Liberty. http: //www.econlib.org/library/ Malthus/malPop4.htm (accessed January 17, 2003).

Mansfield, Edwin. 1963. Size of firm, market structure, and innovation. *Journal of Political Economy* 71 (December): 556–76.

Mansfield, Edwin. 1964. Industrial research and development expenditures: Determinants, prospects, and relation of size of firm and inventive output. *Journal of Political Economy* 72 (August): 319–40.

Mansfield, Edwin. 1968. *Industrial research and technological innovation.* New York: W. W. Norton.

Markham, Jesse W. 1965. Market structure, business conduct, and innovation. *American Economic Review* 55 (March): 323–32.

Marshall, Alfred. 1890. *Principles of Economics.* Macmillan, 1920. Library of Economics and Liberty. http: //www.econlib.org/library/Marshall/marP0.html (accessed January 19, 2003).

Marx, Karl. 1844. The King of Prussia and social reform. By a Prussian, *Vorwarts!* In *Marx: Early political writings.* Ed. Joseph O'Malley, 97–114. Cambridge, UK: Cambridge University Press, 1994.

Marx, Karl. 1845. Feuerbach. In *The 'German Ideology.'* Reprinted in *Marx: Early Political Writings.* Ed. Joseph O'Malley, 119–81. Cambridge, UK: Cambridge University Press.

Marx, Karl. 1887. *Critique of political economy.* 1st English ed. Vol. 1 of *Capital.* Moscow: Progress.

Mason, Edward S. 1951. Schumpeter on monopoly and the large firm. *American Economic Review* 33 (May): 139–44.

McCormick, Robert. 1985. Colleges get their athletes for a song. *Wall Street Journal,* August 20, 27.

McCormick, Robert, and Roger Meiners. 1987. Bust the college sports cartel. *Fortune,* October, 235–36.

McCormick, Robert, and Maurice Tinsley. 1987. Athletics versus academics? Evidence from SAT scores. *Journal of Political Economy* 95 (October): 1103–16.

McDonald, John. 1964. Sears makes it look easy. *Fortune,* May, 120–21.

McGee, John S. 1958. Predatory price cutting: The Standard Oil (N.J.) Case. *Journal of Law and Economics* 23 (October): 137–69.

McGee, John S. 1971. *In defense of industrial concentration.* New York: Praeger.

McKenzie, Richard B. 2000. *Trust on trial: How the Microsoft case is transforming the rules of competition.* Boston: Perseus Books.

McKenzie, Richard B. 2005. The legal fit of "the Microsoft problem": Antitrust or copyright law? Faculty Working Paper, Merage School of Business, University of California, Irvine.

McKenzie, Richard B., and Roman Galar. 2003. The importance of deviance in intellectual development. *American Journal of Economics and Sociology* 63 (January): 19–49.

McKenzie, Richard B., and Dwight R. Lee. 1991. *Quicksilver capital: How the rapid movement of wealth has changed the world.* New York: Free Press.

McKenzie, Richard B., and Dwight R. Lee. 1998. *Managing through incentives: How to develop a more collaborative, productive, and profitable organization.* New York: Oxford University Press.

McKenzie, Richard B., and Dwight R. Lee. 2000. Monopoly as a coordination problem. In *Public choice essays in honor of a maverick scholar: Gordon Tullock,* 125–36. Boston: Kluwer Academic.

McKenzie, Richard B., and Dwight R. Lee. 2006. *Microeconomics for MBAs: The economic way of thinking for managers.* Cambridge, UK: Cambridge University Press.

McKenzie, Richard B., and Thomas E. Sullivan. 1987. Does the NCAA exploit college athletes? An economic and legal reinterpretation. *Antitrust Bulletin* 32 (Summer): 373–99.

McNulty, Paul J. 1974. On firm size and innovation in the Schumpeterian system. *Journal of Economic Issues* 8 (September): 627–32.

Milgrom, Paul, and John Roberts. 1992. *Economics, organizations, and management.* Englewood Cliffs, NJ: Prentice Hall.

Mitchener, Brandon. 2003. Europe's case on Microsoft may be too late. *Wall Street Journal,* November 13, sec. B.

Modigliani, Franco. 1958. New developments on the oligopoly front. *Journal of Political Economy* (June): 215–32.

Murphy, Kevin J. 1986. Top executives are worth every nickel they get. *Harvard Business Review* 64 (March–April): 125–32.

NCAA. 2003. http://www.ncaa.org/wps/portal (accessed June 18, 2003).

Nelson, Phillip. 1970. Information and consumer behavior. *Journal of Political Economy* 78 (2): 311–29.

Nelson, Richard R., and Sidney G. Winter. 1982. The Schumpeterian tradeoff revisited. *American Economic Review* 72 (March): 114–32.

New York Times. 1985. Editorial: Colleges majoring in scandal. April 17, A22.

Nolan, Richard L., and David C. Croson. 1995. *Creative destruction: A six-stage process for transforming the organization.* Boston: Harvard University Press.

Nozick, Robert. 1974. *Anarchy, state, and utopia.* New York: Basic Books.

Nutter, Warren G., and Henry Adler Einhorn. 1969. *Enterprise monopoly in the United States, 1899–1958.* New York: Columbia University Press.

Oakley, Allen. 1990. *Schumpeter's theory of capitalist motion: A critical exposition and reassessment.* Hants, England: Edward Elgar.

Ochoa, Tyler T. 2002. Patent and copyright term extensions and the Constitution: A historical perspective. *Journal of the Copyright Society of the U.S.A.* (March) http://www.law.asu.edu/HomePages/Karjala/OpposingCopyrightExtension/constitutionality/OchoaJC S-TermExtArt.pdf (accessed April 23, 2003).

Olson, Mancur. 1965. *The logic of collective action: Public goods and the theory of groups.* Cambridge, MA: Harvard University Press.

O'Reilly, Brian. 1993. Novell faces the battle of its life. *Fortune*, August, 81.

Osborne, Dale K. 1964. The role of entry in oligopoly theory. *Journal of Political Economics* 75 (June): 396–402.

Parcelle, Mitchell. 1995. Millionaires find resort is too rich for their blue blood. *Wall Street Journal*, February 1, sec. A.

Pashigian, Peter B. 1968. Limit price and the market share of the leading firm. *Journal of Industrial Economics* 16 (July): 165–77.

Penner, James E. 1997. *The idea of property in law*. New York: Oxford University Press.

Perelman, Michael. 1995. Retrospectives: Schumpeter, David Wells, and creative destruction. *Journal of Economic Perspectives* 9 (Summer): 189–97.

Pfeffer, Jeffrey, and Nancy Langton. 1988. Wage inequality and the organization of work: The case of academic departments. *Administrative Sciences Quarterly* 33:588–606.

Pindyck, Robert S., and Daniel L. Rubinfeld. 2005. *Microeconomics*. 6th ed. Upper Saddle River, NJ: Pearson / Prentice Hall.

Porter, Michael. 1980. *Competitive strategies*. New York: Free Press.

Proudhon, Pierre-Joseph. 1840. *What is property?* Cambridge, UK: Cambridge University Press, 1994.

Radner, Roy. 1987. Decentralization and incentives. In *Information, incentives, and economic mechanisms: Essays in honor of Leonid Hurwicz*, ed. Theodore Groves, Roy Radner, and Stanley Reiter, 3–47. Minneapolis: University of Minnesota Press.

Reuters. 2005. Harry Potter VI flies off shelves. *CNN Money*, July 18. http://money.cnn.com.

Ricardo, David. 1817. *On the principles of political economy and taxation*. London: John Murray, 1821 Library of Economics and Liberty. http: //www.econlib .org/library/Ricardo/ricP3a.html (accessed January 14, 2003).

Robbins, Lionel. 1946. *An essay on the nature and significance of economic science*. 2d ed. London: Macmillan.

Roberts, John. 2004. *The modern firm: Organizational design for performance and growth*. New York: Oxford University Press.

Roberts, Paul Craig. 1995. A minimum-wage study with minimum credibility. *Business Week*, April 22, 22.

Robinson, Joan. 1933. *The economics of imperfect competition*. London: Macmillan.

Robinson, Stanley D. 1980. Recent antitrust developments. *Columbia Law Review* 80 (1): 1–42.

Rohlfs, Jeffrey H. 2001. *Bandwagon effects in high technology industries*. Cambridge, MA: MIT Press.

Romer, Paul M. 1994. New goods, old theory, and the welfare costs of trade restrictions. *Journal of Economic Development* 43 (February): 5–38.

Rosenberg, Joel B. 1976. Research and market share: A reappraisal of the Schumpeter Hypothesis. *Journal of Industrial Economics* 25 (2): 101–12.

Rubin, Paul H. 1990. *Managing business transactions: Controlling the costs of coordination, communication, and decision making*. New York: Free Press.

Sanjay, Kathuria. 1988. *Market structures and innovation: A survey of empirical studies of Schumpeterian Hypothesis.* New Delhi: Indian Council for Research on International Economic Relations.

Scherer, Frederic M. 1965. Firm size, market structure, opportunity, and the output of patented inventions. *American Economic Review* 55:1097–1125.

Schmookler, Jacob. 1959. Bigness, fewness, and research. *Journal of Political Economy* (December): 628–35.

Schumpeter, Joseph A. 1934. *The theory of economic development.* Cambridge, MA: Harvard University Press, 1951.

Schumpeter, Joseph A. 1939. *Business cycles.* New York: McGraw-Hill.

Schumpeter, Joseph A. 1942. *Capitalism, socialism, and democracy.* New York: Harper.

Schumpeter, Joseph A. 1949. Science and ideology. *American Economic Review* 39 (March): 345–59.

Schumpeter, Joseph A. 1951. *Essays: On entrepreneurs, innovations, business cycles, and the evolution of capitalism.* New Brunswick, NJ: Transaction, 2002.

Shughart, William F., II. 1990a. *Antitrust policy and interest group politics.* New York: Quorum Books.

Shughart, William F., II. 1990b. Protect college athletes, not athletics. *Wall Street Journal,* December 26, B6.

Smith, Adam. 1759. *The theory of moral sentiments.* London: A. Millar, 1790. Library of Economics and Liberty. http: //www.econlib.org/library/Smith/smMS2 .html (accessed March 23, 2003).

Smith, Adam. 1776. *An inquiry into the nature and causes of the wealth of nations.* Ed. Edwin Cannan. London: Methuen, 1904. Library of Economics and Liberty. http: //www.econlib.org/library/Smith/smWN0.html. (accessed January 14, 2003).

Smith, Vernon L. 1982. Markets as economizers of information: Experimental examination of the "Hayek Hypothesis." *Economic Inquiry* 20 (April): 165–79.

Solow, Robert M. 1957. Technical change and the aggregate production function. *Review of Economics and Statistics* 39 (August): 312–20.

Stigler, George J. 1968. *The organization of industry.* Homewood, IL: Richard D. Irwin.

Stigler, George J. 1975. *The citizen and the state: Essays on regulation.* Chicago: University of Chicago Press.

Sullivan, E. Thomas. 1982. The economic jurisprudence of the Burger Court's antitrust policy: The first thirteen years. *Notre Dame Law Review* 58:16–18.

Sullivan, E. Thomas. 1984. On nonprice competition: An economic and marketing analysis. *University of Pittsburgh Law Review* 45:402.

Sullivan, E. Thomas, and Jeffrey L. Harrison. 1988. *Understanding antitrust and its economic implications.* 3d ed. New York: Mathew-Bender.

Sullivan, E. Thomas, and Herbert J. Hovenkamp. 1984. *Antitrust law, policy, and procedure.* Charlottesville, VA: Michie.

Summers, Anita A. 1968. *The organization of industry.* Homewood, IL: Richard D. Irwin.

Summers, Anita A., and Barbara L. Wolfe. 1977. Do schools make a difference? *American Economic Review* 67:639–52.

Teece, David. 1977. Technology transfers by multinational firms. *Economic Journal* 87 (June): 242–61.

Tellis, Gerald J., and Peter N. Golder. 2002. *Will and vision: How latecomers grow to dominate markets.* New York: McGraw-Hill.

Tullock, Gordon. 1965. *The politics of bureaucracy.* Washington, DC: Public Affairs Press.

Tullock, Gordon. 1967. The welfare costs of tariffs, monopolies, and theft. *Western Economic Journal* 5 (June): 224–32.

Tullock, Gordon. 1971. Public policy as a public good. *Journal of Political Economy* 79 (July–August): 913–18.

Tullock, Gordon. 1972. *Toward a mathematics of politics.* Ann Arbor: University of Michigan Press.

Tullock, Gordon. 1980. Efficient rent-seeking. In *Toward a theory of the rent-seeking society*, ed. James M. Buchanan, Robert D. Tollison, and Gordon Tullock, 97–112. College Station: Texas A&M University Press.

Tullock, Gordon. 1983. *Economics of income distribution.* Boston: Kluwer Nijhoff.

Tushman, Michael L., W. H. Newman, and Elaine Romanelli. 1986. Convergence and upheaval: Managing the unsteady pace of organizational evolution. *California Management Review* 29 (1): 1–16.

Tushman, Michael L., and Elaine Romanelli. 1985. Organizational evolution: A metamorphosis model of convergence and reorientation. In *Research in organizational behavior* 7, ed. L. L. Cummings and B. M. Staw, 171–222. Greenwich, CT: JAI Press.

Underkuffler, Laura S. 2003. *The idea of property: Its meaning and power.* New York: Oxford University Press.

U.S. Bureau of the Census. 2007. *Statistical Abstract of the United States: 2007.* 126th ed. Washington, DC.

Vaidhyanathan, Siva. 2001. *Copyrights and copywrongs: The rise of intellectual property and how it threatens creativity.* New York: New York University Press.

van Lohuizen, Jan. 2001. Voter/consumer research. Washington, DC: Americans for Technology Leadership, http://www.techleadership.org/LatestNews .asp?FormMode=Release&ID=34 and http://www.techleadership.org/ toplines.pdf (accessed July 8, 2001).

Vaughn, Karen I. 1980. *John Locke and social science.* Chicago: University of Chicago Press.

Vaughn, Karen I. 1996. Economic policy for an imperfect world. *Southern Economic Journal* 62, no. 4 (April): 833–44.

von Mises, Ludwig. 1949. *Human action.* Irvington-on-Hudson, NY: Foundation for Economic Education, 1996. Library of Economics and Liberty. http://www.econlib.org/library/Mises/HmA/msHmA23.html (accessed April 18, 2003).

Warren-Bolton, Frederick R. 2000. Direct Testimony: State of New York *ex rel. Attorney General Dennis C. Vacco, et al. v. Microsoft Corporation.* Civil Action No.

98–1233 (TPJ), p. 21. http://www.usdoj.gov/atr/cases/f2000/2079.htm (accessed February 22, 2003).

Weistart, John C., and Cym H. Lowell. 1979. *The law of sports.* Indianapolis: Bobbs-Merrill.

Weistart, John C. 1985. *The law of sports (supplement 1985).* Charlottesville, VA: Michie.

Wells, David A. 1889. *Recent economic changes, and their effect on the production and well-being of society.* New York: Da Capo Press, 1970.

Winston, Clifford. 2006. *Government failure versus market failure: Microeconomics policy and government performance.* Washington, DC: AEI-Brookings Joint Center for Regulatory Studies, American Enterprise Institute, and Brookings Institution.

Wittman, Donald. 1995. *The myth of democratic failure: Why democratic institutions are efficient.* Chicago: University of Chicago Press.

Worley, J. S. 1961. Industrial research and the new competition. *Journal of Political Economy* (April): 183–86.

Yoder, Edwin. 1985. College athletic system corrupt. *Greenville (SC) News,* June 28, 4A.

U.S. Court Cases

Appalachian Coals, Inc. v. U.S., 268 U.S. 344 (1933).

Aspen Skiing Co. v. Aspen Highlands Skiing Corp., 105 S. Ct. 2847 (1985).

Beef Industry Antitrust Litigations, 600 F.2d 1148 (5th Cir. 1979), *cert. denied,* 449 U.S. 905 (1980).

Berkey Photo, Inc. v. Eastman Kodak Co., 603 F.2d 263 (2d Cir. 1979), *cert. denied,* 444 U.S. 1093 (1980).

Broadcast Music, Inc. v. CBS, 441 U.S. 1 (1979).

Buffalo Broadcasting Co., Inc. v. American Society of Composers, 744 F.2d 917 (2d Cir. 1984).

Chicago Board of Trade v. U.S., 246 U.S. 231 (1918).

Continental TV. Inc. v. GTE Sylvania Inc., 433 U.S. 36 (1977).

Copperweld Corp. v. Independence Tube Corp., 104 S. Ct. 2731 (1984).

Fashion Originators Guild of America, Inc. v. FTC, 312 U.S. 457 (1941).

FTC v. Indiana Federation of Dentists, 106 S. Ct. 2009 (1986).

Gunter Hartz Sports, Inc. v. U.S. Tennis Assoc., Inc., 665 F.2d 222, 223 (8th Cir. 1981).

Hennessey v. NCAA, 564 F.2d 1136, 1151–53 (5th Cir. 1977).

Kior's, Inc. v. Broadway-Hale Stores, Inc., 359 U.S. 207 (1959).

Lorain Journal v. United States, 342 U.S. 143 (1951).

Mackey v. National Football League, 543 F.2d 606 (8th Cir. 1976).

National Society of Professional Engineers v. U.S., 435 U.S. 679 (1978).

NCAA v. Board of Regents, 104 S. Ct. 2948 (1984).

NCAA v. Board of Regents, 104 S. Ct. at 2969, citing R. Bork 1978, 278.

Neeld v. NHL, 594 F.2d 1297, 1298–1300 (9th Cir. 1979).

Northwest Wholesale Stationers, Inc. v. Pacific Stationery and Printing Co., 105 S. Ct. 2613 (1985).

Smith v. Pro Football, Inc., 593 F.2d 1173, 1179 (D.C. Cir. 1978).

Telex Corp. v. IBM, 510 F.2d 894 (10th Cir.), *cert. denied*, 423 U.S. 802 (1975).

Transamerica Computer Co. v. IBM, 698 F.2d 1337 (9th Cir.), *cert. denied*, 104 S. Ct. 370 (1983).

U.S. v. Addyston Pipe & Steel Co., 85 F.271 (6th Cir. 1898), *aff'd*, 175 U.S. 211 (1899).

U.S. v. Griffith, 334 U.S. 100 (1948).

U.S. v. Machinery Corp., 110 F. Supp. 295 (D. Mass. 1953), *aff'd*, 347 U.S. 521 (1954).

U.S. v. Microsoft Corp., 00–5212, 00–5213 U.S. Ct. App. (D.C. Cir. 2001).

Cited U.S. Congressional Bill

U.S. Congress. House. H.R. 5213 Committee on Education and Labor, Committee on Energy and Commerce. *A bill to establish the Congressional Advisory Commission on Intercollegiate Athletics*, 99th Cong., 2d sess, July 21,1986; see 132 Cong. Rec. H4690 (daily ed. July 22, 1986) (statement of Rep. Thomas A. Luken).

Index